LIBRARY
OLD TESTAMENT STUDIES

641

Formerly Journal for the Study of the Old Testament Supplement Series

DAVID'S CAPACITY FOR COMPASSION

A Literary-Hermeneutical Study of 1–2 Samuel

By Barbara Green

LONDON • NEW YORK • OXFORD • NEW DELHI • SYDNEY

T&T CLARK
Bloomsbury Publishing Plc
50 Bedford Square, London, WC1B 3DP, UK
1385 Broadway, New York, NY 10018, USA

BLOOMSBURY, T&T CLARK and the T&T Clark logo are
trademarks of Bloomsbury Publishing Plc

First published in Great Britain 2017
Paperback edition first published 2018

A catalogue record for this book is available from the British Library.

ISBN: HB: 978-0-5676-7358-9
PB: 978-0-5676-8492-9
ePDF: 978-0-5676-7359-6

A catalog record for this book is available from the Library of Congress.

Series: Library of Hebrew Bible/Old Testament Studies, volume 641

Typeset by Newgen Knowledge Works (P) Ltd., Chennai, India

To find out more about our authors and books visit
www.bloomsbury.com and sign up for our newsletters.

to those—especially whom I know and love—
who struggle with the journey from arrogance to compassion

CONTENTS

Figure   viii
Abbreviations   x

Chapter 1
RELEVANT METHODOLOGIES FOR CONSTRUCTING AN ANCIENT FICTIVE WORK   1

Chapter 2
WHY A KING? CHOICES OF SAUL AND DAVID (1 SAM. 8–18)
  EDGES AND STRUCTURES   33

Chapter 3
COMPETITION AND CHOICES: KINGS INTERLOCKED (1 SAM. 19–26)
  CONSTRUCTING PLOTS   69

Chapter 4
PRESENCE AND ABSENCE: DAVID AND THE DEATH OF SAUL: (1 SAM. 27–2 SAM. 1)
  THE NARRATOR   111

Chapter 5
DAVID CONSOLIDATES HIS RULE: (2 SAM. 2–8 AND 21–24)
  CHARACTERIZATION   139

Chapter 6
FRUITS OF ARROGANCE: DAVID'S POOREST CHOICES (2 SAM. 9–14)
  CONVERGING FIVE TOOLS   183

Chapter 7
FRUITS OF SUFFERING: DAVID EXPERIENCES COMPASSION (2 SAM. 15–20)
  CONVERGING THREE TOOLS   217

Chapter 8
DAVID GOES THE WAY OF ALL THE EARTH (1 KGS. 1–2)
  THE SIXTH TOOL: NARRATIVE ANALOGY   247

Chapter 9
RECEPTION AND CONSTRUCTION OF DAVID IN A WESTERN PAINTING
  READING VISUAL ART   277

Bibliography   295
Index   306

FIGURE

Figure 9.1 Giovanni Battista (Giambattista) Pittoni, *David before the Ark of the Covenant, ca.* 1760. Oil on canvas. Uffizi Gallery, Florence; Photo Credit: Finsiel/Alinari/Art Resource, NY.   279

ABBREVIATIONS

AB	Anchor Bible
Bib	*Biblica*
BSac	*Bibliotheca Sacra*
BibInt	*Biblical Interpretation*
CBQ	*Catholic Biblical Quarterly*
HB	Hebrew Bible
Int	*Interpretation*
JBL	*Journal of Biblical Literature*
JSOT	*Journal for the Study of the Old Testament*
JSOTSup	Supplement Series
NT	New Testament
OT	Old Testament
RevExp	*Review and Expositor*
SBL	Society of Biblical Literature
SJOT	*Scandinavian Journal of the Old Testament*
ST	*Studia Theologica*
TynBul	*Tyndale Bulletin*
USQR	*Union Seminary Quarterly Review*
VT	*Vetus Testamentum*
VT Supp	*Vetus Testamentum* Supplements
ZAW	*Zeitschrift für die alttestamentliche Wissenshaft*

Chapter 1

RELEVANT METHODOLOGIES FOR CONSTRUCTING
AN ANCIENT FICTIVE WORK

1 Initial Considerations

How will we engage with the story of David, situated amid many methods clamoring for our use? Various challenges and opportunities arise when we attempt a fresh reading of an ancient classic, with many constructions inviting development. Biblical writers themselves offered various ways of seeing and showing the royal hero: The Chronicler represents David as being concerned primarily with feats relating to worship and warfare (1 Chronicles). Certain psalms lift up moments of David's life to picture him variously: for example, caring for the safety of the Ark of God (Psalm 132). The books of Samuel are less adulatory, neither avoiding to name the king's great failures nor moralizing dramatically about them. Early postbiblical Christian commentators read David allegorically or typologically, seeking ways in which he resembled and thus prefigured Jesus.[1] Jewish ancients, lacking that particular agenda, queried other details of the life presented in the biblical text.[2] The David narrative in the books of Samuel is spacious, hosting a variety of possibilities for basic views of the main character.

Early modern commentators became interested in mining from the narratives the early history of the biblical people, to present Iron Age Judah and Israel.[3] Recent

---

1. Consult the vast critical work of H. G. Reventlow, surveying both Christian and Jewish readings throughout the period of reception and response to biblical texts: *History of Biblical Interpretation,* vol. I. *From the Old Testament to Origen,* trans. Leo G. Perdue, vol. II. *From Late Antiquity to the End of the Middle Ages,* trans. James O. Duke (Atlanta: SBL Press, 2009).

2. Matthias Henze, ed., *A Companion to Biblical Interpretation in Early Judaism* (Grand Rapids, MI: William B. Eerdmans Publishing Co., 2012) provides such detail.

3. The early work of historians shows this trend, for example, John Bright, *A History of Israel,* 3rd ed. (Philadelphia: Westminster, 1972). Historians Israel Finkelstein and Neil Asher Silberman, *David and Solomon: In Search of the Bible's Sacred Kings and the Roots of the Western Tradition* (New York: Free Press, 2006) show a later phase of historical thought. For work more conversant with challenges of postmodern historiography, consult Lester L. Grabbe, "Reflections on the Discussion," in Grabbe, ed., *Enquire of the Former Age: Ancient Historiography and Writing the History of Israel* (London and New York: T&T Clark International, 2012), 263–75.

modern writers have been more critical of David than early ones, noting with a certain zeal his abuses of power.[4] Toward the end of the twentieth century, modern literary scholars found the textual material centering on David a rich banquet for interpretation, and their work remains foundational and fruitful.[5] More recently yet, scholars freshly conscious of the importance of reader perspectives have explored the narratives, focalizing named concerns, for example, feminist and postcolonial matters.[6]

Often these interpretive projects overlap and collaborate, though not always. The interpretation of the stories of David in 1–2 Samuel offered here will engage primarily contemporary literary methods, aiming to use, synthesize, and surpass the foundational work done at the end of the last century.[7] I will for the most part set aside historical issues that remain central for many scholars. Historical and sociological data are surely embedded within the biblical story, set as it is and produced as it was in specific time and space. But there is such a range of

4. See, for example, Steven L. McKenzie, *King David: A Biography* (Oxford and New York: Oxford University Press, 2000) and Baruch Halpern, *David's Secret Demons: Messiah, Murderer, Traitor, King* (Grand Rapids, MI: William B. Eerdmans Publishing Co., 2001).

5. Those studies include: Robert Alter, *The Art of Biblical Narrative* (New York: Basic Books, 1981); Yairah Amit, *Reading Biblical Narratives: Literary Criticism and the Hebrew Bible* (Minneapolis: Fortress, 2001); Shimon Bar-Efrat, *Narrative Art in the Bible* (JSOTSup 70, Sheffield: Almond Press, 1989); J. P. Fokkelman, *Narrative Art and Poetry in the Books of Samuel:* vol. I: *King David. II Samuel 9–20 and 1 Kings 1–2* (Assen, The Netherlands: Van Gorcum: 1981); *Narrative Art and Poetry in the Books of Samuel:* vol II: *The Crossing Fates: I Samuel 13–31 and II Samuel 1* (Assen, The Netherlands: Van Gorcum, 1986); *Narrative Art and Poetry in the Books of Samuel:* vol. IV: *Throne and City. II Samuel 2–8 and 21–24* (Assen, The Netherlands: Van Gorcum, 1990); David M. Gunn, *The Story of King David: Genre and Interpretation* (JSOTSup 6, Sheffield: JSOT Press, 1978); Robert M. Polzin, *Samuel and the Deuteronomist: A Literary Study of the Deuteronomic History. Part Two: 1 Samuel* (San Francisco: Harper & Row, 1989); Meir Sternberg, *The Poetics of Biblical Narrative: Ideological Literature and the Drama of Reading* (Bloomington: Indiana University Press, 1985). These and other works like them are critiqued by Greger Andersson, *Untamable Texts: Literary Studies and Narrative Theory in the Books of Samuel* (London and New York: T&T Clark, 2010).

6. The material may be sampled in a work like Athalya Brenner, *Samuel and Kings: A Feminist Companion* (The Feminist Companion to the Bible, Second Series 7, Sheffield: Sheffield Academic Press, 1994–2000), and Uriah Kim, *Identity and Loyalty in the David Story: A Postcolonial Reading* (Sheffield: Sheffield Phoenix Press, 2008).

7. The previous footnotes sample the range of literary biblical work; secular literary theory was developed by scholars such as Mieke Bal, *Narratology: Introduction to the Theory of Narrative*, trans. Christine van Boheemen (Toronto: University of Toronto Press, 1980); Seymour Chatman, *Story and Discourse: Narrative Structure in Fiction and Film* (Ithaca: Cornell University Press, 1978); Gérard Genette, *Narrative Discourse: An Essay in Method*, trans. Jane E. Lewin (Ithaca: Cornell University Press, 1980); and Shlomith Rimmon-Kennan, *Narrative Fiction: Contemporary Poetics*, 2nd ed. (New York: Methuen, 2002).

possibilities for discerning those coordinates, such uncertainty and dispute about particulars, that their discussion tends to swamp other interests once they get a foot in the door. The setting may be from around the eleventh century, with a likely time of production culminating not earlier than the late sixth or early fifth centuries BCE, a large and not very well-known period.[8] The reading attempted here can manage without needing to pin down the context more closely. I do maintain that the struggle between Judah and Benjamin, so prominent in the David story, will have had urgent contemporary relevance to the group that produced it, whether we can know that concern in detail or not.[9]

Since such minimization of historical specificity can seem irresponsible, let me offer an analogy. Consider Shakespeare's *Antony and Cleopatra*, a play written in the seventeenth century about events that took place in the first century CE, as presented by Plutarch around a century later, available to Shakespeare in a summary and to us in several volumes.[10] As we watch the play, to what extent do precise historical questions consume us? If we can assume that Plutarch has the tangle of relevant events presented adequately as backdrop scenario for Shakespeare's drama, does that setting suffice for us to engage with the basically fictive presentation of persons and their interactions offered by the play? Do we learn more about the *play* when we study the *history* more closely? Not necessarily. Do we learn more about *history* when we probe the details of the *play* itself? Again, not really. Our situation with the present topic is similar. A second way to think about the interpretation project: consider a visit to a museum, featuring the art of Rembrandt. As we look at the paintings, we can try to peer through the works to ask what Netherlandish scene or whose well-worn face is represented, or we can appreciate the detail of the depictions as we have them. Ideally we can do both. But often different "muscles" are involved, and to search for historical referents can distract massively from looking at what has been portrayed, which is clamoring for our skilled observation. My point is to suggest that as the set of reliable historical data correlating well with the narrative is actually diminishing, we may and must consider issues more relevant, specifically with literary and hermeneutical theory.

This present work, in certain dialogue with opposing views, wagers that David can be seen as flawed but willing to learn from mistakes, as amassing and misusing power but also capable of turning toward wisdom and compassion. The intent of this book is to offer such a portrait from the biblical material to readers who

---

8. To approach this vast set of research, consult Philip R. Davies, *The Origins of Biblical Israel* (Library of Hebrew Bible, Old Testament Studies 485, London and New York: T&T Clark, 2007) and *Memories of Ancient Israel: An Introduction to Biblical History—Ancient and Modern* (Louisville: Westminster/John Knox Press, 2008).

9. Elizabeth Vandiver, *Greek Tragedy* (Chantilly, VA: The Teaching Company, 2000), DVD, *passim*, discussing the classic Athenian dramas, suggests how while reworking ancient and mythic themes, the fifth-century playwrights also offer issues from the Persian or civil wars as well.

10. Geoffrey Bullough, ed., *Narrative and Dramatic Sources of Shakespeare*, 8 vols (London: Routledge & Kegan Paul, 1957–75).

wish to consider it. As will be explained shortly, the philosophical assumptions underlying this interpretation count on readers bringing particular concerns to an ancient text, constructing what is of existential value—carefully and critically to be sure, but not neutrally. The point I want to offer, the portrait to unfold, is that the character David is shown to turn from an initial and appropriate young *naïveté* toward a propensity to use and even manipulate others. Once confidently dependent upon God, who assists him variously, David comes to act with arrogance and contempt toward others, including the deity. Checked, and painfully so, David struggles to act from graciousness, sometimes managing and sometimes not. After some signal failures, he seems able in the end to act with appropriate integrity. This book concerns that journey of his, invites readers to avoid easy valorization or vilification but to experience these struggles with empathy.

We can, then, think about rereading the biblical story of David in terms of the parents begetting and birthing it: modern literary study and philosophical hermeneutics. Each forebear needs brief attention, in fact a quick tracing of its own genetic heritage as well. The modern and, specifically, the current literary methods have arisen from pioneering work both within and outside the biblical corpus. Since that story is not so well known as it might be, I include here a brief synopsis of how the Bible became recognized as literary as well as historical and a brief introduction to the philosophical issues involved in interpretation of ancient texts.

2 Modern Literary Methodology

a Roots of the Present Literary Study of Biblical Texts

1. Ancient Theorists Plato and Aristotle (427–347 and 384–322, BCE, respectively) remain the best place to begin. Plato thought that poets offered truth/reality deficiently and derivatively from a perfect eternal form, producing not reality but appearance, verbal representation. What exists eternally and what is represented by mortals are ontologically distinct, and to confuse them can only be dangerous. Literary mimesis—storytelling, poetry, drama—is even farther removed from truth than are other human expressions and activities, with such writers lacking the philosophical rigor to understand what they are doing: rendering copies of copies. Consequently, poets seek to please audiences, and audiences likely miscue from culturally embedded art to imitate what they are shown, and not beneficially. Plato concluded that poets and writers, unable to speak truthfully, needed either censoring or even banishment from an ideal state or society.

Aristotle, approaching the same issue from a more descriptive and classificatory angle, suggested that artistic language should be judged by its own criteria, distinct from other expressions of culture, with each utterance evaluated on its own merits rather than as belonging to a particular class or expressing a specific morality. Not driven, as was Plato, by the sense that the poets' representations were false and their impact harmful, Aristotle examined the question of how audiences responded when hearing the words or watching the suffering of others enacted fictively and artistically. He concluded that viewer responses were actually to their own suffering and vulnerability rather than to that of characters encountered in art. Right and wrong did not come into it. Andrea Nightingale, summarizing her essay on these two giants, notes: "Ironically, Aristotle rescued literature by writing a dry philosophical treatise; Plato attacks literary texts while producing some of the most complex pieces of literature ever written."[11] These two thinkers can be seen as setting forth major issues that continue to be relevant to any discussion of literature: language, the nature of representation, truth and its varieties, relations among author, text, and readers.[12]

The Hebrew biblical tradition, roughly contemporary with these two thinkers and their writings, evidently did not theorize like the Greeks, who so dominated classical thought and have influenced the agenda ever since then. Hence the issues just raised by the two seminal thinkers do not surface explicitly in the Bible. The most comparable matter might be the nature of the Hebrew poetic tradition (using "poetic" to cover the Bible's artistic language, whether poetry or prose), including the form and function of Hebrew rhetoric.[13] Scholars can read the language, describe the strategies, and speculate about their impact, but the ancient writers themselves do not lend a hand to the meta-discussion, while surely providing the raw data for it.

2. Modernity As we proceed quickly toward the literary turn shaking up biblical studies midway through the twentieth century, we can ask how literature was studied academically before the several key changes relevant to biblical studies. Surprisingly, before the turn of the last century (1894 at Cambridge University and 1911 at Oxford), there was not much formal recognition of English literature as a serious subject for academic study. Generally, the English literary tradition was approached in terms of what is called "liberal humanism" (comparable to the Great Books tradition familiar in the United States), where literature was assumed to underwrite and endorse a common morality valued by "middle-class" educated citizens (not elite or "lower-class" values). Since the two great universities were effectively controlled by the Church of England, an easy bridge linked established

11. Andrea Nightingale, "Mimesis: Ancient Greek Literary Theory," in Patricia Waugh, ed., *Literary Theory and Criticism: An Oxford Guide* (Oxford: Oxford University Press, 2006), 37–47 (46).

12. Faiza W. Shereen, "Form, Rhetoric, and Intellectual History," in Patricia Waugh, ed., *Literary Theory*, 233–44 (235), distinguishes the thought of these two great thinkers as "lumping" (Plato) and "splitting" (Aristotle). That is, where Plato sees reality as *a priori*, synthetic, and unified though diminishing as it fades from the realm of forms, Aristotle situates poetry under imitative arts and then divides it into narrative and drama, each with subcategories and constituent parts.

13. The most useful recent summary is probably Jack R. Lundbom, *Jeremiah 1–20: A New Translation with Introduction and Commentary* (AB 21A, New York: Doubleday, 1999), 68–92, 121–40.

Christianity and English literature—with the great works offering a sort of pale religion.[14] Literature could also be studied somewhat philologically (a process akin to how the Bible has been studied) and historically as well. There was no agreed and established tradition of critical study of the literature per se, with a couple of early modern essays by Sir Philip Sidney and Samuel Johnson providing a base, supplemented eventually by the theorizing of romantic poets (late eighteenth to nineteenth centuries, with their keen interest in the artist's expressivity). Victorian poets (late nineteenth century to early twentieth century) added commentary that came to form a stable tradition of thought on the nature of literary study.[15] But note: This is late!

Once the two leading British universities took on the challenge of teaching literature, it took one classic shape (sometimes called Practical Criticism) in England and a slightly different but clearly related form in the United States (best known as New Criticism). This phase of study, dominating from the 1920s or so until the 1960s, can be usefully, if generally, characterized, as its issues continue to be debated up to the present. Granting national, regional, and personal differences among those who wrestled with these matters, we can single out several motivating and grounding concerns that structured this phase of theory: (1) a perceived threat from scientific thought and research and from technology and "mass culture" that seemed to threaten the values of humane letters; (2) the vexing problem of clarifying some critical process for the study of literature without turning literature into science; (3) the clarification of literature in relation to other disciplines, so it might seem a field with its own integrity rather than part of history or classics; (4) the consideration of who actual readers were, such as might be assisted (or informed!) as to best procedures for forming a critical common mass of readers; (5) the emergence of some of the hermeneutical questions that remain fraught (e.g., when we read a work, whose voice and views are being represented or perceived; whether literature has a stable meaning); (6) the reconsideration of some perennial questions rooted in philosophy (e.g., what is literature, how does language represent experience); and (7) the need to develop appropriate curricula for advanced study.[16]

These general modernist concerns prominent in both centers of the study of English literature (associated signally with F. R. Leavis of Cambridge University and less clearly with Northrop Frye of University of Toronto and Harvard and

14. Peter Barry, *Beginning Theory: An Introduction to Literary and Cultural Theory* (Manchester: Manchester University Press, 1995), 12–14, provides some background. He reminds us that until the dawn of the twentieth century, the degrees granted by "Oxbridge" were divinity, mathematics, and Greek and Latin classics, though certain other centers of study, University College, London, and other major urban campuses did provide formal instruction in English literature. The formal study of literature is a late phenomenon.

15. Barry, *Beginning Theory*, 22–25.

16. For efficient summaries of issues presented summarily here, consult Patricia Waugh, "Introduction: Criticism, Theory, and Anti-Theory," in Waugh, ed., *Literary Theory*, 1–33. The volume provides plentiful information on all phases of these issues.

Robert Penn Warren of Louisiana State University, Yale University, and University of Chicago at Champlain) took hold—again with some variations not immediately relevant here—tending eventually to agree on several specific norms and practices: (1) the proper subject matter of literary study is not philology or some other specifically language-related study; (2) historical and social considerations are not relevant to the work being studied; (3) the point is, rather, to do a close and careful study of the words on the page; (4) such study ought not result in effusive or extensive paraphrase but must be explicit about both underlying principles and analytical process of interpretation; (5) philosophical explorations into the roots of literary issues are not to be sought or stressed; (6) the valorized style prefers showing to telling; (7) beginning with the assumption that the author of a piece is the important participant, there emerged a focus on the text but without any noticeable awareness of or interest in particular readers (though some of the seeds that would bear fruit about readers had actually been sown).[17]

Nicholas Birns, writing on these same matters, has coined the term "resolved symbolic" to epitomize what seemed to gather consensually at this period, though to be vigorously contested shortly.[18] Birns clarifies that his term encodes the belief that a text on its own can deliver a consistent meaning that is extensive, complete, adequate, coherent, indissoluble, accounting for all the details of the particular literary work. A text's interpretation can be complete, finished, settled—authoritatively. It is a view that "theory" will shortly challenge, and massively.

Though these issues raged in English departments throughout much of the broad first half of the twentieth century, they did not emerge visibly in biblical studies for several decades, even as recently as the 1980s. The direction that critical literary biblical study took was somewhat distinctive, since the vast weight of historical study of the Bible all but eliminated issues that were genuinely "literary."[19] When a literary phase emerged, it was largely focused on close reading, stressing a number of the points listed above as central to British and US practical and new critical procedures. Understandably, it de-emphasized historical contexts, exploited the possibilities of attention to the words on the page, eschewed issues addressed by philosophy and theology, and provided shape for new curricula. Philology remained—remains—important, but the effort to name and show the function of literary tools and methods was primary, with philology subsumed into that effort. The early literary biblical scholars explicitly or implicitly assumed themselves to be correct and normative for all readers, allowing little space for difference of opinion on their judgments. This literary phase, late and intense

17. More detail on these matters may be sought in Barry, *Beginning Theory*, 15–16 and 27–31, as well as in several of the chapters in Waugh, *Literary Theory*.

18. Nicholas Birns, *Theory after Theory: An Intellectual History of Literary Theory from 1950 to the Early 21st Century* (Peterborough, NY: Broadview Press, 2010), 15, 171.

19. Biblical studies named one of its projects "literary criticism," but the endeavor was primarily the quest for historical circumstances of the production of texts, such as those texts (sources) comprising the book of Genesis and eventually in other places. So "literary" criticism of the Bible was thoroughly historical, until the term was reclaimed in the 1980s.

(for those who participated), rather quickly opened up to the "theory" phases of general literary criticism that I am about to describe. That is, the "new critical" phase was short-lived in biblical studies and soon fruitfully enhanced by the waves of issues pounding the beach from the 1960s onward.

3. *Critical Turn* Next, crucially, comes the seismic shift from the late 1960s, continuing at least until the end of the twentieth century: the decisive move toward theory. Large steps again must suffice to sketch the complex change. We can name the three "masters of suspicion," already much sooner than mid-twentieth century undermining some treasured certainties of previous eras by pointing out the ubiquity of pernicious ideological distortion and the blindness of those infected by it. Friedrich Nietzsche (1844–1900) espoused the human will to power over Christian ethical values established or commonly understood, maintaining that the religious ethos—far from salutary—was actually detrimental to human thriving: God is dead. Karl Marx (1818–85) saw history as a great process of classes inevitably conflicting as they compete for social and economic goods. Sigmund Freud (1856–1939), writing on the human mind and consciousness, taught that what we suppose and value about ourselves and our reality is not to be trusted, springing as it does from the repressed, perverse, and shameful and masked by our own proclivities. Premoderns had no such notions, while postmoderns can scarcely escape them.

More proximately, we can cite the pervasive influence of two later major theorists: Michel Foucault (1926–84) and Jacques Derrida (1930–2004). Considered together, this pair can introduce us to "theory." The work of such European thinkers, often seeming alien and obscure to the scholars in English-speaking centers, sought to explain literary and philosophical processes more deeply than had been done before, bringing into the conversation topics largely undreamed by the academics absorbed in more "gentlemanly" discussion of language and literature. Theorists, in this new sense, insisted upon the urgent relevance of certain classic and especially newer philosophical questions and issues for literary and social encounters, making them freshly and intensely explicit, while critiquing or dismissing much that had seemed clear, settled, and preferred. Theory seemed to many an enemy of literature, scorning values that those who espoused them supposed to be common, good, and obvious, if they thought about it at all. The turn to theory tore the wiring from much that had seemed settled, certainly from Birns's "resolved symbolic."

Foucault most notably called into question classification systems and categories, challenging accepted concepts of neutrality, aiming to expose and make explicit, clear, and acknowledged the multiple, if hidden, influences on social realms (e.g., in his early work on medicine). He called attention to the constructedness of all systems, insisting that "natural" was a dubious and even pernicious notion. To investigate the long past of realities was to see the many alternatives to present assumptions, to restore the past to possibility. He studied the reality and scope of power—including the ways it guards its own status and banishes threats—thus undermining social structures, literary canons, and great works by showing them arbitrary and non-innocent. Foucault was and remains massively influential in life and literature.[20]

Derrida, for his part, questioned established hierarchies, showing the instability of any meaning that counts on a fixed relation among participating factors, surely but not exclusively in language. Words do not have inherent meaning but establish themselves provisionally, relationally with other realities, with whatever seems to stand near them to prop them up. Choosing an odd and archaic word, "deconstruction," he gave it new life as he used it to name the process of picking away at foundations to expose the instability, provisionality, and constructedness of what appears to most people as stable, set, and normal. Questioning the claimed binaries of structuralist thought, he set such factors into endless play, demonstrating both their difference in relation to other elements and their ever deferring to settle into fixed relationship. Thus he challenged the confidence of many in inherent or even stable meaning. His demonstration of language as inescapably slippery and meaning as ever unstable and inadequate posed—poses—a significant challenge to literature.

In more specifically literary terms, three other thinkers who added to the attack on the resolved symbolic can be sampled briefly: Harold Bloom (b. 1930) vigorously refuted tenets of New Criticism, called for a creative misreading of the past tradition, and introduced labyrinthine rabbinic exegetical principles into the process of literary interpretation. Roland Barthes (1915–80) offered structuralist implications for the understanding of literature (language and literature as understood as a system of signs controlling expression), distinguishing between a work (produced by an author and read as authorized) and text (constructed by readers), working out the implications of "the death of the author" by prompting a narrator to challenge the relevance of the actual composer. Wayne C. Booth (1921–2005), a neo-Aristotelian, reordered the reading of fiction, introducing an implied author whose presence destabilized the actual author and welcomed an intentionality that was neither fallacious nor reducible to the opinion of the one who wrote the text. Booth also introduced the notion of an unreliable narrator. Each with many others as well moved the production and study of literature out of closed and clear systems to name and celebrate ways more open, multiple, and unsettled, and to complicate the negotiation called reading.

b Late Twentieth Century and Beyond

1. Cultural Criticism Influenced by vistas opened by these powerful thinkers and no less by social revolutions of the latter part of the twentieth century, many more specific fields of inquiry and discourse emerged, each with a rich and somewhat open focus: the *political*, alert to the tremendous ravages of the twentieth century and aiming to bring awareness and even remediation to situations of oppression and violation; the *regional*, conscious of the vast and ongoing power of the colonial

---

20. Birns, *Theory*, ch. 1, explores the contribution of Foucault in helpful detail.

experience, past and present, manifested in cultures of oppressed and oppressor; the *ethnic*, alert to riches available when cultures other than those prominent and dominant in the West are explored and valorized; the *class conscious*, emerging from the voiced experience of subalterns that became suasive; the *gender-linked*, beginning with feminist concerns and widening to explore gay and queer experience; the *psychological*, investigating realms off-limits to casual exploration and needing the enhancement of other social sciences, for example in trauma theory.[21] In a word, these "micro-climate" issues, especially as they continue to proliferate and combine, offer biblical studies a huge array of questions and methods to bring to bear on classic texts. Scholars have moved from asking what biblical texts say about the lives of biblical women to ask how texts embed values that can—even must—be critiqued, moving to how the perspectives opened by these modern and postmodern issues help us construct and interpret the biblical text afresh. The point here has been to suggest the immeasurable impact of modern theory on the study of literature, on classics, and surely on the biblical text, with its status as beyond classic. To attempt study without awareness of these matters is foolish, however they may be taken up or sidelined. Concomitantly, any sense of "doing it all" is futile.[22]

2. Reader Theory How did the reader enter transactions that, until the end of the twentieth century, had seemed solely the domain of author and text? Again, by way of naming a few high points, we can follow the trail of the powerful author, first giving way often in a somewhat smudged manner to the presence of a text before finally being pronounced dead and irrelevant to meaning as readers begin to negotiate discourse more boldly. That is, as it becomes more apparent and accepted that the intent of the author is both difficult to ascertain and largely irrelevant, and as the unitary role once understood as the author's is split among a real and an implied author as well as with various kinds of narrators, uncertainty and ambiguity flower wonderfully though not uninhibitedly. As the quality of language and literature is shown ever unstable and in need of construction, the reader's importance—and skill—comes to be acknowledged, indeed required. Since the point here is simply to map the factors with which an interpreter of literature may and must contend, we can visit two moments in reader theory for a sense of key issues.

Early among these is an effort to map the actual process of what a reader does when encountering ambiguity. For this move we can consider two theorists, Wolfgang Iser (1926–2007) and Stanley Fish (b. 1938). Iser, a German, but with broad exposure in English, was trained as a phenomenologist, and he was intent on describing what happens as readers engage with texts. He assigned a significant role to both text (even author, on occasion) and reader, showing them mutually

---

21. These all have substantial discussion in Waugh, *Literary Theory*, parts II and III; in Birns, *Theory*, chs. 3–7; and in Anthony C. Thiselton, *Hermeneutics: An Introduction* (Grand Rapids: William B. Eerdmans Publishing Co., 2009).

22. Birns, *Theory*, summarizes Derrida in ch. 2 of his book.

interactive, each pole partially constituting the other.[23] The text offers a set of options, from which the reader selects; and the reader activates a particular set of choices, making fresh meaning. Iser's most famous contribution to reader theory is the concept of "indeterminacy," that is, gaps. Such *aporiai* emerge throughout complex literary texts—generated as viewpoints collide, intersecting at plot, narrator, characters, and reader—though of course in another sense they are not "there," being gaps. Each reader negotiates these multiple sites, not once but repeatedly, anticipating, retrospecting, revising, and rejecting. Readers, each theoretically distinctive, have particular repertoires with which they read; texts, also highly dense, have conventions that demand attention. A reader cannot consult a text to ascertain from it whether its cue is being well construed, nor can a text intervene to prevent a reader from a poor choice or to encourage or praise a good one. Readers will tend toward coherence and consistency, Iser held, but readings will also be particular and distinctive. Readers will likely identify with characters. The effect of reading is the appropriation of meaning, specifically including self-knowledge.

Iser is famous for his analogy of our "reading" of the starry splatter of the night sky, where one might see a plow, another a dipper. But ultimately he held that the sky determines our choices.[24] That is, pushed to choose, Iser accorded primacy to text over reader, thus skating closer to New Criticism than he might sometimes sound, shying away from the notion that there are no textual constraints on a reader. But he insisted that a text can cue a reader to fresh insight and activate the reader's imagination in unanticipated ways. His reader of interest is abstract and theoretical rather than particular and real.

Though Iser's limits are not difficult to demonstrate, Reader-Response scholar Robert Holub nonetheless points out several achievements for which Iser can take credit: He theorized about the actual reading process in some detail—notably the negotiation of gaps, drawing attention to a process more complex than a simple negotiation of the meanings of individual words. He made clear that readers must engage their own understandings if they are to interpret literature, and not simply seek the accumulation of what others have said. Texts proffer constructs for negotiation rather than insisting upon dogmatic strictures. Iser, holding an appointment at a US university, helped make the continental philosophical antecedents of his work more familiar to US readers.[25] It is easy to see his appeal for many biblical readers, for whom textual constraints are not optional.

---

23. Iser's implied reader is thus substantially textual, little prone to historical-social particularity.

24. S.R. Suleiman, and I. Crossman, *The Reader in the Text: Essays on Audience Interpretation* (Princeton: Princeton University Press, 1980), 21.

25. Robert C. Holub, *Reception Theory: A Critical Introduction* (New Accents, NY: Methuen, 1984), 106.

Stanley Fish was labeled as "the point man" for Reader-Response theory in the United States, likely true at one time.[26] As a literary scholar, Stanley Fish seems to find basic agreement with what Iser says on a number of points: meaning as event; reception as constituting a work; a reading process that anticipates, reviews, and modifies; the text as the dominant partner; and reader specifics as not particularly important.[27] But during the 1970s and 1980s, Fish boldly labeled the "affective fallacy" (which we will examine shortly) as itself a fallacy. This position marked a substantial shift in his thought, moving him to adopt a much more antiformalist stance, privileging the role of the reader and asserting that there is nothing prior to reading, to interpretation, and indeed nothing remaining after it. The reader's experience comprises interpretation. In that sense, "response" is not so well named. If the indeterminate gap is Iser's signature concept, interpretive communities fill that role for "middle Fish." Readers are cued not so much by texts as by conventions that characterize the groups to which they belong. Those constraints shape readers, who activate them when engaging the text. The conventions are not individually but communally determined, not explicitly chosen so much as imbibed or swum into. Fish thus insisted upon the importance of context and situation for all interpretation, though theorists moving in the direction of cultural studies find him seriously deficient in actually exploiting such particularity. Again, the appeal for biblical studies is clear.

Clashing early in their careers, these two spent some effort to pinpoint, if not resolve, their differences. They generally agree, if one thinks of the large continuum of possible interpreters, that all perception is mediated. But Fish basically negates Iser's indeterminacy theory, suggesting that there is no real indeterminacy, since any reader is thoroughly immersed in and constituted by assumptions before reading occurs. No reader can step out of these constraints. And, Fish continues, there is nothing determined, since before a reader engages it, even the text on the page—and any gap—has no existence outside of reader construction.[28] To talk about gaps "in" the text misses the point, for Fish. Readers are always already constrained and constraining. Iser, unwilling to concede that point, was thus left arguing for or positing a text that does exist prior to a reader. Perhaps more to the point, or more simply and reductively, Iser reveals that he handed priority to the text in matters of constraint, whereas Fish locates it unambiguously in the

---

26. Vincent Leitch, "Reader-Response Criticism," in Andrew Bennet, ed., *Readers and Reading* (Longman Critical Readers, London and NY: Longman, 1995), 32–65 (38).

27. Leitch characterizes Fish's thought in the early 1970s, in "Reader-Response," 36–37.

28. For more detail, see Holub, *Reception Theory*, 102–06 and his *Crossing Borders: Reception Theory, Poststructuralism, Deconstruction* (Madison: University of Wisconsin Press, 1992), 25–28. Another practical way to demonstrate the workings of these matters is explored in Nevada Levi DeLapp, *The Reformed David(s) and the Question of Resistance to Tyranny: Reading the Bible in the 16th and 17th Centuries* (London: Bloomsbury T&T Clark, 2014), 176–89, who uses reader and text theory to explain how those with diverse political views can use David's dealings with Saul to authorize their positions.

reader. To some extent, they were eventually talking on different levels. But their cumulative contribution was significant.

3. *Comprehensive Challenges* How to be alert to the "theory" explosion but not overwhelmed by it? It can seem overwhelming to a reader—indeed, to this writer—to digest all this information that both frees and constrains our reading. The point here is more to recognize how much has happened in the modern period and how foundation-shaking this "recent" critical conversation has been than to envision mastery or expertise across its range. No serious scholar can disregard theory, move along as though it had not happened. Though there is talk about theory's decline and some life "after theory," that moment may not be looming in biblical studies, which tends to run a bit behind the discourses it comes to sense as relevant.[29] And in any case, the path forward must come *through* theory, not circle around it. A biblical scholar must customize this mass of insight to his or her particular commitments, develop additional competence in what is deemed most useful by engaging the original works implied here. Those working with Homer and Shakespeare will proceed differently from those whose specialty is metafiction; those interpreting texts not only ancient but also functioning as Scripture have particular challenges in addition to those adumbrated here. What follows is my own customization, adapted to my commitments, interests, situation, and circumstances. I have become a substantial skeptic about historiography and some of its moves in standard biblical study, having attended to it over decades and continuing to monitor it with some openness. I am also not particularly interested in diverse readers, nor in the history of reception. I am wholly cognizant of the appropriateness of diverse readers interpreting from life circumstances and appreciative of the enriching of the biblical text that has resulted from such reading (e.g., feminist and postcolonial). I celebrate the impact of such interpretation on a text considered normative and formative. I simply do not choose to do much of it myself, though we will look at nonverbal interpretation of the David narrative.

Before leaving the general story of how modern literary study came to be adapted to biblical study and moving to introduce the particular tools we will use, I want to offer one more general contribution of literary thought. In the fresh insight bubbling from the intersection of modern theory with a former confidence in the "resolved symbolic," two fallacies were proclaimed by theorists. I want to reposition them, to call attention to the process of biblical study adapting what it received from broader literary study, staking a position for postmoderns who are also committed, intentional, responsible readers of biblical texts. Called the *intentional fallacy* and the *affective fallacy*, these positions on certain sets of issues encourage us to ask again about meaning in texts: What is it, how does it work, who manages it? Briefly and summarily, the *intentional fallacy* claims that it is invalid to assume that we can reduce a work to the intention of its author; the *affective*

29. See Birns, *Theory*, ch. 7; for specifically religious issues, consult Jens Zimmermann, "*Quo Vadis?* Literary Theory beyond Postmodernism," *Christianity and Literature* 53.4 (2004): 495–519.

fallacy asserts that a work's impact on readers is irrelevant to it. Thus flatly stated, we can likely agree. But in both instances, the trajectory of insights accumulating throughout the twentieth century helps us to nuance the conclusions here, to see and say more. In biblical studies, authorial intention has played a central role that shows little signs of abating, for example, the theology of the Priestly writer or of the writer of the Fourth Gospel—both legitimate and respectable projects. Similarly, how readers respond to what they read remains central in the deep appropriation of the biblical text. So the point here will be to nuance both "fallacies" a bit, so we can gain from the issues they pose.[30]

The utter sundering of author, text, and reader from each other is not tenable, with its limits reached, perhaps, in some of the discussions around the death of the author and the turn to the reader. If, basically, the three partners (author, text, reader) remain inseparable in various ways, the issue is to weight the participation of each—a choice also depending heavily on the genre of the text: in a technological manual of directions, the author's intent is more crucial than in a poem; in the production of a drama, audience response is far more crucial than in a private journal. We can talk about a distinction between the utterer's meaning and the utterance meaning, and we will do well to query the interpreter's frame of reference as well—again, insofar as these are available and with appropriate awareness of how little we may know even about ourselves, interpreting, let alone about an ancient text and multiple authors. It may be possible and important to deduce or construct the plan of an author at least provisionally from cues discernible in a text. Various efforts may be adjudicated, with some deemed more persuasive than others. The psychological processes of ancient authors are far out of reach, though some of the other extratextual historical and social circumstances may be available for construction. If a modern poet is writing about the First World War, for a reader to know something of that conflict is useful—even crucial. The work of J. L. Austin in speech act theory reminds us that the utterance "I do" takes on a special and legal meaning in particular circumstances, where speaker intent surely signifies. We can hear a narrative voice offer an opinion and name a plan, as Luke's Theophilus does at the beginning of Acts of the Apostles, but we are not thereby constrained to accept the statement as cleanly authorial. The special case of irony also slows us down from being too categorical about intent. How do we decide if a text "is" ironic? Some texts may have been so authored; many can be so read. But are there textual indicators guiding the choice? They are notoriously difficult to find, name, exploit—not least when we are dealing with an ancient text.

The concern implicit here, perhaps unknown to traditional and to "new" critics but familiar more recently, is that a text can become so unmoored from everything as to mean nothing or support anything. This point helps us to think carefully about where meaning resides: if not in the mind of the author, is it "in" the text? Can a reader construe just about anything from a text? Does the triad of

---

30. See Peter Lamarque, "The Intentional Fallacy," in Waugh, ed., *Literary Theory*, 177–88, and Chris Baldick, *The Oxford Dictionary of Literary Terms*, 3rd ed. (Oxford: Oxford University Press, 2008), 5, 169–70.

author, text, and reader function rather as a team, with a reader making meaning from what a text proffers, as artistically crafted by a skilled author? As we think about ways in which language has been shown complex and rich, unstable, and multivalent, we have new ways of thinking about how artists, texts, and readers interact. The whole turn to the reader, discussed above, offers a radical critique of the claim that the impact or effect of a work is off-limits to its consideration. So as biblical studies makes use of these points, critical nuance is wanted.

c Literary Tools for the Present Study

Dependent upon and flowing from these issues emerge some specific literary assumptions and tools that will guide the present interpretation.

1. General The most basic literary concept to be named and drawn upon is *narrativity*. Narrativity comprises the set of features marking and distinguishing narrative from other genres (e.g., drama, lyric poetry), signaling that a narrating voice recounts a tale to us in some sort of significant temporal sequence, likely involving causal relations among characters and events. Presented for our consideration is a series of events (not simply situations), clothed in subjects and predicates, interrelated in one way and not another.[31] Storytelling may be second only to the capacity for language itself as marking our characteristically human condition.[32] Perhaps outside our propensity to narrate events, we scarcely know our experience or achieve consciousness.[33] Narrativity—whether we are participating as writers or readers—gives us opportunity to establish order when faced with the challenge of chaos and affords us satisfying occasion to wrestle mystery and incoherence into something knowable and manageable, enhancing our capacity and thirst to understand and make meaning. Narrative presents us with complexity, demands that we negotiate the zigzagging of time, the uncertainties

---

31. The typical ways for relations among events to be postulated include by continuity, contiguity, or causality. That is, events are not simply piled together but are interrelated in some way, with the particular choice crucial. Knowledge of Hebrew grammar and syntax helps us determine what we can and cannot assert and where we may offer possibilities. For good introductions to this vast topic of narrativity, see H. Porter Abbott, *The Cambridge Introduction to Narrative*, 2nd ed. (Cambridge, UK: Cambridge University Press, 2008), chs. 1–2; consult also Suzanne Keen, *Narrative Form* (New York: Palgrave Macmillan, 2003), chs. 1–3 (121). Luc Herman and Bart Vervaeck, *Handbook of Narrative Analysis* (Lincoln: University of Nebraska Press, 2001) present their study of narrative in chronological order, with their introduction and ch. 1 providing basic concepts.

32. For various claims about the ubiquity, multiformity, and staying power of narrative in human culture as appraised by various scholars, see Abbott, *Cambridge Introduction*, 1–3 (and his first two chapters); Herman and Vervaeck, *Handbook*, 1–10; Keen, *Narrative Form*, 1–5 (and in fact the first two chapters).

33. This is a vast topic and not wholly relevant here, but for some discussion on it, consult Abbott, *Cambridge Introduction*, 1–12.

of causality, and the endless depth of personages who seem like ourselves. As we find ourselves identifying with one character or averse to another, we feel entitled to our perceptions and assessments, even while recognizing that we are presented with "zones" of characterization not so very much unlike the ones we operate from our own consciousness. Narrative, specifically verbal fictive narrative as has been under discussion here, is a profound human activity, allowing us to make meaning as we explore representation.[34]

To identify narrativity as basic presents us next with the challenge of naming participant roles in the basic narrative writing/reading process. Adapted from general literary theory by Jerome Walsh, this parsing of narrativity, extending from authoring through reading, can be conceived as shared among six paired and participating entities.[35] At the left end of the process stand the *real authors* of a text. In the case of ancient classics, we may not know who those were, and so a name is provided, which becomes traditional. When we call Homer the author of the *Iliad* and *Odyssey*, we understand that "he" did not create those texts simply or privately. Some actual, historical persons produced the material we call 1 Samuel 8 through 1 Kings 2, with no shortage of effort to identify their hands, and no lack of possibilities. In the modern period the material that embeds our David story has generally been credited to an entity called the Deuteronomist (or Deuteronomistic historian).[36] But consensus and clarity are lacking, and as already indicated, I do not choose to come any closer than to say that the authors or editors of the material likely lived between the eighth and sixth centuries

---

34. R. Ruard Ganzevoort, "Introduction: Religious Stories We Live By," in R. R. Ganzevoort, Maaika de Haardt and Michael Scherer-Rath, eds., *Religious Stories We Live By: Narrative Approaches in Theology and Religious Studies* (Leiden, Boston: Brill, 2014), 1–17 (3). Other essays in the volume explore ways in which narratives help us make meaning with fictive religious narratives.

35. Jerome T. Walsh, *Old Testament Narrative: A Guide to Interpretation* (Louisville: Westminster John Knox, 2009), 2–9 explains his model and provides a schematic which I simplify here. For additional discussion, not focused on biblical material, consult Keen, *Narrative Form*, chs. 1–3 (1–54, discussing the model on 33) as she opens these questions in a slightly different way, as do Herman and Vervaeck, *Handbook*, 16–22. The articles on "Implied Author" by Ansgar Nünning and "Implied Reader" by Emma Kafalenos in David Herman, Manfred Jahn, and Marie-Lauren Ryan, eds., *The Routledge Encyclopedia of Narrative Theory* (London and New York: Routledge Taylor & Francis Group, 2005), 239–40 and 240–41 provide additional nuance.

36. For a recent discussion of this topic, which emerged and has developed over the past one hundred and fifty or so years, consult Thomas C. Römer, *The So-Called Deuteronomistic History: A Sociological, Historical and Literary Introduction* (New York: T&T Clark, 2007). Even those who remain generally satisfied with this understanding question whether the hand that produced most of the material in the Deuteronomistic history, as it is called (extending from Deuteronomy through 2 Kings), is to be identified with the skilled artist of the David materials.

BCE, with their specific situations and plans unable to be specified with much more precision.

Real or actual readers are all receivers of the narrative, extending from those for whom it was composed (*intended readers*) to us, reading in the third millennium of the common era, with these readers diverse over time and culture. So *real authors* create texts, and *real readers*, many over millennia, in the case of the David story, read them. Real authors and real readers mark the edges of the process of narrativity.

More relevant for present purposes is the next layer of storytelling, called the *implied author*. This is not a flesh-and-blood person but a logical concept, almost a placeholder. The implied author, to simplify a complex and disputed matter, is an abstraction standing in for all of the vast, even infinite planning that can be understood as comprising a great literary work, what H. Porter Abbott calls "a sensibility behind the narrative that accounts for how it is constructed."[37] The implied author is the one who, by definition, is responsible for precisely the material under present consideration, who coincides exactly with the design of this narrative. Even if we were to learn, somehow, that the same historical person also wrote other material, it would make no difference to our sense of the implied author, whose sole narration is stipulated as 1 Samuel 8 through 1 Kings 2. The concept of implied author allows us to talk about the shaping of the whole work without needing constantly to raise all the uncertainties of historical process. The implied author of the particular David story as told in 1–2 Samuel is responsible for all the artistry of that work and no other.

The *implied reader*, theoretical like the implied author, is one who "gets" all the moves orchestrated by the implied author, is a perfect partner for the creative skill generating the narrative, and is able to grasp and manage all the artistry of the work and interpret it adequately. It is impossible for any actual reader to manage such a feat, so again, this role is artificial but logically desirable. The implied reader position reminds us that actual readings are always partial and provisional, relieving us of any attempt at mastery or completeness.

The *narrator* is the voice we read on the page, whose words we can underline with a yellow pen, should we so choose. The narrator of the text under present consideration is not a character in the story but tells events over the heads of its characters. Again, controversy and alternatives are not lacking, but in this study, we will stipulate that the implied author delegates the actual narrating to the narrator—that is, in the design of the material, an *extradiegetic narrator* (existing outside the narrative rather than as a character within it) who is the main voice to carry the story. But very often others—characters within the story—are given responsibility for the telling. A narrative is thus typically nested, with our challenge being to discern whose voices we are hearing and how to appraise them. The implied author, responsible for the whole work, is that "personage" who delegates

---

37. Abbott, *Cambridge Introduction*, 235.

to the narrator the job of uttering certain information.[38] The narrator employs various strategies rather than simply providing "plain" information, choosing how we are informed. A carefully refined tool, as we shall see, is the question of angle of perception or utterance.

The *narratee* is the match, or set of matches, for the nested narrator: the one, specifically, to whom a particular utterance is addressed, for whom it is crafted so also likely intended in some way, historically specific in a way that lies beyond the interests of this study.[39]

The practicalities of the six-member reading model are easier to grasp if we consider an analogy. In his complex and sophisticated presentation of the US Civil War, the work's *actual author*, Ken Burns, designs and directs a huge audiovisual *narrative* to offer a rich if partial edition of a vast historical-social event.[40] Though he has many other epics to his credit, for example, the story of baseball, a study of certain Roosevelts, his *implied authorship* or responsibility for simply *The Civil War* means we can consider that work on its own merit without needing to examine it in relation to other works Burns has authored. In his production of this key internal crisis faced by the United States, Burns orchestrates multiple voices to narrate the epic. The main *narrator* is a contemporary historian, David McCullough, who becomes recognized visually or auditorily as the consistent voice holding the narrative together. He introduces other narrating characters to assist: songs are sung, letters read, poems recited, wistful or boastful comments offered, newspaper clippings testify—each distinctive visually on the DVD or by change of music or accent. The invited speakers (some twenty voices, including Studs Terkel, Garrison Keillor, Kurt Vonnegut) voice nineteenth-century texts from within the epic told (so *intradiegetically*), while McCullough is not part of the earlier event but tells it from outside (*extradiegetically*). All this narrative diversity

38. Literary study spends a great deal of time on kinds of narrators (e.g., Keen, *Narrative Form*, 38–41); useful as well is Robert Scholes, James Phelan, Robert Kellogg, *The Nature of Narrative*, 40th anniversary ed. (Oxford: Oxford University Press, 2006), 84; consult also Herman and Vervaeck, *Handbook*, 80–101. For present purposes, the matter is not so complex as in modern fiction.

39. Walsh, *Old Testament Narrative*, 99, offers the useful example (elaborated a bit by me) of a family helping the teenaged daughter prepare for her first formal dance. The circumstances prompt her father to recollect taking his eventual wife to her first formal dance. The dad will narrate that recollection in one way to his daughter, but if questioned by a son who is very young but vaguely aware of what is happening, he will recount it a bit differently as the son's capacity to understand is obviously not the same as his sister's. Later, perhaps, he will narrate his recollection to his wife, again slightly differently. Thus there are three narratees, each able to hear the narrative as sculpted for his or her ears. I posit that the narratee in this story is a listener who understands the issue of the struggle between Judah and Benjamin in a way that is largely off-limits for later readers. For present purposes, the narratee does not need specifying, since my concern is with real readers.

40. Ken Burns, *The Civil War*, aired September 23–27, 1990, Florentine Films, WETA TV DVD.

offers intricate and infinite contributions to *The Civil War*, with nuance varying, depending on whether the words offered are from McCullough, from a Southern soldier, a Northern war widow, and so forth. Each of the intradiegetic narrators, participating from documents that witness to actual experience in the war (cf. the contemporary historian McCullough), makes a particular contribution to the presentation. It matters who is talking, and not all characteral utterances are equally reliable. Were we to eliminate any of these nested voices, we would be diminished in receiving what is on offer.

There are surely many other ways to offer a narrative of the historical event, and so the choice of the actual author to produce what he did, and the production itself as authored implicitly, constitute it as a unique narrative work. The medley of voices, each distinctive and speaking from a very partial experience, sets this narrative up to be heard on various levels and weighed as to contribution. The viewer (or hearer) of *The Civil War* may come to esteem some speakers above others for insight, or to know that some soldiers may speak more directly of battle outcomes and some widows more perceptively about what is already diminished, even before the war ends.

To conclude the analogy: The real readers are all viewers of the piece. The implied reader is one fully alert to the vast design of the piece, a sort of Ken Burns double, we might suppose. The narratee is the vast and generally educated audience set to whom the piece is addressed. Part of the genius of Burns is to be able to "narrate" so widely. It might be more useful to ask who is *not* a narratee, and to that query, I would say the pitch is *not* to a pro-war Marine.

Two other fundamental distinctions can be offered here, to be made relevant as we proceed. The first is the distinction between the *time of setting* and *time of production*, again particularly crucial for classics, where later readers are reminded not to assume that the setting of the story can be relied upon to provide details of its actual context. If the narrative has been thrown back earlier in time, as it were, over the shoulder of the teller or writer of it—a habit much beloved of biblical composers—then we cannot assume that any of the narrative details is reliably derived from the setting; it is much more likely to have come from the time of the narrative's production into the tale in which it is extant. If modern North Americans are reading a novel set in the nineteenth century, they immediately recognize the time gap and do not fall into chronological confusion. When most moderns read materials set in the second millennium BCE, the differences between that era and hundreds of years later are likely blurred, so that they may easily confuse one period with another.

Second, the vital differentiation between *what events are narrated* and *how they are provided*, the *story/discourse distinction*, will be made useful as we proceed. Unlike the setting/production differential, story and discourse are a modern insight, enunciated in the 1960s and developed in various ways thereafter. The basic insight exploits the distinction between the "what" of the story and the "how" of the discourse, between events as logically needing to occur, and as represented. Thus a narrative has events and existents that can be understood as having happened in an orderly and reconstructible way, and those may be disclosed by a narrator to a reader in some other order, for artistic purposes. When we are dealing with a fictive narrative, we need to recall that there are not necessarily "real" or actual events lying behind their recital, retrievable in some way. But in the narrative that concerns us here, the artistic skill of the narrator to manage what we know and how we learn of it remains valuable and productive in a way that may not pertain to certain modern material. Particularly useful will be the matter of discrepancy of knowledge: between characters and reader and among characters.[41]

One way to anticipate collaboration among these participants is provided by Scholes, Phelan, and Kellogg: "Meaning, in a work of narrative art, is a function of the relationship between two worlds: The fictional world created by author and the 'real' world, the apprehensible universe. When we say we 'understand' a narrative, we mean that we have found a satisfactory relationship or set of relationships between the two worlds."[42] When we make appropriate discrimination between and among providers and levels of information and anticipate ways in which we are invited to be "writerly" as we read (rather than choose the more compliant "readerly" mode), we become active, conscious, and intentional meaning-makers with the texts we interpret. We can never arrive at perfection or completeness, but to the extent that we are aware of our many choices, we will be provided for more richly than might otherwise be the case.

Another way to anticipate collaboration is to be *specific*. Alert to the power and productivity of narrative, and freshly reminded of the instability and openness of meaning, I have selected seven particular literary methods or tools, all both classic and freshly conceived, venerable but still generative. The seven could have been more or fewer, and in fact one of the salient characteristics of them is how they overlap, are closely interrelated, cannot be definitively pulled apart. The seven are: (1) establishing the edges of a work embedded in a larger work, with the implications of starting *in medias res* rather than *ab ovo*; (2) determining the presence, function, and impact of multiple structures: likely one large and comprehensive plan and several smaller ones; (3) mapping multiple plot possibilities; (4) detailing *narrator* characteristics; (5) examining *character construction* in all its diversity; (6) attempting a compound device, tentatively named *repeating, refracting plot elements*, which allows us to discern and revalue crucial elements as they recur; (7) transposing a presentation from one era to another and from a verbal to a visual genre. My aim (for myself and for you) is to read responsibly, to remain alert to our moves and our privilege in so proceeding, and to be changed as well by what we construct.

41. Dan Shen, "Story-Discourse Distinction," in David Herman, Manfred Jahn, and Marie-Lauren Ryan, eds., *The Routledge Encyclopedia of Narrative Theory* (London and New York: Routledge Taylor & Francis Group, 2005), 566–68.

42. Scholes, Phelan, and Kellogg, *Nature of Narrative*, 82.

3 Hermeneutics and Transformative Reading

a Basic Issues

We come to the second "parent" of the process of reading: philosophical hermeneutics, particularly as related to the turn to language in the modern period, suited for ancient texts while remaining normative and formative for many working with them. How can we name the dynamics most suited to reading and interpretation? Philosophy, since and even before Plato and Aristotle, has been taken up with the metaphysical questions of what is real and truthful, with epistemological issues of how we know and express what we know. Since the scientific revolution, the Enlightenment and their offspring—all presenting fresh and steep challenges to philosophy—new insights into the nature and function of language also provide fresh possibilities for approaching the understanding of texts.

Some basic questions: What does it mean to interpret a text? What is the desired and anticipated outcome of interpreting texts, particularly ancient texts with which readers have little immediate cultural familiarity?[43] Is such distance problematic or productive—perhaps both? Is scientific understanding the most useful model or analogue for the interpretation of artistic texts? Is anything historical relevant, and if so, how? Insofar as scientific processes value objectivity, rigorous method, and repeatable or verifiable results, are such features germane to texts, able to be managed? Does the interpreter stand largely outside the interpretive process, such that interpreters are exchangeable and results readily shareable? What sort of gain is expected, desired from the engagement of text and reader: objective meaning, insight into what has been interpreted, self-knowledge—or some blend of those? Are texts simply objects to be studied, or are they partners, to be engaged, somewhat (though not exactly) in the way one person engages another person? If the partner analogue is more suited than the scientific objectivist model, how does a conscious interpreter begin to engage with an ancient text? In other words, how should distance be overcome? How should subjectivity be maintained? How can the interpreter avoid simply reinscribing the shortcomings of a textual partner? What is the best way to theorize about the participation of the interpreter in the text?

If, as seems likely the case, scientific and objective modes of inquiry are not most apt, is there some process preventing an utter slide to relativity and absorption in the pleasing mirror, rather than seeking the gaze of a "textual other"? Conversely, what stops the interpreter from simply dismissing an ancient text that will very often appear by later standards deficient in some major way (e.g., sexist, elitist, violent)? Can a process, if not a tight method, be offered and used, critiqued, and improved? Is experience relevant, and if so, how? If multiple interpreters approach a challenging text, what shapes insight that emerges? How can an interpreter be

43. The issue here is not whether readers are familiar with texts, having heard them many times; the relevant gap is between the originating circumstances of the ancient biblical texts and the cultural circumstances of later readers, where there is so much we do not readily understand.

suitably open to change? These issues, clearly closely related to the questions just considered, need unfolding.

b Development of Hermeneutics

Hermeneutics is the branch of modern philosophy explicitly concerned with meaning, with processes of interpretation. The field derives its name from Hermes, messenger between Greek gods and mortals, charged with helping the humans understand the gods. As the vast field of philosophy struggles—even flails—with all the issues classically associated with knowing and experiencing reality, truth, and being, here the narrower concern is to understand how *language* is part of the quest to participate fully and responsibly in *appropriating insight from and with* texts. Insofar as we understand what we are doing when we interpret and can gain skill in that endeavor, we are likely to do it better, more perceptively and fruitfully. Hermeneutics and the philosophers we will sample—particularly their insights into human language and texts—offer us insight into how we use, even live in, language. Insofar as we may understand the stories of David to be rich and complex about human experience, narrated with insight and skill, we are moving deeply within the realm of Being. With hermeneutics, we will penetrate as closely as possible what we most need to know to interpret deep texts skillfully, supplementing literary moves to explore how our characters come to wisdom and how we, constructing them, may do so ourselves. Challenged to introduce adequately the issues that will be assumed and utilized in this reading of the David narrative, we are faced with a discourse even more vast than historiography and literary theory, with only a relatively small portion being relevant here.

Anthony Thiselton is perhaps the most prolific current hermeneutics scholar working with the specialized subfield of biblical interpretation as well as being thoroughly grounded in its interface with the broader philosophical tradition. He unfolds for us how hermeneutics helps us to explore how we read, understand, and appropriate biblical texts, especially insofar as they were written in a time and culture substantially different from our own and have been steadily and variously interpreted for some twenty-five hundred years.[44] Hermeneutics was once considered to comprise basically the exegetical tools and procedures for reading biblical texts.[45] But not inappropriately, as over time the challenges to such reading

---

44. Thiselton, *Hermeneutics*, 1. This particular volume works well in present circumstances since it revisits some frames of interpretation familiar from both historical and literary methodologies, thus assisting us to see interrelationships among our three basic sets of tools.

45. Exegesis is the name given to our managing reading ancient texts with a number of tools still important for biblical work, now considered insufficient, though necessary. It might be useful to consider by way of analogy a complex task like preparing a formal meal: some basic things are necessary to do—washing and peeling vegetables, sifting flour, blending ingredients for a sauce; those are, analogously, exegetical tasks. But there is much more to do, tasks more complex and challenging, if the whole meal is to emerge suitably; that process we can liken to interpretation.

accumulated, so did the understanding of hermeneutics, until it developed into a general process of interpretation of texts, not necessarily limited to linguistic art, though surely focusing primarily there while asking larger questions about modes by which humans understand. As early in the postbiblical period as we know about, the rabbis had rules for their reading, as did the early Christians, though their ways seem simple by comparison with what we have available to help us by the twenty-first century. But we can discern that from early times onward the understanding and passing on of texts was a major mode of human knowing. We also know from general literary criticism that only in the twentieth century was the participative role of the reader recognized and welcomed, challenging the assumption that all those educated and privileged enough to be reading would derive the same basic insight. Modern hermeneutics practitioners are much more alert to and appreciative of the vast array of influences affecting readers than were the ancients. To read the deepest and wisest of our classical texts, those most copied and cherished over time, is constitutive of being human.[46]

From before Plato and Aristotle and surely since, lovers of wisdom have been grappling with matters held to be most fundamental and crucial to human existence. Among those are questions related to what is real and true, how we know what we know, how humans are related with all else that is, classically summed up as the bond between and among creator and creation. Up until the modern period, questions about human beings had been virtually inseparable from notions about the realm of the divine, with thinkers wondering about the ways in which the nature of God—specifically the monotheistic and generally benign deity of the Jewish and Christian traditions—was implicated in human nature, knowledge, and experience. The categories of Aristotle in particular, as appropriated by Thomas Aquinas and other Christian thinkers from the Middle Ages onward, became so "canonical" that once they began to be questioned seriously and shown as substantially wanting, there came a crisis for religion as well as for all other areas of human life challenged by modern analytic discoveries. The European scientific revolution and the age of Enlightenment challenged the foundations of philosophy and much else, leaving thinkers of the eighteenth and nineteenth centuries to find ways of explaining reality other than those derived from Plato and Aristotle and adopted by Christian theology. That is, the universe as explained by Galileo, Newton, Darwin, and eventually by Einstein was so radically different from what had seemed solidly in place previously that philosophers were challenged to explain human knowing in radically new and technically precise ways, an effort and process extending over several centuries. Though the steps from classical and medieval philosophy through early modern into language philosophy do not seem unexpected or new when our major interest is in the interpretation of texts

---

46. For a wonderful study of the cross-cultural and cross-temporal phenomenon of generating and canonizing language, see Wilfred Cantwell Smith, *What Is Scripture?: A Comparative Approach* (Minneapolis, MN: Fortress Press, 1993).

composed of and mediated through language, it is worth recalling that much of the long history of philosophy has broader interests.[47]

c Hermeneutics' Turn to Language

Early work in language philosophy began not so much as an end in itself but rather as an exercise in logical precision aimed to clarify and establish certain positions more accurately than before.

The topic of representation is not new, though it emerges freshly in modernity. By mid-twentieth century, philosophers like Ludwig Wittgenstein and Ernst Cassirer had written extensively on language. Cassirer, in particular, makes clear that language is not simply a tool used by humans but that language itself shapes human experience. Cassirer characterized humans as constituted by the various symbol systems in which they find themselves: linguistic, mythic, religious, and artistic. To understand ourselves requires recognizing how we swim in the symbolic, including language.

We recognize the classic concern about what happens when human experience is expressed artistically, often in language, perhaps written by one person who will have drawn it from a tradition that had been communally shaped over time and then received by others—not least by those who might contest it. Once a text exists and comes into the hands and lives of others who may not know as much about its origins and scope as ideally could be wished, how do such receivers understand it? How does a text achieve, contain, or proffer meaning? How does language, specifically written language, gather and express experience and also fall short, even fail to do so in some basic way? As readers engage with a rich text, especially one that did not grow up in their midst or they in its developing days, how can suitable understanding take place? Will not inevitable blindness and clumsy errors vitiate any good that might come to those who inherit such tradition? How do any of us begin to understand well what we do not already know? How do we make the strange familiar and the familiar strange enough so that we can begin to see well? To what extent can we devise patterns and processes to help us with our ignorance, and with the contrary parts of ourselves that misperceive and distort, not least when such texts challenge us to embrace what we do not prefer? How do we integrate old and deep texts with our own lives in ways that are not wholly solipsistic? Are texts objects for us to conquer, or do we do well to approach them more relationally, consider them more empathetically, and open ourselves to being transformed by them? Contrary to or at least very different from the ways of much modern science, hermeneutics calls us to *participate* in just these things, not simply manage them.

47. A quick visit to broader philosophy will immerse us into matters like: What is the nature of the human mind? Can God be a deceiver? What is the basic substance of reality? Can good come from evil? How does the mind know? What can be known? Are there reliable foundations? Those are not strictly hermeneutical matters but classically philosophical.

We are headed for activity where text and reader engage each other, where a toggling process of explanation and understanding helps reader and text move closer to each other—assisted by all the moves we know are important to make in biblical studies: care with the original languages, apt knowledge of the originating cultures, consultation with experts, and submission of our work to the appraisal of others. All of these crucial matters underlie the hermeneutical procedures under discussion here. Suspicion is called for as we proceed, a sort of distancing from what seems easily available, protecting both text and reader from something too facile, too arid, too removed from the human existence of which our texts speak and which we live. We come to see how communal a process is interpretation, how transformative it can be, depending on the depth of engagement.[48]

Granting significant presence to the reader (though allowing appropriate space as well for authorial artistry and textual richness), what limits guide the reader? Much that is needed has already been suggested in the portion of this chapter on literary criticism, with its eventual welcoming of the reader. Interpreters are not all the same, and readers with different qualities, skills, interests, and experience coming from various cultural matrices will construe texts with apt diversity. Though offering responsibility to the reader can seem and even be hazardous, it has rather been observed that forbidding, silencing, or cordoning off diverse readers while concentrating the classic texts in the hands of a few is no antidote to poor reading. Indeed, a case can be made that to sequester texts does more harm than to allow to be engaged more liberally. Experts will and should be consulted, and to be such a scholar is indeed a privilege and a serious responsibility. But the ancient texts are not so fragile that they will fracture or spoil in ordinary hands. Those who love classic texts deeply need to find ways to enhance interpretation skills, and those who wish to be good readers need to invest time in learning what will best avail. Multiplicity and lack of tight determinacy are not an inevitable foe, nor is the willingness to consider historical context and authorial trace.

As we are invited to consider and to learn the skill and art of interpretation, we will see ways in which diversity has already enriched the tradition and should continue to do so. Hermeneutics is basically an open process, not a closed one. As the circle of interpreters has grown, so has the large interpreting community learned more about what is involved in the study of classic traditions. As philosophy has wound its way at least in the West, much has been offered, tested, rejected, affirmed, and expanded. We are not without many good teachers. Ancients as well as many moderns trust that the project of hermeneutics will not go badly astray. To consult the long history of the reception of the biblical text should—generally speaking—encourage us to carry on as have our forebears. As we move from modes of reading primarily allegorical and typological into others

---

48. Thiselton, *Introduction*, ch. 1 elaborates these points in his introduction. See also David Jasper, *A Short Introduction to Hermeneutics* (Louisville: Westminster John Knox, 2004), ch. 1, and Stanley E. Porter and Jason C. Robinson, *Hermeneutics: An Introduction to Interpretive Theory* (Grand Rapids, MI and Cambridge, UK: William B. Eerdmans Publishing Co., 2011), ch. 1.

more classically Aristotelian in the hands of scholastic thinkers, proceeding next in the Renaissance and Reformation to consider issues that seemed more existentially situated, modern study has shown us many things to consider as we read.

Sandra Schneiders, New Testament scholar and proficient hermeneut, offers several criteria which, taken together, will serve as a suitable guide for our hermeneutic endeavors.[49] She names two that are global marks of good interpretation—proper attention to what is possible and what is not possible to do with a text, and an acknowledgment by others of the fruitfulness of a reading. She then lists others: a reading should account for a text as it is, needing little complicated rearranging in order to work; it should be consistent and valid for a whole text, not require a special maneuver for some part of a passage; it should be compatible with what is generally known and accepted from other relevant sources; it should proceed responsibly, draw upon and name appropriate methods. By way of paraphrase, we might say we should be leery when a reading proceeds too unexpectedly "from left field" but remain open to and eager for fresh insight about classic texts.

So what line of general hermeneutical insight made the crucial turn toward work that will be most productive and practical for contemporary biblical scholarship?

1. Friedrich Schleiermacher The study of modern biblical hermeneutics usually is seen as beginning in the nineteenth century with the work of Friedrich Schleiermacher (1768–1864), the first to make the interpretation of Scripture project basically correlative with thinking, thus moving hermeneutics beyond exegesis and philology, beyond specific and finite method and rules. Though, compared with much we have been considering, he remains too fixed on recovering authorial intent, historical circumstances, literary processes, and even precise textual effect, we can appreciate that even to consider such things as important marked a major step forward.[50] Working in the same general period that saw the emergence of the critical study of biblical texts, he expressed the view that there was a common hermeneutics of texts, not a special set of assumptions and procedures exclusive to the Bible. For him, the interpretive process came to be a moving among philologies or linguistic issues and these he called psychologies, catching the romanticist interest in communing with expressive processes of an artist. With Schleiermacher the topic of interpretation of texts slides closer to the questions literary theorists were grappling with—a step that needs taking before we can arrive at a theory more directly helpful to present concerns about interpretation. He articulated the sense that reading (interpreting) was an art (not a science), was creative, much as

49. Sandra M. Schneiders, *The Revelatory Text: Interpreting the New Testament as Sacred Scripture*, 2nd ed. (Collegeville, MN: Liturgical Press, 1999), 164–67.

50. Thiselton, *Introduction*, 158–61, appraises Schleiermacher's contribution. A fuller study, Richard Palmer's *Hermeneutics* (Evanston, IL: Northwestern University Press, 1969), 84–97, provides an additional perspective.

was writing. He argued that both writing and reading are triggered by a desire to be known and to know.[51]

2. Martin Heidegger The second crucial thinker to consider is *Martin Heidegger* (1889–1976), whose challenging and abstruse thought was the immediate impetus for the work of the two scholars for whom we are heading.[52] Heidegger widens and deepens the interpretation project from the understanding of entities and texts to the more radical question of being, Being, and being-there, seeing hermeneutics as more ontological than epistemological. He valued the more existential and historical over the more abstract and general, sought to understand written material in its particular contexts, and to see interpretation itself as situated. The "signature concept" of at least the early Heidegger is *Dasein*, which means the human's being-there, being where one actually is. In working out the properties of *Dasein*, Heidegger distinguishes inauthentic existence from an authentic being-there that is awakened, chosen, usually as a result of struggling with human challenges, the greatest of which is a recognition of finitude and mortality. The human life project is, comprehensively stated, a quest for authentic Being.

The later Heidegger came to talk about language as quasi-divine, as more than the sort of practical tool many think it to be. Central for our purposes is his claim that human existence itself is radically hermeneutical, that interpretation is a fundamental human activity, his urging that meaning and truth are not graspable objectively but found and received relationally. The process of understanding begins not abstractly, nor is it accomplished in a clear step; it starts from where the interpreter finds himself or herself to be and proceeds not neutrally, not as though pursuing an object, but relationally and provisionally, always struggling toward authenticity. Heidegger is difficult and controversial—not least for his Nazi politics—and the point here is not to understand him so much as to see him as a necessary step between Schleiermacher and Gadamer and Ricoeur.

3. Hans Georg Gadamer Gadamer (1900–2002), a student of Heidegger, was a humanist as well as a philosopher, maintaining a lifelong interest in Plato while

51. For this thinker, consult Thiselton, *Introduction*, 148–61; Jasper, *Short Introduction*, 84–86; Stanley E. Porter, and Jason C. Robinson, *Hermeneutics: An Introduction to Interpretive Theory* (Grand Rapids, MI: William B. Eerdmans Publishing Co., 2011), 24–33. After Schleiermacher, others continued to develop and sharpen his insights, and considerable work was done on the New Testament and the presentation of Jesus, scholarship associated with the names of Barth and Bultmann, eventually of Fuchs and Ebeling. Though, inevitably, work on interpreting the figure of Jesus is not so readily transferrable to other texts, these insights about textuality advanced the field of hermeneutics, bringing it to a certain maturity in the early twentieth century and preparing us to single out the work of the two scholars generally considered most helpful for the current understanding and interpretation of biblical texts, a subset of texts in general, even of ancient texts.

52. Thiselton, *Introduction*, includes in ch. 11 on Gadamer most of what he says about Heidegger. See also Jasper, *Short Introduction*, 104–06 and Porter and Robinson, *Interpretive Theory*, 57–69.

acquiring a penetrating grasp of the whole Western philosophical tradition and a capacity to advance it usefully.[53] Like his teacher, he considered interpretation and understanding as central to human existence, as a deeply humanizing (though not specifically religious) quest, granted it was always provisional, historical, and temporal rather than complete, abstract, and objectifying. He refused both the dominating scientific knowing and the reductive abstract Cartesian philosophy with their claimed certainties, as least relevant to understanding the humanistic tradition. Building on insights of Schleiermacher, Gadamer saw that understanding is approached circularly, as one begins to know from what is known while gradually widening the entry foothold. Though the sciences hold that past scientific insights once seen false are virtually useless, Gadamer showed how in the humanities understanding emerges from an accumulated past that continues to be a substantial and valuable participant in what we know. Being rooted in and composed of much that has preceded us in our cultural tradition is not a barrier to understanding but an aid. The inherited framework we gather and receive helps us order what we know and allows us insight, rather than being a barrier to circumvent.

Thiselton moves through a summary of Gadamer's major work, *Truth and Method*, offering its key insights cumulatively. The title pushes back against the claims of those for whom a clear scientific method is desirable. Gadamer, a Platonist, maintains that truth, when it comes, arrives more indirectly, more by way of question and response than by a defined method. Truth is not so much acquired as engaged, appropriated. Comparing textual interpretation to immersion in graphic art, he also helpfully likened it to playing a game: A player enters a game which has preexisted that moment, follows the rules that are in place, and loses him- or herself in the particular game being played, not in some abstraction of it. Giving oneself over fully to its processes, becoming absorbed in it, the particular experience enjoyed is far from the objectifying process of scientific method or rote exegesis, but neither is it merely a subjectivist or solipsistic quest. The player is shaped by what he or she experiences, neither simply imposing self on the game in some way nor wandering through it superficially and with no impact registered.

Gadamer takes issue with certain insights of Schleiermacher, finding them too fixed on trying to understand something that was the experience of another, too intent on the romanticist confidence in the recovery of the expressivity of the original speaker or writer of a text—so tempting for the biblical project as well. Rather, and crucially for Gadamer, we can only understand within the horizon of time and space we inhabit, can only really hope to see from where we actually stand—not from some abstract or alien place. As a student of Heidegger, Gadamer values our Being-where-we-are-given-to-be as the place from which we view a horizon and begin, provisionally and by degrees, to approach and understand provisionally and processually, building from what we know to learn what we have not known before. We begin "there" rather than nowhere, situated rather than in a past we have not inhabited. Gadamer is optimistic about the flow of the

---

53. For a discussion of Gadamer, see Thiselton, *Introduction*, ch. 11; Jasper, *Short Introduction*, 106–08; Porter and Robinson, *Interpretive Theory*, 174–84.

tradition as a series of horizons for us to approach, seeking to fuse ours with those offered by others—texts included—as we meet them. Horizons shift, and time and space change. Reading ancient texts in this way makes clear the phenomenon of historical consciousness: our particular, situated, existential way of understanding that is neither simply a retrieval of some past era nor a solipsistic imposition of our own moment upon something else.[54]

Gadamer is also more optimistic than some about the possibility of an interpreter standing near another subject (human or text), seeking to see from as shared a point of view as possible, standing in the shoes of another, so to speak, or close. He urges the effort to do so—again, a gradual one as the processes of explaining and understanding toggle. He, likely after Plato, urges that questions open us in a way that more general sets problems do not, that the formation of the existing and awakened human being comes through a lifetime of asking questions, attempting to answer them, listening to cues, being changed by what we hear. Discussing, analogically, how we come to understanding by way of conversing with another speaker, he maintains that written texts, with their particular challenges, are the proper domain of hermeneutics. Thus does Gadamer introduce us to *interpretation as formative of human experience and being, interpretation as lifelong and open, ultimately transformative for those who "play the game" seriously.* There is no end point, no declaring completion. As Thiselton concludes, "Everything is hermeneutical; everything requires interpretation."[55]

4. Paul Ricoeur Finally, what can we learn from Paul Ricoeur, and why is he the endpoint of this brief hermeneutic investigation? Paul Ricoeur (1913–2005) is generally recognized as the most valuable hermeneutical theorist for those who work with biblical texts, though it is probably also the case that few biblical scholars have appropriated his thought as well as might be done. Ricoeur had the advantages of significant life experiences (not all of them pleasant but surely productive), the opportunity and ability to learn deeply from the long philosophical tradition, and the occasion to interact with many vibrant people (Derrida was his student assistant at one point). Ricoeur was a perceptive learner, a creative synthesizer, an alert critic, and hence able to gain from virtually everything that passed beneath his eyes. He is classified most fundamentally as a phenomenologist (after Husserl and Heidegger), questing for the significance of lived experience. If, as seems the case, his most consistent interest was the human will, he investigated that topic broadly and deeply, including as it does human choice and freedom, guilt and

---

54. The relevance of this key insight for historical biblical studies and for literary criticism will be clear, thus reminding us why hermeneutics is as crucial for biblical studies as are historical and literary methods.

55. Thiselton, *Introduction*, 226. Perhaps surprisingly, contemporary literary theory arrives at this same basic insight, along another route. Called the "Ethical Turn," its character is discussed by Liesbeth Korthals Altes, in David Herman, Manfred Jahn, and Marie-Lauren Ryan, eds., *The Routledge Encyclopedia of Narrative Theory* (London and New York: Routledge Taylor & Francis Group, 2005), 142–46.

fallibility, and the expressions of those in language and texts. The human quest for self-understanding that interested Ricoeur also opened up for him the human imagination, articulated in language, notably in narrative. Among his many achievements are writings on biblical narratives, some early in his life, others late and collaborative. He was also a committed and active Christian, a perspective that allows him a particular authority when he speaks of transformation as available from the human process of interpreting great texts, including the biblical.[56]

Ricoeur's fruitful appropriations of the tradition and his creative insights in regard to it were several, some named here. A key basic insight is that apparent differences are not necessarily dichotomous, that a patient and creative inquiry, shifting among modes of investigation and between interpretive steps in the appropriation of a single artwork, will often show related matters and issues— meaning—that might, at the surface, seem opposed. Schneiders credits Ricoeur as being the source of the massively utilized and helpful insight that sees engaged biblical narrative as comprising *three worlds*: behind the text, within the text, moving from the text to engage the reader's actual existence.[57] Ricoeur produces fresh and original work on both *metaphor and symbol*, looking deeply into their structures and explaining how he sees each as mediating meaning. For Ricoeur, metaphor must be understood not at the level of words but as an assertion, a sentence, with a subject and a predicate. A metaphoric claim seems foolish or false at the literal level, but when approached beyond that stage and asked to disclose something deeper, it has a fresh and unexpected truth to convey. The combination or clash of apparent falseness and deeper truth generates insight in a perceptive reader, who anticipates and desires rather than misses or refuses deeper meaning. Metaphor thus conveys what cannot quite be said literally.[58] Symbol, so far as I can see, functions for Ricoeur somewhat analogously, while drawing from extralinguistic reality in a way that metaphor does not appear to do.

One of Ricoeur's most mature and extensive studies is on time and narrativity, where he inquires into ways in which human temporality structures narrated time (a topic of deep interest to Heidegger). For Ricoeur, the key is the capacity of the human imagination to create and recreate events, to blur, productively, the real and the imaginary in order to explore, fictively, the human potential for good. Drawing on earlier insights, he sought to move beyond interpretive understandings that were fixated on the abstract mind or historical circumstances of originating people

56. Thiselton's *Introduction*, ch. 12, focuses on Ricoeur; see Porter and Robinson, *Interpretive Theory*, ch. 5. Kevin, Vanhoozer's *Biblical Narrative in the Philosophy of Paul Ricoeur: A Study in Hermeneutical Theology* (Cambridge: Cambridge University Press, 1990) and Schneiders' *Revelatory Text* provide specific bridges between his more general ideas and their use for interpreting texts. Their overviews are invaluable but general. I am chagrined and disappointed to say that none of Ricoeur's biblical writings appeals much to me, but I much appreciate the readings that others have done using his general insights and interpretive moves!

57. Schneiders, *Revelatory Text*, 129, note 20.

58. Ibid., 30–31.

or events. He avoided the hopeless quest to recover what cannot likely be known, while at the same time appreciating the importance and ongoing significance of primordial existents and their recitals. He thus avoided the pitfalls of positivistic historicism, on the one hand, and facile and inauthentic solipsism on the other. How to talk about ancient events so that their impact remains powerful without aiming or claiming to rest in their historical specificity is clearly a key topic for biblical texts. Ricoeur showed the need to approach primordial past events (we might instance the Hebrew Bible experience of exile and return, or the Christian last supper of Jesus with his disciples before his death) as having a reality that transcends the actual originating events themselves, while taking them seriously and counting on their value. The project of narrativizing and ritualizing such events, thus adding to a thick discourse generated over time, adds significance for interpreting participants.

Perhaps most useful for present purposes is his elaboration of the complex process of interpretation, which owes much to Heidegger and Gadamer while making key changes as well. With Gadamer, Ricoeur comes to the insight that written tradition is distinctively different from other modes of linguistic expression (like conversation). Like both his mentors, Ricoeur talks about dialogical processes to help an interpreter make meaning *with* a text. That process has discrete moments: An effort to explain a text critically, then the moment of letting understanding accumulate; an active interrogation of a text by a reader, who queries all that is relevant, and then its insight is received through the framework of the interpreter; the textual words are made strange and approached with some suspicion, and then they are recognized as familiar, deep and meaningful.[59] In Ricoeur's own words: "Hermeneutics seem to me to be animated by this double motivation: willingness to suspect, willingness to listen; vow of rigor, vow of obedience."[60] Throughout the process, the text is not the interpreter's object, nor is a scientistic method invasively brought to bear on it. Questions are posed respectfully, with the assumption that the classic text has something valuable, even fresh, to offer a reader, who also brings to it queries its earlier interpreters may not have posed. Horizons can coincide.

By-products of this process, named by Ricoeur, are several: He speaks of *distanciation*, the fact that the language of the text, once written, is distanced from its original author, from its circumstances of production, from its first referents and receivers. Concomitantly, a responsible reader will not so sever the possibility of understanding what might be relevant from the past that she or he is blind to what the text needs to maintain. Ricoeur's *surplus of meaning* is his claim that the very processes of interpretation lose or generate meaning for and from the interpreter's present that goes beyond the earlier events and appropriations of texts. A reader, participating in this hermeneutical quest, may emerge with a sort of second *naïveté*, a capacity to receive and appropriate fruitfully a text even on the far side of all the critical work done with it. This moment is not a rejection of

---

59. Ibid., 142–48, 157–59, 169–78 explains the process in some detail.
60. Ricoeur, *Freud and Philosophy: An Essay on Interpretation*, trans. Denis Savage (New Haven: Yale University Press, 1970), 5, quoted in Thiselton, *Introduction*, 233.

all that has been learned but a capacity to hear truth despite or beyond problems encountered—within certain limitations. The disciplined and loving process of interpreting a deep text has the capacity to generate deep meaning, and it is this experience that can be, over time, transformative of a reader—all the more when the text is claimed as sacred Scripture—but the process works with deep texts (think of works by Dante, Shakespeare, Dickinson, and many other examples) and their skilled readers as well. Difficult, challenging texts, so engaged, are often able to find or create in readers a greater capacity for fresh and transformative insight, understanding, even compassion, most particularly if characters within the narrative are thus engaged as well. Though it includes knowledge, the process goes beyond the acquisition of it, such that the gain is not simply or even primarily information but insight. Insight, accumulated, transforms.

4 *Implications*

The point of providing this historical and theoretical background is to ground the reading about to emerge—its aims and processes. To substantially exclude the historical, except for maintaining the ongoing and urgent relevance of the conflict between Judah and Benjamin, is unusual when discussing "historical" books. To highlight the extensive and complex literary facets available for interpretation of a rich text—privileging seven particular tools—challenges both readers and me to exploit them well. Skillful use of the methods deriving from literary theory will allow fresh construction not only of David but also of the deity, with whom David is so interdependent. Finally, the processes of hermeneutics authorize and assist a reading grounded not only by the text but also in the ethical and spiritual choices of myself as interpreter—you if you so choose. My wager that David can be shown as a flawed human being with deep moments of turning toward God and as demonstrating compassion while often falling short of that capacity as well opens up space for an interpreter. Such a reading is salutary for me, perhaps also for others.

Chapter 2

WHY A KING? CHOICES OF SAUL AND DAVID (1 SAM. 8–18)
EDGES AND STRUCTURES

1 Introductory Considerations

How can we think afresh about David's kingship as narratively presented? Why a king? Why Saul of Benjamin's Gibeah, David of Judah's Bethlehem? How and where does the story of kings begin? Our question here is neither about how royal institutions, structures, and persons actually came to be selected, nor about the relationship of the presentation in Samuel and Kings with that of Chronicles. Ancient tales tend to start in "the" middle of things, since "the" starting point is not clear, and may vary with the poet or audience. Basic story lines were, for ancient audiences, generally known, with interest centering on how an old story might be ordered and shaped so as to sustain, even nurture, interest. In this chapter, we will consider the early part of the David story, noting how it starts and suggesting its uncertain endings, offering observations about its general shape or structure. These first two tools, prepared as they have been by the introductory material on contemporary literary study and the spacious invitations of textual hermeneutics, will assist our study of David's early days.

2 Literary Theory

a Edges

A biblical story like David's starts in the middle in at least two "weight-bearing" senses: First, though we can point to the moment David is introduced, the narrative is already a tangled mass before he emerges. Readers are challenged to place this new character into the midst of developing, even determined events. Though much of David's backstory remains untold, certain hints are to be made productive later. David's story ends in the middle as well, as we wonder how Solomon will manage his father's legacy. A classic and also canonical narrative functioning as Scripture in living communities has been read and interpreted for some 2,500 years, with at least part of that vast accumulation—good and bad—still attending it. A reader must remain disciplined about allowing the narrative to present fresh possibilities and close off dead ones.

In modern literature, the beginning and ending of a work seem clear, bounded by the covers of the book.[1] The Bible, by contrast, is an anthology, developing over hundreds of years. Starting with Genesis and ending variously, depending on which canon is being read, the challenge of discerning the start and finish of a particular story uncoiling within the whole seems unrelated to problems faced by postmodernity.[2] Similarly, though moderns may encounter a wholly fresh story spun by a new writer, for ancients presentations were generally familiar, so that to consider where a story started and stopped was already complex, if not confusing. The theoretical challenges of opening and closing may pertain especially if the material were performed and heard, rather than written and read.[3] Though the ancient and modern narrative situations seem unrelated, the theoretical discussion of boundaries—extending at least from Aristotle to the present—can be helpful in flushing out problems that the edges of ancient texts may embed.[4]

1. Beginnings Where one chooses to start, is conscious of starting, matters,[5] with the diagnosing of a beginning not to be assumed as corresponding to the beginning of a telling.[6] We can reliably think of the manner of beginning as

1. Postmodern theorists argue that the matter is far from simple. For issues important in general though not so pertinent here, consult two essays in Brian Richardson, ed., *Narrative Beginnings: Theories and Practices* (Lincoln: University of Nebraska Press, 2008); Niels Buch Leander, "To Begin with the Beginning: Nabokov and the Rhetoric of the Preface,"15–28; and Melba Cuddy-Keane, "Virginia Woolf and Beginning's Ragged Edge," 96–112.

2. Biblical books as now extant not only began orally but then also spent part of their lives as scrolls, with edges determined somewhat by length rather than simply by content. S. Douglas Olson, in *Blood and Iron: Stories and Storytelling in Homer's Odyssey* (New York, Leiden, Koln: E. J. Brill, 1995), 228–39, speculating on book divisions, shows them being less obvious than they may seem to readers accustomed to how the material is now split.

3. Perhaps "the Gilgamesh story" illustrates that most clearly, existing even now both as broken and partial tablets of episodes and as a long tale where the episodes are strung together. It is likely that the individual units preceded the composite one (as indeed the shorter physical tablets are older), but evidence is inconclusive. To have as extant a long tale, segmented now into episodes on tablets, with an apparently appropriate order does not mean they began that way, rather suggesting that the "whole story" may not have had the privileged status that we like to give it. For more details, consult Andrew R. George, *The Epic of Gilgamesh: The Babylonian Epic Poem and Other Texts in Akkadian and Sumerian* (London: Penguin Books, 1999).

4. Brian Richardson, "Introduction: Narrative Beginnings," in Brian Richardson, ed., *Narrative Beginnings*, 6–10, implies that Aristotle was relatively untroubled by the challenges under discussion here: "A beginning is that which does not itself follow anything by causal necessity, but after which something naturally is or comes to be" (7–8); Horace famously commends Homer for starting his epics as he did, in the middle rather than from the start (8).

5. Francis M. Dunn, "Introduction: Beginning at Colonus," in Francis Dunn, and Thomas Cole, eds., *Beginnings in Classical Literature* (Cambridge: Cambridge University Press, 1992), 1–12 (9).

6. Abbott, *Cambridge Introduction*, 55–60, 230; Keen, *Narrative Form*, 16.

made primarily by the author and as varying by genre, though recently it has been understood that readers are also responsible for such choice.[7] It may seem that when an author begins somewhere, somehow, other options are thereby put off the table.[8] But an opening offers a cluster of information, stated and implied, already multiple and ambiguous. A narrative may begin from some point of story events, or it may begin by highlighting discourse,[9] with the implied author's challenge being not how to surprise the audience but to arrange matters freshly and brilliantly. Author and reader were thus freed for innovation, since material could be provided in many ways and with multiple effects possible. Authors and narrators did not need to provide all the pertinent information, since audiences of old brought considerable background to wherever a particular story seemed to begin. The same may hold for us, when we already know an ancient story well and almost forget to notice where we are plunged into it, how the opening beckoned us. The challenge is to stay alert for fresh detail or new complexity, to hear more skillfully how a backstory elucidates a given matter, to resist assuming information that comes to mind from another source. As Brian Richardson notes, there is no formula for how to begin.[10]

Additionally, an author (real or implied) has two basic choices: To start *in medias res*, "in the midst of things" that have already transpired, or to relate *ab ovo*, from the egg, from its inception.[11] We might even suppose that an author may start with the ending.[12] Each choice has particular opportunities and challenges. This basic decision is made by the implied author, who must then provide appropriately what is needed as it is needed and in the manner that works most effectively: with relevant information provided lavishly, sparingly, or not at all, for the moment.[13]

Theorists list some ways in which an *ab ovo* beginning can be managed: Exposition can be provided, delayed, omitted, or can be hinted or provided

---

7. Brian Richardson, "Origins, Paratexts, and Prototypes," in Richardson, ed., *Narrative Beginnings*, 11–14.

8. Diskin Clay, "Plato's First Words," in Dunn, and Cole, eds., *Beginnings*, 113.

9. Brian Richardson, "A Theory of Narrative Beginnings and the Beginnings of 'The Dead' and *Molloy*," in Richardson, ed., *Narrative Beginnings*, 113–14, offers us this distinction, adding that a story (modern or ancient) may also begin in some prefatorial way.

10. "Theory of Beginnings," in Richardson, ed., *Narrative Beginnings*, 113–14.

11. Chris Baldick, *Oxford Dictionary*, 167.

12. Brian Richardson, "General Introduction," in Richardson, ed., *Narrative Dynamics: Essays on Time, Plot, Closure, and Frames* (Theory and Interpretation of Narrative Series. Columbus: Ohio State University Press, 2002), 1–7 (2), offers us the views of Edward Said, who feels strongly that beginnings are privileged, while Peter Brooks insists that the ending is what governs all.

13. Boris Tomashevsky, "Story, Plot, and Motivation," in Richardson, ed., *Narrative Dynamics*, 164–78 (169–70). James Phelan, "Narrative Progression," in Richardson, ed., *Narrative Dynamics*, 211–16 (211), notes that the material is provided within the story or not.

partially.[14] Though explaining matters from the start is easier for a new reader, an author is challenged to manage that feat without being tedious or exposing things a reader would gain by struggling to discern. If a narrative begins *in medias res*, the moment selected for entry should be emotionally rich, able not only to catch but also to sustain interest over the length of the narrative. To start at a place of crisis or drama is to demand the reader's attention and also challenge him or her to seek flashbacks and backstories in order to clarify what is happening. The starting point should be both emotionally gripping and intellectually stimulating, so that problems are immediately proposed for the receiver of the text to ponder, indeed for the writer of the narrative to create.

A quick look at Homer—perhaps most like the David storyteller—adds texture to the subject. He begins both epics clearly enough, by invoking the Muses in proems. These two addresses appear to indicate the themes adequately: the anger of Achilles and the workings of the gods for the *Iliad* (1.1–8); the challenges of what became a solo homecoming for the hero in the *Odyssey* (1–12). And yet, upon closer examination, those starts may seem defective, inadequate to the complexities of those works.[15] A reader might assess that the *Odyssey* actually begins when Odysseus begins his narrative in book 8 rather than when Homer opens the tale.

So with our material involving David, overlapping three biblical books: We might start the David narrative with the first king, appearing in the book of the Judges, or perhaps at the moment when Saul is anointed—or in between. It might seem obvious that his story begins when David is anointed, in the middle of 1 Samuel, in the midst of many events and situations. Though we can say it begins when we meet David at his anointing, it can just as well be said to begin with the firing of King Saul for a series of things he did. There is no deep access to David's challenges without knowing what happened with Saul. The David story, alternatively, may be said to begin when David subsequently arrives at Saul's establishment, which happens successively.

2. Endings The concluding of a work is no less complex a matter, though better studied and more diverse in type. Aristotle, as usual, provides early advice, urging that endings be clear, neither relying on artificiality nor attempting to

---

14. Boris Tomashevsky, "Story, Plot, and Motivation,"169–70; James Phelan, "The Beginning of *Beloved*: A Rhetorical Approach," in Richardson, ed., *Narrative Beginnings*, 195–212 (197–200), offers another schema differentiating among exposition, launch, initiation, and entrance.

15. For detail on this discussion, see Victoria Pedrick, "The Muse Corrects: The Opening of the *Odyssey*," in Dunn, and Cole, eds., *Beginnings*, 39–62. She suggests that in both poems, the invocation falls short of introducing the poem. Sheila Murnaghan, "Equal Honor and Future Glory: The Plan of Zeus in the *Iliad*," in Deborah H. Roberts et al., eds., *Classical Closure Classical Closure: Reading the End in Greek and Latin Literature* (Princeton: Princeton University Press), 23–42, agrees that Homer's war poem extends beyond the avenging of honor and also beyond Achilles's anger.

mete out to humans strict justice or obvious deserts.[16] As moderns love the question of whether or not there can actually be a beginning, whether or how starting at it is possible, so are contemporary theorists insecure and uncertain about closings.[17]

Don Fowler lists a number of criteria once considered adequate: A narrative can end at its last section or conclude when a reader's sense of satisfaction is indicated. It ends to the extent that the ending is final, that its initial questions are answered, or to the degree that it has seeded some new critical readings. But, upon further reflection, he claims that those points are tangled rather than discrete, as we observed about inceptions as well.[18] Theorists suggest several abstract ways in which material may be brought to a conclusion. Some have to do with story: characters marry, die; as some bid farewell, shown successful at their quests, or not. Other choices rise more from discourse: a work can circle back to the place it began, can repeat structurally some aspect of its beginning, may tangentially pick up on a previously undeveloped detail.[19] A story beginning with a problem or a quest will end with its resolution in some way, even its failure. Massimo Fusillo specifies that an ending should be characterized by completion, integrity, and coherence, moves that authors may make by returning to the beginning in some way, offering a closing that parallels the opening, moving beyond it tangentially or closing it down, perhaps with the perspective or words of a particular character.[20] To end a narrative is not the same as bringing it to closure, as James Phelan notes, a point he made about beginnings as well.[21] Though readers tend to like clear endings, those are neither always provided nor required to be. Endings can be deferred, like deceptive cadences, to borrow a term from music.[22] Deborah Roberts specifies that authors may refuse an ending, or perhaps allude ahead, even plant clues as to alternative future plans for characters whose lives have been under discussion.[23]

It has been suggested that certain of most famous ancient classics struggle to end well without perhaps succeeding, each adding an unsatisfactory coda to the climax

16. Brian Richardson, "Introduction: Openings and Closure," in Richardson, ed., *Narrative Discourse*, 251–55.

17. Massimo Fusillo, "How Novels End: Some Patterns of Closure in Ancient Narrative," in Roberts et al., eds., *Classical Closure*, 209–27.

18. Don Fowler, "Second Thoughts on Closure," in Roberts et al., eds., *Classical Closure*, 3–22 (3–4).

19. For possibilities here, consult James Phelan, "*Beloved*," in Richardson, ed., *Narrative Dynamics*, 197–200; Peter Rabinowitz, "Reading Beginnings and Endings," in Richardson, ed., *Narrative Dynamics*, 300–13 (304–05).

20. Fusillo, "How Novels End," in Roberts et al., eds., *Classical Closure*, 210–11.

21. Phelan, "Narrative Progression," in Richardson, ed., *Narrative Dynamics*, 214.

22. Peter Rabinowitz, "Beginnings and Endings," in Richardson, ed., *Narrative Dynamics*, 304–09.

23. Deborah H. Roberts, "Afterword: Endings and Aftermath: Ancient and Modern," in Roberts et al., eds., *Classical Closure,* 251–73 (262–69).

of the tale.[24] As with openings, Homer's conclusions have been discussed usefully. Some question whether the *Iliad* would have done better to conclude without the spectacle of the funeral games, while others allege that since a main concern has been honor due to Hector, the games provide apt closure.[25] Similarly, some find that the *Odyssey* would have ended more satisfactorily with the reunion between Odysseus and Penelope, though others counter that the hero's subsequent leaving home is necessary for certain other matters to be concluded. Again, though the points are provocative, readers' views are diverse, leaving it difficult to assess these endings in any absolute sense.

The issue of the conclusion of the story of David is complicated and enriched by the anthological and yet closely woven nature of the extant text. We may feel it ends when David dies. But as the start of his tale is a matter of discernment, we may choose to follow the narrative through to the decisions Solomon makes about carrying out his father's wishes, and we will do well to remember the rather mysterious fates of the last of the Davidic kings—Josiah's progeny. A question to explicate is how well the basic problems of the narrative have been resolved by its various endings. Those working with the David material are faced with the decision about whether and where to include the material of 2 Sam. 21–24. All these choices make a substantial impact on the story's understanding. As we will see when we get to the matter of plotting, the more relevant "strings of story" we can manage, the richer our experience will be.

b Edges of the Story of David

How, then, shall we later receivers choose our beginning? What do we know of him before we meet David? How is kingship spoken of, outside of the material in 1–2 Samuel? Our narrative is escorted and enhanced by what lies outside its most obvious edges. As we step aside from the chronological recital that perhaps disproportionately influences modern reading, what can we say about kingship as remembered into tradition?

1. Rare but hidden in plain sight A few points can be made strange for our reconsideration. There were no kings in the first four or five generations, from Abraham and Sarah through the offspring of the sons of Jacob, no kingship in the days of Moses and Joshua. Law presented as Mosaic raises approvingly the possibility of kingship in Deuteronomy 17, without making it important or

---

24. Patrick Colm Hogan, *The Mind and Its Stories* (Cambridge: Cambridge University Press, 2003), 123–31. So the hero Gilgamesh is found somewhat inexplicably or unsatisfactorily back in his kingdom, building walls; Homer ends the *Iliad* not at the death of Hector but at the funeral games; the *Odyssey's* final book finds its hero on the road from Ithaca.

25. Murnaghan, "Equal Honor," in Roberts et al., eds., *Classical Closure*, 23–42.

providing much positive description of it, rather by warning against the dangers of a foreign king who might accumulate goods, to excess.

The matter is slightly more complicated in the book of Judges. There kingship is four times explicitly described as *lacking* (17:6; 18:1; 19:1; 21:25). When it becomes briefly *present* in the person of Abimelech, son of Gideon/Jerubbaal—himself the son of a father who refused an offer of reigning over his kin and the brother of one who riddled about it—the experience is not positive (Judg. 8–9). The parable or riddle accompanying the elevation of Abimelech seems to suggest that competition and selectivity were not intense, with the first applicant accepted. That first king dies ignominiously, and the experiment, if such it was, is not repeated in the narrative for a while.

Skipping past the books that *do* feature kingship (where, as is commonly observed, reports are rarely good), we note that the story of kings ends in the death or exile of the last of the crowned heads, or enigmatically, with the reprieve of the last surviving king sprung from prison to sit—slightly better dressed and fed than previously—among peers though in a foreign land (2 Kgs. 25:27–30). Brief references in Haggai (1–2), Zechariah (4), and Ezra (2–5) raise only to dash the possibility that a Davidic leader takes up a position after the exile to Babylon and return from there. Kingship is valorized in certain psalms (e.g., 2, 18, 45, 72, 89, 110, 144) but vilified in a number of prophetic texts (notably in Jer. 21–23). So as we assess the long trajectory of time from Adam and Eve, or Sarah and Abraham, down to the end of the biblical period, the time of kings is brief: an interlude, and not a happy one, though once kings lack, there emerges occasionally a wish or hope for an anointed leader.

2. *Kingship ubiquitous* But, oddly, we may observe that in another sense, a pervasive royal presence is rehearsed. Certain kingship motifs are pressed into service before the institution appears, with a number of its elements visible, clothed as alternative leadership. By the time we meet Saul, we have already seen much of his story hidden in plain sight, granted in a scramble of motifs, with the royal identity not immediately obvious. It is those fuzzy edges of David's kingship story we will now peruse, briefly.

Having made uncertain and unfamiliar the beginnings of our David narrative, we can circle back to consider in slightly more detail three extended narratives of pre-royal leadership (two from the book of Judges and one from early on in 1 Samuel). Again, the concern is not facticity or redaction but the play of language as we prepare to meet both kingship and Saul as prelude to David. If we consider ourselves as "pushing off" from these three narratives, what kind of a start might they offer to the choice of a king? Common to the three episodes is the threat from outside the clans of Israel and disunity and disorder from within. Leadership assignments are varied and never successful for long. Should a judge seem successful, when he dies, old problems or worse ones spring up. There is no hereditary leadership, and such sons as narrated do not seem promising in any case. Weak leadership and the presence of many opponents make a potent blend.

Judges 6–9 is a long narrative, filled with details, much irrelevant to the stories of Saul's and David's selection. But certain motifs stand out:[26] With Gideon and Saul, we meet three generations of males, Gideon being a son and also a father (Judg. 6:11) as Saul is, explicitly: son of Kish and father of Jonathan (1 Sam. 9:1–2). Gideon resembles Saul at first, an unwilling or reluctant leader, hiding from and resisting the responsibility thrust upon him by God's agents, who are patient of Gideon's various attempts to gain certitude (Judg. 6:12–32; 1 Sam. 10:22). In each case, the man who began hesitantly to take military leadership action becomes eager for it, all reluctance seemingly vanished. As a son, Gideon is almost put to death (Judg. 6:30–32) as Saul's son Jonathan is (1 Sam. 14:38–45); but in each case there is a reprieve, derived from the son's military skill and people's gratitude. A son's relation to the father's leadership emerges a bit differently in the two stories, since Abimelech grabs kingship violently (Judges 9) while Jonathan will evade it (1 Sam. 18–19). But the first sighting of Jonathan shows him framed in competition with his father, a role he lacks conspicuously later. The motif of vanishing troops is present in both stories (Judg. 7:1–8; 1 Sam. 13:8), though Gideon dismisses his soldiers, while Saul panics when he sees his troops slipping away. Each man is provided a proleptic vision, and though Gideon's encourages and strengthens him (Judg. 7:9–14) and Saul dies of his (1 Sam. 28:15–19), a case can be made that what Saul learned was salutary if unwelcome.[27] Gideon's lapse into idolatry (Judg. 8:27) and his son's grabbing for kingship accompanied by the death of his brothers echoes Saul's frustration at being unable to secure reliable access to God (1 Sam. 28:6)—efforts of Ishbosheth to claim the throne once he is the sole survivor of his father's sons (2 Sam. 2–4). Abimelech is addressed not by a prophet but by an enigmatic speaker (Judg. 9:8–20), as Saul has the ambiguous words of Samuel to confuse him (e.g., 10:8). In time, both sets of words are proven true. God's spirit troubles both Abimelech and Saul (Judg. 9:22; 1 Sam. 16:14), and each man is opposed by former allies who try to trick him so as to gain military advantage. Finally, each asks to be killed by his armor-bearer (Judg. 9:54–55; 1 Sam. 31:4), though in each case, the matter is not completely straightforward.[28]

26. David J. Pleins, "Son-Slayers and Their Sons," *CBQ* 54 (1992): 29–38, calling attention to the work of Peter D. Miscall on narrative analogy, suggests consideration of the relationship between larger blocks of material than are usually compared, urging that the point is not to discern the compositional strategy but other literary relationships among sets of texts. See also Keith Bodner and Ellen White, "Some Advantages of Recycling: The Jacob Cycle in a Later Environment," *BibInt* 22 (2014): 20–33. They demonstrate the presence of shared motifs, comment on the impact, and suggest reasons for the phenomenon, offering several examples and references of similar work by others.

27. See Barbara Green, *How Are the Mighty Fallen? A Dialogical Study of King Saul in 1 Samuel*, JSOTSup 365 (Sheffield: Sheffield Academic Press, 2003), 422–34, for the case that Saul learns via the Woman of Endor, who helps him engage the dead Samuel to learn the very information he needs to die responsibly on the following day.

28. Jonathan's armor-bearer is conspicuously present in the episode that leads to Jonathan's being condemned to death, as is Saul's. There are additional motifs as well, from

Consider the following questions: What does it mean that young kingship looks dubious? How are we to construe the sense that God's acquiescence to kingship and clear designation of Saul ends up being so disastrous? How shall we correlate the narrative relating how a father (Gideon) refused kingship but his son (Abimelech) arrogated it to himself and killed rivals with the father-son relationship of Saul and David, similarities alerting us to consider representation rather than referentiality? How does a parable or a riddle refract each narrative? Insofar as Saul's reign and the fate of Jonathan are rehearsed in the earlier story, the abundance of common motifs is not accounted for simply due to the presence of similar topics. A shadow falls forward onto Saul, both as contrasted with Gideon and when compared with Abimelech. Said more generally, the emergence of kingship is shown negatively, whether by comparison or contrast. There are no good endings: not for Gideon, not for Abimelech, neither for Saul nor Jonathan. The choice of Saul (and of David) begins or may seem to begin with Abimelech.

A similar set of echoes arise from the final story in the book of Judges, when we get the backstory for the tribe to which the first king belongs. In chs. 19–21 (another long narrative filled with more detail than is pertinent here), the book of Judges manages to cast Saul of Benjamin as an unlikely choice for a leader—not in an actually positive sense, as we will see when David overcomes his status as youngest to become king, but in a negative way, emerging as he does from a thoroughly disgraced tribe. We count strikes against the first king's tribe in these last three chapters of Judges.

The first step is an outrageous action by Saul's tribe against the others, and the muster of the eleven against the one (Judges 19). In recent critical discussion, emphasis falls heavily on the outrage done to the woman not only by men of Gibeah but by her father and her husband, but here the relevant point is the rape of the woman and the insult offered "her men" by those of the Benjamin tribe. The eleven tribes seem to agree—rare in Judges—that the insult to the Levite, as it were, must be avenged. God, consulted as to particulars, seems unhelpful at the start, since the single tribe, Benjamin, prevails over all the others, unexpectedly. But on the third attempt, thanks to more skillful maneuvers, the eleven wipe out nearly all the men of Benjamin (Judges 20). Once the small tribe is defeated and slated for extinction through lack of progeny—a disgrace as well as a threat—the others regret the possible disappearance of even the guilty Benjamin group and twice contrive to secure women for the survivors of the internecine conflict so that Benjamin can produce sons, granted from stolen and "outsider" women. Thus Benjamin offends egregiously, is blamed and excoriated, suffers defeat and decimation, and avoids extinction only when the eleven other tribes, pitying him perhaps for reasons of tribal solidarity rather than for any quality of his, help them acquire two sets of women somewhat dishonorably, to avoid a tribe breaking away

---

later in the story of Saul (e.g., his pursuit of a group from which one escapes to eventually thwart him). I am dealing here primarily with the Saul material before David is introduced. For a close study of this sort of motifs shared by Samson and Saul, see Edward L. Greenstein, "The Riddle of Samson," *Prooftexts* 1 (1981): 237–60.

from the whole group, Israel. The original deed of taking one woman, improperly, is rounded off by the taking of six hundred (Judges 21).

Again noting the presence and insistence of the motifs rather than trying to track their likely original referentiality, what do we see? No matter the guilt and ignominy, the Benjamins must survive, but why? Benjamin continues only due to assistance from the eleven, who have just all but wiped their smallest brother out. There is no sign of Benjamin's denial of what happened, no suggestion that it was not heinous. That others may also have been blameworthy does not exonerate the Gibeah men of their misdeed. Reprisal, though deserved, needs a limit. Hidden within the confusion of tribal membership at the start of the story (a Levite from Ephraim marrying into a Judah clan), we discern the motif of Judah against Benjamin. At the end, the eleven are forced to strategize if they are to win, as though little Benjamin is almost more competent than they are even with YHWH's help. That is, it takes three tries and trickery for the defeat, though the defeat is massive when it finally happens. Two plans are required to resolve the problem of the near-wifelessness and sonlessness of the Benjamins: first the abduction of women from a group (Jabesh-Gilead) that never disqualified itself by oath; and second, the setting up of the Shiloh raid that allows additional women to be taken. Can anything good come from Shiloh? Is this not yet another disaster for Benjamin? The whole episode shifts past the seizure of one woman and the shaming of "her men" to the near elimination of a tribe. In fact, if improper seizure of a woman was the original problem, it is compounded in the end by more of the same.

The impact of these motifs, when lifted from the mass of other detail, prepares us for a most negative impression of the first king being a man of Benjamin, no matter his parentage, height, or appearance, or the number of times and ways the choice of him is ratified. This choice cannot turn out well, it seems. The point I want to suggest—to offer rather than try to demonstrate comprehensively—is that the royal story of David has roots tangled in the story of Saul, which has its roots intertwined in the sorry tales of the judges. Where does the David story begin? Much earlier than 1 Samuel 16, though that is one of its beginnings. Saul of Benjamin was born to fail as a leader, as kingship will stumble repeatedly before collapsing.

3. Motifs shared: Eli and sons, Saul and sons A third narrative filled with royal motifs opens the book of 1 Samuel while seeming in many ways to resemble material in Judges.[29] Elkanah is presented dynastically (1 Sam. 1:1–2), fifth in line, with Samuel being sixth, Joel and Abijah seventh. Elides are also implied as dynastic, with typical priestly names, though their specific lineage is provided forward rather than backward, extending until the last of them (Abiathar and his son, Jonathan) support

---

29. David Jobling, *1 Samuel, Berit Olam Studies in Hebrew Narrative & Poetry* (Liturgical Press, Collegeville, MN: 1998), 29–37, working with this same concept of uncertain edges, talks about this material as the "extended book of Judges," continuing into 1 Samuel as far as ch. 12. He also calls attention to the lack of fit many see between 2 Sam. 21–24 and the rest of the David story (36–37). I often appraise material quite differently than he does, not least since our methods diverge somewhat.

the Adonijah cause (1 Kgs. 1:25, 42).[30] The early Elides are drawn thoroughly bad, from the impotent and permissive father to the abusive and blasphemous sons. Eli's sons have nothing good said about them, even when in what is arguably their finest moment—their effort to win a battle with the Ark—they lose it and their own lives as well. Their father is shown deficient when, positioned in his chair at the Shiloh shrine, he cannot discern what Hannah is asking, though he blesses it, redundantly, it would seem (1 Sam. 1:12–17). He cannot land a corrective word on his sons, though he is warned and seems to understand what is wanted (2:22–25; 3:11–18). In his last scene, blind but hearing too much, he falls, accompanied by almost all remaining of his line (4:12–22). The best that can be said of Eli's leadership and his house is negative, rehearsing Saul's rule.

Other characters can be compared: Samuel's mother, Hannah, correlates with Samson's unnamed mother (Judges 13; 1 Samuel 1). Elkanah resembles Manoah, each knowing less than his wife, each running ineffectually behind his spouse in terms of knowledge and insight. The respective sons generally correspond as well, Samson and Samuel managing leadership but not with signal or sustained success. This welter of motifs and analogy makes a negative impact, while starting the long royal narrative. Worship at Shiloh seems most dubious, both in Judg. 21:15–24 with stolen women and in the beginning of 1 Sam. 2:12–17, with illicit and immoral liturgy.[31] The Ark, positioned at Shiloh at least narratively, is misused as it is made to witness the Elide sons sin at Shiloh, by being lost in battle, by becoming a misbehaving and dangerous guest, first to Philistines city-states but later to non-proper Israelite caretakers as well, until it recuperates under Abinadab and can go into David's city. It is difficult to feel optimistic about young Samuel being trained by Elides. Indeed, he eventually places his two bad sons into position illegally, since judgeship is presented as divinely appointed, never inherited. What Samuel does learn at the shrine is, arguably, not priesthood and not judging but how to be a prophet to a king: to speak powerful and unwelcome words to authority (1 Sam. 3:11–18).[32] Hannah's prayer (what she asks and gives thanks for: 1 Sam. 2:1–10) thematizes the whole long story: things are not what they seem but can be reversed—good things go bad and bad things go good—high beings topple and lowly ones may expect to rise. Hannah also voices the insight about the differences between receiving and grabbing but also the possibility of the dismissed slipping back into line to become receivers again.

30. Jobling thinks the Elides are presented as Aaronids, *1 Samuel*, 53, though I am not so certain.

31. On that point: the Jabesh-Gilead favor we will see with Saul is tainted for the same reason (Judg. 21:1–14).

32. Jobling, *1 Samuel*, 57, thinks, oddly to me, that Samuel renders judgeship triumphant and has "comprehensively solved all Israel's problems, both internally . . . and externally." I, on the other hand, see the Ark in trouble, Shiloh devastated, leadership ineffectually or at least vaguely presented, worship abused, and Samuel making the classic error of appointing sons after himself and evil sons at that.

The point: The beginning of the story we are reading is fuzzy-edged. Events narrated in Judges and those leading to the request for a king are constituted by common and consistent motifs. The David story begins long before we meet any king.

4. *Frayed endings* If the epic of David seems to gather itself slowly and comprehensively before beginning, how does the long story conclude? Does the story of David's presence and power with YHWH's people come to a proper finish? When might we consider that the narrative of Judah and Israel with kings is over? Though it seems out of place here, we need briefly to consider where our story of David ends, if it does, such as it does. The point will be, again, not really to promote a choice but to suggest that the narrative of our concern trails past the death of David, announced with amazing brevity in 1 Kgs. 2:10–11.

Simply to name a few trailings: Perhaps David's "life" is not over until his heir, Solomon, carries out his father's wishes (so until 1 Kgs. 2:46). Or, with David's temple-building disappointment (2 Samuel 7) in mind, we may want to take the story to Solomon's successful completion of that task (up through 1 Kings 10). We may choose to conclude David's story with its sins against women by considering Solomon's women in 1 Kings 11. Perhaps the foolishness of Solomon's son, Rehoboam, leading directly to the dissolution of what had been a unified venture (1 Kings 12), brings David's uniting of those elements full circle. We might say, simply to reinforce porous or uncertain edges, that David lives on in the deeds of some of the great kings—Josiah (2 Kgs. 22–23) or Jehoiachin (25:27–30). We may glimpse David and his dead sons (and Saul with his) in the death of Jeroboam's firstborn (1 Kings 13), or in the poignant notice of the deaths of King Zedekiah's sons (2 Kgs. 25:7). Even the implied matter of the returning exiles refusing the leadership of the Davidic Zerubbabel and continuing from the late sixth century to be kingless is not disconnected from the story that only superficially ends when David draws his last breath, with the Zerubbabel story hinted in the misadventures of Saul's last son, Ishbosheth (2 Sam. 2–3). The point is that the ending is not clear, with the latter boundary to the story being as fluid as the front one. If the story starts *in medias res*, it ends enigmatically there as well. The challenge is to continue to ponder how the narrative has been and can be positioned amid all the other information we have. Before we begin, we are already immersed in the story of royalty.

Considering once more the major differences between starts and finishes of ancient and modern stories, I suggest that helpful points are raised from modern fiction about the challenges of edges. A useful way to think about this basically unresolvable issue comes from posing a question faced by a historian who plans a book on the Second World War in a context where—for a few decades—those who will read it already know a fair amount about that conflict and their views will vary: where to begin, to end? There are no inevitably obvious places, though some seem more feasible than others. An author makes a choice to begin—perhaps even at a middle place and then back up or zigzag along as needed, or from some point that seems more satisfactorily first than other places.[33] In a sense, there is no absolute beginning place, no natural start, and no inevitable end. It must be chosen by the writer and agreed to by the reader. The point is to exploit that feature usefully.

3 Structures

1. Theory Biblical commentators, perhaps exceeding other narrative scholars, love to discover and lay out story floor plans or skeletons, at macrolevels and microlevels. It is rare to pick up a volume produced by biblical scholars in the past few decades and not find structures for consideration, whether shaped by form critics in search of form/genre indicators or by rhetorical scholars thirsting for the pitch and flow between speakers and hearers. As was true of our first tool seeking to discern the edges of a narrative, the analogous concerns of moderns for shape seem to resemble little the simpler moves of scholars of ancient texts. And yet insight is available. To contemporary secular theorists we will briefly turn— their work on boundaries and frames claimed as rising from cognitive theory and computer models—before looking at the simpler if more detailed work of biblical scholars working on structure. The theory available on structures is clearly related to the question of edges, though distinct as well, as will be procedures of plotting related to both edges and structure. All the tools overlap and collaborate.

Those theorizing presently offer us several ways of thinking about structure: Structure may operate "nestedly" or concentrically, as in the analogical example of Russian dolls. The story-discourse distinction is one such pattern, though it resists visual mapping. Narratives often offer layered language, beginning with an implied author who delegates to an extradiegetic narrator, who hands the responsibility to intradiegetic voices who may share it in various ways—all of which are offered to the alert reader.[34] The challenge is to attend to the levels consistently and carefully, noting the impact of places where the frames are violated.[35] The *mise-en-abŷme*, where a whole narrative is repositioned and re-angled in some fresh way, provides another example of the structuring process, to which we will return.

The simpler and more classic effort of biblical scholars to map the design of their ancient texts shows some of the same features, others as well. The best and most exhaustive structure queries of scholars on extensive texts rise not so much

---

33. Philippe Carrard, "September 1939: Beginnings, Historical Narrative, and the Outbreak of World War II," in Richardson, ed., *Narrative Beginnings*, 63–78.

34. Marie-Laure Ryan, "Stacks, Frames, and Boundaries," in Richardson, ed., *Narrative Dynamics*, 368–76, offers various ways of discussing and showing these issues exemplifying Scheherazade's voice in *Arabian Nights*, among others.

35. William Nelles, *Frameworks: Narrative Levels and Embedded Narrative* (New York: Peter Lang, 1997), 121–57, discussing the phenomenon in complex modern fiction, shows how quotation marks (with the text showing perhaps as many as eight sets) signify.

from source or redaction quests but from the effort to discern form or genre and to see comprehensive evidence of the rhetorical purpose or teaching of a text.[36] Robert O'Connell claims that intricate, consistent, repeating, formal patterning makes visible the set of devices by which we can discern the argumentation of the authoring hand and strategizing aims. Structural cohesion promotes rhetorical development, argumentation designed to evoke response.[37] Another study of chiastic structures in biblical prose suggests that they function as part of characterization, allowing spoken discourse to show evidence of careful planning and deliberation.[38]

The classic and comprehensive study of this feature by Jerome Walsh discusses kinds of structures, presumed rationales behind them, and likely functions they accomplish.[39] Briefly, he demonstrates with examples spanning the entire Hebrew Bible that our awareness of the various "architectural" cues—some as small as sounds and others the size of many chapters of narrative—helps us see what is being said, specifically how it is managed. He offers the many relationships made visible when we note repetition— whether chiastic or concentric, where patterning recurs and replicates. Some repetition is practical, marking the edges of a frame; other is more elaborate and detailed.[40] Walsh then shows how disjunction can be suggested even within the many relational sequences, reminding us that our use of commas, periods, dashes, paragraphs, and chapters accomplishes the same goal.

36. Robert H. O'Connell has worked long and carefully on the structures of the book of Isaiah: *Concentricity and Continuity: The Literary Structure of Isaiah*, JSOTSup 188 (Sheffield: Sheffield Academic Press, 1994); further work occurs in *The Rhetoric of the Book of Judges*, Supplements to *VT* (Leiden and New York: Brill, 1996).

37. O'Connell, *Isaiah*, 19–29, 235–42; he makes the same claims more compactly in *Judges,* 3–7. There, usefully here, he suggests that Judges is to support the leadership of David over against that of Saul: "Indeed, the deliberative patterning of events and phraseology used to characterize Saul and David in 1 Samuel seems to be a deliberate stratagem of the Judges compiler/redactor" (7).

38. Elie Assis, "Chiasmus on Biblical Narrative: Rhetoric of Characterization," *Prooftexts* 22 (2002): 273–304. He provides numerous other examples and references to studies from both testaments and wider literature. An effort to bring some order to the tendency of scholars to see chiasm everywhere is suggested by Craig Blomberg, cited by Gordon H. Johnston in "The Enigmatic Genre and Structure of the Song of Songs," Part One, *BSac* 166.662 (April–June 2009): 174, note 25.

39. Jerome T. Walsh, *Style and Structure in Biblical Hebrew Narrative* (Collegeville, MN: The Liturgical Press, 2001).

40. Walsh, *Style and Structure*, 7–114. Jack R. Lundbom, in *Biblical and Rhetorical Criticism* (Sheffield: Sheffield Phoenix, 2013), 167–68, also specializing in structures, says the following: "Repetition is the single most important feature of ancient Hebrew rhetoric, being used for emphasis, wordplays, expressing the superlative, creating pathos, and structuring both parts and whole of . . . discourse. Its importance can hardly be overemphasized. Repetitions can be sequential or placed in strategic collocations to provide balance."

Biblical structures can use scenes, character presence and absence, time and place notations, and interrupted sequences to break units into manageable pieces.[41] Finally, Walsh shows how conjunctive cues overcome disjunction to reestablish connectivity.[42] His study is filled with examples of the various structures so produced, including many from the story we are about to read. To consider multiple structures of the same text portions demonstrates that structural mapping is not simplex or merely classificatory but a way of working out complex relationships. There is no "the right" structure. We are being nudged in the direction of seeing that the discernment of complex literary structures is a collaboration between implied author and real readers, with the leadership perhaps uncertain, a point to be taken up again when we talk about plotting.

2. Structure of the David narrative The most extensive work on the present narrative structures has been provided by Jan Fokkelman, who has written extensively and intensively on the corpus comprising 1 Samuel 1 through 1 Kings 2. He provides for us a useful macrostructure, offered here and adapted as needed.[43] Fokkelman offers a template (for prose passages), a "12-note scale," where a passage can be identified in units of descending size: book or composition; sections/cycles; acts; scenes; scene parts; sequences/speeches; sentences; clauses; phrases; words; syllables; sounds.[44] It is difficult to imagine a finer sieve for observation. Since language functions at these various levels and often works simultaneously at several of them, the comprehensive schema is able to accommodate analysis in various aspects. Structures are like floor plans and skeletons, indicating a good deal of information in one way while removing clues to other kinds of information. But as we would not likely purchase a house without paying careful attention to the blueprints—nor purchase it simply on the basis of such scrutiny—so this large-scale presentation is useful. At the very least, structures force careful attention to verbal detail. As we may anticipate, structures are related to the presentation of the implied author and narrator as well as to our eventual investigation into plot. But, alerted by the work of contemporary frame theory, we can see that the mapping of physical structures can be highly useful to show many features beyond the verbal ones most popular with biblical scholars. The following structure will guide the present book.

41. Walsh, *Style and Structure*, 117–72.

42. Ibid., 175–90.

43. Jan P. Fokkelman published his work on the material of the books of Samuel and Kings out of Bible order; so in this outline I will replace his numbering of what he calls acts with fresh numbers corresponding to Bible order. I will generally maintain his divisions but renumber and somewhat simplify his subtitles. The outline presented here is taken from the table of contents of three of his four volumes on the biblical material, collectively called *Narrative Art and Poetry in the Books of Samuel* and specified previously by volume (above, ch. 1, note 5).

44. Fokkelman, *Crossing Fates*, 15. The first chapter of this volume (1–21) discusses these matters in detail.

- 1 Samuel 8–12 Act One
  - — Choice for Kingship
    - ○ 8:1–6 People Request a King
    - ○ 8:6–9 Prophet and Deity Discuss the Request
    - ○ 8:10–21 Prophet and People Discuss the Request
    - ○ 8:21–22 Deity Affirms the Request

  - — Seeking and Finding a King
    - ○ 9:1–4 Quest Undertaken
    - ○ 9:5–10 Journey to Zuph
    - ○ 9:10–14 Journey to the City
    - ○ 9:15–25 Encounter of Prophet and King-to-be
    - ○ 9:26–27 Journey from the City
    - ○ 10:1–8 Journey back through Zuph
    - ○ 10:9–16 Quest Completed

  - — Saul Selected as King and Acting as King
    - ○ 10:17–29 Saul Becomes King Publicly
    - ○ 11:1–15 Saul Acts as King

  - — Kingship Definitively Inaugurated
    - ○ 12:1–2 Samuel Presents the King
    - ○ 12:3–12 Samuel Reviews the Past
    - ○ 12:13–25 Samuel Reiterates the Basic Demand

- 1 Samuel 13–16 Act Two
  - — Saul's Rejection
    - ○ 13:1–22 Saul Loses Support
    - ○ 13:23–14:23 Jonathan Creates Conditions for Victory
    - ○ 14:23–46 Saul Isolates Jonathan

  - — 15 Second and Final Rejection of Saul

  - — David Anointed King
    - ○ 16:1–13 Samuel Anoints David
    - ○ 16:14–23 David Comes to Court

- 17–19 Act Three
  - — 17:1–54 Shepherd Boy as Champion
  - — David Enters Saul's Household Afresh
    - ○ 17:55–18:5 David and Saul's Son
    - ○ 18:6–16 David and Saul's People
    - ○ 18:17–30 David and Saul's Daughters

  - — Antagonism Intensifies, Subsides, Festers
    - ○ 19:1–7 Jonathan's Mediation

- o 19:8–18 Spear and Trap
- o 19:19–24 Pursuit by Saul Frustrated

- 20–23:13 Act Four

  — 20 Covenant between David and Jonathan

  — David Fleeing

  - o 21:2–10 David at Nob
  - o 21:11–16 David Flees to Philistia
  - o 22:1–5 David in Adullam

  — Saul against the Priests and David at Keilah

  - o 22:6–23 Saul Exterminates the House of Nob
  - o 23:1–13 David Relieves Keilah

- 23:14–26 Act Five

  — Pursuit: Ziph to En-Gedi

  - o 23:14–18 David in Horesh
  - o 23:19–28 Narrow Escape at Ziph
  - o 24 David and Saul Meet at En-Gedi

  — 25 Pursuit Re-Presented

  — 26 Final Encounter at Ziph

- 27–31 + 2 Samuel 1 Act Six

  — David in Keilah as Philistine Vassal

  - o 27:1–28:2 David as Achish's Vassal
  - o 29 David: Ally or Opponent?
  - o 30 David Pursues Amalekite Plunderers

  — Saul's Demise

  - o 28:3–25 Saul Consults a Medium
  - o 31 Defeat and Deaths at Gilboa
  - o 1:1–16 David Learns of Gilboa
  - o 1:17–27 David's Lament for Saul and Jonathan

- 2 Samuel 2:1–5:5 Act Seven

  — Whose Dominion?

  - o 2:1–11 Exposition
  - o 2:12–32 Day of Warfare

  — Generals Keep their Kings Occupied

  - o 3:6–21 Abner Shifts to David
  - o 3:22–39 Death of Abner

- ⸺ One Man's Breath Is Another's Death
    - ○ 4 Fate of the House of Saul
    - ○ 5:1–5 David Becomes King over Israel

- • 5:6–8:18 Act Eight

    - ⸺ Jerusalem, David's City
        - ○ 5:6–16 David's Conquest
        - ○ 5:17–25 David Defeats Philistines
        - ○ 6 David Brings the Ark to Jerusalem

    - ⸺ God Grants the Kingdom a Future
        - ○ 7:1–17 David Receives an Oracle
        - ○ 7:18–29 David Prays in Response
        - ○ 8 Summary of David's Military Successes

- • 9–12 Act Nine

    - ⸺ Triangle of David, Ziba, Mephibosheth
        - ○ 9 David's Concern for Jonathan's Son
        - ○ 16:1–4 Ziba's Concerns
        - ○ 19:25–31 Mediation

    - ⸺ War, Sex, Violence
        - ○ 10 War in Ammon
        - ○ 11:1–27 Adultery, Cover-up, Murder

    - ⸺ Confrontation, Repentance, Mourning, Harmony, Victory
        - ○ 11:27–12:15 Nathan's Words
        - ○ 12:16–25 Death and birth
        - ○ 12:26–31 Settling with Ammon

- • 13–14 Act Ten

    - ⸺ David's Children
        - ○ 13:1–22 Lust to Hatred
        - ○ 13:23–38 Absalom's Revenge

    - ⸺ Interventions
        - ○ 13:39–14:24 Wise Woman
        - ○ 14:25–33 Intermezzo and Reconciliation

- • 15–20 Act Eleven
    - ⸺ Absalom Rebels and David Flees
        - ○ 15:1–12 Preparation and Outbreak
        - ○ 15:13–31 David's Flight
        - ○ 15:32–16:13 Three Encounters

— Absalom and Two Counselors
  - ○ 16:15–17:14 Council of War
  - ○ 17:15–23 Escape of David

— Outcome on the Battlefield
  - ○ 17:24–18:18 Preparations
  - ○ 18:19–19:1 Report of Outcome and Mourning of David

— Joab Intervenes
  - ○ 19:2–9 Joab's Words
  - ○ 19:9–16 David's Relationships

— David's Journey Back
  - ○ 19:17–24 Shimei
  - ○ 19:32–41 Barzillai

— Schism between Israel and Judah
  - ○ 19:41–20:3 Dispute and Secession
  - ○ 20:4–22 Joab's Role

- 21–24 Act Twelve[45]

— Two Crises of Crime and Punishment
  - ○ 21:1–14 Bloodguilt and Atonement
  - ○ 21:15–22 and 23:8–39 Anecdotes and Lists
  - ○ 24 Census and Punishment

— Great Hymn and Short Poem
  - ○ 22 Praise and Thanksgiving
  - ○ 23:1–7 Last Words of David

- 1 Kings 1–2 Act Thirteen
  — David Decides about Succession: 1 Kings 1
  — David's Last Wishes
  - ○ 2:1–12 David Instructs Solomon
  - ○ 2:13–25 Adonijah's End
  - ○ 2:28–35 Joab's End
  - ○ 2:36–46 Shimei's End

4 Choosing Kings

Having recognized the subtle but pervasive way in which the story of kings emerges from within a wider narrative stream and how it counts on our noticing

---

45. This material will be considered out of its biblical order.

a variety of narrative hints before it commences in earnest, we approach the long story of David, well-prepared to hear it deeply attentively.

a A Closer Look at the Story of Saul: 1 Samuel 8–15

Our next way to reflect on the capaciousness of the David narrative is to reposition what we have of Saul. As is well known, before David is chosen king—the point at which our story of David most obviously begins—Saul has reigned, with Samuel presented as both initiating and terminating Saul's rule. Part of our closing in on David's story—while recognizing its productive overflow—is to consider how the Samuel-and-Saul material pre-capitulates David's narrative. Insofar as the story of Saul is a reprise of Judah's later experience of kingship, a miniaturized and re-angled presentation, then it functions also as a foreshadowing of and prequel to David's rule and will resemble it, if oddly. What is most useful to hear, first from the final transition of judges to a king and then from the change from Saul's reign to David's rule? How can we weight the Saul material so that it readies us for the David narrative that will occupy us in the main portion of this study?

This narrative of the hiring and firing of Saul as first king is the immediate context for the rise of David and hence the most relevant place to look for issues remaining central. I have written on this material with a focus on Saul and continue to think much as I thought at that time.[46] Here the question is re-angled: If David's story begins in the midst of the Saul narrative, what Saulide genetic heritage does the long David narrative privilege most prominently? Since the focus of this present study is not Saul, I will stipulate summarily as I think suits, not discuss it in detail or seek to demonstrate points about his early reign. Again, my purpose is not to seek historical data but to observe and mine how material seems to have been presented. We can consider five coordinates of the topic of pre-David kingship.

1. Kingship sought The narrative of the books of Samuel (and beyond) and surely that of 1 Sam. 8–15 is foundationally about kingship as an institution before it is about the king. The players in the royal drama are several and key: God, Samuel the prophet, the people, Saul, the brief *Torah* about kingship in Deuteronomy, the Philistines' threat, internal factors such as those belabored in Judges. The narrative challenge is to show the asking and granting of kingship and king as inherently compromised. Most commentators offer good points about what was not straightforwardly negotiated, and those are useful in terms of characterization and plot.[47] But given the trauma that kingship becomes, it cannot be easily spoken of. That it is minimally approved in Deut. 17:14–20, though with more negative than positive detail attending the concession, testifies to the complexity of the matter. That God expresses hurt and disappointment as well as acceding to the request (1 Sam. 8:7–9) thus makes narrative sense. That Samuel himself is not presented as proceeding in a straightforward way suits the story being told. That

---

46. Green, *Mighty Fallen*, chs. 3–4.
47. See Jobling, *I Samuel*, 59–67.

is, when we hear him report back on his encounter with God and do not hear him repeat God's words but something else, we catch the implications (8:6–18).[48] The elders who asked for a king may adduce the wrong reasons (to be like the nations) as well as right ones (the Samuel-sons are not suitable as successors to their father), and they seem persuaded not a bit by what Samuel warns (8:4–20). Kingship involves dynasty, or at least stability of leadership, a fraught problem from judges, and surely it remains so in this section where Jonathan is first disestablished as royal heir in 13:13–14, then condemned to death by a paternal oath (14:39–45), finally reprieved but not released from the immediate consequences of the curse. When we see and hear Saul's son elsewhere in the narrative of Saul, after ch. 14, Jonathan is intent on establishing David's rule rather than his own. Jonathan lives under sentence of death, a position his father assigned him, though Saul resists acknowledging either Jonathan's state or his own responsibility for it.[49]

2. Saul set up Saul's kingship is a *mise-en-abŷme* or a small representation of the larger story of kingship.[50] The issue is not simply *what* wrong Saul did, but *how* is Saul *shown* to have done wrong, since he is an epitome of kingship, and kingship practiced poorly. Kings under- or overreach, Saul first among them. Saul's failings will be symbolic and corporate in some way, not simple and personal. Eli, though a priest and not a king, is also a dynast, and the story of his fall[51] and the failure of his house is a prequel here, as David's story will be both sequel to the Saul narrative and prequel to many other narrative lapses of royal sons. Eli's incapacity or unwillingness to manage his sons will be recapitulated with Saul and David and their sons. Kings fail, royal houses do, kingship will.

3. Kingship's inherent negativity Kingship is asked and given ambiguously, by design. Elders are adamant, a prophet is offended, the deity disappointed and disgruntled. Communication is confused. The implied author could have designed and the narrator related a clearer story if clarity were the point. But the narrative need is for ambivalence, from the start. So all the efforts to place responsibility cleanly are slightly misguided. Is someone mightier than Samson and Samuel needed to fight Philistines? Likely so, but Philistines will remain a problem, as

48. The narrator does say that Samuel told everything (8:10), but the represented speech is not a match (8:11–18); Samuel is shown to report on the specifics of 8:10 only in 12:17, if at all. For a more detailed discussion, see Polzin *Samuel and the Deuteronomist,* 82–83.

49. The infertility of Michal, the assassination of Ishbosheth, the incapacities of Jonathan's son, Mephibosheth, all contribute to this claim about the defunct or fallen house of Saul, surely a live issue at the time of the production of this material, even if we do not know quite how so.

50. For this wonderful trope, see Lucien Dällenbach, *The Mirror in the Text,* trans. Jeremy Whiteley with Emma Hughes (Cambridge, UK: Polity Press, 1989) and David A. Bosworth, *The Story within a Story in Biblical Hebrew Narrative* (Washington, DC: Catholic Biblical Association of America, 2008), 1–36, 158–65.

51. For a brilliant and allusive reading of the episode where Eli, learning of the loss of the Ark, falls to his death (1 Sam. 4:12–22), see Polzin, *Samuel and the Deuteronomist,* 49–54.

Saul cannot defeat them and David actually even joins them, temporarily, though finally he is said to have vanquished them (2 Sam. 5:17–25). Is kingship approved? Ambivalently, with multiple and deep reservations. It is a brilliant presentation.

4. *One thing needful* As the choosing of Saul moves uneasily along, there comes a point where Samuel reduces the matter to what can be called the one thing needful: 12:20–25. The one positive qualification in Deuteronomy 17 is that the king study and copy the law, promote and do it, make it operative. Though one thing only, it is of course the "thing" that no king can accomplish, nor can God, even when God promises to "install" it in human hearts (e.g., Jer. 31:33). Granting the difficulty of the charge, still, Saul is never presented as making any attempt at this single responsibility. In fact, his portrait is conspicuous for having little relation with God and none with God's Torah. Saul and God are consistently shown at cross-purposes. Saul and the kingship he epitomizes fail massively at the one thing needful.[52]

As the story develops, David will not have Saul's cardinal sin of non-relatedness with God. The second king's key weakness will root elsewhere. But it hardly needs demonstrating that "kingship" as it unfolds has more incumbents resembling Saul than David. David, even if with a heart like YHWH's, fails to obey, while others do worse, even Hezekiah and Josiah (good fathers though with recalcitrant and backsliding sons). I maintain that the Deuteronomy-laced story in which the David narrative is embedded is negative to kingship, to the institution itself. The alternatives may be no better: Judges do poorly as leaders, and over time we learn from history if not from texts that priesthood becomes corrupt as well. Prophets are a mixed lot, as are governors. So the issue may lie deeper than the title or job description of the leader. Jeremiah has perhaps spoken well commenting that the human heart is more bent that anything, above all (17:9). Be that as it may, the record of kings is notoriously poor. That divine discourse occasionally rhapsodizes about royal privilege (2 Sam. 7:13–16) does not rebut or resolve the difficulties.

5. *Fatal misjudgments* Finally, as we move to the end of this sketched review of pre-David material on Saul, I think the presentation of the critique of him—the firing first of his lineage (13:14; 14:39–42) and then of himself (15:23) and his refusal to accept either situation—is shown as occasioned by dire royal misjudgment and disobedience to deity and prophet in the most serious matters: worship and war. There are many explanations of who did and failed to do precisely what in ch. 13,[53] or

---

52. Students tend to feel the unfairness of the ease with which David communicates with the deity, both before and after the priest with the ephod joins him, contrasted with Saul's much less successful efforts. But, I counter-pose, if the point of the presentation is to show kings as congenitally deficient in the one thing needful, then Saul cannot be adept at it. It is not a matter of fairness or fault.

53. For a brief consideration of the views of scholars on this matter, see Green, *Mighty Fallen*, 234–39.

perhaps why God required so violent a deed for the Amalekites.[54] But the portrayal remains: that Saul disobeyed twice and was fired, if not quite removed, from his post. His literary characterization extends this flaw in various ways, which can be summarized in the statement that Saul could never align with God's ways.[55] I find Saul a tremendously appealing character despite his many shortcomings. But that he is a failed leader is the crux of the matter.

So as the curtain drops briefly in 1 Samuel 15 to be raised shortly, the agenda seems full. The point offered here is that there is neither a firm start nor finish to the narrative we will work with, and though we will set edges, they are provisional, unstable, easily placed elsewhere. We will never finish reading the possibilities of the recounting we have, nor should we wish it.

b A Closer Look at the Choice of David: 1 Sam. 16–18

1. Introductory observations We finally meet David and engage with the narrative of his anointing and gradual arrival at the court of King Saul. Having just reviewed the fluid edges of our story and recognized that it matters where we choose to start and stop, we begin as David emerges into the comprehensive story that has already hinted where he might be welcome and where resisted. The deity's nudging the prophet toward Bethlehem marks the beginning of our effort to interpret David, to show him desirous of multiple, conflictual, and shifting things—pitched already against a story that began without him. The ending of this first section is less certain, is set variously by commentators, but we will stop at the end of ch.18, with David chosen and qualifying for leadership in diverse ways, not yet much resisted or resisting. The general shape or structure of the unit I have broken out here for scrutiny seems determined primarily by episode:[56]

- 16:1–13: David, son of Jesse, is anointed;
- 16:14–23: David becomes Saul's healer and armor-bearer;
- 17:1–56: David becomes a military leader;[57]

54. Consult Sternberg, *Poetics of Biblical Narrative*, 482–515 for a superb close study of this narrative.

55. For a thorough study that seeks to offer a more positive portrayal of Saul than he usually receives, centering on the material of chs. 13–15, consult the work of Dawn Maria Sellars, "An Obedient Servant? The Reign of King Saul (1 Sam. 13–15) Reassessed," *JSOT* 35.3 (2011): 317–38. The points are worth considering, though the quest to rehabilitate Saul's kingship seems misconceived to me.

56. For an alternative, see Antony F. Campbell, S.J., "Structure Analysis and the Art of Exegesis (1 Samuel 16:14–18:30)," in Henry T.C. Sun et al., eds., *Problems in Biblical Theology: Essays in Honor of Rolf Knierim* (Grand Rapids, MI/Cambridge, UK: William B. Eerdmans Publishing Co, 1997), 76–103.

57. For a small structuring of 17:1–23, see Walsh, *Style and Structure*, 149–50. Fokkelman, *Crossing Fates,* 143–201, discusses this section of narrative (17:1–18:5), demonstrating interesting points, most of which were also available by other kinds of scrutiny. In other

- 17:57–18:16: David becomes Saul's "son" and Jonathan's "brother";
- 18:17–30: David becomes Saul's son-in-law and Michal's husband.

As previously suggested, there is always more than one way to show structure in a useful way. Here the point is to show the impact of cumulative arrival of David at Saul's court and his gradual preparation for replacing his erstwhile host. My specific interpretive wager and thesis is to see and show how characters in the David narrative provide occasions for insight, wisdom, and compassion, as suits biblical narrative. David, though steeped in patriarchy and power, is shown to learn and extend wise compassion. His journey toward such a goal is leisurely and indirect—even perverse, and not every reader will be persuaded. David's desires in our first section focus on relationships rather than on positions or things. He has diverse agendas with various people with whom he interacts. The challenge is the radical incompatibility among those aims. As we watch the young David with his own birth family, then with King Saul, with Jonathan, Michal, and others in Saul's household, we will see his desires emerge, grow, later. We will note as well those with whom David has minimal relationship: his father and brothers, the prophet Samuel, Saul's daughter Merab, and Saul's wife, Ahinoam of Jezreel. What is most remarkable in this initial unit is how little David actively wants but how intent he can become when, twice, he acquires some agency.

Both to illustrate and expand these initial points and also to break into the narrative, we can review some of the general ways by which the narrative proceeds, and suggest diverse ways in which the implied author manages discourse choices. The extradiegetic narrator is the primary teller of events in these chapters, with modes of discourse varying. The narrator takes responsibility for certain utterances that might be considered problematic, for example, communicating what God thinks, says, and does. That is, the narrator simply says that God spoke to Samuel as though God were a character on an even level with the humans—clearly not quite the case. The narrator's introducing God's discourse and desires into the narrative without special incident is in itself a claim.[58] We see it operative in one way in ch. 16, where the narrator "hands the microphone" to the deity (vv. 1–3, 7, and 12), who then discourses with the prophet. Though the deity is not quite

---

words, his observations do not rise exclusively from his observations about structure, though they likely presented themselves as he was working carefully with the structure of the long section.

58. Those familiar with biblical conventions are not startled that God speaks easily to the prophet Samuel, since that is what prophets do in the Bible: hear and mostly heed the deity, try to persuade other to do so as well. But in narrative terms, the narrator's ease and the implied author's not making this interaction remarkable offer a claim about reliability. I think we are not to speculate about whether Samuel was mistaken here about what God wanted. That is, though we may have many questions here, suspicion that the prophet miscued is not among them. For another view of the matter, consult Joe E. Barnhart, "Acknowledged Fabrications in 1 and 2 Samuel and 1 Kings 1–2. Clues to the Wider Story's Composition," *SJOT* 20.2 (2006): 231–36.

on par with other actants, the narrator presents conversation between deity and prophet as though God were a plain-speaking participant. The narrator does a similar though not quite identical thing in 16:14 and 23 when "he" (as I shall characterize this narrator) provides information about God's doings, or those of God's spirit: A good spirit leaves Saul to attend David, replaced by an evil spirit who attends Saul, at least intermittently. More information we are not given, and these spirits have no consciousness presented, as God does. We may (and will below) ask how we are to understand that the narrator knows such things, but that he claims to do, unproblematically, is clear. The narrator takes responsibility for the situation; God does not explain.[59]

Having singled out for special attention the narrator's presentation of God and soon to call attention to the distinctive way in which the narrator will shrink his own presence in ch. 18, simply adding clarifying detail to a scene mostly narrated by characters, it seems that the rest of this material is dominated by the narrator. Characters speak only occasionally if strategically, to make crucial and vivid points or to move the action along by what they say. Again, this design is offered here as implied authorial choice, so that we can keep the levels of discourse straight and orderly—the narrator not being "in" the story but a voice telling it. Though we will review and in fact make nuanced these matters when we turn seriously both to the narrator and to characterization, they are part of general narrativity as well. With this small bit of narrative theory in mind, we can look at this first section of our long narrative, meet David, and spend enough time with him to register significant changes in him, offered to us from a variety of narrative angles. We can examine the shifts in him in three sets of material: first, within his own family; second, as part of the household of the reigning king; third, as it becomes likely that even from advantageous positions, he will not easily thrive there. David is generally compliant in this section, shifting to determine his own path only twice.

2. Anointed king The scene is sketched, with minimal but strategic character discourse. Elders voice fear when Samuel arrives in Bethlehem (16:4). Samuel speaks for God (16:5, 6, 8, 9, 10, 11). Jesse has one line (16:11), to indicate that yes, there is one more son than has been presented. The implied authorial design builds to a secret, uneasy, unexpected, even unwelcome event. As we watch David selected by God for anointing by a prophet (16:1–13), he is primarily *seen*, that verbal element being the motif word of the general unit (this section and beyond).[60]

---

59. In other genres, this transaction is made more complicated, for example, when prophets disagree among themselves about what God wants. We may also recall that earlier in 1 Samuel the young Samuel struggles to learn the ways of God's communication (1 Samuel 3). When Samuel is pressed by Eli to reveal what God has communicated, Eli—who cannot have welcomed the content of the words—disputes neither their truth nor provenance.

60. See Robert Alter, *The David Story: A Translation with Commentary of 1 and 2 Samuel* (New York: W.W. Norton & Company, 1999), 99. Besides the main Hebrew root for seeing (*r'h*), the verb *nbṭ* (take note) is used, also *bqš* (seek), the verb *ʿyn* for eyeing, the verb *qll*

David is so young and minor that he is not invited to the sacrifice to be presided over by Samuel, is not mustered with the rest of Jesse's sons, and is missed by no one until the sons have run out unexpectedly before the prophet scrutinizing them. Only then is the youngest summoned from his job of tending animals, already seen ahead—"pro-vided"—by God for some good quality of heart that is not yet clear to any, even to us.[61] That he is fine-looking is perhaps a surprise but not necessary.[62] The boy acted upon by deity, prophet, and spirit makes no response to any event or person. His name is not even spoken by the narrator until David has been made king. The complete lack of agency and subjectivity compounds these other literary features to suggest that until anointed and for a short time to come, David is small, unseen, young, silent, subordinate, as minimally involved in his selection as is conceivable. The contrast with Saul's choosing, which took place over four chapters and numerous episodes of 1 Sam. 9–12, is provocative.

3. Introduced to Saul's palace There is not much dramatic development in the next section (16:14–23), but enough to remark. Again, characters speak little. When King Saul needs a healer, servants of his household raise the matter and know a candidate, with one of the palace people attesting his qualities: good at music, skilled in war, a man of valor, well-spoken, and good-looking.[63] We catch a general impression of candid concern shared among players, with Saul's courtiers speaking directly if carefully to the king (16:15, 16, 18), while the king responds (16:17, 19, 22). The five qualifications are more than what we heard from David's family, and they are evidently convincing to Saul. The "old" king requests David. Jesse of Bethlehem, evidently willing as well, sends his son to the king. "He loved him," the narrator tells us ambiguously (v. 21). Saul makes David his armor-bearer as well as minister to the troubled royal moods experienced, result of the departure

---

for appraising negatively, plus the focalizer *hinne*, to direct the reader to appraise from the point of view of the character or narrator (whoever is speaking). In the narrative schema I am suggesting we use, this is the implied author collaborating with narrator and characters to see and show David.

61. Scholars have queried the meaning of the words attributed to God in 1 Sam. 13:14 and here at 16:7, discussing this idiom, whether it means that God acted according to God's own choice or whether there is some alignment between the deity's heart and that of David. For the discussion see Mark George, "Yhwh's Own Heart," *CBQ* 64 (2002): 442–59 and Benjamin J.M. Johnson, "The Heart of YHWH's Chosen One in 1 Samuel," *JBL* 131.3 (2012): 455–66. Fokkelman, *Crossing Fates*, 121, directs us back to the place (13:9) where God claims to have chosen already a better (good-er) man. See below as well for Eliab's contribution to this matter of David's good heart.

62. Keith Bodner, *1 Samuel: A Narrative Commentary* (Sheffield: Sheffield Phoenix Press, 2009), 171, reminds us to consider whose appraisal this is, concluding that it is Samuel's. The particular challenges and benefits of discerning viewpoint will be explored later as we consider character.

63. Thus do the characters, Saul's servants, collaborate with others to testify that the choice of David participates in "good"-ness.

of God's good spirit from Saul, as we have been told. David is still presented as passive, but as we hear his attributes recited, we get a better glimpse than before, as we do when we see evidence of his two roles at Saul's court. As Bodner observes, Saul is the first character to name David.[64]

Three more points pertain here: First is the deep and symbolic nature of the king's armor-bearer, a position to function several times in the narrative ahead. It is more a position to be filled than offering much interest in who fills it. Here David takes the role for Saul, as others will do later. Narratively speaking, all armor-bearers remain linked. When Saul will beg his unnamed armor-bearer to kill him many chapters from now, we will remember that the role was once filled by David: implied authorial artistry. Second, though here we are told that David's music is initially soothing to Saul, we know as well that, shortly and permanently, David's presence will not soothe but rile the king. David's place and role at court, approved and welcomed—even invited—by Saul, will turn to a torment for him, fault of neither or of both. Fokkelman shrewdly names the role as that of a Trojan horse.[65] David will be both balm and bane for Saul, with agency unclear beyond what has already been told to us by the narrator: the good and evil spirits are somehow from God. The third point, related as well, is the question of the syntax of 16:21: "He loved him." Who loved whom? Saul loved David or David Saul? This is a famous early crux in our story, and it has been sorted to suggest that the syntax is ultimately ambiguous, perhaps purposefully so as to allow us to be justified in thinking that either one of them loved the other or that each loved the other.[66]

A basic "platform" for David's goodness thus emerges, witnessed by deity, prophet, old king, and his servants, narrated by the extradiegetic voice, and orchestrated by the implied author. David has tortuous roads ahead of him, but our first sense of him offers a capacity for at least a simple goodness, an alignment of some sort between the being and/or choice of the deity and the heart of the chosen one.[67]

4. *Armed and qualifying as hero* The next unit, bringing David again from his father's sheep to Saul's presence, is the long ch. 17, where David emerges quite

64. Bodner, *1 Samuel*, 174.

65. Fokkelman, *Crossing Fates*, 135.

66. G.C.I Wong, "Who Loved Whom? A Note on 1 Samuel 16:21," *VT* 47 (1997): 554–56 sorts the following: Not only Saul but also David has been subject in the chapter; vv. 21 and 22 may be constructed with parallel structure but need not be; in v. 21 David is the clear subject of three verbs and Saul the clear referent in the predicates, but that need not implicate the fourth occurrence; there is no help from gender or even really from context; the versions and translations can be consulted and may be suasive but are not decisive. Wong himself likes the mutuality translation, but considers it optional.

67. Jason S. Derouchie, "The Heart of Yʜᴡʜ and His Chosen One in 1 Samuel 13:14," *Bulletin for Biblical Research* 24 (2014): 467–89 offers that the matter hinges on whether the preposition *k*/like is adjectival or adverbial: whether God selects as seems best to him or if there is some sort of match between selecting and selected. It may be undecidable, inclusive.

clearly and changes, before our eyes, from passive to active, boy to man. We see a boy arrive at the battle site, sent by his father with supplies for his older brothers, clearly still a stay-at-home and sent-on-errands son, in contrast to his oldest siblings. We seem justified in inferring that this is his first trip to the battle site, since he registers surprise and indignation at what reaches his ears. He talks like a boy, asking about rewards and seeming distracted from hearing what has just been answered, such that it needs repeating (vv. 26–27). Reproached by his older brother, David, boy-like, twists away in a quasi-denial, quasi-rebuttal of the charge.[68] We may think that his exclamatory question, "'Who is this uncircumcised Philistine, that he should defy the armies of the living God?'" (v. 26), cutting right through to the heart of the problem Goliath poses—how the refusal or incapacity of Saul to challenge the Philistine is an affront to God—is precocious, given that no one seems to have voiced it before and someone hearing it now takes the speaker right to Saul.[69]

There, fearlessly, David speaks to the king with both directness and tact, urging that "no one" be afraid, that "your servant" will fight the Philistine. The conversation between king and shepherd boy shows David wiser, braver, more attuned to God, surely the actant with more initiative and courage. Saul seems easily talked out of his hesitation to permit what David offers (vv. 31–37), persuadability being a persistent characteristic of Saul (except when he is stubborn). The arming scene is a classic and weighted moment, a man's equipping a boy to do his own job, suiting the boy to fight the giant in place of the tall king. But no sooner do we glimpse David dressed in the king's identity than we see him refuse it, articulating—as the narrator also summarizes—that he is not accustomed to the royal gear. The point, both practical and symbolic, offers us David hesitating between boy and man, moving off as a boy for the last time, armed with simple weapons that have presumably worked well for him in the encounters he has just claimed as his *resumé*. Arguably, we also glimpse Saul and David contesting over who is king, though taking opposite sides from their later positions on the matter: Saul here pressing David to royalty and David refusing will reverse shortly. Once more we see a boy through the eyes of the giant, who sneers at him in our hearing (vv. 43–44). David's rejoinder to his opponent's vaunting may be boyish boasting (vv. 45–47), though since it turns out to be accurate, we do well to hear it as serious. By the end of the scene, David has

---

68. As noted above, though, we can also with our fuller knowledge of the whole story hear these utterances as somewhat double-voiced, suggesting the mature as well as the young David. Bodner also suggests that part of Eliab's narrative job is to abet the implied author in making us suspect that David's heart needs scrutiny: "Eliab and the Deuteronomist," in Bodner, ed., *David Observed: A King in the Eyes of his Court* (Sheffield: Sheffield Phoenix Press, 2005), 10–24; Bodner uses slightly different language, but the point is the same: two speakers share responsibility for the assessment.

69. As Fokkelman points out, *Crossing Fates*, 164, David himself and his brother minimize the possibility of David's success, which Saul's men take much more seriously.

killed a fellow-human, whether with the stone the boy picked up or with the sword the giant lost control of and the young man wielded makes little difference.[70]

The long episode of the battle with Goliath the Philistine is distinctive in some ways (amount of narrator description), though not in basic narration choices. Characters (David's father at 17:17–18) speak strategically to initiate action needed, as Saul and Abner do at 17:55–56, to render prominent and uncertain the key point: whose son is David. David's oldest brother sneers (17:28) to suggest conflict and to prompt David's first utterance of several rebuttals that push blame away from him (here v. 29), and Saul's men speak directly at v. 25 to announce a key datum: The man who slays the giant can expect to marry a royal daughter. We sense that, since that information is important for the story, it is stressed by being queried by David, who just heard it (v. 26).[71] In fact, since this is David's first quoted speech, it has singular importance. David's first direct discourse asks about rewards for successful deeds, as well as about removing insult to God! The narrator provides the repetition by summary (v. 30). The main speakers, narrating the more structurally important information, are Goliath (vv. 8, 9, 10, 43, 44), who speaks with defiance, rudeness, arrogance, and ignorance and Saul, who speaks (vv. 33 and 37) for a position David will argue him out of.[72]

A trailer from this long episode, intertwining with the next one where Jonathan reappears, shows David suddenly more guarded with Saul, who has just asked afresh and in a flashback of some sort who this young man is.[73] David claims Jesse of Bethlehem as his father, but Saul commandeers him now (again) for his own household (16:19; 17:55–58; 18:2).[74] Thus does David begin his process of becoming "Saul's son," not merely his musician and armor-bearer. So granting the length of the scene, it is still a short space of time to watch David grow from boy to man, from subaltern to agent, from designated object to speaking subject. In narrative terms, this achievement has been communicated by implied author, narrator, and other characters, prompting and witnessing to the speech of David

70. In mythic terms, that is in the "grammar" of such scenes as this, the arch villain or hero's opponent must be slain by his own sword, as Goliath here experiences. The implication (or inference) is that the sword-carrier has in some ways brought about his own death, a sobering and instructive thought.

71. Repetition in all its myriad shapes is one of the primary tools of both implied author and narrator, as similarities, as well as divergences, can be exposed to useful effect.

72. There is surprisingly little shared discourse between Saul and David, though the general impression is, I think, that they converse a lot. A similar point can be offered about David and Michal, who have exactly one exchange in our hearing (2 Sam. 6:21–22).

73. Since we are talking about artistic representation of a potential-laden moment and not facticity, it is not of concern that in the narrative we are reading, Saul does not seem to know who David is, though we have seen them in close contact. If one "first meeting" between these two is good, two is better. Would that there were more to relish and appraise!

74. Fokkelman, *Crossing Fates*, 194–98 makes a number of useful observations about the construction of this material opening in ch. 18, positioning it a bit differently from my choices.

himself. My choice has been to show David first as the chosen king and then how he went on, by degrees, to choose the throne, for himself.

5. *Invested by Saul's son* Chapter 18, interweaving David with Saul's children and various other groups among the king's people with a complexity not evident in the structure we are using, offers us access to nascent desires attending the young hero.[75] As the long Goliath scene ends, the king reconsiders the identity of the young fighter with new eyes (17:55, 56, 58), raises the key question of the moment: whose son, whose man, whose heir? Jonathan sees David as his self, the narrator tells us—not as a rival, upstart, heir to Saul's own royal position—and gives his own royal equipment to David (18:1, 3, 4) as we saw Saul offer *his* armor previously, distracted as we may have been by the impracticability and illogicality of the scene. Women in song make David a hero, though not inevitably more than that (18:6–7).[76] Israel and Judah love him (18:16). Saul takes David from his father—he makes him his own son (18:2) and his fighting man (18:5, 13). But almost at once Saul sees David as an usurper (18:8), and envisions and anticipates him as dead (18:11–12), though ineffectively. It is a dizzying journey for David, at least in narrative terms. David's speech dominates in quantity (17:26, 29, 32, 34–37, 39, 45–47, 58) and in importance, as we shall examine shortly.

6. *Made Saul's son-in-law* The betrothals of David to the daughters of Saul (18:17–30) comprise a revealing set of verses, on which I have written previously.[77] They offer another sort of discourse still, full of ambiguity and complexity, where no

---

75. Polzin, *Samuel and the Deuteronomist*, 179, characterizes it as "ragged shifting."

76. The character of the brief song has been well discussed, the issue being whether it can be discerned that the song is disrespectful of Saul's honor as he claims. See Michael Patrick O'Connor, "War and Rebel Chants in the Former Prophets," in A. Beck et al., eds., *Fortunate the Eyes that See: Essays in Honor of David Noel Freedman in Celebration of His Seventieth Birthday* (Grand Rapids: William B. Eerdmans Publishing Co., 1995), 322–37 and Fokkelman, *Crossing Fates,* 209–221 for a discussion showing uncertain that Saul's inference is justified. This is a moment to suggest some nuances of Hebrew syntax: The song, which we will hear again, twice, is articulated by the women as follows: verb ("slain"), the subject ("Saul"), the objects (a word for lots of people, sometimes "thousands," sometimes a collective unit); the parallel lines offers its match, though with verb omitted but carrying over from the first line, so understand ("slain"), subject ("David"), object (another word for a big or numerous group, sometimes translated as "myriads"). It is not immediately or inevitably obvious that Saul has been insulted, since he is named first and given credit. David comes second. Since neither of them slew more than one, there is exaggeration for both. The words of the Hebrew object do not immediately demand zeroes to be counted, indeed as the word "myriad" in English is usually a word suggesting "lots" rather than presenting its zeroes for immediate calculation (perhaps somewhat like the word "gazillion"). We can also doubt if the women would sing a song to insult their king. The point is that if the song is less uneven in Hebrew than in English translation, Saul's taking offense marks his over-reaction.

77. See Barbara Green, "The Engaging Nuances of Genre: Reading Saul and Michal Afresh," in Timothy J. Sandoval and Carleen Mandolfo, eds., *Relating to Text: Interdisciplinary*

speaker provides information directly.[78] Before looking more closely at David, a brief illustration of story and discourse is in order, to sample and appreciate both the difference between them and also their capacity to collaborate. In terms of story information, we learn that David, after certain negotiations, marries Michal, daughter of Saul (18:20–30). But if we note how we are provided with that information, several discourse points emerge. First, we have already heard Saul's men, when discussing the apparently inadequate incentives for engaging the Philistine giant, opine that one of the rewards for success will be betrothal to a royal daughter (17:25). The woman is a prize, to be earned and awarded, yet also a goal to be slowly sought. We do not hear Saul promise a daughter, but his men say it, and the narrator calls attention to the comment by having David query it (vv. 25–27), after which the narrator affirms that those who had first said it repeated it, without quite taking responsibility for the truth of it. The men may be speaking truthfully—or be mistaken, or lying.[79] This information, that David has already "earned" a royal daughter, adds significant texture to the negotiations regarding Saul's daughters: first Merab, then Michal. Arguably, Saul has not kept his word or been slow to do so, but of course it was not actually *his* word but that of his men. Does Saul renege on a commitment or not, and if so, what do the shameful overtones add to his own dishonor, to David's strategies? As negotiations continue, they are managed by a messenger rather than face-to-face, introducing more opportunities for ambiguity. All of this is implied authorial design, exploiting both the play of narrating voices and the story/discourse differential.

Though the negotiations over Merab are briefer and uncertain (18:17–19), the material involving Michal is fuller, allowing her, in time, to emerge more clearly as a character than does her sister (here, 18:20–30, eventually in 19:11–17 and in 2 Sam. 3:12–16 and 6:16–23). As is well noted, Michal is *talked about* in ch. 18 by the narrator, who reports that it was told to Saul that she loved David, and that Saul was initially pleased.[80] Michal is implicitly discussed by Saul and David through the

and Form-Critical Insights on the Bible (London and New York: T&T Clark International, 2003), 141–59.

78. Fokkelman presents this section as a scene within a story within a major act (as shown on the structure above). He says in *Crossing Fates*, 242: "There is practically no single element in the story that does not have a clear counterpart or parallel. A structural reading implies here that the dialectics between all these pairs is exploited and that a good interpretation cannot be situated anywhere other than in the *inter esse* of their correspondences." That is, though again I myself observed much of the detail he derives from structure, I had not noted the pairing. His careful structure of vv. 20–30 is on 239–40.

79. Since we are viewing a work of art, we cannot necessarily ascertain which of these options is the likeliest. One of the factors that moves narrative is readerly construction of who knows what, speaks sincerely, and so forth. We can say, in terms of the discourse, that though we never learn whether Saul's fighting men are citing him correctly or not, we eventually see David married to a royal daughter.

80. Here, I insist, against virtually everyone else, that the narrator does not vouch for the truth of the statement. We cannot claim, as many do, that Michal loved David. It is said that

intermediary words of servants, allowing us to exploit the uncertainties of nested narration: extradiegetic narrator, two main characters—Saul (talking both to himself and aloud to others), David parrying cryptically—the messengers ferrying these words. Clearly enough Saul has two plans in regard to David-married-to-Michal: what he says aloud (be the king's son-in-law) and what he says to himself (be dead, killed by enemies that Saul sends David to fight).

As the narrator reduces his own presence, David shows himself a skilled negotiator, placing few cards on the table, thus prompting the king to make his own hand plainer. David's crafted reply to Saul's proposal (v. 21) is highly ambiguous, an exclamation or question and undecidable at that: "'Is it a small matter, do you suppose, to be the king's son-in-law, when I am a poor man and of no consequence?'" (18:24). The interrogative utterance is loaded with possibilities, running from a genuine and true statement of unworthiness all the way to being an ironic and even bold rejoinder to the king, reminding him implicitly that son-in-law to the king is something already promised unreliably to the slayer of Goliath and then to the putative partner for Saul's firstborn daughter. It is impossible to select or eliminate options definitively, and readers will proceed as they choose, making David coherent here as seems best. David's reply—actually, the reply returned as from him to the king by the messengers—prompts from Saul the price to be paid: one hundred Philistine foreskins, information challenging David wordlessly to accomplish, doubling it. The episode ends as the narrator reports Saul's knowing YHWH is with David and that Michal loves him.[81] The king is more afraid and more hostile to David, who is more successful and more esteemed by others (18:25–30).

7. Implications of David's introductions As we move toward the completion of this early material, we can observe some other moments of Saul with David. Saul's favorable impression turns most clearly when his self-talk constructs the song of the women to be disrespectful of him compared to David (18:8). The narrator, in the know, has here and sooner (16:14, 16, 23) said that an evil spirit is part of Saul's trouble, without clarifying just what is entailed thereby. The narrator asserts that Saul, from that moment on (18:9), eyes David, a condition specified by actions. Shortly after the king's interpretation of the women's song, Saul is shown hurling his spear at David, who is playing the harp as the king raves (18:10–11). With minimal agency, the musician avoids the king's spear, and the narrator notches up Saul's fear, recognizing, the narrator supplies, that Saul knows that YHWH had left Saul for David (v. 12). More actions: Saul sends David away from the palace to march with the troops (18:13–15), but David's success again disturbs Saul as it pleases others. The betrothal attempts follow (18:17–30), embedded in

---

she did, said passively, with no one taking responsibility. The rumor is all we know. The skill of artistry is to tell us something of Michal but not show it, contrasted with both telling and showing how Saul is to be viewed.

81. Again, that Saul believes this to be so need not mean it is so. We have not heard it from Michal herself, nor will we.

this pattern of Saul's trying to place David at lethal disadvantage. The details of David's reaction to these moves are not communicated, only enough to suggest that he avoids death while obeying Saul's orders. That is, with the exception of taking on Goliath and acquiring a royal wife, David is generally acted upon; only as he manages these two exceptional moments does he manifest initiative. The first seems youthful and naive; the second, more mature and calculated, hosting at least the possibility of David's manipulation of the royal positions.

4 Conclusions and Transition

We can step back and draw some early conclusions about our narrative: its manner of presentation and our constructions of its artistry as we bring two literary tools to its analysis. My ultimate goal is to trace David's journey toward compassion, such as it is discernible.

a Methodological

1. Edges The early narrative, starting both remotely and proximately, does not offer much help. David's own story is already deeply embedded in the story of kingship, the uncertainty—flexibility—of starting place affecting how we meet the main character. Kingship, with the concentration of power that inevitably and invariably attends it, seems an unlikely school for compassion. We have seen the matter of dynastic sons already compromised before Saul adds a son to his household and know that the line of dead royal scions winds through the David narrative until the end of the story of the kings. Does Saul's acquisition of David mark the final ending of Saul's dynasty, or does the addition of another "son" to the house of Saul, another "brother" for Jonathan, urge us to read differently? Does the general setting of the David stories offer a backdrop where better—recall how "good" functions as a motif word—dynastic sons than Eli's Hophni and Phinheas and Samuel's Joel and Abijah may still hope for grace? Or are dynastic sons the problem, the implication or inference that one can inherit and perform leadership well with no qualification besides common blood? Can David become a surrogate Saul-son as he is made Jonathan's brother, Michal's husband, Saul's son-in-law?

2. Structure The structure of the long narrative, offered to us so far as a vast blueprint, will need specification in terms of plot dynamics: simple sequence, provocative contiguity, ominous causality.[82] Without adequate discussion of these nuances, we will flounder. But already we have noted some odd time features. David seems to arrive at the court of Saul at least twice, offending logic but suiting the significance of the moment. Does David arrive when, invited by courtiers and

---

82. Continuity: an enemy is slain, a song is sung; contiguity: a song is sung and a hearer takes offense; causality: a hero's offense at the words of a song provokes his fear and suspicion that a rival wants his position, and so he acts to stop it.

king, he becomes Saul's armor-bearer? Or do we prefer the moment when he earns his status as commander, having performed a feat of valor? The odd time notations clustering around the end of the Goliath episode—where David deposits Goliath's head in Jerusalem, where he is sent on exploits before the Goliath-troop returns home—are provocative: textual problem, rough redactional seam, perhaps more. David joins Saul's family at least twice more—connected with a son and a daughter—possibly Saul's spouse as well. The general structure can offer these points, but we will need finer tools to mine them adequately.

b *The Narrative of 1 Sam. 16–18*

A few key issues can be restated as we begin to read the David narrative, its hero perhaps poorly positioned for the journey toward compassion. But since we are not first-time readers but already shaped by the narrative we have, it is all the more important to read critically and to let the tools in our hands be of service to us. Even to raise fresh questions that we will discard stretches our imaginations to see points that we rushed past unheeding before. The material we have worked on so far, three chapters, has presented us, first, with no small process of change in David from the small sheep-boy acted upon by authorities to the careful negotiator we have just seen in the betrothal scene. There is, second, an intricate interlocking among characters: David and Saul most obviously, but really David with the whole household of Saul—while in conspicuous contrast, not with his own family. Those who think Saul long outstays his time read one way,[83] and I am suggesting another: that the old king's presence is necessary while David learns his role. As I hope is clear, our quest is not for the historical threads we may tease out about these foundational events but to plumb as deeply as possible their representation in language. David's apprenticeship with Saul may not guide him well on his journey toward compassion, not so well as his caring for animals.

Third, in this present chapter we also opened up the tremendous variety of witnesses made available when we distinguish among our sources of information, notably here implied author, extradiegetic narrator, and narrating characters. Though this feature of narrativity needs and will receive closer consideration shortly, we watch as the narrator emerges as an artistic speaker, offering us some information generously (e.g., Saul's feelings) and withholding other (intent of the women's song after the Goliath-defeat, the attendant circumstances involving the betrothal between Merab and David, Michal's desires), standing behind some of what he says unambiguously (Jonathan's love for David) and seeming distanced about other things (Michal's love for David). The word "unreliable" does not quite suit (more on the concept later), but we can say that the narrator is partial, in two senses of the term: favoring some characters and not disclosing all we might like to know. As characters narrate intradiegetically, we are given much to sort and ponder. Who among them is truth-telling: Samuel? Who is conflicted, such that utterances are compromised: Jonathan, and perhaps David? Which of them is self-

---

83. Jobling makes this claim in *1 Samuel*, 79–93.

deluded, claiming hopes as realities: surely Saul, but others as well? Commentators have long observed the contrast between the presentation of Saul's inner life and that of David, the one offered to us frequently and the other rarely disclosed. This is uneven terrain.

Fourth, the story/discourse discrepancy, offering keen teamwork, opens additional points of complexity. That Saul feels animosity toward David, eventually and even soon, is manifest, but the manner of its representation shows Saul as torn, perhaps irrational, shifting responsibility from David. God's choice of David is clear to us and intermittently to Saul, but the role of God's spirit adds texture to the suggestion or suspicion that Saul is being unfairly maneuvered in some way. Who is responsible here, and how do we make headway in sorting claims? Though the king's servants diagnose Saul's trouble as evil spirit-linked, and the narrator agrees, does Saul acknowledge such a thing? Is the royal reticence a matter of denial, avoidance, ignorance?

Fifth, the portrait emerging shows the complexity of David, though we get an easy start on it, I think. The boy emerges, called forward as an afterthought and a last possibility when more obvious options have disappointed, dwindled. He is acted upon, spoken to and of, while standing silent. Talked about among Saul's servants, his arrival negotiated between "fathers," David arrives and is assigned two jobs, which he does, again, with minimal agency. Even his arrival at the Israel-Philistine standoff shows him simply as a messenger. But here, and briefly, we see him look around, see and hear what others had missed or resisted, speak fearlessly, have a dangerous and signifying plan that he carries out successfully. But then he seems to revert to more passive ways, though now by design and choice rather than innocence. That is, David arrives at the battle as a boy and leaves as a man. Though reverting to his earlier characteristic compliance, it is not quite the same as before. David wordlessly accepts what Saul offers—leadership—and what Jonathan gives him—markers of royal patrimony. David fills positions he is assigned with success, though when love and approval are given by others, at least as the narrator summarizes, David has no overt or reciprocal response. We see him dodge Saul's thrust spear more than once, implying no great change of plans on his part. Amid that phase of his narrated life, we see a spark of agency from him only when he seems, in an enigmatic rejoinder, to counter Saul's efforts to betroth him to a second daughter, and to double the requested bride-price. David, briefly, shows his superiority over Saul as negotiator. We may think the bartering disrespectful and manipulative, or perhaps not. But we have seen David's agency as he manages Saul. And then, he seems to move back to opacity if not passivity.

Sixth, if David has been shown as directed by others, except for engaging Saul over fighting Goliath and marrying Michal, the trend seems to be in the direction of greater agency but also greater privacy. David will, in the narrative ahead, blurt his feelings and views, but rarely, and some will suspect artifice. Saul, on the other hand, is easier to read. That Saul sees David as a royal rival is clear. But to anticipate a point I will develop later: We have heard from the narrator that Saul knows from Samuel that God has chosen another king, fears God is with David rather than with him, and suspects that David covets the throne. We, reading, especially persuaded by what eventually happens, may suppose that Saul should understand that David is Saul's God-designated successor. But the character Saul betrays no such assurance. To know that David is a threat is not the same as understanding that God is backing David to be king and has confirmed him. Thus Saul works to thwart David, signaling minimal awareness of God on this or really any other matter.

Finally, seventh, how to name the conflicting desires, so far? I would suggest that we only twice see David edge beyond simply doing what others have assigned him. The roles he takes to himself—especially Saul's at the battle with the Philistines, which precipitates that signal human action of killing another—mark him moving from his shepherd role, where he claims to have killed predatory animals. To kill Goliath is a different thing, and it will not be David's last such deed. To be the king's armor-bearer and armor-wearer will have lethal consequences. David moves more decisively to claim Saul's daughter and to allow her to displease her father in regard to him, and then to allow the king's son's claim on him, and again to let Jonathan as well as Michal displease his father in the matter of David. Consequences unfurl, for all, and to the next of these we now turn.

Chapter 3

COMPETITION AND CHOICES: KINGS INTERLOCKED (1 SAM. 19–26)

CONSTRUCTING PLOTS

1 *Transition*

In the material just considered, after a long overture hinting of kings and eventually introducing Saul, we watched David being chosen as king by God and God's spirit, by a God-directed prophet. We witnessed him anointed and brought into the household of Saul, first as musician and armor-bearer, then as quasi-son and military leader—and not simply in one battle, significant though that event was. We also saw David become an intimate of Saul's son Jonathan and daughter Michal. Welcomed in diverse ways, David also met opposition from Saul, prelude to more. As early as the return from the Philistine battle, Saul takes offense at a victory song and muses proleptically—with both accuracy and paranoia—that nothing lacks to David except the kingdom (18:8). Twice Saul hurls his spear at David, who dodges it (18:10–11). The narrator adds that Saul feared David and eyed him (18:9, 12), sought ways to be rid of him (18:17, 21, 25, 28, 29), but ineffectually. These early efforts of Saul to counter David seem at first haphazard and spontaneous, but even when more planned, still fruitless. How David is actively resisting Saul remains hidden in the verbal parrying comprising the slaying of Goliath and especially the betrothal to Michal. David's capacity both to obey and undercut Saul's directions and desires becomes visible.

David's journey toward kingship is in some ways leisurely, in others rapid. Our first pair of literary tools helped us appraise both speeds. David enters the story of leadership in the midst of things already long underway, with certain narrative patterns set before he draws breath. The choice of where to start his story and the determination of structure are left to each interpreter; both affect reading. A complex and well-told narrative will be neither obvious in its planning nor simplex, though cues will not lack.

In the material to be considered in the present chapter, Saul's lethal determination reaches the awareness of others, eventually pushing David from the palace. Beginning from episodes involving Saul's son and daughter and finally reaching "his" prophet, Saul's animosity drives David from him. As our last chapter saw David find his way deeply into Saul's kingdom, the present one will track him as he withdraws from Saul—though actually they remain closely intermeshed.

Whether David learns more than strategies of escape and behaviors of retaliation remains to be seen. In this present chapter, we will consider structure again as well as enlivening it with insights from plot and plotting. The section of narrative material to be included here is long, and the choice I made for this book does not necessarily correlate tightly with the Fokkelman structure provided in the previous chapter. The narrative is well suited to queries around structure, being arguably "the same event" repeated several times.

2 Methodology

a Literary Structures

Fokkelman sees and shows this material of 19–26 as part of a larger set extending from 1 Samuel 18–2 Samuel 1, comprising twenty-one units and twenty-nine to thirty smaller named parts; of that expanse, he splits the material of 19–26 featured here into seven units.[1] My purpose now is, first, to sample the sort of careful work he does by instancing a single chapter, offered as typical of his work and scrutinized to remind readers what is available in his vast study of the David material. We will also stress again on why looking for literary structure is important enough to function as one of the seven tools I am exploiting in this book.

1. Chapter 19 sampled Fokkelman splits it into three scenes (vv. 1–7, 9–18, and 19–24) as follows:[2]

The first unit, "Jonathan's mediation, stay of execution," is shown chiastically:

A Saul versus David (v. 1a)

   B Jonathan is fond of David (v. 1b)

      C Jonathan warns David and sends him away (v. 2ab)

      C' Jonathan sends for David and informs him (v. 7ab)

   B' Jonathan brings David before Saul (v. 7b)

A' David serves Saul as before (v. 7b).

The speech at the center of the unit is also shown chiastic:

   A "do not wrong" (4cd)

      B "for his work is very favorable to you" (4c)

         C David's contribution (5a)

---

1. In his *Crossing Fates*, Fokkelman maps and discusses the material throughout the volume.
2. Fokkelman, *Crossing Fates*, 248–58.

X result: Goliath killed (5b)

C' God's contribution (5c)

B' "you saw and rejoiced" (5d)

A' "Why do wrong" (5e).

Fokkelman makes numerous observations about the unit, for example isolating keywords relating to "to pursue," "to kill," "to flee," and pointing out that Jonathan dominates fourteen of the sixteen lines of the unit, succeeding in the rhetorical plea he makes to his father, the king.

The second unit involving David, Michal, and Saul is mapped chiastically as well:

A David fled and escaped (v. 10d)

   B Michal's speech: "If you don't escape tonight" (v. 11bcd)

      C Michal lets David down through the window; he escapes (v.12ab)

         D Michal makes a dummy (v. 13)

            E Saul sends messengers: 1 line speech (v. 14)

            E' Saul sends messengers: 1 line speech (v. 15)

         D' Messengers discover items on bed (v. 16)

      C' Saul's reproach to Michal: 2 line speech (v. 17abc)

   B' Michal's speech: 2 lines of David speech (v. 17d–g)

A' David had fled and escaped (v. 18a).

Special attention is given to Michal's three utterances (vv. 11cd, 17bc, 17fg) as well as to the material not included in the main chiasm (vv. 9ab–10a–d).[3] Motif words are pointed out ("to strike," "to escape," "to flee").

The final unit is not mapped chiastically but laid out in an outline of its sentences:

Introduction: Saul informed of David's whereabouts (v. 19 = 5 lines)
Part IA: Saul sends agents, the Spirit eliminates them (v. 20 = 5 lines)
Part IB: the same befalls the next two groups of Saul's agents (v. 21 = 5 lines)
Part IIA: introduction: Saul to Ramah (v. 22 = 6 lines)
Part IIB: decisive confrontation: Saul seized by ecstasy (vv. 23a–24c = 6 lines)
epilogue by narrator: proverb (v. 24de = 2 lines).[4]

3. Ibid., 258–76.
4. Ibid., 276–87.

Fokkelman goes over with readers the density of the language arrangement, the skill of the repetition of themes of escape, disguise, concealment. He remarks the prominence of the word for death and draws attention to the links between this brief unit and Saul's Samuel-related search in 1 Samuel 10.

2. Utility of discerning structures With all that noted, reinforced by my claim that to read Fokkelman's observations is almost always thought-provoking, I offer two additional points. First, many if not most of his best observations do not come from the structures he isolates. Valuable as they are to prompt careful reading—a point he makes explicitly in asserting that the chiasm of 19:1–7 prompts us to search for meaning[5]—most of his points would be visible without the structures. Fokkelman also tends to go beyond the evidence in his observations, for example, when he speaks of David "pouring out his heart" to bring Samuel up to date at Ramah.[6] He also seems to miss the insight that, when Jonathan reasons with his father about the injustice and infeasibility of his desire to kill David, the incentives Jonathan offers are least likely to persuade and most likely to inflame his father, insecure about David's skills. To map structures is the best way to observe closely what is being narrated, and that Fokkelman has worked out excellent candidates for virtually all the material under consideration here is invaluable. But when I look here for observations arising exclusively from structure that would not have been otherwise available, I find few. Structures are necessary but not sufficient, and they offer a starting place to be enhanced by consideration of plot.

b Plot and Plotting

1. General considerations The long and especially the recent discussion of what comprises plot and plotting has led many to conclude that the process cannot be reduced easily to one comprehensive entity.[7] Though appearing simple at first consideration, plot construction is sufficiently complex that the factors remain incommensurate, all the more so over the broad range of genres and historical periods involved in the construction of theory. The goal of this present section,

---

5. Ibid., 255.

6. Ibid., 271.

7. Hilary P. Dannenberg, in *Coincidence and Counterfactuality: Plotting Time and Space in Narrative Fiction* (Lincoln and London: University of Nebraska Press, 2006), 6–16 provides a sketch of recent theorizing on the matter, concluding that a single understanding is not possible, due to the incommensurability of factors. For an introduction to some of the features not pursued here, see also Dannenberg, "Plot" and "Plot Types," in David Herman, Manfred Jahn, and Marie-Laure Ryan, eds., *Routledge Encyclopedia of Narrative Theory* (London and New York: Routledge, 2005): 435–40.

then, is not to theorize globally about plot but to offer a conceptual model sufficient for grounding the reading I am attempting.[8]

Scholars like to observe that the word "plot" means helpfully (in English) a piece of land, a conspiracy, and the plan of a literary actant; it is a noun and a verb, participating in both identities.[9] Definitions of plot limit those broad edges. Suzanne Keen moves her readers succinctly through the main possibilities: Plot is a sequence of narrated events, or it is the way the narrator tells the story; plot is what the reader understands as the real story.[10] E.M. Forster famously distinguishes between story (the king died and then the queen died) and plot (the king died, and then the queen died of grief), where causality dominates simple continuity.[11] Another way to make that point is to say that plotting happens at the level of story and discourse: The story (sometimes called the *fabula*) is the basic events that happen; discourse (or *sjuzet*) is the way in which those are arranged when narrated.[12] Jerome Bruner adds, recalling Kenneth Burke: "'Story stuff' involves *characters* in *action* with intentions or *goals* in settings using particular means." The story has some set of plights into which characters fall, then some choice of steady state, breach, crisis, redress.[13] Responsibility is shared among authoring entities (implied author and narrator), among contending characters, and by readers (real readers who infer from what is on offer in various ways and see diverse things).[14] Emma Kafalenos, with misleading simplicity, suggests that whenever something happens to attract our attention, we begin to speculate about what caused it, to try to understand its causes and consequences.[15]

2. Story and discourse Plot is implicated in the general narrative models under consideration here, being usefully distinguishable as story and as discourse. At the story level, plot is understood as the events that happen in the story, among

8. Omitted here are the long history of the topic, a grammar or typology of existing plots in literature, a formula that claims to be right for all plots, or a concept that aims to specify the workings of plot by some factor like gender or culture. For a historical overview of plotting, see Robert Scholes, James Phelan, and Robert Kellogg, *Nature of Narrative*, 207–39. They sample the various kinds of plots from the ancient classics of Homer to the modern novel; Dannenberg's introduction provides resources for various other considerations.

9. Peter Brooks, *Reading for Plot: Design and Intention in Narrative* (Cambridge, MA: Harvard University Press, 1984), 11–12.

10. Keen, *Narrative Form*, 73, developed through 89.

11. E.M. Forster, "Story and Plot," in Richardson, ed., *Narrative Discourse*, 71–72.

12. Jerome Bruner, *Actual Minds, Possible Worlds* (Cambridge, MA and London: Harvard University Press, 1986), 17. These are standard but highly useful concepts in narratology.

13. Bruner, *Actual Minds*, 20–21, emphasis his.

14. Marie-Lauren Ryan, "Cheap Plot Tricks, Plot Holes, and Plot Design," *Narrative* 17.1 (2009): 56–75 (56), names just author and characters, dealing typically with later works whose authors are known.

15. Emma Kafalenos, *Narrative Causalities* (Columbus: Ohio State University Press, 2006), 1.

the characters—specifically including their stated and enacted plans; it can be abstracted as what needs to have happened in the order that is logical, whether we are provided with each move or not and whether we learn the moves in that order or not.[16] At the discourse level, the word "plot" takes on a more technical sense of the way in which the story events are disclosed to the reader, whether by design of the implied author or as narrated by a voice not acting or existing as a character in the story. The implied author plot design is comprehensive and available to the most sensitive (implied) readers in subtle ways (e.g., by structure, by analogy, by rhetorical device), whereas the narrator's role is more direct, being a specific "underlinable" narration. What may seem insignificant at the story level can be crucial for discourse.[17]

Phelan and Rabinowitz offer an additional distinction in terminology which may be useful: They combine plot dynamics (the instabilities and complications related to characters and events) and narratorial dynamics (tensions arising from discrepancies of knowledge among author, narrator, and the audiences envisioned by [implied] author and narratees) into a new category called textual dynamics. These dynamics are encoded in the text, rather than being constructed by (later, unintended) real readers.[18] The second large set remaining is readerly dynamics.

While structuralist literary theory (narratology) was satisfied to discern, map, and offer these insights in a rather static way, later postmodern theory finds the reader's role increasingly important. Actual (real) readers must make sense of the (implied) authored and narrated plot, in several ways. First, as we will see when we turn to the work of Emma Kafalenos, real readers, when consulted, testify to various choices, and cannot be relied on to take the most theoretically obvious pathway. And real readers, as they proceed, can be seen to revise their sense of how the plotting works repeatedly as they proceed and likely over time, when they return to a classic to reread it. Thus plot, or plotting (a better word), is more fluid,

---

16. The classic detective story provides good access to these levels. Such a work needs to have a precise and detailed set of events that must have happened within the story and among the characters—the crime and the solving of it—but which, for the sake of the genre, are not revealed to some of the characters or to the reader until the end of the work, where they are often reconstructed and presented both in the story and as part of discourse strategy. The way in which the work is planned relies upon these story events while keeping them mostly obscured—though hidden in plain sight—until they are made clear at the end, usually in the recital of the one who solved the mystery. The design of that process, both steps of it, emerges as discourse.

17. James Phelan and Peter Rabinowitz, "Time, Plot, Progression," in David Herman et al., eds., *Narrative Theory: Core Concepts and Critical Debates* (Columbus: Ohio State University Press, 2012), 57–65 (59).

18. Phelan and Rabinowitz, "Time, Plot, Progression," 59. They are specifically interested in managing the racism of Mark Twain's *Huckleberry Finn*, though the issue they name is also relevant for certain authorial traces within biblical texts that later readers do not wish to appear to endorse.

more dynamic, and more participative than was once understood. The reader takes responsibility for constructing the plot, and readers will do that job with various results. Plot is in certain ways unstable.

3. Plot factors Theorists supply various technical terms for talking about the events of plot: for example, as kernels and satellites or as nuclei and supplements, in each case with the first of the named pair being the more crucial move while the second type expands it more peripherally.[19] That is, plots are seen to proceed in terms of major and constituent pivots (kernels or nuclei) and subsidiary ones (satellites or supplements). Another way to think of the plot events at their various levels is by imagining plot strings, crossing and tangling in various ways, whether contributing centrally or as offering "red herrings." If a tangle of plot strings composes and threads a story—those of various characters, that of the narrator, the moves of the implied author and the various paths available to readers—we need to inquire when each started and how it is resolved, as well as to ask how plots cross.[20] Plotting thrusts reading partners (authors, narrators, characters, readers) into overlaps and discriminations of sequence and continuity, causality and conflict, all to be variously negotiated.

Implicit but deserving mention is the unevenness of information as a narrative proceeds to unfold plotlines. Who knows what at a given moment, and who is not in the know—with what set of effects?[21] Discrepancies between what is disclosed to readers and story-actants need scrutiny, as does unevenness of knowledge among characters. Clearly, the tool of plotting is more challenging to explain and explore than were the two previous tools of discerning edges and structure, as will be our engagement with narrators and characters. Plots typically involve tension, reversal, and recognition of major insight—or, of course, the failure to manage these on the part of at least some.

4. Temporality A major insight currently discussed as central by most theorists is plot's inherent temporality: things happen in story time[22] and are narrated in

---

19. This terminology comes from Seymour Chatman and is elaborated by Abbott, *Cambridge Introduction*, 22–23 and Keen, *Narrative Form*, 79.

20. This discussion can be sampled in Abbott, *Cambridge Introduction*, 55–66; Keen, *Narrative Form*, 77; Scholes, Phelan, and Kellogg, *Nature of Narrative*, 111–12; Walsh, *Old Testament Narrative*, 17, has a chart that talks about the plot of the determination of David's successor (1 Kgs. 1–2), but that plot string—a virtual rope—has been in play for nearly the duration of the David story.

21. See Abbott, *Cambridge Introduction*, 46–49, Walsh, *Old Testament Narrative*, 14–17.

22. In simpler theory, time is simply part of setting: certain closed-circle murder mysteries take place in a stately home over a winter weekend when all ingress and egress are cut off by a blizzard. It becomes clear that the perpetrator is a guest and prisoner of the house. Time is a winter weekend in a blizzard, between the arrival of the last guest and the coming of external authorities onto the scene when the weather breaks.

discourse time.[23] Time relations among characters do not easily coincide with nor can they be easily correlated with the reader's participation in time. The basic and still influential work distinguishing the modes of narrative time (at both story and discourse levels) was provided by narratologist Gérard Genette, elaborated by the next generation of theorists. Time proceeds differently at story and discourse levels, with the discrepancy being productive of insight at both levels. Brooks and Ricoeur both stress the dynamism involved in plot, aiming to move the plot discussion into deeper channels than sometimes sought. Brooks maintains that plot is driven by desire, whether that of author, actants, readers, with meaning emerging only as readers make sense of what is provided in temporal succession, pursuing that line as it develops.[24] Ricoeur makes the noun "plot" into a verbal, maintaining that *emplotment* or plotting is a better way to talk about what happens, pushing beyond the more static structuralist conception of plot with its set notion of limited actant roles.[25] Phelan and Rabinowtitz, collaborating, say: "We regard the progression of the narrative—its synthesis of textual and readerly dynamics— as the key means by which an author achieves his or her communicative purposes and the story of progression as a key source of insights and understanding how a narrative creates its effects."[26] Progression, they continue, calls attention to the logic of textual movement from beginning through middle to ending; the reader's experience of how story and discourse are mutually engaged calls attention to the workings of reader effect.[27]

5. Gaps One additional point can be raised as part of this initial and theoretical discussion: How is information provided—or not—in what order, leaving what kinds of gaps, and for whom? Gaps, discussed in Chapter 1 with the work of Iser, are places where information of one kind or another is not available. Walsh organizes the general phenomenon usefully: Some gaps are inevitable simply because completeness is impossible, while others are artistic, for example, those related to characteral motivation.[28] There are gaps of fact, information withheld from the reader, with greater or lesser impact; gaps of motivation are the richer to explore and the more likely to allow diversity of interpretation; gaps of continuity are also provocative, not least as the distinctive "open" Hebrew syntax is made

---

23. Keen, *Narrative Form*, devotes a chapter (6) to time facets of narrative, as does Walsh, *Old Testament Narrative* (also ch. 6); see also Abbott, *Cambridge Introduction*, 55–66.

24. Peter Brooks, "Narrative Desire," in Brian Richardson, ed., *Narrative Dynamics*, 130–37.

25. Paul Ricoeur, *Time and Narrative*, vol. I., Kathleen McLaughlin and David Pellauer, trans. (Chicago and London: University of Chicago Press, 1984), 65–68. See also Ricoeur, "Narrative Time," in Richardson, ed., *Narrative Dynamics*, 35–46.

26. Phelan and Rabinowitz, "Time, Plot, Progression," 58.

27. Ibid.

28. Walsh addresses kinds of gaps in his *Old Testament Narrative*, ch. 7, as does Keen, *Narrative Form*, 81, also providing excellent practical questions for plotting, 85.

productive for readers. Walsh's discussion shades into what he calls ambiguities rather than gaps: semantic moments where the precise meaning of a word is undecidable, and syntactic snarls, where the Hebrew refuses precision.[29] These gaps and ambiguities are not quite the same as the puzzles of fact arising in ancient narratives that intended audiences would have understood but which moderns find baffling. Those can be resolved at least partially with reliable historical information. Literary gaps are crucial to note and manage, and to welcome other readers to resolve alternatively.

6. *Narrative causality* Before turning to the plotted narrative material under consideration in this present chapter, we must sample the work of Emma Kafalenos on narrative causality for use in the repetitious set of stories involving Saul, David, and the pursuit we are about to consider. Her primary concern is with readers' discerning narrative causalities and the impact of narrative context on such perception. Referring to what we have distinguished so far as story and discourse, she says: "Narratives determine the context in relation to which we interpret the events they report."[30] Narrative is provided *sequentially* (i.e., in some chronology), and the particulars of such sequencing influence our insight. The shaping of readers' interpretations is inevitable, whether the reader is aware of it or not. Additionally, we receive information *incrementally*, a second process that influences our sense of causality. These two inevitable facets of narrative experience—that we receive information in some particular order and that it accumulates—prompt us to revise as we read. Kafalenos next provides us with a set of ten functions, or positions within causal sequence, that she finds adequate for mapping the process she wants to demonstrate and explore.[31] Her epistemological concern is how the information we receive through narrative is shaped by the (manner of) representation through which we receive it and through which, as competent readers, we construct both temporal and causal relationships: "A vocabulary of functions enables identifying, naming, and comparing interpretations of an event's consequences and causes."[32] She adds: "Because the causal relations between a given event and related events and situations depend on which events and situations the interpreter considers related, and on the given event's chronological position among the related events and situations, an event can express one function in one narrative and another

29. Walsh, *Old Testament Narrative*, 65–80.

30. Kafalenos, *Narrative Causalities*, vii. She explains her concern in the preface (vii–xiii) and sketches her model in ch. 1 (1–26), then explicating her insights in subsequent chapters with various literary works.

31. Kafalenos cites the influence of structuralist scholars Tzevetan Todorov (working with the *Decameron*) and Vladimir Propp (mapping Russian folktales), situating her work more carefully in relation to theirs than is relevant here (*Narrative Causalities*, 4–6). She offers a set of ten functions (or sites, positions) which she maintains are adequate for mapping narrative's sequential and incremental representation of a sequence of events.

32. Kafalenos, *Narrative Causalities*, 6.

function in another narrative," a quality she calls functional polyvalence.[33] The ten functions are named and characterized abstractly as follows:[34]

> **A/a:** destabilizing event (or reevaluation that reveals instability)
> **B:** request that someone alleviate A/a
> **C:** decision by C-actant to attempt to alleviate A/a (the C-actant is the character who performs function C)
> **C':** C-actant's initial act to alleviate A/a
> > **D:** C-actant is tested
> > **E:** C-actant responds to test
> > **F:** C-actant acquires empowerment [D E F are also called donor events]
> > **G:** C-actant arrives at the place or time for H
> **H:** C-actant's primary action to alleviate A/a
> **I:** (or **I neg**) success or failure of H.

She clarifies that a function is a position of causal sequence, with the ten functions locating positions/sites/stages along a path leading from disruption of equilibrium to new equilibrium. A complete sequence includes functions A, C, C' H, I and may include B, D, E, F, G. Functions represent events that change a prevailing situation and initiate a new situation.

She next sieves a brief and simple folktale narrative usefully through her ten-functioned structure, demonstrating both its usefulness and its potential for nuance, while citing the perceptions of her students (real readers) to manage the story and the functions fruitfully, to choose relations consensually, that is, moving beyond first impressions to use the structure skillfully, aided by questions.[35] She also clarifies the intricate and enmeshed relationship between the story (her *fabula*) and the discourse (her term is "representation"): The discourse (representation) is authorially provided, and the construction of the story (*fabula*) is what readers provide. Discourse (representation) can be provided from diverse angles, influencing the reader construction. She concludes on an ethical note:

> Understanding how fictional narrative[s] shape our interpretations of reported events can make us more competent readers of narratives that report events in our world (in response to which we may need to act, or to refrain from acting), and more competent interpreters of events we observe in our world (in response to which we may need to decide whether to intervene).[36]

Without my needing to claim that her functions are fully adequate, the challenge will be to see what they produce in terms of insight.

---

33. Ibid.
34. Ibid., 7.
35. Ibid., 9–17.
36. Ibid., 17.

3 Plotting and David's Flight from the Court of Saul

a Macrolevel: Story Events

At the macrolevel and primarily in terms of story events, the plot of this large section of material comprises Saul driving David from him, David fleeing Saul; Saul remains the visible king, and David remains king-invisible.[37] David, arriving at Saul's court gradually, is also slow to leave it; Saul, who once invited and welcomed David, is deeply conflicted about being quit of him, not very skilled at it. At a first reading, we might anticipate that once David has left Gibeah, he will not encounter Saul again, but that is not how it works out in our narrative. We shall look at the dynamic in ten uneven sections, where we have a series of durative situations or scenes where David, homeless, is looking for a place to settle, presumably to wait out Saul's reign. But in each case an event, narrated, stirs him to move on. If we pose the narrative problem as how to plot, engagingly, "the same" situation repeatedly—Saul tracks David who comes to circle behind him—we can appreciate the challenge of showing the same event several times, with enough consistency so that we register a perennial problem for David—and for Saul as well—but also that we perceive variety and suitable progress. The repetition may seem to risk *David's* life but actually heightens the likelihood that David will take the matter of *Saul's* life and reign into his own hands. David himself articulates that danger near the end of the sequence. The repetition/variety shows how the initiative or advantage passes from Saul to David, so that by the end of this long section (more than two hundred verses), David most clearly has the mastery in their chase and yet breaks off from fear of what he has learned. He is given several opportunities to learn, and these we will examine.

I will offer a simple schema to function for the story-level various plot episodes we have here, though the more complex of them will develop it additionally as needed, ultimately drawing Kafalenos's functions into use to talk more explicitly about story-as-discoursed. But a skeleton that works for the ten events of interlocked choices we have here is: *an initial situation, a plan formulated*, then *the plan executed*, with *outcome narrated*. The clarification of what repeats allows us to look, first for whose plotting we are watching and how the resistance proceeds, and who succeeds. We will also be able to watch the variation among the sameness and select for the basic change in dynamism as it occurs.

I assume here this sense of the macrolevel design by the implied author and spend time primarily on character plotting, watching carefully what the narrator adds for the benefit of readers. The artistry of the entire work under consideration here aims, I suggest, to show Saul massively incapable of the one thing he needs to do, which is to "grow" *Torah*-observance among his people (cf. Deut. 17:14–20). Hence he must and will be replaced by David, with YHWH's assistance. Saul's refusals to yield here only compound the problem of his kingship, and those

---

37. Fokkelman, *Crossing Fates*, 248, makes that observation but does not note that the subtlety of David's skill at drawing Saul to him is also evident.

moves are detailed in this section. The question being explored is whether and how David is a worthy king, with my sense of the point under construction being that he is a worthy man in a role that is itself flawed. As previously claimed, it is my sense and my challenge to show David resisting arrogance and learning compassion, a feature slow to emerge. We see here, I think, David experiencing some behaviors from Saul and others from Saul's household but learning most particularly when he has his episode with Nabal. Compassion it is not, but it is a step in self-awareness, which puts David on the path toward gifts that lie on the other side of self-knowledge.

b Ten Narrative Units

1. Jonathan dissuades Saul from killing David: 19:1–7 The narrator summarizes the first *initial situation:* Saul's son and servants are made privy to and asked to participate in Saul's resolution to see David dead.[38] But, the narrator adds, Jonathan delighted in David. The tangled plot strings expose conflict between the aims of father and son, intensified temporally from the end of the Goliath scene where Jonathan made David a *peer* and perhaps a *prince* by giving him his own gear, while Saul sought to commandeer him as *son* and *surrogate*, though certainly not as heir. Though we can very briefly see those two acts of welcome by Saulides congruent, as early as the welcome home from the battle Saul sees David as a threat in a way Jonathan never does. So against his father's plan to kill David, Jonathan's *formulated plan* is, first, to position David safely as witness,[39] then to dissuade his father from his plan for David's death. Jonathan's *plan-execution* strategy is to appeal to Saul's self-interest: Saul ought not sin against one who has not only not sinned against him but done him positive good, and at great risk to himself. The Saul we have been watching seems unlikely to be persuaded by reminders of David's capacity to do what Saul was unable to do, or by David's willingness to undertake what Saul refused while being taunted about it repeatedly (17:8–10, 23). That Jonathan ascribes David's victory to God is plausibly tactful, but to say that Saul rejoiced is a response we did not witness. Jonathan is either naive here or disingenuous, but the *outcome narrated* shows him successful: Saul hearkened to Jonathan's words and swore, in direct discourse and invoking God, that David should not be put to death. The second outcome is that David and Saul are in each other's presence, as before. "As before" was not so good, as we recall and will revisit shortly. Jonathan is shown successful, if perhaps not skilled, and Saul's basic indecision about David is reactivated.

2. David escapes Saul's spear: 19:8–10 Arguably part of David's being "in Saul's presence as before" includes David's continued success with Philistines who war against Saul. It is the scenario seen in ch. 17 extending to 18:5 and pertains here,

---

38. As Bodner explains, *1 Samuel*, 202–03, the syntax is not so revealing as we might wish, though the general intent is clear: David to die.

39. Bodner, *1 Samuel*, 203, takes it as a scene for David to see, not hear.

where Saul should feel torn, as was clear enough in 18 if not 17. Saul has indicated in the hearing of the reader that his plan is for Philistines to kill David, sent to fight them (18:21). In any case, perennial (temporally extensive) Philistine threat and Davidic success against them set the *initial situation,* which culminates in Saul's *plan*—to pin David to the wall with his spear while David plays the harp. This moment is a doubled and plausibly conflicted one for Saul, who once agreed to or requested David to his side to provide music (16:17). The narrator names the evil spirit from God as the agent of Saul's deed—perhaps of his failure to accomplish it. The *outcome* is David's flight—not simply his dodging as before—to his own house shared with Michal—not too far a move, but more decisive than exposure to Saul's aimed spear. David is being inched from Saul's entourage.

3. *Michal prevents Saul from killing David: 19:11–17* Saul's next move is to send messengers to guard David in his home until next morning, when he should be killed. We need not ask why a morning killing is better than a night execution, rather simply note that temporal delay allows escape. The urgency seems grasped by Michal, whose single sentence to David names Saul's *envisioned plan*: "'If you do not save your life tonight, tomorrow you will die'" (v. 11). Plot strings snarl as Michal executes her *counterplan*, siding with her husband against her father, acting at once to take advantage of the king's delay. David, wordless, chooses the first option, moving a bit farther afield. Michal's plan seems to comprise gaining her husband time to escape her father, as she attempts not so much to divert as delay Saul's knowledge of David's flight. She seems indifferent to her own safety, addressing the king with near-rudeness. If Saul grows more overt about his plan to kill David, Michal is as clear about her plan to save him. What is more complex here than we have seen with either Jonathan or the evil spirit is her motive. To her father's "'Why have you deceived me?'" she voices a quotation attributed to David: "'He said, "Let me go; why should I kill you?"'" (v. 17).[40] This we did not hear, reminding us that David does not speak in this whole chapter. We may think that "he" has endangered her life, or that he, as quoted, is disclaiming intent to bring lethal harm to his wife, daughter to the king: "Why should I be the cause of your death?" he may be understood to have said. Against a majority of commentators who continue to remind us that Michal loved David, I reiterate that she *was said* to love him and that *rumor* was told to Saul. But we are no closer here to knowing her feelings than ever, while her actions are astute, inventive, bold. The *outcome* is that her husband survives.

4. *Samuel and God's Spirit stop Saul from harming David: 19:18–24* Whether v. 18 belongs with the past or this present scene is not important, except that the only *initial plan* we see here is David's choice of refuge with Samuel. Saul's *plan*,

---

40. Contra Alter, *David Story,* 121, who names it a pure invention by Michal. I reckon that is too literal a conclusion, granted we do not hear it said. Mark S. Smith, in *Poetic Heroes: Literary Commemorations of Warriors and Warrior Culture in the Early Biblical World* (Grand Rapids and Cambridge: William B. Eerdmans Publishing Company, 2014), 70, calls Michal a "key human female."

consistent if not subtle, is to send messengers to take David, an intent thwarted by the presence of prophetic inspiration, resulting in the incapacity of the messengers to act to bring David to Saul. The king's next *plan*, also thwarted, is to take the matter in hand himself, but he fails in the same way his messengers did. The *plan executed* thus fails, but the fresh *outcome* is David's removing himself from Samuel's presence to make another attempt with Jonathan.

To comment briefly on the four scenes of this chapter is to underline that persistent if ineffective plans for David's death are made by Saul; the plans to preserve David's life come from Saul's putative or previous allies—his son and daughter and God's spirit—who make clear that they are on the side of David's survival. Though Jonathan and Michal do well, God's spirit must be noted as also managing skillfully, named in 19:9 and implied in 19:20–24. David enacts no clear plan except to remove himself gradually from danger, so far succeeding.[41] What he is thinking is not revealed, except insofar as we note him moving consistently from Saul's reach, inept as it is so far. That we, reading, are not concerned about his safety does not mean securing it is not a major plot objective.

5. David ascertains more certainly Saul's determination to kill him: 20:1–42 This is a long unit, which I have previously discussed at length, to show it a set of fifteen utterances (exchanges) between Jonathan and David aiming and succeeding to clarify Saul's intent in regard to David.[42] In the midst of these exchanges, Jonathan and Saul speak to each other.[43] The chapter moves from David's initiative and question, concluding with the two friends agreeing that there is no chance for David to reclaim his place in Saul's court. Here I will use our simple grid to discuss not so much the speech but the plotting. Only now, after the four shorter scenes just considered, initiative returns to David, who for the first time since the betrothal of Michal shows resourceful agency. David approaches Jonathan with a plan, which is ours to discern over Jonathan's head, as it were.

Pushing off from the *initial situation*, David asks Jonathan (20:1) what he has done or how offended, that Jonathan's father seeks David's life. It may be construed as a "straight" question, asking for information that lacks. It may also be seen as a rhetorical prompt for Jonathan to account for his father's moves, which is what happens: On the basis of the close bond between himself and his father, Jonathan

41. Alter, *David Story*, 122, points out what we are calling a discourse move: that the narrator "bares" Saul and "covers for" David. It is a good example of the narrator's unevenness, which we may overlook when words like "omniscience" are used.

42. Green, *Mighty Fallen*, 301–21, with a briefer exposition in "Experiential Learning: The Construction of Jonathan in the Narrative of Saul and David," in Roland Boer, ed., *Bakhtin and Genre Theory in Biblical Studies* (Atlanta, GA: SBL Press, 2007), 43–58. For a treatment of it focusing on its several questions, see Kenneth Craig, "Rhetorical Aspects of Questions Answered with Silence in 1 Samuel 14:37–28:6," *CBQ* 56 (1994): 221–39.

43. Alter, *David Story*, 123, reminds us that this is David's first speech to Jonathan. It is worth our recalling that though we may subconsciously fill in more than we are given, the exchanges between characters are often unnaturally minimal.

protests that if *he* does not know of Saul's intent to harm David, it cannot be so. It may seem difficult for us to see how Jonathan can be in such denial, except insofar as we recall that what we last saw Jonathan witness was Saul's assurance on oath that David would not be put to death (19:6). That Jonathan is not visible in the material just considered where Saul relapses allows the inference that he was not present. Jonathan's insistence also makes sense if we credit that he does not want his father and his friend at odds. David, on the other hand, is in little doubt about Saul's intent without understanding the root or persistence of it.

Alternatively, if David is to be read as plotting to prod Jonathan into recognition that Saul does not wish him well, then to shatter the trust the son feels for his father is required. To Jonathan's refusal to imagine that his father could wish harm to David without Jonathan knowing of it, David counters strongly, bluntly, perhaps unkindly: "'Your father knows well that I have found favor in your eyes, and he thinks, "Let not Jonathan know this, lest he be grieved." But truly, as the Lord lives and as your soul lives, there is but a step between me and death'" (20:3). That is, from whatever reactive or proactive motive, David takes aim at the bond of closeness Jonathan has just claimed with his father, and shows it baseless. If this second supposition seems reasonable, we see it also succeeds with Jonathan, who declares himself willing to put David's view of things to the test. So David's *initial plan* is to get Jonathan as his helper in flushing out Saul more definitively than before. David wants certainty, a difficult thing to gain from Saul, who has trouble sticking to a course for long or actually accomplishing it.

As we ponder the plans of the two characters here and the attendant gaps, speculating because we cannot quite know, we can think a bit farther out to their longer-range objectives: If Jonathan is planning for David to be king, as seems so in material ahead (e.g., 23:17), he will want to help David survive as close to the court as possible. If David can be seen as wanting to split Jonathan from Saul and divert him to David's own side—for which I see little evidence—then this present project shows that outcome unlikely, unrealistic. These two points are undecidable, but in terms of exploiting the narrative as we have it, to speculate on the characters' plans is vital. The implied author will have it in mind, and here I think that Jonathan is shown remaining loyal to both father and friend and consistent in not wishing to inherit his father's position. David is shown surviving to whatever end he sees for himself—though we must note that he never speaks aloud or silently about his own anointing, and never alludes to it.

As the plotting by these two characters develops, it is not difficult to follow, especially if we eliminate the distractions of secrecy and timing that attend their conversation and the language of mutual fidelity that they pledge.[44] The *plan* David formulates is to provoke Saul into reaction when David, who presumably under normal circumstances should be at Saul's table, is absent at the New Moon. How will Saul respond to such a situation? David counts on a verbal response from the king,

44. The secrecy is understandable, since Saul is publicly hunting David. The words of fidelity of each to the other and the other's kin (20:8–18) are important both to shape the character of each player and to remind us of why David brings Jonathan's son into his court.

on Saul's questioning Jonathan, who will then explain that he, Jonathan—asked by David to go rather to his own father, Jesse's, table—granted that permission. If Saul is agreeable, they will learn of it. If Saul is angry—at the absence, at learning that David approached Jonathan for a waiver from the expected attendance, at Jonathan's presuming to grant it, at David's choosing his own father's house over the king—then they will have learned that result (20:5–7, 18–23). There is little indication of what outcome either character expects or desires, though they seem to agree that something will precipitate from their managing the volatile Saul, in fact more than one thing. I maintain that David aims to get firm information, likely a confirmation of what he has been experiencing from Saul's attempts on his life. Jonathan, in my view, may hope to show David that Saul is well-disposed toward him, as he managed to demonstrate recently, if briefly to David and readers (19:1–7).

We can see a bit more about plot design here and appreciate its scope. What is being offered to Saul is provocative, in that it tests sonship—whether David is Jesse's son or Saul's, whether Jonathan is a loyal son to his father or betrays his father for his "brother." The scenario also tests Saul's authority, since it shows David resisting Saul's patronage and managing his affront with Jonathan's rather than Saul's permission. If Saul can hope that the son (-in-law) he is pursuing will be afraid not to come to his table on a feast, he will be disappointed and shown outmaneuvered. Also contesting here are the strategizing capacities of the two men, as demonstrated in the betrothals of the king's daughters. If we construct Saul as having thought himself capable of rendering David vulnerable through marriage to Michal, he was forced to acknowledge, according to the narrator, the opposite outcome. Similar here.

The *plan is executed* (vv. 24–33), much as its design potential indicated likely. When David is absent on the first night of the feast, Saul accounts for it to himself, his lack of confidence betrayed, perhaps, in his self-talk, doubled to reassure himself: "'Something has befallen him; he is not clean, surely he is not clean'" (v. 26). But when David is missing a second night, Saul's language reveals that he had not convinced himself that David was legitimately absent: "'Why has not the son of Jesse come to the meal, either yesterday or today?'" (v. 27). Jonathan performs as agreed, though again it is not clear with what hopes and what awareness. That Saul erupts underlines the offense he is feeling: David's request of Jonathan to spend the feast in Bethlehem, commanded by a brother and not even by his father (vv. 28–29). Saul's anger is directed toward the son who *is* at his table, prompting language we have not heard from Saul so explicitly, stressing his determination that Jonathan will rule after his father. That we have heard Saul told twice that such an outcome is unlikely (13:14; 15:28) and that we have heard Saul commit his son to death for a breach of an oath (14:39, 44) seem brushed aside in Saul's sense of events. Jonathan, departing from the script we witnessed but reverting to David's language at the start of the scene (20:32 re-voices 20:1), attracts a spear-thrust from his father, such as David has experienced three times already, thus equating the two in Saul's succession-defeating action. Jonathan flees, from his father, back to his friend.

Before commenting on the outcome, a few more words on the enactment. If, as indicated above, David's desire is at least for certainty, he seems to have generated it. Saul is clearly considering David a threat to Jonathan's rule, and Jonathan-with-David a threat as well. If David's goal was to demonstrate his father's animosity to Jonathan, that, too, has been accomplished—uncontrollable anger at both sons. If Jonathan has needed persuading that Saul does not wish David well, it seems manifest. As a plan executed, it is highly successful, showing Saul feeble in his own position, let alone in being able to secure a position for Jonathan.

The *outcome narrated* is clear, as we move past flurries of arrows and words of mutual commitment. We are deprived of hearing Jonathan describe the scene to David, with the narrator's note of mutual weeping needing to suffice. The narrator has already told us, "And Jonathan . . . was grieved for David because his father disgraced him" (v. 34). The earlier note of solidarity between the two (18:3) allows for Jonathan to feel the disgrace for both of them, perhaps for Saul as well. Other outcomes: the bond between the two young men is strengthened, extended to their heirs. The two split, to meet only one more time. Jonathan returns to his father, and David moves farther afield. If David can be seen assessing his clarification, he has it— such as Saul can provide consistency or certainty. David is, narratively speaking, able to see progress in what Jonathan knows about his father's plans for David. But also clearer are the loyalties of the two young men toward the descendants of the other, as such need will arise. If Saul can be envisioned as assessing his state, it would be to see that his children side with David over their father's desire to be rid of him. The narrator has told us a lot, not so much as we might like, but the basic edges are clear. The implied author has, again, shown Saul unfit to rule and David forbearing to some extent, though a case could be made that David exhibited brutality in his exposing Saul to Jonathan as he did. Saul's desires are clear, but David's are hidden, except to survive and have some clear choices.

6. More witnesses learn of Saul's intent to destroy David: 21:1–22:23 The next scene is long and complex, forking in a way new to the story to show David doing one thing, while Saul does another—yet they tangle.[45] David continues his planning role as seen in ch. 20, though seems unable to sustain it effectively; outcomes escape his control. Others respond to his moves, which continue difficult to read with certainty. Where uncertainty abounds, reader options abound as well. I will offer my best sense of David's plotting choices, recognizing that other readers will construct differently here, where the authorial cues are not so clear as they often are. The challenge is to discern—suggest—causality.

The *initial situation* seems clear: David is definitively and now resolutely on the run from Saul's palace, with no more indecision about escaping Saul's reach. He arrives alone at the shrine of Nob, to be greeted by a trembling priest, Ahimelech, a great-grandson of Eli (21:1–2). Bodner asks why the priest should be shown fearful and suggests we will soon learn that a Saul-man is present at the shrine as

---

45. Alter, *David Story*, 136.

well, and that the priest fears how the confluence of participants will work out.[46] I am satisfied that David's status as unattended suffices to raise the priest's suspicion, since that is what the two discuss. David claims, to soothe the fearful priest, that he is on an errand of "the king" (name unspecified), a secret one, and that he will be joining companions. The priest's dropping the topic and cooperating reassures me that he is content with what he was told.[47]

The *plan formulated*—beyond flight—is more difficult, but crucial to speculate about. David presumably wants something from the priest, and his visit will have far-reaching consequences. But his specific plan remains opaque, uncertain even as it happens. He asks of the priest two things: First, food; second, a weapon. The first of these matters is managed in vv. 3–6. He is given food, once he assures the priest he will respect the customs surrounding it.[48]

The narrator chooses the moment between David's requests (v. 7) to call attention to the presence at the shrine of the Edomite Doeg, presently in the employ of Saul. The information, of course, is for us, not for the characters.[49] Doeg is thus placed by the narrator to witness the next mini scene, and for readers to be

46. Bodner, *1 Samuel*, 223–24, introduces the narrative technique of delayed exposition: Though we are told the priest is nervous as David arrives, we do not learn the reason until Saul's herdsman is named several verses later; on the other hand, if what alarms the priest is what he says—that he is unaccustomed to receive David unattended, there is no time discrepancy.

47. Pamela Tamarkin Reis, "Collusion at Nob: A New Reading of 1 Samuel 21–22," *JSOT* 61 (1994), 59–73. Bodner discusses this scene and the Reis reading at length in "Revisiting the 'Collusion at Nob' in 1 Samuel 21–22," in Bodner, ed., *David Observed*, 25–37. Their basic agreement is that (*contra* most interpreters) the priest and the royal fugitive do collude against King Saul, each knowing the other's situation and intent, an alliance reasonable, Reis says, due to the importance of the priestly group at Nob for any resistance to "the state." Their construction is careful and plausible, though not convincing to me. What Reis is doing (and what Bodner does with consistency and brilliance) is what we are doing as well: studying the representation and seeking, with the tools at hand, to make good use of it.

48. Those customs are not so clear, and this scene has generated substantial discussion about the loaves, the licit consumption of them—indeed, by no less a commentator than Jesus himself (Mk. 2:25–26), who biblical scholars like to show as having made an error in naming the priest! Among many useful places to look for discussion on the point, consult Fokkelman, *Crossing Fates*; P. Kyle McCarter, *1 Samuel: A New Translation with Introduction, Notes, and Commentary,* AB 9 (Garden City, NY: Doubleday, 1980), 349–50; Diana Edelman, in *King Saul in the Historiography of Judah*, JSOTSup 121 (Sheffield: Sheffield Academic Press 1991), 164, notes the passages where bread has been mentioned: 10:4; 14:27; 16:20; 17:17.

49. Hebrew syntax calls this a circumstantial clause, providing a sidestep, a pause in the forward movement of the action between David and Ahimelech the priest. The same verb is used of Doeg's presence as was offered about David's supposed companions and their suitability to be given shrine bread: the verbal root *ʿṣr*, suggesting a range of "restrained/detained/kept." For some commentary to suggest the texture of what has been provided,

informed that he is there, presumably also known to the priest but not necessarily to David (though we will learn in time that he did see Doeg).

David's second request of the priest is for a weapon (vv. 8–9). His words are almost offhand: "'And have you not here a spear or a sword at hand? For I have brought neither my sword nor my weapons with me'"[50] He receives more than he asked, as Goliath's sword is offered him by the priest, evidently put into David's hand, though we do not quite see it happen.[51] David comments on the quality of the sword and seems to approve the priest's giving it to him. But, in narrative terms, that the sword—so important as a mythic item—has no further explicit use suggests to me that the sword and the food are incidental to David's plan unfolding somewhat uncertainly at the shrine.[52] The narrator assists again, relating that the sword is wrapped in a cloth behind the ephod, and allowing us to hear the priest urge David to take the sword. We are not told that the priest handles the ephod to get to the sword, thus plausibly appearing to a watching, foreign, suspicious witness to have done a consultation for David. But I think we are entitled to picture the moment in just that way, as is the skulking Doeg.

My own sense is that, though collusion between David and Ahimelech cannot be disproven, it is neither the only nor the best construction. David has been shown in the past to have helpers, though Jonathan is the only one David actually selected (or if Samuel at 19:18–24, we do not see enough to make much use of that occasion, since Samuel remains virtually absent from the representation). On every other occasion (so far), others take the initiative and David receives, without displaying much agency. So my sense of David's plan is that he approaches the shrine in need of food, perhaps desirous of the Goliath sword, though gaining it seems more incidental, almost an afterthought. Once David sees Saul's servant, he enacts a scene that Doeg reports. That the priest, when asked, says the sword is behind the ephod suggests to me that the priest is implied narratively to handle the ephod to get the sword, and that manipulation is what Doeg is shown and claims to have been witness to. Against Reis, who says the giant's outsized weapon would be impractical,[53] I suggest that its status reminds any seeing it how David came by the sword, reinforcing for us how David is growing more comfortable with armor and weapons that once seemed too large. David need not have planned and I maintain is not shown intending harm to the priest, but harm happens, and David bears some responsibility for it—will claim some, shortly. That David asks and receives two things which receive little further development prompts me to look for a third,

---

even though we can and must proceed without solving this completely, consult Fokkelman, *Crossing Fates*, 352–59, assaying his reasons as well as his information.

50. Alter, *David Story*, 70–72, has reminded us that narrative speech is almost inevitably stylized, not natural.

51. The last we saw of that sword was in David's hand, though he was said, proleptically, to have put weapons in his tent in Jerusalem (17:54).

52. Alter, *David Story*, 70–72 notes that Hebrew narrative tends to be spare, nothing not needed is provided. Hence these details signify.

53. Reis, "Collusion," 68.

given if not asked. So bread, a sword, and the appearance of a consultation, all of which Doeg will report to Saul and Saul will query with the priest (22:9–10). David departs, provisioned and armed, moving toward Gath.[54] Doeg departs, with information of varied quality, returning to Saul. The narrator has ably assisted both men. The *plan executed* is more authorial than characteral, and relies upon reader skill and ingenuity. Why David wants Saul to think the priest has helped him with consultation is plausibly to imply divine help.

The *outcome* splits, a technique to be utilized in the material ahead. David's arrival at and departure from Gath and Doeg's arrival and report at Gibeah are roughly synchronous. David's *outcome* substantially generates Saul's opening situation. First we follow David. In 21:10–15 he, perhaps with Goliath's sword, arrives in Goliath's former home, to be recognized by the giant's former compatriots. How should they recognize the fugitive except that he is carrying the sword? Why do the men of Gath misidentify David as king of the land, except that he is the Israelite who slew their hero and so, arguably, the king, by somewhat the same logic as Saul construed the song?[55] Strangely if realism were the main criterion, but with great narrative suitability, the Gittites voice the song the women sang for David and Saul. The words thus sung, the narrator tells us, frighten David, who presumably does not expect to be recognized. As Bodner queries, why is David alarmed by the song rather than pleased?[56] I think the narrative joins are tight here, if implicit rather than stated. The narrator shows us that David neither desires nor anticipates being recognized, and has not supposed that showing up with the famous sword would identify him (or if he is not carrying it, they recognize him in any case). Had not the narrator revealed that David was surprised, we might have expected more shrewdness from him, or perhaps a different reaction.[57]

David's next if somewhat extemporaneous move is to simulate madness by gestures of scrabbling and drooling. The "mad king" identity is often subtle as well as occasionally overt, possibly a comment on certain royal individuals or perhaps on Davidic monarchy as a whole, even on dynastic kingship as an institution in general: Besides (king) David, who has not adequately thought through his appearing at Gath, we have blind or coy Achish, who seems to take the simulation at

54. Technically we are not told that the characters saw him, but David later tells the priest's surviving kin that he himself had seen Doeg. We do not learn of it until later, both when it is strategically powerful and when David, remarking, has surely learned more than he knew at the moment of first seeing Doeg.

55. See Craig, "Rhetorical Aspects," 221–39. Fokkelman, in *Crossing Fates*, 365, maintains that both Saul and the Philistines misconstrue the women's words; but the song has a life of its own, once the women have sung it, and their intent does not control meanings. But as the Philistines were shown astute if ignorant about the Ark, so here: David *is* king, though the Philistines, unlike readers, have no way to know of it factually. As with the Ark, "the uncircumcised" know more about identities than those better positioned to understand.

56. Bodner, *1 Samuel*, 229.

57. Craig, *Asking for Rhetoric*, 79, thinks David becomes somehow detained at Gath, another way to ponder his behavior.

face value, prompting as it does from him a sneering and imperceptive remark. He scolds his men, almost jovially, for adding another madman to his establishment. And we have King Saul, who is about to do the maddest deed we will see him perform (among various contenders for that status in his story).

The theme of David with the men of Achish—David sheltering with and assisting Philistines—is an important one in the story.[58] Though David can see, and we are shown, that his coming to Gath has not been a wise move, and though he departs, he will return at the end of our current section of material. Even at the disadvantage registered here, he is safer than elsewhere. His later choice to return to Achish (at the end of ch. 26) will seem justified, if counterintuitively. David's lack of foresight is saved by the implied author of this long story featuring more than one mad king, who shows David shrewd enough to know he must now flee the establishment of Achish as well as that of Saul. So the outcome for David continues to be safety, at least for the moment, as he moves toward Adullam and allies (21:1–2), thence to Moab and to another king who helps him (22:3–4), on to a helpful prophet who warns him to flee back toward Judah (21:5), when his whereabouts reach Saul's ears. That David does not manage this planning very effectively is made clear but also retrieved, so to speak, by whoever is guiding David in the story—God's spirit, not implausibly—and the authorial genius.

If there is a further David-plan, its edges are well-concealed. Though on occasion capable of planning (ch. 20), David has also been shown planless when fleeing to Samuel at Ramah (19:18–24). Since we are talking about representation, the issue is not whether there might be a plan but rather that none is disclosed to us. That David stumbles to Gath without anticipating the outcome there and that he never seems to do anything with the sword of Goliath suggests to me no comprehensive plan.[59]

The second *outcome* of the Nob encounter and the *situation* beginning a scene featuring Saul occurs at his palace, where the king sits, berating his people over both the lack of help and the actual disloyalty he claims to be experiencing in the matter of David. In narrative terms, this scene is initiated by Saul's learning that David is once again closer than before, or not under the protection of a foreign king—something geographically strategic that we may have trouble picking out, knowing the geography and implied conventions less well than the teller of the tale (22:6).[60] The scene about to unfold is carefully plotted, in my opinion, not least for showing Saul massively unsupported by those from whom he expects help, though later we may be surprised at how much help he receives about David's whereabouts. As previously stipulated, that Saul epitomizes a failed dynastic institution is what

---

58. Jobling, *1 Samuel*, 10, calls more attention to the Philistines' importance than do most commentators, discussing them in their own chapter of his commentary.

59. Fokkelman, *Crossing Fates*, 355, astutely notes that in a single move, David both includes and excludes the priest.

60. The map provided by McCarter, *1 Samuel*, 352, whether accurate in each detail or not, is helpful for envisioning David's moves in this part of the narrative.

the implied artistry of the piece most consistently shows. This present scene is arguably the nadir of Saul's rule.

With David on the move, Saul is seated at his home base, holding the spear he has occasionally thrown ineffectually at sons David and Jonathan, surrounded by men he will accuse of disloyalty. The scene, like virtually all of the material in this long section, is about information: Who (including ourselves) knows what, and how may such information or lack thereof be managed strategically, by various witnesses? To state that in slightly different terms: How does the narrative move, both as narrator and characters unfold it? Here the main planner is Saul. His opening salvo is an accusatory question, delivering several rounds:

> "Hear, now, you Benjaminites; will the son of Jesse give every one of you fields and vineyards, will he make you all commanders of thousands and commanders of hundreds, that all of you have conspired against me? No one discloses to me when my son makes a league with the son of Jesse, none of you is sorry for me or discloses to me that my son has stirred up my servant against me, to lie in wait at this day." (21:7–8)

Saul asks or accuses his tribe about motivation: How might they anticipate profit by choosing David over Saul, whether they have actually been rewarded or not, anticipated it realistically or not? That David has nothing to bestow yet is clear, but Saul suggests that David already owes Saul's own tribesmen for alleged disloyalty. Then before that rambling accusation can be answered, Saul adds motive to his construction of the deed done: Is it to gain such rewards from David that Saul's own tribe have conspired against him by withholding from him information about Saul's son and David—and specifically, Saul accuses—that Jonathan has set Saul's own servants against him. To reshuffle and distill that charge: Is Jonathan conspiring with David to set Saul's people against him, and do none of Saul's men tell him, since they anticipate gaining rewards from David? It is easy to dismiss Saul as a mad king, so before we move in that direction, we have to ask if Saul's words contain any truth.

Saul's people, charged here with disloyalty and venality—such as Samuel spoke of when warning against the costs of monarchy (8:11–18)—stand silently, not responding to the king's accusations, leaving us to ponder what they may be supposed to know but not say. *Is* David conspiring, with Jonathan? That behavior we did witness clearly in ch. 20, less clearly with a priest in ch. 21 at Nob. *Is* Saul notified of it by anyone? Again, so far, we have seen Jonathan's armor-bearer who might have spoken to Saul but evidently does not. The priest will provide information shortly when asked. In the pursuit scenes ahead (23:1, 13; 24:1, 26:1), Saul will seem to have a good deal of information from helpers, though not from his own closest people.[61] Saul may be understood as referring to narrative moments when his men approved David (18:16). We cannot know exactly what events Saul is speaking about, whether his charge is groundless or partially accurate. But

---

61. Bodner, *1 Samuel*, 240, calls these "pockets of loyalty."

before Doeg speaks up, we must note that none of the men of Benjamin replies, including Jonathan, if present. Silence is often a weighty if enigmatic reply, and so it is here.[62] None denies the charges, though we can offer several ways to read their silence. If Saul's plan is to gain information, he fails so far; if it is meant to reinforce the charge he makes, he is doing well. Saul's objective is not so clear here, but if it is to stir some response, he succeeds, while of course failing terribly at leadership.

For now Saul is given information, though not by one of his own tribesmen. Doeg's words take over: "'I saw the son of Jesse coming to Nob, to Ahimelech son of Ahitub, and he inquired of the Lord for him, and gave him provisions, and gave him the sword of Goliath the Philistine'" (22:9–10). Doeg says what we have seen him witness, reversing the order, presumably making the most serious of the charges—consultation with the deity—first.

Bodner, again naming the move, says that Doeg's testimony is another instance of delayed exposition; that is, the narrator has withheld information that could have been presented earlier, concluding that Doeg claims, now, to have seen the two together and alleges that the priest consulted for David. The problem, Bodner suggests, is whether we are given narrative cues to believe that Doeg speaks sincerely or that he is lying (though he could be sincere but mistaken). On the side of our disbelieving Doeg is that the narrator did not himself tell us what Doeg claims to have seen, placing the priest's patronymic in Saul's mouth, reminding us that this is an Elide, a member of a house we heard condemned earlier in the story (1 Sam. 1–3, in various ways).[63] That is, though this scene involves plans of Saul and David, it also catches the curse spoken to the Elides much earlier (2:29–36).

Spending no more words, Saul shapes his *plan* from Doeg's information and summons all the priests of Nob to him, to question Ahimelech about not *whether* he has consulted for David but *why*, and naming the outcome: that David is conspiring against Saul (v. 13). That is, on his way to ascertaining motive and outcome, Saul names the charges: the food, the sword, and the inquiry of God. The priest—first trembling before the lone David but accepting reassurance that the young man's mission was legitimate and represented the king and that the lone suppliant would be joining others shortly—seems now less fearful and more naive as he responds to Saul, both failing to deny the main charge and managing to verbalize and valorize the skills of David and Saul's reliance on him (vv. 14–16).[64] The priest's response to the king's question is a brilliant sentence, in its capacity though not designed to offend. The priest, signaling to me his innocence, re-intonates rhetorical logic we heard from Jonathan at 19:4–5: Who is more trusted than David, the priest asks, saying precisely the wrong thing to soothe or dissuade the king. Not just this time, he adds, implying or leaving us to infer that consultation took place beyond our

---

62. For an insightful discussion of the impact of questions answered with silence, see Craig, *Asking for Rhetoric*, 49–72.

63. Bodner, "Collusion at Nob," in Bodner, ed., *David Observed*, 32–34.

64. If one follows Bodner and Reis here, the priest should register in some way that the thing he was nervous about has happened. That is, the priest should be more guarded and eager to excuse himself, not less.

knowing it. To me the priest sounds simple and credulous, very little alert to what is about to happen. If he is attempting to cover guilt by a show of innocence, he errs to attempt it. The priest, planless himself except perhaps to hope to please or flatter Saul, says exactly the wrong things about himself and about David as well as about Saul. Had we not been informed of the ephod, handled by the priest to get to the sword, we might suppose that Doeg has lied, fabricated the inquiry—which is indeed what many suppose. Implied here is the matter of who in Saul's entourage knows that a breach has occurred between Saul and David. That, too, is a narrative matter and ultimately undecidable. We can allege sociological information to say that such secrets do not keep well at court. Or we can say that the point is that Saul is drawn to feel that the secret is safe enough to be dangerous to his enemies.[65] So only at the end of his testimony to David does the priest seem to say: If there is more, I'm not to be held responsible.[66]

But Saul, so starved for information, responds to what he has been told, informed both by his chief shepherd and by the priest.[67] He appears to take the priest's rambling sentence as an admission of guilt and pronounces a death sentence, ordering his men to kill the priests but again getting no cooperation from them. He must rely on Doeg for action, thus compounding his sense of royal impotence to witnesses if not to himself (22:17–19). The scene, we may note, is unreal: One man kills eighty-five men, with only the last escaping.[68] That is, in a scene where royal power might be on display, powerlessness is manifest. Finally, adding to Saul's problems, if not at once, is a narrative note for us (not for Saul): a survivor flees to David (22:20–23), who will make good use of him. *Outcomes* pile mostly negatively for Saul.

How to proceed? Certainty eludes us, appropriately so. The implied author and narrator have not presented the material unambiguously, so options remain open. The challenge is to think it out as clearly as we can do and to name *our* moves, so that others and we can "check our math."[69] At stake are the responsibility of Saul for the death of a house of priests, the culpability of the priest Ahimelech for his

---

65. Part of what we are shown about Saul is that, whatever we may think of his leadership qualities, he always has people to help him, right to the very end of his life, where a woman risks her life for him and three of his sons die with him.

66. Reis characterizes the scene, using terms of madness (paranoid rage) and lack of self-control (maudlin self-pity) to characterize Saul. She portrays Doeg as having realized he was duped at the shrine and now seeing an opportunity for positioning himself more advantageously Reis, "Collusion," 69–70. She concludes, 72–73, with the questions she considers her reading strategy has solved.

67. This view, of course, rests on her earlier hypothesis that David and Ahimelech are colluding about something, and it is implicitly false.

68. There is another motif here to watch for: Before all the information is quite extracted from a witness, he is killed. Might we anticipate, construct, that he had more to say?

69. We may recall situations where, doing math problems, we claimed to have the correct answer but were not credited with it until and unless someone could check our work to see by what steps we arrived at it.

own fate, and the question of David's own accountability for his part in the death of the priests, in Saul's action, and so forth. This is a very dense ethical moment in the story, and we need to appraise carefully.

I have written elsewhere about Saul's character zone as it culminates (temporarily) here, my sense being that Saul's character is sketched as a royal entity (person and dynasty) that fails, he is intended to fail. This moment intensifies his radical unsuitability for the role for which he has been selected, anointed, and confirmed, and from which he is eventually fired. Ahimelech, in my view, is best characterized as clueless. At the shrine, the priest is manipulated into giving David bread, handing him the Goliath sword that has been behind the ephod, such that he is seen—arguably, since this moment is not described explicitly—handling the ephod in David's presence. That the priest is flustered when shouted at by King Saul and speaks unwisely and ambiguously, praising David to Saul and not really answering the crucial question, fits this appraisal. That we have seen Ahimelech's kin, Eli, Hophni, and Phinheas in dubious action and condemned by several voices earlier means we are not much surprised here when this Elide scion cannot avoid the trap he has been caught in.[70]

But David: What can we say of him in this scene at Gibeah? How do the last few verses trailing from this scene (vv. 20–23) help us read him? The main point of this study (my reader's plotting, as it were) is to sketch the complexity and conflictedness of David's needs and desires, his narrative portrayal as a character spacious enough to host and give insight into broad humanity. First, what happens: In the scene of the slaughter of the priests, Abiathar, son of Ahimelech, flees to David, he alone to tell the tale. Why to David?, we may ask: Arguably it is his best viable choice. Possibly Abiathar, like so many of Saul's people, reveres David.[71] The implied author does not give Abiathar's discourse, so we have only the narrator's words: "He told David that Saul had killed the priests of the Lord." Only David speaks, offering us a rare moment of reflection: "'I knew on that day, when Doeg of Edom was there, that he would tell Saul.'"[72] Tell Saul what, David? That you met by plan? That you met at David's sole initiative, the priest unaware?) That he gave you bread? That he allowed you Goliath's sword? That he handled the ephod in your presence? That he consulted for you? That he was staged to appear to consult for you? David concedes something significant though generally, without

70. Bodner, *1 Samuel*, 235, among others, reminds us that once we know Ahimelech is an Elide, we cannot be hopeful about his survival.

71. At the very end of the narrative of David, this priest will choose against David's naming his son Solomon to be king, siding with the self-proclaiming Adonijah. It is a long-deferred piece of information, but likely relevant, since the presumption is that we know the whole story. When we see this lone priest-survivor here, we "recall" how his story will end (1 Kings 2).

72. Bodner, "Collusion at Nob," in Bodner, ed., *David Observed*, 35–36, names it as another instance of delayed exposition, since in theory David might have said it at the time. This is also our confirmation that when the narrator revealed Doeg's presence (21:8), it was done through the eyes of David.

clarifying details, not enough to allow resolution of these issues, even when he adds, "'I have occasioned the death of all the persons in your father's house'" (v. 22). What is he claiming here? Is this statement "rhetorical," in the sloppy sense of a pointless flourish, a dramatic accusation of himself, rather than naming the violence of the king and his Edomite shepherd? Is it rhetorical in the more precise sense of the term: David says it strategically, before others can say it first. How do we appraise David's words? And he makes one more concluding claim, offering Abiathar protection in his, that is, David's, company, despite that some will seek their harm. Do we impute kindness here? Guilt? Surveillance? Is hospitality and fellowship an admission and apology? Does David again promise more than he can really manage? As almost always, David's motives are not easy to name without uncertainty. Is David truly sorry for his role in the death of the Elides, though we know that it had been pronounced long ago?

On his journey toward fuller agency along the ethical paths he traces, David will come to toggle between arrogance and generosity, as though unable to grow either without lapsing into the other. Here we have a sample, more complex than David with Saul over fighting Goliath, with Saul over betrothal to Michal. An action of David's, undertaken as many assist him, has seriously negative effects on the Elide priests, determined already in the knowledge of readers and coded for eventual betrayal of David when he is about to die. Here, in the narrative present, David's unintended betrayal of Ahimelech brings him a benefit, as we are about to see in detail. His own response is partial and incomplete, but present. As usual, David remains opaque. Arrogance is perhaps not central in his characterization, but perhaps a tendency to use what others offer at their cost to his own gain.

7. Saul and David compete unevenly: 23 This chapter is not so elegantly narrated as are virtually all other parts of this section, but the main point is clear enough, at least in terms of theme and coherence.[73] God is helping David, who asks help and responds to it. Saul, asking none, receives none, his fulsome religious language notwithstanding. Sensing the unit as a circle rather than an outline, I suggest we look at it as follows: vv. 1–5, 6, 7–12, 13–15, 16–18, 19–27. In terms of general theme, it shares with the rest of the material in this unit Saul's pursuit of David and David's flight from Saul, intensifying the question of the uneven knowledge of the two protagonists. As already demonstrated, pursuit is a long-running theme, and its persistence (with three more pursuits ahead of us) sends us back to recall the prominence of Saul's attracting David: begun when he brings him to his house and makes him armor-bearer, when he requisitions him from Jesse of Bethlehem, when he sets him over the king's fighting men, when he betroths him to his daughters. In each case, the pursuit goes awry in some basic way, with King Saul

---

73. For detailed and generally useful comments about its complex structure, Fokkelman, *Crossing Fates*, 416–51, is not to be missed. Antony F. Campbell has frequently noted that some narratives we have seem more like hastily sketched notes, as prompts for stories rather than developed and polished ones: "The Reported Story: Midway between Oral Performance and Literary Art," *Semeia* 46 (1989), 77–85.

being shown increasingly incompetent, at least in the matter of securing David. This chapter also manages the "who knows what and how did he learn it" question with the motif of consultation of the deity, a theme prominent previously: when Samuel consults YHWH over the request for a king, when Saul is reselected as king after having been anointed secretly, when Saul is chosen by lot, and when Saul consults to ascertain why a battle has gone awry and who is responsible. There is, as well, a geographic emphasis here, as noted earlier, thanks to the practical map of McCarter, which shows David moving (whether luring his quarry or being pressed by trackers) toward the southeastern wilderness by degrees here: Keilah to Ziph to Hachilah hill at Horesh to the Maon wilderness. So, though moving in shorter spurts, the material fits its placement well.

The *initial situation* faced by both actants is pursuit and escape: Saul pursuing, David escaping. The *plans* are not highly detailed beyond those two poles. David is informed about a Philistine raid[74] by unspecified persons. Consulting the deity with a yes/no query, he receives a clear yes though it is opposed by his men. Re-consulting, he receives a similarly clear affirmative response, which he obeys to great success. We note that David asks, God answers, with the resistance coming from David's men, who may lack the access to God's voice that David has, or perhaps they lack his confidence.[75] In any case, their fearful response is accommodated this time and will not recur in the same way. David and God are communicating well, with other humans at the periphery. David's plan appears to be survival, not more.

Saul's plan is to capture David at Keilah, informed as he is that David will be there. Saul relishes the illusion that God will assist him. Narratively speaking, as David is provided information by unknown persons in v. 1, so Saul is informed here (v. 7). But whereas David is able to consult about what he learns, Saul has primarily himself to converse with, and so he does, but imperceptively. Whereas David is told truly even though those with him miscue, Saul is miscuing by himself, thinking that David will be trapped in the city where he has gone to help, anticipating that God has delivered David into Saul's hands as he enters a blind alley. Saul acts, but David, learning of it and once again following up with an ephod-assisted and a triple consultation, asks the right questions, receives clear responses, and dodges his adversary. Saul, learning of it, avoids the foray. This is an interesting time/space question, since the king's planning ahead and anticipating an outcome is completely thwarted and in fact prevented by the information David has. The unevenness of the two men's knowledge is stressed. David, warned, avoids Saul's hand (23:7–8, 13). Each has human allies, wanting to be helpful. But with divine communication, thanks to the priestly ephod that arrives in the hand of Abiathar fleeing Saul after the king has slaughtered all his kin, David survives Saul's pursuit.

---

74. The chapter ends (vv. 27–28) with a similar intrusion of Philistines, with Saul to the rescue, presumably ineffectually, since he never foils them. By definition, they are his nemesis.

75. Exactly how the consultation works we of course do not know.

In what Bodner labels a narrative deferral and Christopher Paris calls a narrative obtrusion, we learn in the midst of inquiries that David has not only the priest Abiathar but also an ephod that he has carried away from the slaughter of his kin.[76] Presumably it has arrived at David's side with the sole fugitive, but only now, when it becomes particularly relevant, is our attention drawn to the means and hence reliability of David's information. The narrative deferral or obtrusion allows the narrator, anticipating what a reader needs, to provide it.[77] That is, right after we are shown a scene of confusion, where character doubt may distract us, we, reading, understand that God's response to David's question is clear and reliable. Once we learn that the priest has the ephod, we are conspicuously reassured that David knows what he is doing and is guided by God's reliable word. David is thus contrasted with his men, who may doubt, and especially with Saul, who, being priestless[78] is also ephodless, indeed, God-lacking.

Moving from Keilah toward the southern wilderness (vv. 14–18), David avoids Saul's search, thanks, the narrator says, to God who does not let him fall into Saul's hands. David knows where Saul is, while Saul searches unproductively for David. And though Saul cannot find David, Jonathan, we are told, comes to him and encourages him. Bodner points out that, contrasted with Saul who ruminates falsely in vv. 7 and 21–23, David's only words are his questions to God.[79] And, again contrastively, Jonathan voices a language opposite of what his father is saying and doing. This is the last encounter of David and Jonathan, and Jonathan's words strike most commentators as odd. Does Jonathan say what he reckons David needs to hear: That David will be king, that Saul will not capture him, that Jonathan will be his "second," and that Saul knows it well? In terms of who knows what and how, this is a most intriguing moment, to which David makes no verbal reply. Is the scene a response to David's unvoiced doubting that he will ever be king? We need to recall that as a character, he cannot yet have our reader's assurance about it. Is David afraid that Saul will destroy him? Again, though *we* see ahead to the culmination of Saul's failure to do so, the character David does not stand where we do. He will, in ch. 26, reveal something more to us than he does here. Does Jonathan think he will assist David, or does he think David wants to think so? Does he himself want to think so? Is Jonathan correct in his saying that Saul knows what lies ahead for David—perhaps what we heard him ask or exclaim in 18:9: "'All he lacks is the kingship!'" Jonathan's claim, whether right or wrong, reminds us that Jonathan has remained with his father, having left Saul only to make this quick final visit. We may also think back to Saul's accusation to his own men about his son: colluding with David and none to inform him (22:8). Saul is indeed hampered

76. That the ephod is mentioned only in v. 6 does not mean it was not the mode of inquiry in vv. 2–4.

77. Christopher T. Paris, *Narrative Obtrusion in the Hebrew Bible* (Minneapolis, MN: Fortress Press, 2014).

78. Bodner observes, *1 Samuel*, 223–24, that Saul had priestly (Elide?) assistance back in ch. 14, but certainly not now, since he has eliminated all but the one helping David.

79. Bodner, *1 Samuel*, 240–41.

by lack of information, but we may feel that he has driven informants from him, consistently and resolutely. But to remain loyal to both men, as Jonathan basically does, accusations to the contrary, is not a small achievement.

The rest of the chapter proceeds with additional general *plans, intended but not much implemented*: Saul has human helpers (23:19–26) who seem poised to help him catch David, who is hastening, planlessly to avoid him. But a messenger summons Saul to cope with Philistines, and David escapes (vv. 27–29).[80] These matters might have been developed to a higher level of artistry, but the point is clear. *Outcomes*: David eludes Saul. That we, reading, are confident of David's safety and place little confidence in Saul's efforts does not mean that the characters are shown to share our views, reminding us that we do not have full access to theirs. The pattern continues (vv. 19–28), as human informants tell Saul where David is and offer to help him, should he wish to come down and attempt a capture. Saul is glibly grateful, blessing his benefactors and urging that they do their reconnaissance with care, since, Saul adds, "'It is told me that he is very cunning!'" David's hiding spots are to be investigated, so that when the king appears, David can be taken even if sheltered among his tribe of Judah. But as Saul approaches, David learns of it (his mode unspecified but effective) and David drops farther south, not to his people at all. Saul learns that move and pursues, coming close: the two are separated only by a hill, when word comes to the king that the Philistines have raided his land and Saul must go back, as he does. If this appears to us as David's closest escape, it is not a situation he remarks.

The repetition makes summary unnecessary, so here it remains to comment on David's agency. The most singular thing is his access to the priestly ephod and its resources, thanks to the presence of the fugitive priest. We need to recall that Abiathar is an Elide and to "pre-member" that he will ultimately choose against David, so some shadows are present here, if barely noticeable. David's access to God's plans works well here, but this also will not continue, for some reason we still have to ponder. Since the tide is about to turn, I think we can see David, massively assisted here, most resolutely avoiding Saul's reach, determined to evade his opponent. He does not respond to Jonathan's word that the narrator called encouraging, but that we heard that word gives us an insight to David's state that we would not otherwise have had. If Paris is correct, that the narrative obtrusion is to keep readers from a slip, what might we have supposed without it? That David is on his own, lavishly guided by God is the most obvious thing. A next question: When David stops consulting, is he *then* on his own? If Saul's clearest characteristic here is that God does not help him and David's—so far—is that if God *does* help him, what next for me? How shall we construe him—them—when David ceases to ask God for assistance?

<hr />

80. That narrator provides no detail here leaves open the matter of the source of the message to Saul. Perhaps, analogous to a "divine passive" in a verb form, where the agent is implicitly God, the anonymous messenger is also of God.

8. *Saul's indecision about killing David: 24* That these next three chapters fit thematically into the material under consideration is obvious enough: pursuit, with pursuer and pursued becoming ambiguous, even switching places and roles; their discrepancy of knowledge, with David favored. The David-and-God-in-consultation motif vanishes, though—a most provocative detail. Since I have written on this material previously, in a slightly different context but which is useful for present purposes, there is no need to repeat all that work here.[81] Rather, after stipulating to several things, I will look at some key moments in these chapters, so as to offer suggestions about David's motivation not germane in my earlier treatment that focused on Saul. The stipulations are as follows: First, pursuit continues, intensifies, and reverses: By the end of the whole unit (19–26) but even in ch. 24, David is able to approach Saul without Saul anticipating it, so that David is the tracker and Saul the tracked. That Saul breaks off pursuit after they talk is also clear here, but not really new. Second, there is a progression, largely absent in the material just examined. As we hear David ruminate in 24 and then in 26, his situation will change, as we will see by 27:1, which both ends this long section and begins the next one. Saul's words show him somewhat "stuck," unable to continue to go after David but also not able seriously to desist from it, until David vanishes into Philistine territory and those foes of Saul muster for their final blow to Israel's king. Saul can neither complete the hunt nor abandon his quest for David. Third, the intervening chapter (25 between 24 and 26) is a *mise-en-abŷme*, but much more: a dreamlike unit where elements shared with the chapters flanking it are recognizable but also changed from how they appear to one awake. The characters are familiar but distorted, their motivations much intensified, more available for our insight, though perhaps not theirs. Fourth, David's language betrays much more of what he is thinking and desiring than we have seen before. In our quest for David's desires and their tangle, we have arrived in fertile ground, finally.

Looking now specifically at 24, we will also add the Kafalenos schematic to the grid already in use: The *initial situation* (destabilizing event, **A**) facing David is Saul's fresh approach to David with a large contingent of men, having been notified anonymously again. Saul arrives at En-gedi in the southern region, coming again close to where his prey is hiding (24:1–3). The *plan formulated* (request for alleviation, **B**) is offered by David's men, who seeing Saul when he is not aware of them, encourage David to take advantage of the uneven positions and knowledge of the two. David's men claim that God had already approved such a hostile move: "'Here is the day off which the Lord said to you, "Behold, I will give your enemy into your hand, and you shall do to as it shall seem good to you"'" (v. 4). David (as **C**-actant), wordless for the moment, inflicts a symbolic wound on Saul, cutting the edge of his robe (**C'** act to alleviate the situation), without the latter knowing of his opponent's presence, counterintuitive though such a thing may seem at the realistic level. But the narrator at once reports that David's heart reproaches him for doing so (the testing, **D**). He himself voices that sentiment to his men, saying, "'God forbid that I should do this thing to my lord, the Lord's anointed, to put forth

---

81. Green, *Mighty Fallen*, 367–410.

my hand against him, seeing he is the Lord's anointed'" (v. 6; the oath or prayer may be his acquisition of empowerment **F**).[82] But he has, in fact, done it and will make use of the scrap of robe shortly, suggesting to me that self-reproach does not yet run too deep. What David has also clarified in labeling his deed is that an offense against God's king is not the same as a deed aimed against someone else. The person of God's anointed is to be respected, and David falls short here, in deed if not in word as well.

David, emerging now behind Saul for a confrontation (**G**), demonstrates a *plan* with one desired outcome (persuade Saul to break off pursuit) but two modes, one minatory, the other conciliatory. Following the king from the cave where they have been enclosed together, David simultaneously threatens Saul with the severed garment and placates with language, asks Saul to witness what, in fact, the king has not seen. Making obeisance to his opponent—who is presumably still attended by three thousand men—David asks the question he has earlier presented to Jonathan, maintaining that though others tell Saul that David is against him, it is not so: "'Why do you listen to the words of men who say, "Behold, David seeks you hurt?" Lo, this day your eyes have seen how the LORD gave you today into my hand in the cave; some bade me to kill you but I spared you'" (vv. 9–10 [**H**: the primary action to alleviate situation A]). That is, David counters, more threatening than before: I could have done worse than I did, as others encouraged me, worse than attacking the royal garment. To imply that a situation might have been worse is a threat, however else it may register. David again asserts his own innocence and Saul's guilt, offering a proverb and an oath to buttress his own claim to innocence of seeking no harm to Saul. The precise intent or aptness of David's pair of proverbs is not so easy to understand, but some blend of self-exculpation and other-accusation seems likely.

If David seems to be positioning Saul to accept his (David's) version of things before the witnesses who have assembled, as well as before God, he seems, again, to succeed. Saul weeps, concedes right in what David has said, reiterates David's logic that he is innocent in regard to Saul, who is guilty in regard to David, matching David's proverbial speech with a figure of his own: "'For if a man finds his enemy, will he let him go away safe? So may the Lord reward you for what you have done to me this day'" (v. 19). And, startlingly, Saul acknowledges that he knows that the kingdom will be established in David's hand and begs that his own line not be cut off, to which David agrees, as he has already sworn to Jonathan (vv. 21–22). Saul's plan of killing David is thwarted, and David's objective of eluding Saul's grasp is also met, a pattern running at least since 18:11. If David wishes to know specifically what Saul holds against him, he does not learn it. Insofar as David needs Saul to understand Saul's own motivation if he is to change behaviors, David fails. He has bought some time but not as much as it may seem, if this scene is examined without reference to the other places where Saul ceases his

---

82. Fokkelman, in *Crossing Fates*, 461–63, notes that this is David's longest speech, even though it omits what Fokkelman called David's palpitations: his second-guessing his own deed.

hostility toward David, only to commence it again shortly. So the *outcome* here is substantially the status quo: Saul, pursuing, can be deflected (perhaps both **I** and **I neg,** success and failure). David, pursued, can avoid capture but not end pursuit. The responses of the pair, however, are more extreme than before: Saul's words of concession uttered before the group he has assembled for pursuit; David's act of violence against Saul's person, both done and made use of before he lets his quarry go—escalation, on both their parts. Saul can be said to have gained, in the sense that he has lost nothing except a round. David has won nothing he has not been offered before. Saul reigns, for all that he has indicated some glimmer about the future. David is on the run, as before. The narrator affirms that outcome: "Then Saul went home, but David and his men went up to the stronghold," at En-gedi, presumably. There is no guarantee that more of the same lies ahead, as of course it does.

9. David rehearses killing Saul: 25 Standing briefly with the implied author, we may ponder how many more pursuit scenes can be wrung from the material, given that we have already examined at least eight. How many more times the same story can be rendered freshly into discourse? But there are two more to examine, each moving action that could seem stalemated (or stale) into crisis. That readers are not worried for David's safety does not mean that he as a character is not shown concerned, and so we need to observe him with his own point of view in mind. That Saul is coming ever closer to David and with more men endangers David in one if not two ways, and to those we now turn.

This chapter is extensively commented upon and in many contexts, with diverse methods, signaling its mysterious ambiguity.[83] Bosworth includes it in his book exploring the literary feature of *mise-en-abŷme*, showing how this chapter represents another portion of its fuller self, in miniature, offering a different, even distorted angle (e.g., mirrored), in effect a paradoxical duplication, whose purpose and effect are to foreshadow, recapitulate, or offer a retrospect.[84] I think it is all that, and more.

I have written of it, interpreting it both as a genre distinct from what we have been reading—perhaps a dream or a reverie—and also as tightly related.[85] Calling attention, as many do, to the lack of fit between what David has been doing and the seemingly clumsy introduction of new characters and scenario (whose details do not advance the matrix story, except that Abigail marries David and bears him a son who never figures in the succession), I drew attention to the ways

---

83. Perhaps the most useful place to get an overview of scholarship on 1 Samuel 25 is Mark E. Biddle, "Ancestral Motifs in 1 Samuel 25: Intertextuality and Characterization," *JBL* 121.4 (2002): 617–38. Biddle summarizes ways in which Saul and Nabal seem analogous (626).

84. Bosworth, *Story within a Story*, 71 and 109 within 70–117.

85. Green, *Mighty Fallen*, 367–410; also "Enacting Imaginatively the Unthinkable: 1 Samuel 25 and the Story of Saul," *BibInt* 11.1 (2003), 1–23. In those two pieces, the focus was on the character Saul; here, my concern is David.

in which the character Nabal is a thinly disguised Saul; Abigail resembles the Jonathan-like presence mediating between "Nabal-the-Saul" and his opponent; and the character named David is David-out-of-control, galloping to do his worst to "Nabal-the-Saul" who has so affronted him. As we are presented with David becoming increasingly alert to the dangers of the royal pursuit—moving from a concern that *Saul might kill him* to a realization that *he might kill Saul*—this scene of ch. 25 appears as a grotesque and carnivalistic representation of the chase of kings. I present it as like a dream (almost an allegory), where familiar elements of deep concern present themselves though uncharacteristically, perhaps irrationally, provocatively, revealingly.

The narrator begins (25:1) by setting this episode after the death of Samuel, a moment signaling a major change of some sort in the power struggles of the characters featuring in this story of young kingship.[86] The character David (whom I will also name artificially to remind us that ch. 25 is not "straight" narrative) engages a wealthy if churlish man with a beautiful wife. The *initial situation* for Nabal-the-Saul is to maintain what he has, even through a season of vulnerability (shearing sheep in a neighborhood where outlaws are present [25:2–4]). If he can avoid paying for protection, he will want to do so (vv. 10–11). Whether he hires assistance is not clear in the narrative, though it is alleged and some testify that protection occurs (vv. 14–16).[87] This ambivalence catches well the tangled justice issue between Saul and David. The *initial situation* for the David is to survive in the wilderness and support those with him. One way to do so might be to provide protection service, though we do not quite see it happen, granted, it is alleged verbally, remaining an active if elusive factor within the story. Our challenge is to assess carefully and productively this prominence of an unverified motif. To put it in terms of the dominant narrative rather in the short-range purposes of this story: How is Nabal-the-Saul not only dependent upon the David but also indebted, owing him in some way?

For the *plan formulated*, we listen to the David, who sends men to request payment from Nabal-the-Saul for services claimed as rendered. The language sent from the David to Nabal-the-Saul is courteous at the surface, urging him to consult his own men about the contested claim, asking remuneration for "son David" (vv. 2–8). The bill is presented respectfully enough, as we hear David instruct his messengers (vv. 5–9). The narrator offers us the directions and summarizes the

86. Bodner, *1 Samuel*, 258–59, says this note comes only once Saul has acknowledged David's claim. I think each of Saul's acknowledgments is fleeting. Jobling notes, *1 Samuel*, 92, that Saul is indecisive but not insincere, an assessment with which I agree.

87. Scholars are split on this, resolving this major gap variously. For example, Biddle maintains, by intertextuality and analogy, that David resembles Laban of Genesis and is thus unjust in what he claims of Nabal ("Ancestral Motifs," 624); a contrary view is expressed by Mary Shields, "A Feast Fit for a King: Food and Drink in the Abigail Story," in Tod Linafelt et al., eds., *The Fate of King David: The Past and Present of a Biblical Icon*, (New York and London: T&T Clark, 2010), 39 within 38–54, who states unequivocally that he is running a protection racket.

implementation, but we hear another witness verify—or testify—that the request was a reasonable and just one (vv. 14–16). Without providing absolute clarity, the plotting inclines us toward crediting the David rather than Nabal-the-Saul.

When that message is delivered to him in summary by the David's men, Nabal-the-Saul answers rudely, dismissively, insultingly, denying the David any claim on his resources; the David's men bring back this news, the moment again summarized by the narrator rather than replayed by the narrator (vv. 9–12). Since we, reading, cannot actually verify crucial narrative facts, we need to note the disagreement and where it roots. Nabal-the-Saul's words (vv. 10–11) raise issues we have heard before, and of course from Saul: Who is David, son of Jesse, and what is he to me? On the run? What do I owe him of my heritage? The response seems to assume that, justice aside, the Nabal character can in fact accomplish his goal, which is to hang on to what is his without surrendering any of it to the David. Nabal's *plan executed* is simply to resist paying the bill presented, to avoid a dispreferred situation.

The *plan executed* by the David now moves into its next phase. He shows every sign of being determined to collect on what he feels is owed, even at the cost of the lives of every male in Nabal's household (vv. 12–13 and 21–22). He arms and moves toward Nabal-the-Saul with four hundred men, leaving two hundred to guard the gear (v. 13)—aggressive pursuit. The narrator is toggling the scenes here, so that we can watch the impact on various characters. The plan of the David to execute a whole household is what we saw Saul do in ch. 22. The roles of these protagonists are reversed from what we have been watching—scrambled, dreamlike.

If Nabal-the-Saul does not have a survival *plan formulated and executed*, his household provides it for him, as we are made privy to another scene happening simultaneously. One of Nabal's men relates to his master's wife, Abigail, whom I will also call "the-Jonathan," his version of what has happened. The young man testifies clearly that what the David and his men claimed from Nabal-the-Saul is justified, due, and owed. We may note that this is our only verification of the matter, and we can weight the word of the servant as seems best (vv. 14–17).[88]

The next *plan formulated and executed* is Abigail-the-Jonathan's, who moves to pay the outstanding claim, generously, with no sign of feeling it diminishes the household. She assembles, with the servant's help, goods from the storeroom and moves them toward the David, without telling her husband (vv. 18–20). Having heard about the problem, Abigail-the-Jonathan moves to pay what her husband has withheld, offering perhaps more than has been owed—though it is difficult to tell[89]—moving it all toward the David, who is galloping with hostile intent toward them all (vv. 18–20). That the response of Nabal-the-Saul to the presence and demand of the David has endangered the household, and that he seems not to care

---

88. This, like the matter of what the priest of Nob did and did not do, is undecidable. Scholars have various views on it, which are valuable for serving to indicate how the interpreter is assuming, supposing, and reasoning.

89. The question under negotiation in the story is what *is* owed of Saul's goods to David.

about their situation (v. 17) seem noteworthy. Thus the onus of harm to befall the household is placed on the owner, not on others.

As the two opponents converge more closely—thanks to the moves of the one—we are given access to the David's language and hear him restate his grievance: "'It was all for nothing that I guarded the man's possessions in the wilderness, that nothing he owned is missing, while he paid me back evil for good. May God to thus and so to him, and more, if by morning I spare a single male of his people'" (vv. 21–22). Intercepting the David en route to destroy Nabal-the-Saul—the aggressor mouthing curses and reviewing injustices as he goes—Abigail-the-Jonathan takes responsibility for paying what the David claims and Nabal-the-Saul refuses, taking the responsibility on herself and blaming her husband as well (vv. 23–25). The meeting of the David and Abigail-the-Jonathan is presented to us, with her bowing before the David, claiming some responsibility or solidarity verbally while also seeking to mitigate consequences looming. She distances herself from her husband in most unlikely language (were we hearing realistic speech of a wife to another regarding a husband), maintaining that she has not been part of the unjust transaction, and claiming that the most important request she makes is that the David refrain from shedding the blood of Nabal-the-Saul. She offers the goods she has taken from their household as due the David, and begs God to provide the David an enduring house (vv. 23–27).

Her next words and in fact the David's response trouble commentators (vv. 29–34), who tend to find them objectionable for one reason or another.[90] But what Abigail-the-Jonathan says to the David is that his life is bound up in the bundle of life dear to YHWH and that the David's opponents will not prevail against such care, recalling perhaps words exchanged between David and Jonathan in chs. 20 and 23. The David's pursuers will not succeed in what they attempt, however the situation may appear, and Abigail-the-Jonathan begs a place with the David when God will have accomplished God's purposes. But the David must also take care not to shed blood needlessly by taking into his own hands what is God's care. The David blesses his benefactor, crediting that actant with staying David's hand from injustice. The David accepts the largesse and promises well-being to Abigail-the-Jonathan, who returns to the side of Nabal-the-Saul (v. 35), after matching her language to the David, imploring him to avoid the sin of bloodguilt which he has come close to doing (vv. 26–31). Her talk is of the importance of David resisting to kill a man who may—or may not—deserve retribution. Her rhetorical strategy moves to stress God's role in preserving David from killing a whole household. She insists that the blame fall on her, that David has more at stake than his quarrel with Nabal-the-Saul, and that when God shall establish a house for the David—will have made David prince over Israel—it will not be at the price of this particular bloodshed.

---

90. Useful is the analysis of Ellen van Wolde, "A Leader Led by a Lady: David and Abigail in 1 Samuel 25," *ZAW* 114 (2002): 355–75; she speaks of the language working at two levels as she discusses this portion of the chapter (362–67).

The passage is much commented upon, and for many reasons. Here, we can note that it ranges toward topics clearly related to David's larger and farther-off plans. In effect, since we are dealing with the process of plotting, with Abigail reminding the David (and us) that his objectives and goals are larger than retaliating, perhaps unjustly or dishonorably—it remains uncertain—against one man by destroying a whole household. Whatever may be owed by the master to the David, the whole household must not die of it. She remarks, enigmatically, that without David's own intervention, his enemies will be slung as from a sling while the David will be bound in a bundle in the care of God. Commentators are not too pleased with David's verbal response (vv. 32–34), again, for various reasons. But what he in fact says, directly, is that she has indeed restrained him from what he was about to do, and that it would have involved bloodguilt. That, I think, is key, whether the manner is the death of the one or the many. So the David abandons his plans of reprisal and settles for his first objective: to gain goods for his people. Additionally, he gains a wife (vv. 39–44), having lost Michal through what Saul chose to do. He has also, outside our knowing how, gained Ahinoam of Jezreel, most obviously Saul's wife and the mother of his children. In terms of plotting, an heir for David is the concern of multiple planners, and as Michal is subtracted, others are added who might assist.

The story is not yet complete, since Nabal-the-Saul still lives, even though the David is in the midst of taking his goods from him: food, men, spouse, honor. Abigail returns to the household from which she had departed and finds its leader drunk and feasting like a king (the narrator nudges us). Plotting shifts to the question of what to do about Nabal-the-Saul. Who has a plot for his removal? The implied author, the narrator, the David and Abigail-the-Jonathan—perhaps even the man himself—all have an interest here, Abigail not least by asking David to remember her when he should have come into his kingdom (v. 31). Abigail defers her news briefly, so that when next morning she tells her husband "these things," his heart dies within him (vv. 36–37).[91] "About ten days later the Lord struck him and he died," the narrator reports (vv. 36–38), unreliably, I maintain, in the modern and technical sense of that term:[92] deliberately offering us a perspective at odds with the overall shape of the implied author's work. My point here is that everything we are offered about the Nabal-the-Saul suggests that he dies of his own massive, persistent, and determined "heart trouble."

91. For a major study on these Nabal motifs, especially his heart troubles, see Marjorie O'Rourke Boyle, "The Law of the Heart: The Death of a Fool (1 Samuel 25)," *JBL* 120.3 (2001): 401–27, where she sees Nabal as suffering the fate of Moses's Pharaoh.

92. As we will explore in the next chapter, the narrator can be called "unreliable" when his specific information is at odds with the rest of what is provided. To credit the death of this character to "struck by Yahweh" disregards a good deal of information about the link between the manner of his life and his death. But what is rehearsed in this comment is the language we have in David's mouth as he ruminates on the fate of Saul in 26:10: It is one of the possibilities that David names as alternative to his own temptation to slay Saul, and not, of course, the one that will eventually happen.

The news goes to the David, who blesses God and marries Abigail (vv. 39–40). Thus is a whole set of *outcomes narrated*: the David saved from guilt with his justice claim satisfied; Abigail-the-Jonathan performing a crucial set of services for David, her life and progeny now intertwined with his; Nabal-the-Saul, unable to manage realities, learning what has happened to his goods at the hands of his own people, is dead. God is credited as active, by Abigail, by David, by the narrator (vv. 39–44). The narrator informs us, wrapping the chapter in real time as it was opened (25:1, 43–44), that David now has two wives: Abigail, Ahinoam of Jezreel, and that Michal had been given to another man. As has been well discussed, the only Ahinoam in the Bible is Saul's wife.[93]

It seems difficult to miss that it rehearses the key issues shared among Saul and his household (in their various roles) and David and his followers. The issue to be settled—rehearsed in strange space among characters and for readers—is not any longer how to resolve matters between Saul and David such that the pursuit ends, but how Saul will be removed. The blame misses being on David directly—a pattern to repeat in the material ahead (at least until the death of Uriah). If we, reading, feel that the David is innocent of Nabal's death, we may reconsider later. It seems to have become moot to learn definitively whether the claims presented to Nabal are just or not, whether the David is justified to request resources from Nabal's goods or not. If the David extorted from Nabal, the whole episode reads differently. If we saw Saul removed from kingship by the end of ch. 15 and his dynasty "fired" prior to that (13:14), the question before us was: How will Saul terminate? If we saw David anointed in ch. 16, our question was when and under what circumstances will David take the throne? That we know the general coordinates of the story does not excuse us from thinking about the specific and intricate plotting of it. The dialogue between David and Abigail (25:24–34) has made manifest that there are justice issues to mind, whether we think we have seen them in the story of David and Saul or not. Now, with one episode of pursuit to examine, we draw close to the heart of what has been explored in this long set of material from chs. 19 to 26.

In this present study, suggesting that David is shown as gaining ethical texture as he grows agency, the playing out of his choices since ch. 21 and up to ch. 26 seems clear. David's persistent objective is primarily reactive: to escape Saul's reach, especially when it seems lethal, from where Saul interprets the women's song (18:8) and at various moments thereafter. As David first moves out of range, his plans are not skillful, endangering others besides himself, indeed, far worse than himself. Saul's willingness to kill seems manifest—though we must not lose sight of the fact that it never happens, despite multiple opportunities. As David makes fresh decisions, named geographically, we may infer that he is learning what is needed, and by the time we get to chs. 23 and 24, especially when David has a priest with an ephod, David is skilled at eluding Saul. When David shifts from

93. Jon D. Levenson, "1 Samuel 25 as Literature and History," *CBQ* 40 (1978): 11–28. Jobling, *1 Samuel*, 123, also reminds us that Nathan's words in 2 Samuel 12:8 speak of "your master's wife into your own bosom," so Bodner *1 Samuel*, 272–73.

tracked to tracker—or better, when he is able to both be tracked and to track—he asserts his innocence to Saul, who appears to believe him, or at any rate, to verbally acquiesce. The goal is to end the pursuit, given that Saul is unable to sustain a lethal effort with David. But Saul cannot break off.

But the more subtle change in chs. 24–26 is David's awareness—ours as well—of what he is coming close to doing as he and Saul intersect. In my construction here, David experiences such an encounter in ch. 24, dreams it in ch. 25, and then voices it more directly in ch. 26, to himself and to us, resulting finally in his flight to Philistia. It is a choice he has attempted clumsily at the start of the unit but will seem to work out better for him as we move ahead.

10. David withdraws from the risk of killing Saul: 26 This chapter shares a rough structure with chs. 24 and 25: Saul learns David's whereabouts and pursues him; Saul's initial advantage turns to disadvantage; David reviews options for dealing with Saul; David parries and resists the worst he might have done but not without performing an aggressive action;[94] David engages Saul in conversation; Saul concedes David's view.[95]

The transition between the previous episode involving the household of the churlish man, now dead, and Saul's pursuit of David is the usual anonymous notification to Saul that his quarry has been spotted by people loyal to the king. Saul's *initial situation* requires him to be again in receipt of information he needs to accomplish an objective, which may be named as harassing David without being capable of eliminating him. Saul is nothing if not a denier of reality, though, and so I will call his *plan* the pursuit and elimination of David as a threat, even if such a goal is not a believable plan for a (or for this) reader. *Why* Saul cannot kill David is not clear, but *that* he cannot is manifest. But we join Saul and his three thousand men closing on David, whose *situation* begins in the wilderness, surviving as best he can. David's first *plan formulated* seems to be to learn of Saul's whereabouts without being seen. So before plans develop, we, with David, see Saul and his men encamped, without their seeing him (26:1–5).

David next initiates a visit to the midst of Saul's encampment, accompanied by a witness/companion, his nephew Abishai having voiced his willingness to go. When they arrive and see Saul and his men cast into a deep sleep from God, the narrator later informs *us* (not the characters), Abishai speaks up as have others

94. Polzin, in *Samuel and the Deuteronomist*, 207, observes that David communicates with Saul by gesture as well as word.

95. Green, *Mighty Fallen*, 374–75, developed in detail on the following pages. See also the work of Klaus-Peter Adam, "Nocturnal Intrusions and Divine Interventions on Behalf of Judah. David's Wisdom and Saul's Tragedy in 1 Samuel 26," *VT* 59 (2009): 5–11, who is asking source and redaction questions, as is Steven L. McKenzie, "Elaborated Evidence for the Priority of 1 Samuel 26," *JBL* 129.3 (2010), 437–44, whose comments are interesting. A thorough study and comparison can also be read in Cynthia Edenburg, "How (Not) to Murder a King: Variations on a Theme in 1 Samuel 24; 26," *SJOT* 12. 1 (1998): 64–85. Fokkelmann, *Crossing Fates*, 530–31 and Craig, *Asking for Rhetoric*, 88–89 review structures.

before him, encouraging David once again with theological confidence: "'God has given your enemy into your hand this day; now therefore let me pin him to the earth with one stroke of the spear, and I will not strike him twice'" (v. 8). To be gazing at a sleeping Saul is God's gift to David not to be wasted.

But David indicates at least to me that he has learned something since he last saw Saul, resisting that prompt at once, lacking his prior readiness to harm first and regret later. "'Do not destroy him; for who can put forth his hand against the Lord's anointed, and be guiltless?'" (v. 9). It is a more institutional claim than we saw in ch. 24, where the issue seemed more about Saul and David personally. Here it is about anointed leaders, of whatever name. David's next rumination is, arguably, the most intimate speech we hear from him, his reflection the most exposed. He rehearses four possibilities about the elimination or expiration of Saul, which has emerged as the basic need. If Abishai's plan is not to be accomplished, what to do? David, obligingly—whether still addressing Abner or musing to himself (and for us)—names the options: "'As the Lord lives, the Lord will smite him; or his day shall come to die; or he shall go down into battle and perish. The Lord forbid that *I* should put forth *my* hand against the Lord's anointed; but now, take the spear that is at his head and the jar of water, and let us go'" (vv. 10–11, emphasis added).[96] For the reticent David, the character whose inner life we are shown so sparingly, this is revealing. David appears to appreciate in a way not manifest before the David tangled with Nabal-the-Saul that the real danger is not that Saul will kill him but that he might kill Saul.[97] To experience coming near to doing something and then be averted can be informative, salutary. In a sense, the three options are close to what happens to Saul: the Philistines kill him in battle, and Saul, out of touch in every way with God, dies of that lack/choice of his, dies asking for information and help. But that lies ahead of us. Saul, deeply asleep, has *no plans*.

One more conversation with Saul, but at a remove, seems to be what David now *executes*: His words to Saul lack the markers of respect we heard in ch. 24 as well as the language of overt threat we heard in ch. 25. In fact, David's words are addressed to Abner (whom we met briefly when David killed Goliath) rather than to Saul, suggesting that Abner has not done what he ought have done to protect the king (vv. 13–16). Saul responds, but not because he has been addressed. As the two converse about the potentially lethal removal of water bottle and weapon from

---

96. I prefer this as a rare rumination of David's, a construction reinforced when he is the one who follows his directions about taking the king's lifeline (v. 12). That Saul and his men are in a deep sleep also reinforces my choice to see the Nabal interlude as a sort of deep sleep/quasi-reverie, which of course is not its obvious label.

97. Craig, in *Asking for Rhetoric,* pays attention to this material in his ch. 6, dealing with chs. 24 and 26 but primarily 26. He suggests that once David has enunciated the options for Saul's death, he moves to bring it closer by taking items not only crucial for Saul's survival but also symbolic in the text (pp. 91–94). Of the spear, Craig says (p. 92), "a symbol in this larger story of power and death, or more to the point, the misuse of power which leads to death."

his adversary, David's tone is less conciliatory, more distant, and less courteous (vv. 14–16 to Abner, vv. 17–20 to Saul).

David also adds a second set of new content: After his familiar claim of innocence, he raises the question of whether *God* is inciting him against Saul, or whether it is a *human* temptation, and how to proceed in each instance. David decries the possibility that he will be driven from God's presence, to other gods, he says (vv. 19–20). Craig observes that David registers more feeling here over being deprived of his heritage including his deity than of being pursued by the king.[98] Here David comes as close as he will do to hinting that he is being forced from the heritage for which he was anointed. Saul, as before, repents of what he has been doing and is freshly accused of, promising new behavior (v. 21). David, not shown convinced, returns the two items so crucial for the king's safety in the wilderness and repeats his now-familiar claim: "'God delivered you into my hands but I refrained from harm, and may God do such to me'" (vv. 22–24). Saul rejoins vaguely but not much differently than before (v. 25). As we glimpse the opening verse of the next chapter, we know that David does not expect change *in Saul* but will need to remove *himself*, definitively. David repeats, for the last time, since this is his final encounter with Saul, his statement of innocence, which we may braid together with every such utterance he has shared with Saul—from wordless dodges of the royal spear to this moment. David rehearses, somewhat freshly, his situation, the one that has emerged as most urgent: Who has stirred you up against me: God or human beings? There is no response to that set of alternatives, and David does not seem to expect one, moving on, rather, to his *final plan*, or the outcome of all that has happened: He must move safely out of range of Saul, in both senses of the phrase, lest he lose his heritage with God (vv. 19–20). Saul blesses David, perhaps recalling the blind Eli misreading the prayer of Hannah but blessing it ineffectually. *Outcome narrated*: David goes his way, back to Achish of Gath. Saul returns to his palace, with his death nearby.

4 Implications and Transition

We can draw some conclusions here, both in terms of method and content, as we prepare to move on. For method, five points: First, given the basically simple and repeating plot objective presented, the simple structure used is adequate to lay bare the dynamics between Saul and David. The more complex grid offered by Kafalenos with its capacity to explore plotting from more than one point of view may become useful but is not needed here. Second, the story/discourse distinction reminds us to stay alert to plotting within the story and that is offered and available over the heads of characters, since considering each is crucial. Third, the image of

---

98. Craig, *Asking for Rhetoric*, 101–02. That is, he is upset over it, even though we, reading, may not quite understand what he is saying—which I suggest is more about his future than about his past and more about space than worship.

tangling strings of character plotting, each character generating a knotted string that engages the plans of others, is useful for offering complexity of plotting, prompting us to look for snarls where plans intersect and conflict. Fourth, the matter of gaps: which to work with and why, with those offering possibilities for causality seeming the most crucial. Gaps and ambiguities remain what they are, even when we, reading, seek to interpret them. Fifth, the odd genre-shift represented by ch. 25 is the most galvanizing scene of the set, catalyzing change.

In terms of content, five key factors also emerge: First, the persistent events of this whole unit make evident that David's strength is waxing as Saul's wanes. The pursued and pursuer change positions, shift power. Second, a step in David's journey toward responsible and perhaps compassionate agency is his recognizing that "the problem" is not simply Saul's hostility but his own. David's owning this moment and choosing to refuse harm is important (26:11). As the recipient of much help from others, David may be positioned to ponder how he can offer some forbearance, if not more. Third, David's reverie on the removal of Saul reopens and refocuses the question of what God wants and will accomplish. We, reading, must consider this point at the story level, as those acting within the story struggle to discern what God will further with their information. David has been anointed, but by the end of the material just considered, he can be understood to have wondered about how his royal future will unfold. Fourth, the re-presenting of David's hostility toward Saul in ch. 25, viewed as an unmasking and escalation of the dynamics of previous scenes of pursuit, reveals the extent to which the drive to exact vengeance may consume the players. The intensity of David's hostility toward his opponent and all his household, unmatched by anything seen previously, seems—granted, outside our witnessing his moment of insight—to have shifted his consciousness, such that he makes a fresh decision: to avoid the occasion of Saulide pursuit. But the potential for disregard of others stands out starkly. Finally, fifth, we need to add the occasions of God-language that striate the material we have just read: oaths and promises exchanged among characters, the powerful if transitory functioning of the ephod, the asseverations of Saul and David and supporters, the spirits attending the two principals, and the events of ch. 25. All these testify to God's hand guiding David to refrain from harm, if not more. In terms of compassion and David's capacities, we have seen him more the object of graciousness than the giver of it. Jonathan's gifts to David, from the clothing he bestows to the selfless intervening we see in "Abigail-the-Jonathan," offer David the experience of putting the good of another ahead of one's own immediate interests. David is shown to suffer pursuit at the hands of Saul and to receive graciousness from Saul's family—not least given his life by his wife Michal who lowers him to freedom to her own cost—an experience that we may hope to see blossom in David.

We turn, now to another set of material where David comes closer to kingship, and to consider the role of the narrator.

Chapter 4

PRESENCE AND ABSENCE: DAVID AND THE DEATH OF SAUL: (1 SAM. 27–2 SAM. 1)

THE NARRATOR

1 Transition

In the material just examined, our focus was primarily on processes of plotting, with all the complexity implied and involved. Of the seven tools we are working with, only characterization will ask us to consider so many collaborative factors. We also continued to benefit from noticing structure and to remain aware of all the mysteries in our story generated by the uncertainty of its edges, specifically where in the long narrative in which it is embedded the story of David fits, how it is arranged. In the chapter just concluded, we recognized the unit of chs. 19–26 as comprising ten variations on risks escalating when David and Saul were in mutual pursuit of and proximity to each other. There are other ways to manage the material, but the choice here was to see and show that particular disequilibrium enacted and explored repeatedly, with sameness and variety playing together, eventually allowing a fresh situation to emerge. At the start of the material, David faced danger at court, planned by Saul. Despite early efforts to resolve the hostility, it became evident that David needed to move out of Saul's range, which happened, slowly and by degrees, leading to the scenes of pursuit within a geographically broad area. Without losing the consistency of proximity as the problem, we came to consider how the urgent source of danger lay with David, who risked drawing nearer the killing of Saul, rather than Saul becoming adept at endangering David—which seemed more likely at the start of the unit—hence David's move into Philistine territory, which is the prime venue of the present set of material.

We most usefully considered plot and plotting at the distinct though not wholly separable levels of story and discourse: desires and events managed within the story by characters, choices, and actions as plotted by the implied author and disclosed by the narrator. These diverse patterns of plotting emerged both distinct from and tangled with each other. The key plot-generators are and remain David and Saul though the deity as well, working at a different level, but still within the story. The two humans remain opponents in the material ahead, but they cease to relate specifically with each other. David's plot strings cross with those of other characters. How God is involved—working to assist and to thwart whom—remains to be seen. If the implied authorial plotting seemed basically simple in the past material—one theme with ten variations—we will have more variety and subtlety here, with the narrator charged to tell us what we most need to consider. We will continue to examine the issues of chronology, contiguity, and causality, suggesting rather than pronouncing, leaving readers plenty of space for interpreting and revising.

The narrative unit considered in this present chapter is arranged in a different way from our last set, closer to the unit presented in 1 Samuel 21 and 22, where the implied author and narrator presented two intersecting tracks of plot and narration, following first David as he fled to the shrine at Nob and thence to Gath, where, realizing he would not be safe, he moved farther afield. Saul's chief shepherd Doeg, witnessing the encounter between Ahimelech, priest of Nob, and David, reported his information back to Saul at Gibeah, joining the planning efforts of David and Saul, while allowing David to move around in the southern area while Saul disposed of the priests of Nob whom he judged to have betrayed him. That the lone survivor of Saul's retaliation against the priests—set off by some action of the priest Ahimelech—fled to David ties together the two plot lines. The narrating of simultaneous scenes is not the usual choice of biblical prose, which prefers to manage one scene at a time. In the present material, we will watch the careful narrating of simultaneous scenes once again, attending to how the narrator provides information for us, and why.

Our present challenge is to talk in more detail about the narrator's role and skill, to demonstrate that facet of narration as we look at material from 1 Samuel 27 to 2 Samuel 1. Our tools of plotting will be featured as well, specifically the narrator's capacity to "tile" or overlap two crucial episodes involving King Saul's last days with four scenes showing David to be elsewhere. The point to be suggested and explored here is that and how the narrator shows David as absent in both positive and negative ways. David is not present when Saul dies and is hence innocent of participating in that event. But simultaneously entangled is the accumulating portraiture that shows David both demonstrating increasing agency and simultaneously claiming an alibi, refusing presence, a set of omissions that lead to harm for himself and others. David's capacity to use his agency for harm and for good is also demonstrated, strange blend though it may seem to be.

2 Theory: The Narrator

Though we have not talked in much detail about the narrator, we have already set into place at least two basic pieces of information now to be developed for more precise work. First, we established the case, at least with this ancient and somewhat anthological narrative, for distinguishing among an actual author, an implied author, and a narrator. Though the narrator is the creation of the implied author—who is generated by an actual author—their roles and tasks are distinct, with the narrator being the voice that narrates in a clear and orderly way what happens. In the David narrative, the narrator is simpler than the entity developing in literary theory from classic times up to the present. The theory explicating fully the nature, functions, and effects of the narrator globally in general literature is more complex than we need for our particular material, though informative for our simpler discussion.[1] Also, second, established as generally useful without being pushed beyond a certain point is the distinction between story events, occurring within the narrative and known to at least some characters some of the time, and discourse events, disclosed to the reader specifically by the narrator and, as such, not known by characters. That is, though there are other possible ways to manage this point, for present purposes the narrator is not a character, not a story actant, but a discourse presence. That the narrator also frequently delegates the task of narrating to characters within the story does not alter the stance taken here.[2]

A chart assembled from the facets of the narrator pertinent for the narrative we are considering presently will allow us to ponder the workings of our narrator in the more than one hundred verses we have here, not rigidly or inevitably but flexibly as the narrator's moves vary from moment to moment. Though certain patterns and preferences will become visible, to observe carefully what the narrator does at each moment will repay effort. As already noted, the narrator's basic role is to tell (as distinct from showing more comprehensively and subtly), providing information, interpretation, and evaluation in one way or another.[3] That means, at a practical level, we can underline the narrator's language, something not possible

1. Full discussions of the narrator role can be found in Abbott, *Cambridge Introduction*, 67–91; Herman and Vervaeck, *Handbook*, 14–19 and 80–91; Keen, *Narrative Form*, 31–44 and 103–13; David Herman et al., *Narrative Theory: Core Concepts and Critical Debates* (Columbus: Ohio State University Press, 2012), 29–37; Nelles, *Frameworks*, 45–73.

2. It is worth recalling that to isolate even temporarily these narrative features is artificial, since they are wholly embedded in each other. When we talk about the narrator, as here, we are also implicitly talking of the other authoring processes as well as of reading, and we are talking about all the features of narration, for example, plot, character, as we line up what the narrator does.

3. Herman and Vervaeck, *Handbook*, 34. Phelan and Rabinowitz, "Authors, Narrators, Narration" in *Narrative Theory*, 29, characterize the narrator as neither single nor stable, which is a helpful cue to us even with our comparatively simple narrator, reminding us to flush out and question our operative assumptions. I find it more useful to maintain a single identity for the David narrator, while possessing a wide range of strategies.

when we are talking about the contributions of the implied author. Beyond that point, consider a set of choices:[4]

— type of narrator (will remain fixed):
  – by position, we have an extradiegetic narrator, not one appearing as a character within the narrative (who would be intradiegetic);
  – by involvement, the basic choices are homodiegetic or heterodiegetic, referring to the "overlap" between narrator and narrative, to apparent familiarity the narrator has with the world of the narrative; our narrator appears homodiegetic, familiar with what is narrated and not calling attention to gaps of experience;

— properties of the narrator:
  – status and authority: the David narrator's status is high, not really questioned; we might use the word "omniscient" here, taking care that we do not import a divine quality to our understanding as can happen in discussion of biblical texts; our narrator is presumed to be quite fully in the know, which does not determine how much or how little he may choose to disclose to us;
  – visibility, ranging from overt to covert: rarely does this narrator call attention to his own presence, which makes him primarily but not exclusively covert;

— basic tasks: report, interpret, evaluate;[5]

— other factors, strategies, varying from moment to moment, as the narrator manages different characters and situations with diverse effect:
  – adequacy: quantity of information provided in relation to what might be wanted; this varies with characters, as has already been noted;
  – reliability: except for rare circumstances signaling some reason to question it, the narrator here is reliable;[6]

---

4. Again, overlap is unavoidable, but I chose to set up more criteria than fewer so that we can notice as carefully as possible how the narrator proceeds. The basic portion of this grid came from Herman and Vervaeck, *Handbook*, 80–91, with some features subtracted and others filled in. Omitted, for the moment, is the matter of focalization and point of view, which will be added as we move eventually to characterization, where it is most pertinent.

5. Phelan and Rabinowitz, "Authors, Narrators, Narration," in Herman et al., eds., *Narrative Theory*, 39.

6. The matter of narrator reliability is a modern issue and so not so readily useful for classic narratives. The issue is not whether the narrating voice makes a mistake (which would be a deep can of worms in biblical material) but the circumstances under which we may make a case for the narrator to transgress what the implied author has established. See Amit, *Reading Biblical Narratives*, 93–102, though I am not happy with her example. Consult as well Amit, "'The Glory of Israel Does Not Deceive or Change His Mind': On

- time issues: where sequential chronology is transgressed in some direction, whether by flashbacks, flash-forwards, or some other metalepsis;
- space: stance from which information is provided; the narrator stands closer to some characters than to others, an unevenness that has effects;
- attitude: how invested the narrator is in the events related;
- mode of presentation: more inclined to show (mimesis) or to tell (diegesis).

This set of possibilities helps us track our narrator moves and mark our assessment of them.

3 Narrating the Events Common to David and Saul

Roughly half of the material (three chapters: 27 [actually also including 28:1–2], 29 and 30) in our present set involves the time David spent in the company or employ of the Philistine king, Achish of Gath, leaving the other half (chs. 28, 31, and 2 Samuel 1) to take up the final events of Saul's life, with the last of these involving David as well. As already suggested, we have reasonably clear edges here, a useful general structure provided by Fokkelman,[7] plot strings, and narrative, all enabling us to proceed fruitfully here.

I suggest that the narrator, the voice relating those events artistically, has two challenges to shape or problems to solve, both arising from the set of material we just examined, where the danger is propinquity of Saul and David, with the risk of harm-doing moving from Saul to David. Now comes the occasion for the artistry (implied authorial, narratorial, and readerly) to show David as both narrowly escaping the act of killing Saul, while at the same time failing to manifest integrity in some basic way.[8] The narrative challenge is to do both of those things simultaneously, intertwined. I will suggest how these two

the Reliability of Narrator and Speakers in Biblical Narrative," *Prooftexts* 12.3 (1992): 201–12.

7. Though the plan will shortly become more complicated, Fokkelman maps this as an act, split between David as a Philistine vassal (chs. 27, 29, 30) and Saul's demise (28:3–25, 31, 2 Samuel 1). Refer to the whole structure provided above, pp. 48–51, where this is called act six.

8. For two studies of the material offer useful perspective on strategies, without either arguing exactly what I want to show or using narrative tools to the extent I am doing: Walter Brueggemann, "Narrative Intentionality in 1 Samuel 29," *JSOT* 43 (1989): 21–35, and Yael Shemesh, "David in the Service of King Achish of Gath: Renegade to His People or a Fifth Column in the Philistine Army?" *VT* 57 (2007): 73–90.

interlinked tasks are done globally in the six chapters before moving to a closer look at the episodes.

a Edges, Structures, Plots, Narration

Fokkelman's basic structure for this particular set of material, generally affirmed by Firth, is marked by David's exits from engagement with Saul, first by leaving the region where they are likely to interact, and finally as David eulogizes Saul and Jonathan (27:1, 2 Sam. 1:27).[9] But he shows as well a deeper artistry behind that simple structure by demonstrating with two triangles that Saul has basically two events (28 and 31), each of which is surrounded by a pair of David-events (27 and 29 attend 28; 30 and 1 attend 31).[10] That more intricate structure is the one most useful for exploring the material. Fokkelman has also provided a chronology and itinerary—a timeline and mapping—for the story events, showing precise correlation between the David-events and the Saul-events and including Philistine and Amalekite moves,[11] which I will try to offer as clearly as possible. There he demonstrates how the key intersecting story events explicitly cover eleven common days, shared by all the players, making clear how each was occupied temporally and spatially in relation to the other as well as in terms of plot. The large and clearest point established is that David is not geographically present when Saul dies. Since the temporal notations are provided explicitly by narrator language, we can explore them here while we are coming to know the narrator better, without worrying about how they are also the implied author's planning and artistry.[12]

In chart form the information looks like this:

9. David G. Firth, "The Accession Narrative (1 Samuel 27–2 Samuel 1)," *Tyndale Bulletin* 58.1 (2007): 61–83, discusses the unit's general features well, referring us to Fokkelman's work (which we will pick up in a later edition than Firth notes), calling attention to the unusual hypotactic nature of it (rather than paratactic), where the material is correlated with other material rather than moving along in a more straightforward way (68–69); Firth also calls it tiled, in the manner of tiles being overlapped rather than having their edges meet sequentially. Brueggemann wants to consider 2 Samuel 1–4 as part of the unit ("Intentionality," 22–24).

10. Jan Fokkelman, "The Samuel-Composition as a Book of Life and Death," in A. Graeme Auld and Erik Eynikel, eds., *For and Against David: Story and History in the Books of Samuel* (Leuven: Uitgeverij Peeters, 2010), 15–46 (16).

11. Fokkelman, "Samuel-Composition," 15–46. The chart (which I have tried to clarify) comes from *Crossing Fates*, 594.

12. Indeed, Firth, "Accession Narrative," 75–80 shows intertextual links between this material and other narrative, and Fokkelman points out numerous other links implicit in his material (*passim*).

11	days for David	for Amalek (sg/pl)	for Philistines	for Saul
1.	28:1–3, 12	30:13	28:1,4	28:3
	marches north	start raid	assemble at Aphek	sees, fears
2.	(marching)	raid		
3.	(marching)			
	arrives at Aphek			
4.	29:2,11	30:1	29:1,11	
	refused	plunder Ziklag	muster to march	
5.	marches south			
6.	(marching)			
7.	30:1–3, 9		28:5	28:5
	arrives Ziklag			visit at Endor
	begins pursuit			
8.	30:17		31	31
	attacks Amalek	attacked by David	attack Saul	dies
		one with Saul		
9.	30:26		31:10	31:10
	back at Ziklag	he starts south	plunder bodies	hanged at Beth Shan
10.	at Ziklag	moving south		
11.	1:2	1:2 arrives		31:12
	kills Amalekite	killed	lose Saul	body rescued.

To try to present that information once more so as to bring out certain additional points, we can manage the four itineraries: *David* departs Ziklag to join the Philistine coalition on day one and arrives on day four; rejected by the Philistines, he reverses back to Ziklag, arriving on day seven to discover his city raided and moves in pursuit; he finds and attacks the Amalekites on day eight and returns to Ziklag on day nine, where the lone Amalekite joins him on day eleven, to be killed. The *Philistines* are gathering and reject David on day four; they move toward Gilboa and kill Saul on day eight, returning on day nine to plunder the bodies and mount corpses on the city wall, from where they lose them on day eleven. The *Amalekites* raid Ziklag between day one and day four and are pursued, engaged, and defeated by David on day eight; on that same day a single Amalekite is with Saul on Gilboa and leaves, traveling three days to return to Ziglag on day eleven, when he is killed. *Saul* has several days to see the Philistines gathering and fear them, and on day seven he consults the medium, dies on day eight, is plundered on day nine, and his body is displayed at Beth Shan, though rescued and buried on day eleven. Though this summary is slightly more definite than the narrative, it generally holds up, sufficient to demonstrate that David is in the far south when Saul is killed in the north. The first part of my point about the narrator's dual characterization of David is made clear simply in terms of time and space, though in other ways too, as will be suggested by the close reading: David is not present when Saul dies. But simultaneously, there is more, other: deceit, dissimulation, disrespect, violence.

b Narration: Shadow to be Demonstrated

The second issue is a shadow to the first, since the narrator wants, as I construe it, to show David deficient as well as proficient, to suggest how in the several obvious ways Saul fails, David mimics him, subtly. The best way to name this quality suitably is to borrow language from Russian theorist and literary scholar Mikhail Bakhtin, who coined the term "alibi in Being." To live with an "alibi in Being" means for Bakhtin to live elsewhere from where in fact one is situated, to be a pretender.[13] It is a choice to avoid responsibility or answerability for living integrally by claiming an *alibi*, to have been *elsewhere* than at the place where one is required to be, with those terms understood as including more than space. Hence it is a deeply ethical concept, not simply a physical one. The present set of material shows David absent in the positive sense of not at Mount Gilboa when Saul dies. But we will also watch David shown to "alibi" in a negative sense, refusing appropriate presence when he might well have done so. This trait is suggested in several ways, each distinctive, but adding up to what we can call David's shadow, a shape that will grow more pronounced once he becomes king. His shadow emerges in moments or situations where David is shown to resemble Saul at his most deficient, as well as when David undertakes negative deeds proper to himself. Saul's flaws, which David has heretofore little manifested, begin to emerge as he comes closer to assuming his royal status and identity, since they are faults in monarchy itself, not simply in one man or another.[14] The two characters are, of course, drawn quite different from each other, but they share the lethal royal heritage. Hence at this very crucial moment of our story, David simultaneously succeeds and fails, neither for the first time nor for the last.

Before proceeding, we can also anticipate by naming them some of this narrator's default and most obvious characteristics, both to initiate and sample that discussion. These have been placed on the narrator chart (above) and discussed briefly there. As already suggested, our narrator is basically *extradiegetic* and *homodiegetic, authoritative* and *covert,* rarely "breaking frame" to call attention to himself by adding some extraneous note, such as he does at 27:6, 30:27, and 31:7, where a current-to-recital custom is explained from a past decision of David. In terms of jobs most consistently performed, our narrator surely *relates*, often if subtly *interprets*, occasionally *evaluates*—these changes of pace prompting readers' ingenuity to discern strategy by naming the impacts. Among preferred strategies: The *adequacy* of narration varies. We have already noted both the difference in

13. Gary Saul Morson and Caryl Emerson, *Mikhail Bakhtin: Creation of a Prosaics* (Stanford: Stanford University Press, 1990), 451.

14. In Green, *Mighty Fallen*, one of my main points was to demonstrate that and how Saul epitomizes kingship, is more than a human character. For that argument, too complex to be reproduced here, consult 55–115.

displaying the inner lives of Saul and David and the matter of David's wife, Ahinoam of Jezreel, who provocatively shares a name with Saul's spouse. The narrator is generally *omniscient*, in the sense that there appears no limit on what can be told, however restricted inadequate we, reading, may find it. Among the most "visibly missing" information are the circumstances of how Ahinoam of Jezreel came to be David's wife and why Saul's wife is so absent from the narrative where other family members are so active. The few occasions of narrator unreliability must each be argued, with the main one so far being the cause of the death of Nabal.

The *time-linked* character of the material has already been sampled, the narrator's choice to proceed achronically. In terms of *space/distance*, we can observe substantial unevenness: The narrator makes diverse choices in terms of how close he stands to various characters, how much is shared. We hear more intimate reflection from Saul and more than we usually have from David. Other characters, even apparently important ones, do not have their perceptions and feelings noted. On occasion, even when a character appears to receive narratorial attention, we remain uninformed about basic perceptions. Achish of Gath receives considerable discourse, comparatively speaking, though we may not feel quite sure he is as credulous as he seems. The deity is also absent here, with the exception of one utterance. The *attitude* of the narrator to characters will vary, sometimes surprisingly. It is my view that the narrator respects Saul in some fundamental ways, his many problems notwithstanding, a status not provided to Joab, surely not to Amnon. The proportion of *mimesis to diegesis* is uneven, with some scenes vividly shown (e.g., Saul and the necromancer, David and the Amalekite) and others simply given a bare-bones recital (the raid of Ziklag by Amalekites). These points will be ramified and exploited below.

4 Reading the Narrator's Skill

a David's Storyline: Time with the Philistines as Saul Grows More Fearful: chs. 27–29

In the interests of staying focused on David even as Saul is more focally featured (as in chs. 28 and 31), I will use Fokkelman's pair of triangles as the operative structure. So we have the first: David's actions (chs. 27 and 29) on either side of Saul's "first" last event (ch. 28). Here, reading more closely, we will continue to comment on narrator moves, to consolidate the impact of David's "positive absence" while detailing more closely his negative absence, tendency to alibi.

1. David with Achish of Gath: 27:1–28:2 Since this chapter is short and revealing, we will begin by naming the narrator moves in the twelve verses offered. In v. 1 we are offered David's own rumination, provided in the direct discourse of self-talk, such as has been more characteristic of the narrator's presentation of Saul. In v. 2, we are shown the outcome of David's decision, the rather global announcement that he and a large group will cross into the patronage of Achish of Gath, with only two of his companions named (v. 3), one not identified as fully as she might have been. Next, so briefly and with no explicative comment, the narrator informs us that Saul's long-running pursuit of David is broken off, permanently (v. 4). Given the long run royal pursuit had in the previous section of material, this is an abrupt and not very adequate datum. David is next given direct discourse with Achish, making a request for his own city while buttressing it with a question (v. 5), to which Achish concedes wordlessly (v. 6); the narrator breaks frame to reveal that in later times, lying outside the story, the city Ziklag belongs to the kings of Judah (v. 6) and to sum up the total of time David lived in Philistine land (v. 7). In the next two verses (8–9) the narrator summarizes David's actual activity—raids against local populations and complete slaughters of those groups. But next (v. 10) a query of Achish into David's actions is met with false information from David. The narrator names the discrepancy between what is true and what David claims, allowing David private discourse to reveal his motive: the reports of any survivors would be damaging (v. 11). Finally, the private thought of Achish reveals that he draws another conclusion from what he has been told: that David's raids into his own land will earn him the disapproval of his own people, with the result that David will have to remain with Achish. A final exchange between these two allies/adversaries (28:1–2) is offered as Achish voices to David what he has just concluded to himself: that David is to accompany him to fight, to which David replies enigmatically. To summarize the narrator's role here is to show its capacious reach, its manifold influence on the story unfolding.

Having exposed the narrator's moves technically, we now need to go back and consider them in finer detail, both to expose the plotting and to suggest the shadow accumulating around David. Let me offer five points. First, near the end of the previous long section of Saul chasing David chasing Saul, David, ruminating on the manner of Saul's death, seemed to conclude that among the possible ways of it, David's own hand must not be responsible (26:10–11). By the episode's end and simultaneously now at the opening of the present set of material (27:1), he resolves to move out of Saul's reach and into Philistine territory, where Saul will be unlikely to venture. David's self-talk, presented by the narrator, reverts to naming the danger as coming from Saul, perhaps occasioned by the encounter between them that intervened, except that Saul was hardly a serious threat in that last scene. That is, as David's previous self-talk (26:10–11) preceded his actual encounter with Saul, his words of 27:1 follow it.[15] What David claims here, a bit surprisingly at least to me, is that the dangerous party is Saul, not himself. The discrepancy is slight, but it signals to me a tendency we will witness more often with David now, to self-exculpate, sometimes as a strategy to confound others but with some spillover to his own refusal of responsibility. Though it is not untrue that Saul has intended and enacted threats to David, he has also been shown increasingly incapable of it as occasions presented themselves, whereas David's capacities are waxing. David's first speech is "misspeech," reverting to the claim that he is endangered by Saul.

15. Bodner, *1 Samuel*, 283–85, reminds us that David's use of "swept away" re-intonates Samuel's language of 12:25, where he is talking of the dissolution of monarchy, absent basic obedience to Torah.

So David once again seeks refuge with Achish of Gath, as he did in 21:11–16. At that earlier time the move was shown ill-considered: David seems not to have anticipated that he might be recognized as the Goliath-of-Gath slayer, that as a famed Israelite fighter he might be appraised as threatening. Briefly adopting a mad-king disguise, David moved on quickly from Gath, back toward the east. But now, point two, a shrewder David will have learned something even from a mistake, and the narrator is able to imply, I think, that David's present circumstances are more dire than before—hence it makes sense to try refuge with Achish again.[16] The need to escape proximity to Saul outweighs the risks of nearness to the despised Philistines. So the situation from ch. 22 develops in temporal terms: Danger has intensified, and risks can be re-weighted, previous actions reattempted. The narrator, clearly able to report the inner thoughts of kings here, concludes the short unit by affirming that David has reasoned correctly, at least on half of the matter: Once Saul learns that David is with Achish, pursuit stops. Since we do not hear Saul's inner process, we are left to a general inference that he fears the Philistines more than he desires to chase David.

A third narrative subtlety is the narrator's note that David is accompanied by six hundred men (and their families, we understand from before and from what we will learn in ch. 30), but with the naming of only two individuals, David's wives: Ahinoam of Jezreel, whom we may recognize as the woman Saul had married and the mother of his children; and Abigail wife of Nabal, whom I have argued as an equivalent of Saul. Thus the narrator has hinted but not quite summarized: Though David has taken two of Saul's wives as his own, still Saul will not track him into Philistine territory. That David is with these two is part of his "Saul look-alike" character. We can also claim narrator reticence here, since he most conspicuously does not provide detail about Ahinoam, who is to be the mother of Amnon, David's firstborn son, and hence an important player.

Fourth, Achish's drawing in this whole "triangle" is a splendid example of narrative skill, though we can examine him as a narrator-effect on David's shadow—rather than as a character, since his role is comparatively limited in a long story that features many minor characters with more significant roles. Achish is drawn mostly through blurted remarks (27:6, 10, 12; 28:1, 2; 29:3, 6, 7, 9, 10), all suggesting either *naïveté* or disarming shrewdness. That is, Achish is a talker, with virtually no other features provided, except his basic descriptor as Philistine leader. When we met him previously in ch. 21, Achish did not appear to have recognized his refugee, in contrast with men of his court, who at once with prescient error named David as king of the land, appearing also well-informed about what was sung in Israel about Saul and David (v. 12). David, alarmed at their recognition, assumed a false demeanor, while Achish seemed unperturbed by both facets of David's identity: "'Lo, you see the man is mad; why then have you brought him to

16. Bodner, *1 Samuel*, 280–81, reports the views of some who feel, on the contrary, that David's position has been strengthened. Perhaps both insights are useful: David's danger in regard to Saul is greater, and David accompanied to Gath is stronger than David fleeing there alone.

me? Do I lack madmen, that you have brought this fellow to play the madman in my presence? Shall this fellow come into my house?'" The sparring banter made it difficult for us to appraise what Achish did know. That is, his mode of discourse makes him difficult to read definitively, a characterization the narrator sustains in the present set of material.

As David now reappears, Achish is again shown, at least at the surface, credulous. When David acts to secure Ziklag as a base for himself and his own people to inhabit (27:5-6), removed from where Achish can observe his doings closely, Achish's ready granting of it suggests that he is easily duped. The narrator's detailing the discrepancies between what David does and says and what Achish asks and learns, enhanced by the narrator's disclosure of David's deeds, gives us a third negative for David. We again have the impression that Achish seems satisfied, fooled by these claims of David, never imagining, even when David claims to be slaying Judahites, that he might be lying. The narrator intrudes a rumination or utterance of David into this moment, informing us that David leaves no survivors of these forays to bear witness—contrasting David with Saul, who was not able to slay all the humans and beasts of the Amalekites, such that witness to Saul's unsuitability to rule was made manifest to Samuel and to God (a flashback to 15:8). So while the narrator paints David as skilled and clever, Achish as clueless and duped, we also hear of David's efficiency at killing and his doing so covertly while under the patronage of a host. We have another literal alibi from David, claiming to be elsewhere than he is. Alternatively, Achish may be playing a more complex game and David building a false and misleading self-portrait, one who can kill whole populations with impunity—not true, as he learns shortly. The narrator assesses and informs us that Achish trusts David's word about his raids, counting on the harm to accrue to David's reputation and serving Achish by tying David to his side for life. Thus does Achish also come to resemble Saul, supposing that David's subaltern status is secure. Or perhaps David comes to resemble Saul, killing priests and families without pity. Perhaps both are shown. We also, arguably, see Achish dallying with David as David did with Saul when Michal was on offer, or perhaps we see David playing with this new patron king as he did with his former one.[17] Strange resemblances.

A fifth point: David's authorization for these raids is also not provided for us, whether simply from narrator reticence or because we can contrast it with further (and subsequent) consultations of the deity. Saul's primary "footprint" in his long narrative of 1 Samuel 9–31 is his refusal and/or incapacity for hearing God. Here, David seems similar. The literal "alibi-ing" we heard from Saul in regard to his Amalekite encounter makes a ghostly and shadowed encore here. David is bold where Saul was hesitant and obfuscating, but for neither is this good.

The blurtings of the king of Gath are concluded, for the moment, at 28:1–2, where we learn that a wider set of Philistines, of whom Achish is partner, is preparing to take on Saul of Israel once again. Achish's discourse emerges to

---

17. Alter, *David Story*, 171, takes Achish as suspicious of David, though he does not explain why; I do not think it is clear.

remind David that he will be part of such an expedition, to which David replies enigmatically, as has been his occasional wont: "'Very well, you shall know what your servant can do.'" Achish, again with apparent *naïveté*, concludes that David can be made bodyguard for life. The role will never be exercised, and so again, Achish appears a foolish if not mad king. David, promising something that will not come to be and alibi-ing, at least for us who know the story, speaks skillfully with Achish who seems to be missing the subtlety. But the points raised are about David's actions and his loyalty. Many commentators point out that David's deeds abetting the Philistines, the dread enemy of Saul and Israel, would not at the time be so easily excused or overlooked.[18] How do kings talk, and why? Achish would not be the last king to hear what suits him nor the last to shelter behind the choices of others, but he has one more exchange with David, to be heard shortly.

2. Saul with the necromancer and the prophet: 28:3–25 Intervening now is ch. 28, the unit so brilliantly and sympathetically featuring Saul, whose perception of massing Philistines increasingly terrifies him. With our eye here on the narrator's skill in storytelling about David, we cannot focalize Saul but must let him remain ancillary, even where he is clearly the main character.[19] Opening this unit's 23 verses (3–25) with analeptic information about the death, burial, and mourning of Samuel, the narrator joins it to the effort of Saul to gain information and the word he is given. The unit concludes with the final meal of the king's life, provided by, accepted from the woman who has helped him with perhaps the last thing he does need: strength to die well. Between those summarily narrated moments, the characters manage the central scenes of the inquiry: Saul's own voice asks his men for a necromancer; he and she share five quick exchanges; and Saul addresses a question to Samuel and is given a speech in return and falls speechless—or speechless, falls. Thus we can see that this central material is split between effective mimesis and practical diegesis.

The narrator begins with the death of Samuel, our second time to be informed of it (see 25:1). That all Israel mourns the prophet is followed by a note that Saul has proscribed all other means of access to divine information, those considered illicit in Deuteronomic law that generally underlies narrative material of the early kings. Saul has, over the length of his story, gradually lost all means of learning what God desires, and has never shown past 1 Samuel 14 any effort to consult.

---

18. Among the many discussions of these matters, those who aim to sort the literary issues include Brueggemann, "Intentionality," and Shemesh, "Fifth Column." Each distinctively manages David's intent. Shemesh is more global in asserting the many reasons why David's determination to avoid Gilboa is absolute, with any alternative unthinkable (her summary is on 79–89, none of her points seeming particularly persuasive to me); Brueggemann is more alert to nuances emerging from literary theory, though he, too, basically exonerates David from any negative charge; he privileges the threefold verdict of David's innocence offered by Achish (27), which he calls the central interest of the narrative, while recognizing that it does not solve all the problems posed by the material (28–29).

19. My appraisal of 1 Samuel 28 remains as presented in Green, *Mighty Fallen*, 434–44.

He has had to rely on human informers, who have not lacked to him but whose confided words have never sufficed for him to accomplish his objective. Saul is without access to knowing what God wants, let alone being able to do it. The king is now shown freshly fearful of what his mustering opponents may do, and he lacks the only prophet with whom we have ever seen him interact, even if much of their exchange was contentious. Shown substantially unaccustomed to other modes of legitimate inquiry, priestless and ephodless since the events of Nob, Saul gains nothing from dreams or lots. With Samuel dead—Samuel whom we have not heard with Saul since the end of ch. 15, when the prophet fired the king, and who, we infer, protected the fleeing David from the pursuing Saul in ch. 19—Saul's lack of access to God is again stressed first as diminished, then as cut off. Isolation accumulates around Saul. His thirst for information in a word-of-God drought and his fear of what he can know from what he sees drive him to the extreme of consulting illegally, though far from ineffectually.

Saul's language to the woman (starting at v. 8) shows him willing to promise her anything if only she will do what he needs, what he correctly assesses and concedes she is able to do. Intent on his lack, Saul is impatient with her fear—suggested skillfully by the narrator's close description of her reactions—desperate to get her to do what he has forbidden done within his kingdom. I hear Saul brave to name Samuel when the woman agrees to open access to the realm of the dead, when she bids him name a name (v. 11). It is difficult to imagine that even Saul can expect good news from Samuel at this point, and yet he asks, surely a mark of desperation, deftly sketched by the narrator. If we seek small, dense intimations of Saul's failure to rule, this moment—the disguised king slipping away at night to beg a skilled necromancer whom he has banished to raise YHWH's prophet to tell him what he already knows—features powerfully. We are shown that Saul manages better with the outlawed necromancer than he does with the licit means of access to God: Torah, prophet, priest, ephod, other divination means, and dreams.

Samuel, rising from the region of the dead, asserts the pointlessness of his having been disturbed, insensitive to the pathos of Saul's final request of him (v. 15). The moment is given to us with certain drama, the identity of the shade clear to us but uncertain by turns to the story participants. Consulted in death, Samuel maintains that there is no new information, only that which Saul has already refused (vv. 16–18). What Saul lacks is not so much specific data but a general familiarity with and willingness to live and lead amid the language of Torah, epitomized as the king's role in Deuteronomy 17. But Saul's illegal channel, herself able to access the dead, gains him and us basic and crucial information both old and new.[20] That another has been selected by God to replace Saul is old news, and that David is successor is known as well. New news, I allege, is that *God* has supported *David* so

---

20. If we, accustomed to the Deuteronomistic rhetoric quick to condemn any but YHWH-alone as acceptable, anticipate condemnation of this scene, it is not provided, which is a major gap.

that all of Saul's *anti-David efforts* have been *anti-God*, and that time is up.[21] Saul failed and kingship failed, insofar as Saul epitomizes it, from refusal to heed. The old news is not so likely to bring on Saul's collapse, but the new insight that *God* has become *Saul's* adversary—and *Saul God's*—is seriously shocking, combined, of course, with lack of food, as the narrator explains directly (v. 20).

The woman's insistence that the king eat marks the far edge of his part in the story, a match to the meal he shared with the prophet before he was anointed (9:19–24). Though her character is provided by words, this deed of insisting that the king and his companions eat their final meal is shown as a gracious gesture on her part. David is absent from this chapter, except perhaps by our wondering if this extreme of silence into which Saul has fallen endangers him as well. The positioning of this chapter, right into the midst of the inexorable muster of Philistines, is artificial in the extreme, as Brueggemann points out,[22] so before concluding this section of material, we investigate what happens on the other side of ch. 28.

But first: Gleaning information about David offers us three points: David's rule is desired by God and has been assisted, as we already knew but learn again here—as was God's insistence on Saul previously. The silence between Saul and the deity is cautionary, perhaps for David and surely for the institution, as we read the sorry tale of the monarchy as it unfolds. The isolation of Saul, so poignantly described here (and at 31), is provocative at diverse levels.

3. David with and without Achish: 29 Again, we can name the narrator characteristics and strategy before adding their impact. The narrator does two main things here: He first combines the logistical moves of the key players, converging previous notes in a fresh and intense scene. We have been apprised of the Philistine massing (28:1, 4) to which is now added 29:1. We have been told that Saul is aware of and reactive to his opponents' presence (28:5, 15). Now David also arrives at the muster (29:2). The narrator, having gathered these players, now breaks David and his men off from the assembly (29:11). The narrator's second move is to provide a welter of direct discourse, with three overt viewpoints represented, plausibly more, insofar as David and perhaps Achish speak with their own language doubled—saying one thing while meaning another. A closer look sorts these utterances for our careful consideration:

- commanders of Philistines (v. 3): "'What are these Hebrews doing here?'"
- Achish (v. 3): "'Is not this David, the servant of Saul, king of Israel, who has been with me now for days and years, and since he deserted to me I have found no fault in him to this day.'"

21. That Saul suspects David of usurping is well-established; that God has chosen someone to succeed Saul, the king has already been told; that Saul can admit, transiently, that David will succeed him we have also heard. But Saul's collapse on hearing Samuel's word suggests that something is a great shock to him, beyond that he is faint from hunger. His collapse is our signal to hear some fresh news information.

22. Brueggemann, "Intentionality," 25, says the gap is like the (old) experience watching a cliffhanger and having to wait a week to find out what happens next.

- commanders of Philistines (4–5): "'Send the man back, that he may return to the place to which you have assigned him; he shall not go down with us to battle, lest in the battle he become an adversary to us. For how could this fellow [David] reconcile himself to his lord [Saul]? Would it not be with the heads of the men here? Is not this David, of whom they sing to one another in dances?'"
- song of women/of Gittites/of allied Philistines (v. 5): "'Saul has slain his thousands, and David his ten thousands?'"
- Achish (vv. 6–7): "'As the LORD lives, you have been honest, and to me it seems right that you should march out and in with me in the campaign; for I have found nothing wrong in you from the day of your coming to me to this day. Nevertheless the lords do not approve of you. So go back now; and go peaceably, that you may not displease the lords of the Philistines.'"
- David (v. 8): "'But what have I done? What have you found in your servant from the day I entered your service until now, that I may not go and fight against the enemies of my lord the king?'"
- Achish (vv. 9–10): "'I know that you are as blameless in my sight as an angel of God; nevertheless the commanders of the Philistines have said, "He shall not go up with us to the battle." Now then rise early in the morning with the servants of your lord who came with you; and start early in the morning, and depart as soon as you have light.'"

The general Philistines, both the men of Achish as quoted in song and the wider group assembling, testify that David remains an unreliable and undesirable ally, whether as Goliath-slayer or as Saul-man.[23] They urge that David will seek to please or reconcile with his former lord by betraying Philistines, inverse of the appraisal Achish has made when supposing that David was making enemies among his own people by raiding them, as he had claimed to be doing. In both cases, the logic is that David must anticipate among his own people consequences for his actions while with Philistines. What their talk does for us, arguably, is remind us that David belongs with Saul and not with Philistines.

Achish, perhaps surprisingly, talks of David as a deserter—from Saul, we understand—and says that there has been no sign of disloyalty to himself (Achish). In other words, David's defection has been complete. But when the Philistines point out the possible strategy of David just mentioned, Achish breaks off resistance and delivers the word to David, holding firm against David's own objection. David, of course, maintains to Achish his own loyalty, which is to say, he asks Achish to present any proof of David's wrongdoing. Others in the scene are silent.

---

23. These general Philistines remind us, perhaps, of those we find in 1 Samuel 4–6 when they seem shrewd and perceptive about what the Ark of God really "is," contrasted with the awareness evinced by the Elides, who should have known better. Even if the Philistine allies of Achish know little, they are more right than wrong about David and see more clearly than does Achish.

With those narrator contributions positioned, what else can we say about David's moves in the scene? That the Philistines are going to engage the Israelites seems consistent and clear, the discourse mode of describing it resembling the story event: gradual but relentless. There is no basic uncertainty about it. The matter of David's participation is what is negotiated, with the sides seeming clear: David appears to intend to participate, general Philistines to refuse him. Achish seems set on having David—until he refuses him. A question to ask is what we are told that can account for the change of mind of Achish, whose discourse has been unsuspicious of the things we know of David from the narrator and that the other Philistines seem to know from their own story information.

Before taking up the matter of how Achish can be seen to reason, we must ask the same question of David: What is his strategy, demonstrated since he has fled Saul definitively and joined Achish? David's rejoinder to Achish here is bold, resounding differently with Achish than with our better-informed selves. This exculpatory utterance, in a sense, is David's signature alibi.[24] We know he is not the loyal "angel of God" that Achish describes. What is David's game, and what is the strategy of Achish? Is Achish foolish or suggestible, right or wrong?[25] Does Achish wish David with the Philistines, and why? Or is he able to be seen as offering David a clear refusal, so that David is not implicated with the battle? Does David wish to join the Philistines and fight Saul or be excused from it? And since his motive is not exposed, the question comes down to how the narratorial and especially the implied authorial artistry guides us to read, prevents us from reading.

Since various options open up as we consider the crossing plot strings here, let me name what I think most plausible. David does not wish to fight Saul, despite his marching to the muster and his verbal plaint to the contrary. We have seen him with multiple occasions to raise a hand against Saul, and watched his awareness of his own dangers grow until he flees Saul into Philistia. Saul in response breaks off pursuit. David has "had to" dissimulate to Achish, since he needs his protection. What David needs from Achish here, and receives, is a respectable refusal to join the coalition headed to Gilboa. David accomplishes that objective. Achish, we may suppose, wants "his man" with him, but not at the cost of either seriously displeasing his own men or having to struggle to convince them that David is reliable. So, without ascribing to Achish layered strategy or complexity, we see him drop David, even easily. Perhaps he seems a bit disappointed, losing a little face as he is opposed by so many. But it is easier to forbid David than to win over his men, which would cost lesser than if it were to turn out that the general Philistines were correct in their appraisal of David. So Achish dumps David.

As we leave this scene, watching the Philistines go northeast while David journeys to the southwest, what have we seen of David's shadow? Adding to the points we have already suggested, five more follow. First, as many note, "the tradition"

---

24. We heard it from him in 17:29, where David was present, was about to perform, and did take responsibility. So what was once a truthful claim would later become dubious as he continued to mouth it.

25. Alter, *David Story*, 181, reminds us that Achish's language here replays Saul's in ch. 24.

has to be residually uncomfortable about David's Philistine phase and has to seek to position it as advantageously as possible, by having David skillfully evade what would have been massively shaming, which is perhaps already bad enough. Second, we as "writerly readers" have had to work hard to interpret this set of material, have had the occasion to consider carefully and with few clues as to authorial intent this matter of what David deeply and truly desires and what he should desire. David's opacity intensifies. For our interpretation process, to be richly ambivalent on this point challenges us. Third, David is shown a shrewd tactician (to borrow an epithet from Homer), adding vastly to his agency, which we have been tracking. From the boy who approached Saul about the giant, to the young man who negotiated shrewdly for his bride, to the friend who helped Jonathan appraise his father more honestly, this mercenary jockeying with Achish marks a big step ahead. But insofar as we have just witnessed the great silence extending between deity and king, we miss David's consultation here. What we have just witnessed Saul be told, by his prophet, Samuel, is that his refusal to listen has built his isolated failure as king. I think this is a support beam in the story of kings, and David risks being at fault as well. The danger of alibi-speech, refusing responsibility for one's deeds, is that the speaker may become convinced that it is true.

Fourth, and related: David's agency here relies on dishonesty and duplicity. His plotting works because he is able to manipulate one Philistine so successfully, while at the same time serving him badly. David correctly wagers that his strategy will get him what he wants, but it is a risk and not his best moment. In ethical terms, granting that other readers may appraise differently—with some applauding such double-dealing skill on David's part as legitimate and praiseworthy in war—I do not think his dissimulation settles so easily.[26] The issue may be one of strategy and tactics: Tactically, David has done well to bluff and feint here, but strategically, it seems a bad move. We may suppose that even if the Philistines had acceded to Achish and David moved on with them, he would have been able to mount other stratagems to avoid fighting Saul. And finally, fifth, we have had to reconsider from fresh angles the question of where David belongs in relation to Saul's final act as king. We have, likely, slipped from narratorial artistry into what is more accurately conceded to the implied author, but the two are collaborating in any case. Just reminded about the reasons for Saul's failure—for kingship's, in my opinion—we are shown David to dissimulate.

b David's Storyline: David and the Death of Saul: 1 Samuel 30–31; 2 Samuel 1

We move to consider the second half of Fokkelman's two-triangle structure, as the events of Saul's death on Mt. Gilboa are again attended by two sets of David actions. This triad is more complex than the first, and we will again watch what the

---

26. As I was finishing my manuscript, I found an essay by Robert B. Chisholm, Jr., "Cracks in the Foundation: Ominous Signs in the David Narrative" *BSac* 172 (April–June 2015), 154–76, which stresses this shadowy side of David's portrait in the books of Samuel.

narrator does while continuing to build the case for David's absence as a negative feature, shadow to the more obvious point that he is exonerated from responsibility for killing Saul.

1. Challenge to David: 30 This chapter follows sequentially on material we just examined, rather than exhibiting a more complex tiled contiguity. Once the Philistine allies have refused to allow David to march with them against Saul, Achish sends away his "bodyguard for life" and David goes. As noted, though the Philistines are acting to safeguard themselves against any treachery Saul's former ally might perpetrate, they also provide David with his own alibi for not being in their company as they attack Saul and also risk discrediting him in our ears for not helping Saul at Mt. Gilboa. Simultaneously, David's absence from Ziklag when marching to join Philistines at Aphek has left the families of his men vulnerable to attack. In addition to that narrative join, we may observe the following narrator moves: The Ziklag raid-and-recovery event is narrated as a report, basically, with little interpretation and virtually no evaluation, except in the story terms of success in accomplishing the objective of recovering the raided property—that whole group of people and property metonymized simply by reference to David's two wives, first taken, then reclaimed.

The narrative quickly (vv. 1–6) gets the rejected allies back to their base to discover the raid, to name their responses, providing for the first time (of more to come), that David's men blame him. David "strengthens himself in the Lord his God," the narrator says cryptically and homodiegetically, while his men come close to stoning him. Presumably the narrator understands the phrase with insider information we lack, except in most general terms. Learning from consultation involving priest and ephod that success is assured (vv. 7–8), David and men move in pursuit. A problem is met (some too tired to march), faced, and resolved (they remain at the brook [vv. 9–10]). An abandoned Egyptian slave materializes to provide information (vv. 11–16), and with his assistance, the Amalekite raiders are tracked and the raided persons and property are all recovered, though we are provided almost no detail of this scene (vv. 17–20). As the journey is retraced, another problem rises in terms of the fatigued men waiting at the brook, and though criticized again, David resolves the problem successfully, with the narrator breaking from his covert mode to tell us that the precedent holds into the future (vv. 21–25). The episode winds to a close as David, again with God-language, distributes spoils to his various allies (vv. 26–31).

Since David is being drawn by the narrator as double-edged or shadowed—positive features allowing a negative edge to be seen as well—we see that while he succeeds he also gains criticism from his own men for the first time. From the approval following his slaying of Goliath, the narrator has piled at David's name approval of virtually everyone in the story with the exception of Saul. That the present episode turns out well must not distract us from seeing the danger it poses as the families of all of David's men are taken, not simply the two named wives of David, and in fact from noting what, specifically, reverses the situation. That is, anticipating that this scene is David's last before he succeeds to Saul's role in at least a partial sense, we catch the resonance with Saul's early dealings with this same set of people (1 Samuel 15). The narrator continues to offer links between the two kings and among royals, naming the raid terms of the two wives we have seen associated with Saul/Nabal-the-Saul: Ahinoam and Abigail, whose names occur here as the only characters singled out. David, faced with this "Saul experience" and with the first mutiny we have seen from any of those following him, apparently does well. The narrator informs us that, distressed, he seeks strength from God—first such reference in this whole section—and summons the priest with the ephod.[27] Asking two clear questions of God about the pursuit, he receives two encouraging and affirmative answers (vv. 7–8). That is, David here shows the inverse of Saulide behavior, and it works well for him. But Saul has consulted once, early in his reign, as well.

Looking at the unit in closer detail: With ultimate success thus assured, David undertakes pursuit of those who have wronged him, moving after them with plenty of men. But before reaching his destination, one-third of his men are described as too weary to travel, and so David solves that potentially divisive situation by leaving them at a wadi, while he moves on with the rest to track his quarry (we catch an echo of "the David's" behavior in 25:13). Here again, fortune attends him, as a lone Egyptian, slave to the Amalekite raiders but abandoned due to illness, provides David with crucial information that the narrator has already told us: Amalekites busy raiding in the Negev as much as David had been reported as doing (27:10), plundered Ziklag. This lone survivor and witness, narrative twin to the one we will meet in 2 Samuel 1, is helpful, and David both encourages him to provide his information and promises to protect him from harm. Assured by oath that his life would be spared, the Egyptian agrees to lead David's group to the Amalekites and does so, with the result that they find them, kill many, and retrieve all that have been taken from them (vv. 11–20). When David's party, herding all of the recovered property and persons, returns to the brook where the fatigued group have remained, a dispute breaks out as to who may share the spoil recovered from Amalek. Some, evaluated by the narrator "mean and churlish," refuse booty to the group who has not actually retrieved it. Again it is difficult to miss the shadows of Saul's (second) anointing in 10:27, where his people split over his authority. David pronounces that booty is to be divided evenly, despite diversity of roles (vv. 23–25), cf. Saul, who lets churlish dissent go unpunished.[28] The narrator, breaking frame to provide us with later information, assures us the decision became a precedent, but it is also ominous, a second time when David's leadership is disputed—far from the last. The chapter ends with David sending gifts to various allies of his in places he was previously said to have ranged, the narrator now tells us (vv. 26–31), refuting the supposition of Achish (27:12) that David's military forays can only gain him enemies.

So as Saul comes to his final moment as king, David—strangely and in various ways resembling him—experiences his first leadership contention, but reaching

27. Bodner, *1 Samuel*, 310, links David's distress at 30:6 with Saul's at 28:15.
28. Bodner, *1 Samuel*, 314.

for God-words and for divine direction as Saul had earlier done but which he has rarely since managed well. David is, so far, showing himself a better leader than Saul, and yet clouds are gathering. The implied author may be suggesting, by analogue, that kings come and go but some of the challenges implicit in royal leadership remain.

2. Saul's final challenges: *31* As with the Endor narrative, the weighty but scant events of Gilboa bringing down King Saul cannot distract us from the narrative of David's story but must be summarized, spare as they already are in the narrator's recital.[29] The attack of Philistines commences, long promised by the narrator and deferred since 28:1, minus the Judah-allies of Achish, who are safely occupied in the southern region. Virtually no extraneous details are provided. In his first sentence the narrator moves to summarize the fleeing of some, the falling of others, and the deaths of Saul's three sons: Jonathan, Abinadab, and Malchishua—only one of whom we have met (vv. 1–2).[30] That Jonathan dies at his father's side is made clear without being stressed. Saul alone is left, it seems, fighting bravely until wounded by archers (v. 3). Next follows the first and brief narration of his death, provided authoritatively by the narrator (vv. 4–6). Saul, in distress from wounds, asks his armor-bearer to kill him rather than allow the Philistines to do it abusively.[31] The armor-bearer, drawing back from an act of regicide, refuses, and so Saul manages his death by falling on his sword. Witnessing the death of his master, the armor-bearer kills himself, so that the two fall together (vv. 3–6). The remainder of the chapter sketches the proleptic result—Israelite regions deserted and then repopulated by Philistines (v. 7)—and the more immediate outcome— the plundering of the slain by the victorious and the aftermath of those events (vv. 8–13). In terms of narrator choice of time spent, we can see that the aftermath of the battle of Gilboa receives as much time as does the encounter itself.

The first result of the battle shows other Israelite survivors—apparently farther afield (since all at Gilboa are dead)—fled, with the result that their towns are occupied by Philistines, the narrator says with great prolepsis, once again drawing attention to his own presence, moving from more covert to overt, providing later information than belongs to our story. The impact stresses the significance and totality of the king's defeat. By the end of the verse which began with their victory, Philistines inhabit Saul's land, a most provocative suggestion.

The second set of information provided manages to offer Saul a combination of disgrace and honor, of respect amid defeat. It is perhaps a more generous portraiture

---

29. This scene is an amazing example of narrator reticence, since both the general quality of the event (battle) and its principals (Saul and Jonathan) are clearly candidates for a more elaborated narrative. Narrators can be reticent about diverse things, with varying impact. Here, though detail is withheld, the basic facts are not. This is different from withholding "facts" about David's first wife and mother of his firstborn son.

30. That there is yet another son we are also not told here by the narrator, nor ever do we learn—more reticence—why he was not with his father and brothers: more reticence.

31. This is the only direct discourse in the scene, providing us with Saul's last words.

toward Israel's first king than we have heard narrated elsewhere. Ironically, Saul's final defeat by his Philistine nemesis is honorable and dignified, despite their effort to vaunt over him afterwards. Saul's body is stripped of armor and decapitated by Philistines, with both body and armor sent throughout Philistia as announcement of the good news for its inhabitants, human, and divine. Saul's armor is placed in a temple, his body displayed on a town wall. But the Philistine dishonor of the bodies of Saul and sons is almost at once reversed. When the people of Jabesh-Gilead hear the news, they march all night to rescue the royal bodies from the city walls, bury them at Jabesh, and mourn appropriately, thus recompensing Saul's deed done for them at the very start of his monarchy (1 Samuel 11). The narrator's tribute, though terse and prosaic, testifies to Saul's qualities, as will David's shortly—perhaps even more deeply.

In this scene of Saul's death, the implied artistry offers us complex possibilities to show David resembling Saul. The Philistines, nemesis of Saul and erstwhile ally of David, appear successful and triumphant, with the news of Saul's defeat and then the physical marker of it racing around their territory, adorning their walls. But as was the case when they thought they had done well to capture the Ark in an earlier battle, they learn here that it is not so easy to keep their trophies.[32] A second point to watch is that, although we appear to have seen the last of the Saulides, the story will spend much more time on them, as we meet two that were not lost on Gilboa. That is, the house of Saul could be expected to vanish from the David story now, but it persists, unexpectedly, as we move ahead. Third, related to these first two points, Saul's status is inverted at the end of his life.

The narrator, reciting for us, offers some ponderable points as well: Saul's last act is, I think, a brave one. That he can act on his own, finally, to terminate his own life rather than fall into the hands of perennial opponents seems courageous to me. Though at first asking another to help him, Saul seems able to accept the armor-bearer's refusal as an opportunity to act for himself, a struggle that has characterized his kingship. This point continues as those he has helped earlier now assist him, without his asking them to do so. Saul "grows" in death.

As we are gathering implications of events here as pertaining to David's characterization, we carry forward the question of where David belongs as this battle of Gilboa is engaged. That many loyal people die with Saul draws our attention to David, who is absent. That Saul's armor-bearer—a position David once held—cannot help the king, or perhaps does help him by refusing to dispatch him, intensifies the question of David's absence. That the armor-bearer dies with his master reminds us that David does not do so. Again, in rational terms, David has done well to avoid being among the Philistines at Gilboa. But has he done well not to be with Saul?

3. David's challenge to praise Saul: 1 The final event remaining is the report of the death of Saul and the defeat of Israel to David and his several responses. Since the narratorial voice whose authority we have little occasion to doubt has already

---

32. Bodner, *1 Samuel*, 304–06 offers ways in which the Ark episodes echo at Gilboa.

related the scene of Saul's death, readers can focus on David's role and that of the messenger without distractions that would be present, were we not already basically well and reliably informed. This scene, shifting from northeast Gilboa to southwest Ziklag, requires the narrator to coordinate Saul and David's events as well as those of Philistines and Amalekites a final time (vv. 1–2). Reviewing that David has been two days in Ziklag after his defeat of Amalekites—time spent to retrieve what had been raided while he had marched to the Philistine assembly at Aphek—on the third day (our day eleven) a lone and mourning Amalekite approaches David, offering obeisance (v. 3). The narrator slows the scene to have David ask the man's provenance and to learn that the refugee is from the Israelite camp, hence from the battle that David has avoided. A second question from David, who will ask five in this last scene, invites the witness's news (v. 4).

The Amalekite's report differs in certain crucial ways from what we have been told, though not in the basic events, which the man states first: flight, defeat, and death (v. 4). David's third question (v. 5) is to press for certainty: How does the man know the things he claims to narrate? How is he witness to what he reports? We have, again as in 30:11–16, David questioning a lone witness. The first one's words are verified; this one will present evidence as well, though with verification remaining more doubtful.

The man's recital (vv. 6–10) provides his version of recent Gilboa events: Chancing to be at Mount Gilboa, he has seen Saul leaning on his sword with Philistine chariots and horsemen closing in on him. "'And when he looked behind him, he saw me, and called to me. And I answered, "Here I am." And he said to me, "Who are you?" I answered him, "I am an Amalekite." And he said to me, "Stand beside me and slay me; for anguish has seized me, and yet my life still lingers.""" The messenger continues, claiming he has done as asked, agreeing with the king's own assessment that Saul's condition is mortal. "'And I took the crown which was on his head and the armlet which was on his arm, and I have brought them here to my lord.'"

The key matter is not so much the story events but their discourse, and the narrator's calling our attention to it in a most unusual manner. The issue concerns not whether Saul has died but whose hand has dispatched him, who has been present, and who have not. Have Philistines killed Saul, or has an Amalekite dispatched the king? Has Saul killed himself, or has he died at the hands of a foreigner, an Amalekite? Are we to see an armor-bearer having refused to do what the king has asked, with the result that a foreigner steps forth to kill him? Who has stripped the body of the king: Philistines the next day, or an Amalekite at the moment of the killing? Has "the last Amalekite," whom Saul was unwilling to kill (1 Samuel 15), killed Saul? Is it perhaps one of the four hundred Amalekites whom David failed to slay when regaining the families and property of his people who escapes to kill Saul (29:17), somewhat as Saul let the last priest slip away to work for David? That the man who claims to be an Amalekite has the royal items does not mean his narrative about them is true. Who is this runner from the battle: Amalekite as he claims, or perhaps a Philistine? The scene featuring the messenger-witness and David replays for us larger issues that have been on the table for some chapters, about the manner of the death of Saul: how it shall happen, how it must not; who is present and who is absent; who knows and bears witness. David has rehearsed earlier that God might do it, as the narrator claimed God slew Nabal (-the-Saul), or his day might come, or he might die in battle. "'But'," said David, "'it must not be by my hand'." Saul dies in battle, clearly enough, as his prophet, *redivivus*, has promised him would happen. That Saul and his armor-bearer die together is a proleptic comment on monarchy, and that an Amalekite outlasts them both is another. All these possibilities emerge from what the messenger says, proffers, to the man who was not present there himself. Kingship slain, land overrun is a longer and a future story, strangely and prematurely present here.

David's next words (vv. 13–14), emerging only after the narrator tells us that he and his men rend their garments, lament and weep, fasting until evening (vv. 11–12), stress this very matter: "'Where do you come from?' He replied, 'I am the son of a sojourner, an Amalekite'" (v. 13). "'How is it you were not afraid to put forth your hand to destroy the Lord's anointed?'" The question, evidently more important than any answer, is followed at once by David's order that the man be killed for what he did, and thus it happens (v. 15). David addresses the dead man once more, calling down onto Amalekite's own head bloodguilt for what he had claimed to have done, killing the anointed of the Lord (v. 16). Killing this witness before their debriefing is completed, David's first act after he learns of Saul's death is an ominous one.

David, resembling again Saul with the priest of Nob, seals forever the lips of the only witness—of the only man claiming to have been witness—before he can disclose all he knows. But though we can appreciate that, in realistic terms, such a hasty move eliminates information, in this artistic scene, I think we have what is needed, granted we want to know more from a too-reticent narrator. Responsibility for Saul's death hovers over several characters, not factually for us to solve, but to call attention to the larger dynamics which we must query. David, once endangered by Saul, comes to endanger him and flees the land to avoid more encounters with him. He is, in spatial and temporal terms, far enough removed so that he is not suspect. But in the overtones of the narrative, the fact that Saul's crown and armlet end up being presented to David reminds us of his involvement. Technically exonerated by narrator and implied author, David's connection with the death of Saul lingers.

The last thing for David to do for Saul and Jonathan (until we learn of Ishbosheth and Mephibosheth) is to lament their deaths, and so he does. Again, focusing here on the singer rather than on the sung, we see that David's poem, entering the tradition as the Song of the Bow, is at once simple and profound.[33] The refrain, occurring at vv. 19 and 27, its words also resounding within the detail of the verses, names the tragedy as of the people, the land, the cosmos as well as that of the two individuals singled out. David, echoing what the narrator has described when word of the death of Saul and others is carried to the cities and idols of the Philistines (31:9), urges now that the word of Saul's death be

---

33. Smith, *Poetic Heroes*, 267–83 (notes 526–41), comments perceptively on the lament, bringing in usefully the insights of other scholars.

withheld in Gath and Ashkelon, forbidding analeptically what has already been made known. He next interdicts the cosmos from producing rain and dew onto the mountain where Saul, metaphorized by his abandoned and begrimed shield, lies neglected and unattended. The armor referenced is a most poignant image, enriching and enriched by its associations with the king's armor-bearer, unable now and unwilling earlier to carry out his responsibilities.

Saul is praised for his military feats, a point made also already offered by the narrator but undramatically (1 Samuel 14:47–52). It can seem and may be ironic for David to praise Saul's prowess with weapons, when our impression and the literary details attending his characterization accumulate to suggest that Saul was not sufficiently adept with them. But the narrator has just told us that Saul is the last but one of his people to fall on Gilboa, implying great courage and skill. While the cosmos is bidden to remain dry-eyed, the daughters of Israel are charged to weep for the one who provided them with luxury—again, details of Saul's kingly economy we have not witnessed, but likely enough. It is, however, a most impersonal comment from David, who could have said so much more and so much other about Saul.

Jonathan's name is spoken twice: To begin with, David praises father and son, king and prince, as a pair of warriors, swifter than eagles, stronger than lions, never parted—not in death, not in life. Again, the apparently simple and almost trite imagery credits each with the loyalty of the other, possibly also underlining an other, absent. For all that might have divided them and even seemed, perhaps to do, Saul and Jonathan die together, with David far removed. David's second address, far more personal, is to Jonathan as his brother, whose love is recited and characterized as unsurpassed by any other David has experienced. Our first sighting of Jonathan and David was graced by the narrator's appraisal that Jonathan loved David as he loved himself, and David says close to the same here. Whose angle is being reported is ambivalent, undecidable in Hebrew syntax. If such love is the epitome of what it means to be human, it is a fine accolade, again a contrast to what is said of Saul as provident. The poem deserves more than this, but the relevant point here is David's skill in praising these two, so briefly, together, separately, profoundly, characterizing himself as well, in shadow.

5 *Conclusions and Transition*

The objective of this chapter has been to show David's technical innocence as he engages with the death of Saul, while at the same time to suggest that a more negative shadow has also been cast. We have studied primarily narrator moves here, while appreciating that some of the artistry has been contributed by the longer range and subtler ways in which the implied author composes this story. The carefully and explicitly synchronized eleven days narrated for us make the positive point clear: David was not at Gilboa when Saul died. That King Saul dies alone, leaning on his oft-hurled spear, attended by an armor-bearer who cannot do what the king needs (save him) or wants (kill him), has a mixed aspect: Demonstrating

David's innocence, it also registers as a failure of David—made Saul's armor-bearer when they first met, given that armor if briefly when the boy went out to do the king's job, recently at least verbally made subaltern of his Philistine lord.[34] Why is David's presence or absence at Saul's side even a question, and how may we explore its impact? The whole story of David so far shows him in Saul's presence and then withdrawing, pushed out, intersecting with his predecessor and lord until he flees to Philistia. The time spent on presence and absence so far is almost excessive. This shadow joins our wider concern to chart David's capacity for compassion, glimpsed rather minimally so far. Related to his characteral agency, David's taking charge of his own choices rather than awaiting the service of others tends either toward altruism or selfishness. We can summarize and correlate that shadow now, as David prepares to take up his kingly rule shortly.

First, David has, in these six chapters, come to take on a strange resemblance to Saul: He has taken his masters' wives but then also loses them, if briefly; he is involved in the slaughter of whole groups of innocent people, leaving no survivors; he has long stretches where he seems disconnected from God, though these do not accumulate steadily as has Saul's lack of contact with the deity. David is for the first time in this material criticized by his peers, Philistines and Judahites. Though we see that God remains determined that the kingship of Saul will pass to David, we recall as well that God's choice of Saul was also insistent. In the end, he mishandles a lone Amalekite, as Saul has done before him. At a longer perspective, early successes will give way to failures; failure will be reversed as death comes closer.

A second set of shadow factors emerges from David's growing propensity to thrive on duplicity. He lies, alibis, double-speaks, with his escape from the Philistine march against Saul and the Israelites thoroughly dependent on claims that seem utterly false. If earlier we have experienced David as struggling to maintain integrity, I miss that side of his portrait here. David's tendency to claim innocence when it is not so obvious within the story increases and will continue to do so. In his utterances, David dissimulates and cannot be where his words claim him to be. His verbal alibi peaks (for the moment) when he indignantly asks Achish how he has deserved not to be included in the Philistine coalition. Perhaps his duplicity is necessary or admirable, but it is a risky strategy at multiple levels. One of the dangers of proffering dishonesty to others is to come to believe it oneself. David seems in danger of such a slip. To excuse David's duplicity as directed against opponents who seem to deserve it does not convince me at all that it is not a problem.

Third, we have the matter of Saul's final hours, both as he watches the Philistines mass and is shown desperate for what he lacks, what David does have access to: contact with God. The narrative stress on the presence and absence of Saul's armor-bearer at Saul's last moment of need, the invitation to that personage to slay the king—refused, the claim of the foreigner to have done the deed that no one else would do all conspire to suggest that David might have been at Gilboa not as

---

34. The lament's reference to Saul's abandoned shield makes a similar contribution, I think. David was not at Saul's side at the most crucial moment of his life.

a Philistine ally but as a helper to his former friend and patron. Alternatively, that there are no survivors among Saul's men suggests otherwise.

Finally, fourth, as we have been watching the growth of David's agency, of his capacity to plan and act as distinct from receiving the service and gaining the benefits of others' plans, we see him do both of those things. David is shown as a capable agent in this set of material, seizing the initiative more consistently than before, managing his non-presence at Gilboa while relying on Philistines to effect it for him. That David ventured as close as Aphek to Gilboa was risky, signaling a danger to himself if not to Saul. I see no linking of graciousness toward Saul, toward Achish, toward Israel or Philistine fighters, certainly not toward the groups he massacres, leaving no survivor to report or complain. David acts to save his own, again specified by the narrator simply as David's two wives; he spares a lone Egyptian who helps him recover what has been raided, and conspicuously does not extend any kindness toward the man who hands him Saul's royal emblems. The closest David comes to compassion is in the words spoken of Saul and Jonathan, dead. David seems brutalized here. As we turn to the next set of narrative where he reaches for and finally proceeds to the throne, and we look more deeply into characterization, we will consider these issues additionally.

Chapter 5

David Consolidates his Rule: (2 Sam. 2–8 and 21–24)

Characterization

1 Transition

After our careful attention to edges and structures, to patterns and plots, and to narrative technique, we arrive with David at the first point in his story where Saul is no longer present. And yet David's own status is not quite set. We will consider now two sets of material most scholars find rather miscellaneous and consequently rarely treat together. The first is often called David's consolidation of his position, while the second is typically classified as appendix.[1] With the question of these edges in unsolvable disarray, my decision (generally after Fokkelman) to see this material as eighteen distinct though related units suits well enough.[2] Not neglecting structure,[3] plotting, or narrator choices, we will focus here primarily on characters and characterization, exploring the material and the theory with minor characters, so as to be ready for the major actors to emerge in 2 Sam. 9–20. What is needed, prior to getting to the consideration of character theory and its implementation with the narrative, is to summarize and survey the eighteen (mostly) small units for anything that needs noting for plotting and narration.

1. For a discussion of what comprises these two units, how each is grouped or structured, and why this is the least problematic pairing, see Fokkelman, *Throne and City*, 1–22. One of his salient points is that the material of chs. 21–24 needs not to interrupt the question of succession which trails into 1 Kings. Some of the material offered there resembles episodes of chs. 2–8, so the choice to do this material together is not the least sensible. An extensive study of the chapters is also provided by H.H. Klement, *II Samuel 21–24. Context, Structure and Meaning in the Samuel Conclusion*, Europäische Hochschulschriften, Reihe 23 Theologie, vol. 682 (Frankfurt: Peter Lang, 2000), whose primary aim is to offer structures and boundaries as significant for construing meaning, though he also notes the scholarly controversy around placement, 17–59.

2. Fokkelman includes here ch. 9, which I will place with the material that follows it, cued by the presence of Mephibosheth.

3. Fokkelman has structures for virtually all the material included here. Simpler ones can be found in Craig E. Morrison, *Berit Olam: Studies in Hebrew and Narrative Poetry. 2 Samuel* (Collegeville, MN: The Liturgical Press, 2013).

To recall, as well, where we have left David's agency and his capacity for goodness and for harm, we summarize that we first met David acting to soothe Saul and then to take the giant Goliath off the king's hands, as graciously as possible. David, recipient of much kindness from others, showed long restraint about refusing to kill Saul who was continually menacing him, but it came to be a close thing. David, drawing away from Saul's reach while claiming to have been driven from his heritage, joined the Philistines, where the killing he had previously avoided became more familiar to him. Avoiding, ultimately, either to kill Saul or to assist him, David gained this innocence at some cost to his integrity, killing without any sign of compunction whole groups of people and then the man who claimed to have been the slayer of King Saul. David seems to be starting from negative space, if he is to move toward compassion as he takes the throne long, if secretly, promised him by prophet and deity. In this set of material David will overstep seriously in cultic matters and be rebuked more clearly than we will see until his breach with Bathsheba and Uriah.

2 Plotting and Narration: David Consolidates his Position (2–8)

We will consider this material in twelve short units. Here each is summarized, with primary interest in the narrator's presentation of plotting characters singled out for their contribution to David's characterization.

a Choice of David and of Ishbosheth as Kings: 2:1–11:

The narrator dominates this scene, after opening with a pair of short questions spoken by David and even shorter responses from the mouth of God. To consult God has been an occasional strength of David thus far, and that it grounds his first post-Saul deed and his access to kingship is important. Thus can David, with consultation and response, move his people from Ziklag to Hebron, where, with amazingly little attention to detail, he becomes king by action of the men of Judah. What *we* know is that Samuel the prophet anointed David with suitable prompting from God. But the particular scene we witnessed when David was anointed is virtually never alluded to again within the story events of the narrative, surely not now.[4]

Similarly, Ishbosheth is made king of a wider region by Abner, formerly Saul's lieutenant and kinsman, also without divine consultation. This Saul-son had not been anointed previously—or even mentioned—and so, compared with the amount of ceremony and detail attending the selection of Saul, the process for Saul's son is also surprisingly minimal. The narrator's presentation of the inadequacy of Abner's initiative will be strengthened in the material ahead.

---

4. Abner will cite the promise to David shortly (2:19), but as it comes within discourse where he says a number of things not verified elsewhere renders it unreliable, I think.

David's analeptic words of thanks to and proleptic hint of solidarity with the people of Jabesh-Gilead for their deed to Saul and his hint of a future relationship between himself and them go unremarked. Ishbosheth takes no such initiative for their deed done for his father and brothers, and we are implicitly reminded that they all died in battle while he, unaccountably, survived. The narrative strategy, then, is to sketch quickly and contrastively these two newly anointed by a number of criteria.

b Conflict Leads to the Killing of Asahel by Abner: 2:12–32:

Abner, featuring prominently if briefly, emerges again as leader of opposition to David of Hebron. We witness what appears to be first, stylized combat between the two sides where casualties are even, and then to become a more general battle. Between those two moments is the pursuit of the lone Abner—shown fleeing somewhere on his own—by the three sons of David's sister, Zeruiah, with Asahel taking the lead, drawing close, refusing to be warned off by Abner as the space between them shrinks. Abner kills Asahel, and shortly thereafter, the two sides draw back, each to their home territory, with the Saul-men having lost many more than the David-men. Asahel is buried. The narrative ambiguity regarding the battle scenes, with context so uncertain, sets up a crucial question that will develop while remaining contested in the David story until its very end: the particular nature of the killing of Asahel, which Fokkelman ambiguously calls "an incident on the battlefield," also noting that Abner has no good option.[5] Abner is shown here both moving away from his own Saul-side and wishing to avoid a problem with David's Joab, which is what his discourse suggests as his motive for wanting to avoid Asahel. But as this scene ends, Abner has an enemy in Joab, if such was not the case before. The matter is now personal as well as political. If, as we continue to read, we surmise that Abner already planned to deliver the Ishbosheth-men to David, Asahel has made it more difficult than it was already.

c Abner Changes Sides: 3:1–21:

The first five verses may belong better with the preceding unit, as the narrator details the birth of six sons to David and their various named mothers while the young kingdom lives at Hebron. Such achievements mark David's strengthening his royal position. Ishbosheth, by contrast, is shown wifeless and sonless, unable to secure a woman once connected with his father, referred to in the narrative as Saul's woman, not Ishbosheth's. The narrator continues to sketch so that Ishbosheth's weakness and inferiority as king grow. Indeed, Ishbosheth is not so strong as Abner, let alone a match for David. In the present scene, Abner is accused by Ishbosheth of taking for himself Saul's secondary wife, Rizpah, and

---

5. Fokkelman, *Throne and City*, 47–53. Though the killing takes place at a battle scene, it is not unambiguously part of the battle, since Abner runs from the scene. This is a great place to see the narrator refusing clarity so that we must watch the conflict without being able to resolve it cleanly.

Abner responds as insulted. That the narrator handles both sides of this dispute as alleged—neither clarifying nor verifying truth claims—allows us the possibility that Abner may have designed a pretext to fall out with Saul's son. Whether he is to be assessed as guilty as charged or falsely accused—to provoke Ishbosheth to some limit, to shame him, or to alienate him—remains ambiguous.

In terms of plotting, Abner appears to be designing a scenario that will allow him to change sides, indeed, to broker the former Saul people to become David's subjects. With those crucial moves not causally pinned down, Abner informs Ishbosheth of his intent: to transfer the kingdom from the (waning) house of Saul to the (waxing) house of David, citing it as God's sworn word to David.[6] He then opens negotiations with David: "And Abner sent messengers to David at Hebron, saying, 'To whom does the land belong? Make your covenant with me, and behold, my hand shall be with you to bring over all Israel to you'" (v. 12). Though the opening question is ambiguous and susceptible to various understandings, David agrees, on a condition he names to Abner and then moves to demand of Ishbosheth: the reclaiming of Saul's daughter and David's own first wife, Michal. The narrative contrast is once again clear: Ishbosheth is unable to withstand Abner in the matter of Rizpah and David in the matter of Michal, as his father was also bested by David in regard to Michal and Ahinoam (Abigail as well, if Nabal "is" Saul).

Abner next deals with both the elders of Israel and the men of Benjamin, verbalizing on his own authority that they also are ready for David to rule them. We hear them neither demur nor consent. Two possibilities emerge: either Abner, with few or no good choices, must make a bold move, or alternatively, he must move into the camp of David with as little reference to Joab as possible.

d Death of Abner: 3:22–39:

The next episode is handled with a swinging door, seeing Abner out of David's presence as Joab enters to learn what he seems not to have anticipated: that Abner is assisting David. Due at least to the episode involving Asahel's death, this possibility is intolerable to Joab, who first rebukes David and then kills Abner, by quasi-stealth. David and Joab exchange angry and important words, making clear that the issue is whether the Asahel killing counts as a battle casualty or not.[7] David mourns Abner conspicuously, with the sincerity difficult to assess. The narrator, again suppressing some clarity about what is understood to have happened, positions David as either surprised and angry at Joab or, alternatively, as feigning indignation. That David would agree to deal with Abner does not entail his respecting a man who would betray his own side. That David wants what Abner claims to be able to deliver does not involve approving doer or deed. Hence, arguably, David is relieved at the killing of Abner by Joab. But insofar as

---

6. Again, narrator strategy here seems to be primarily to report Abner's words and deed without endorsing them.

7. This matter recurs at the very end of David's story, singled out from among many things he could have named against Joab.

Abner is David's guest and ally, David is responsible for his safety, which Joab compromises. Again, David may be understood as having mixed reactions here, with his verbalized and enacted language at odds with some longer-term strategies readers construct with the characters. In the previous set of material considered, this tendency of David to be, feel, speak, and act at cross-purposes was not a strength for him. Abner, as a plotter, largely fails, not least by incorrectly reading the moves of Joab and perhaps David as well.

Discourse threads this unit: Joab is provided with information he lacks by an unnamed source (v. 23), whether provocatively or not is impossible to tell. Joab, however, also accuses Abner of both deceiving David and seeking information, implicitly denouncing David for his failure to recognize Abner's dishonesty. David makes no reply, though the narrator assures us that David does not suspect Joab's plan, lending credence to the possibility that he is missing some of Abner's doings as well.[8] That Abner underestimates Joab's duplicity is also clear, in that he lets him close enough to him to kill him—a parody of Asahel's approach to Abner.

David speaks when he learns of Joab's deed, to self-exculpate. It seems clear to us, reading, that Joab neither has nor needs David's assistance here. David's oath of innocence and curse on Joab, coming so early in their specific dealings together, is one of the strongest in the Bible:

> "I and my kingdom are for ever guiltless before the LORD for the blood of Abner the son of Ner. May it fall upon the head of Joab, and upon all his father's house; and may the house of Joab never be without one who has a discharge, or who is leprous, or who holds a spindle, or who is slain by the sword, or who lacks bread!" (vv. 26–27)

The narrator, summing up directly, notes that Joab's motivation for killing Abner was the killing of Asahel, though without clarifying what sort of death it was, except "in battle."

The next scene involves the obsequies for Abner, in which David's direct speech is again prominent:

> "Rend your clothes, and gird on sackcloth, and mourn before Abner." . . . And the king lamented for Abner, saying, "Should Abner die as a fool dies? Your hands were not bound, your feet were not fettered; as one falls before the wicked you have fallen." . . . Then all the people came to persuade David to eat bread while it was yet day; but David swore, saying, "God do so to me and more also, if I taste bread or anything else till the sun goes down!" And all the people took notice of it, and it pleased them; as everything that the king did pleased all the people. (vv. 31–35)

8. The character Joab is, in my view, second only to David for complexity in these materials and needs a full-length study to sort some of the patterns. Since his characterization is ancillary to David's, there is a lot of key information not provided. Whether it can be got at with other strategies remains to be investigated. Keith Bodner's *The Rebellion of Absalom* (New York and London: Routledge, 2014) suggests a model for such a project.

David's language is clear about his own situation, less so about Abner's. *Should* Abner die in one way or in another, and why? David's refusal to eat before sundown recalls a similar oath by Saul, which did not end so well for king or his son (1 Sam. 14:24–46).

What those witnessing David and Joab conclude is not so evident, though they seem to respond to David's (ambiguous) cues. The narrator's summary seems clear enough, unless we query it by the standards of modern reliability: Is it at odds with the portraiture of the implied author for us to credit that *everyone* is pleased with *everything* that David did? I find it a suspicious statement, akin to what we saw in 1 Sam. 25:38, where God was named as the slayer of Nabal, overriding prominently and suspiciously the vast data that Nabal self-destructed, his narrow little heart unable to endure his wife's generosity. But the narrator is not finished:

> So all the people and all Israel understood that day that it had not been the king's will to slay Abner the son of Ner. And the king said to his servants, "Do you not know that a prince and a great man has fallen this day in Israel? And I am this day weak, though anointed king; these men the sons of Zeruiah are too hard for me. The LORD requite the evildoer according to his wickedness!" (vv. 37–39)

We will visit this material once more when considering the characterization of Abner. Polzin remarks on the high degree of uncertainty attending all this information.[9] The root of the uncertainty is the narrator's strategy to report without vouching for veracity.

e Death of Ishbosheth: 4:1–11:

The theme of the inadequacy of Ishbosheth pervading the material so far recurs, as the young man's fear already named at 3:11 is registered again by the narrator. Not only the king but also the men of Israel lose heart when they hear of Abner's death—while negotiating at Hebron. Since Abner had already told Ishbosheth of his intent to deliver the Saul-kingdom to David without evoking response and had also secured the consent—or had not evoked opposition—of Israel to the same project, Ishbosheth's fear is understandable. Fresh initiative emerges from the sons of a Benjamin-man, who take the next step when no one else does. In the midst of this sequence, the narrator intrudes or inserts additional information about the house of Saul: There is a Saulide scion besides Ishbosheth, a son of Jonathan who is lame, having fallen when his father and grandfather did, though saving his life when they did not. The note once again draws our attention to the dwindling (but not disappeared) house of Saul and also to the mysterious survival of Ishbosheth, which, however, is about to end. In narrative terms, the detail of 4:4 is later than we might have expected to learn that Jonathan had a son, and earlier than we might anticipate it, since the young man will not feature for a time. The narrative placement is strategic, its rhetorical effect to raise and dash the putative hopes of Saulides.

9. Robert Polzin, *David and the Deuteronomist: A Literary Study of the Deuteronomic History* (Bloomington: Indiana University Press, 1993), 43.

Two Benjamin-men arrive at Ishbosheth's house and behead him, and undetected, they ride south. They evoke Philistines who behead Saul, men of Jabesh who ride hard all night on a quest, and the Amalekite arriving at David's place with presumed good news. They tell David: "'Here is the head of Ishbosheth, the son of Saul, your enemy, who sought your life; the LORD has avenged my lord the king this day on Saul and on his offspring'" (v. 8). Like Abner, they characterize Saulide's presence as hostile to David and offer David God-language for the death of Ishbosheth. As plotters, these two are not so easy to read. It may be that they anticipate pleasing David, or they may want to make him look guilty of regicide.[10]

David's language seems unequivocal and familiar, as he himself draws attention to:

> "As the LORD lives, who has redeemed my life out of every adversity, when one told me, 'Behold, Saul is dead,' and thought he was bringing good news, I seized him and slew him at Ziklag, which was the reward I gave him for his news. How much more, when wicked men have slain a righteous man in his own house upon his bed, shall I not now require his blood at your hand, and destroy you from the earth?" (vv. 10–11).

David's claim is one we have heard before: Evil news for Saul is not necessarily desired by David. We have heard him push this sort of calculation aside at least at chs. 24 and 26, arguably at 25, surely at 2 Samuel 1. As validation, David offers the death of the Amalekite, though also calling at least to our readers' attention that he spares unpunished the Zeruiah sons (Joab and Abishai at ch. 24, Abishai at 26, maybe Asahel at 2 Samuel 2 and Joab again at ch. 3) for their words and deeds. In other words, one Amalekite and shortly two Benjamin-men will die of this offense, while three of his own men remain unpunished, though rebuked.

f David Anointed King of Israel at Hebron: 5:1–5:

The narrator moves key events along swiftly, allowing minimal if crucial character discourse to bring them into sharp and quick relief. This unit, as Fokkelman notes, concludes the Abner plans, as his initiatives are completed by others.[11] Israel's tribes approach David at Hebron, not unlike their approach to Samuel (1 Samuel 8), and claiming kinship, they remind David that he served them well when Saul was king and ask him to do so again. They allege words of God (v. 2): "'You shall be shepherd of my people Israel, and you shall be prince over Israel.'" Though no reply from David is offered, the transfer moves forward as Israel's elders convene at Hebron. David covenants with them and they anoint him. The narrator summarizes here the total years for his reign: Thirty-three at

---

10. For an extensive discussion of this passage, see Pamela Tamarken Reis, "Killing the Messenger: David's Policy or Politics?" *JSOT* 31.2 (2006): 167–91.

11. Fokkelman, *Throne and City*, 144–45.

Jerusalem, seven and a bit more at Hebron. Neither God nor David speaks here, and though the quotation recalls familiar language, we have neither heard it said nor witnessed the elders having heard it.[12]

g *David Takes Jerusalem: 5:6–16:*

For such a key and, indeed, long-lasting event, there is virtually no detail about particulars. The narrator again takes up the recital: David and his men, though unbidden, go up to a Jebusite stronghold defended by those who refuse him entrance, citing a proverb to convey that the city is so secure that even the blind and lame can defend it. But David takes the city, then rearticulates the proverb to imply contempt or animosity for the city's defenders, proscribing them and refusing them access as they had been claimed to deny him. Renaming the city after himself, he builds it up and summons Phoenician Hiram to build a palace. The narrator globally assures us: "And David became greater and greater, for the LORD, the God of hosts, was with him. . . . And David perceived that the LORD had established him king over Israel, and that he had exalted his kingdom for the sake of his people Israel" (5:10, 12). As will become clearer shortly, part of building his house is adding to his dynasty: David with more wives begets eleven more offspring, including Solomon, of whom we will soon hear.

h *David Defeats Philistines: 5:17–25:*

These verses extend a major phase for David, begun in 1 Samuel 17, where he tangles with Philistines.[13] This time, with careful consultation of and precise response from God—even with advice regarding tactics—the dread enemy of Saul is defeated at several places. The narrator stresses David's obedience to God here, plausibly in contrast to Saul, arguably as distinct from his initiative in moving to Jerusalem. Fokkelman calls chs. 5–8 David's apotheosis, crediting his obedience to God,[14] but that is not so clear to me.

i *David Brings the Ark to Jerusalem: 6:1–22:*

A more complex piece follows, contributing to the new king's consolidation of his position. But here we note that the progress is not so smooth, nor is divine consultation sought. David's objective seems to be to bring the Ark to his city,

---

12. Ibid., offers a chiastic structure (2:1–5:5) to show these deeds as prompted by Abner, contrasted with David's initiative about to prompt the next set. A matching one (265–66) shows David as agent in the second part of the material (chs. 5–8).

13. For a detailed discussion of how we are to decide the edges of the material here, 5:17–7:29, see Donald F. Murray, *Divine Prerogative and Royal Pretension: Pragmatics, Poetics and Polemics in a Narrative Sequence about David (2 Samuel 5:17–7:29)* (Sheffield: Sheffield Academic Press, 1998), 26–36 and *passim*.

14. Fokkelman, *Throne and City*, 155.

but he fails badly, and we need to consider how the matter is shown. The Ark, longitudinally considered in the books of Samuel (and into 1 Kings 2), is almost a character, and of all the divine accoutrements, is arguably the most sensitive. The narrator describes David's preparations for its transfer, mustering thirty-two units of choice men to accompany the Ark, treating it as though it were his duty to move it around—behavior we know the Ark has not readily tolerated before. David arranges for the Ark to be brought forth, its transportation resembling what the Philistines had designed for it when they sent it away from their presence (1 Samuel 6). The narrator brings God's name in for the first time, except of course for having stressed thoroughly that the Ark is called by the name of the Lord of hosts who sits enthroned on the cherubim (v. 2). YHWH's anger is kindled against a man, Uzzah, who presumes to assist the Ark and dies of his gesture, indirectly checking the man who is orchestrating it.

David, the narrator characterizes, is angry at God and fearful as well, but there is no engagement between the two. David's question or exclamation is, "'How can the ark of the LORD come to me?'" and his answer seems to be that it cannot. So the Ark is handed over to others, where it remains beneficially for its caretakers; when that experience is told to David, he makes another attempt to move the Ark to Jerusalem.

This second effort is described as more elaborate, more liturgical, more ceremonial, and arguably more respectful. That this second journey is successful is narrated before its process is described, so that our tension and attention can be invested not in its arrival but to the encounter between Michal and David. Commentators have little to say respectful of or sensitive to Michal here, Fokkelman among the least perceptive.[15] Since I will consider her as a minor character shortly, here in terms of plotting, she can be seen here as disapproving—or less than approving—this move of David with God's Ark, resembling, perhaps, the deity. Though David avoids the fate of the presumptuous Uzzah—however well-intentioned his gesture may have been—he does not avoid Michal's critique. She speaks to David for only the second time in our hearing, as bluntly as before. If David has accomplished his goal this time, as seems to be the case, Michal, whom the narrator here calls daughter of Saul, does not praise him but insults the manner of his process. That he presides as priest cannot be the central issue, though his priestly attire is what Michal singles out, accusing David of acting like a common shameless man. Exactly what she means we will investigate below, so here we move to his response—David's only direct discourse to Michal in the entire long narrative.

15. Ibid., 193–205, makes careful observations about the rhetoric of the chapter, ways in which it is distinctive among the materials among which it is placed. My earlier work on this unit is offered in Green, "The Engaging Nuances of Genre: Reading Saul and Michal Afresh," in Timothy J. Sandoval and Carleen Mandolfo, eds., *Relating to Text: Interdisciplinary and Form-Critical Insights on the Bible* (London and New York: T&T Clark International, 2003), 141–59, an effort to try to look in larger than gender terms, though including those.

As the episode concludes, David makes two points (vv. 21–22), the narrator offers one (v. 23), Michal none. David:

> "It was before the LORD, who chose me above your father, and above all his house, to appoint me as prince over Israel, the people of the LORD—and I will make merry before the LORD. I will make myself yet more contemptible than this, and I will be abased in your eyes; but by the maids of whom you have spoken, by them I shall be held in honor."

David says this is about God's choice of David over Saul, David's increasing house over Saul's diminishing one, and appearances seem to be on his side. David's second point is that this deed was done for YHWH, whether doer and deed be appraised as exalted or base. That is a harder claim to validate, since we have not heard David consult on this subject. The Ark does not react against this effort of David to house it in Jerusalem, nor will it when Solomon houses it within the temple. So perhaps its silence indicates consent, or perhaps it is biding its time until monarchy terminates. The narrator ignores that second point to return to the first David offered: "And Michal the daughter of Saul had no child to the day of her death." There is no Saul line through Michal, certainly not involving David, who is prolific as she is barren. Michal's silence and David's last word, affirmed by the narrator, reinforce the point that has not really been in doubt for readers.

j David Proposes to Build a House for YHWH, Who Disposes to Build for David: 7:1–17:

The next two units, though vastly commented upon for other than present purposes, are crucially important in their narrative context, which is where and how we will consider them.[16] The first unit shows David not too dissimilar from his claiming his city and moving the Ark: He has an idea that suits his kingship and moves to accomplish it. The narrator has very few lines in this chapter, but the first (v. 1) is a reminder to us, reading, that God is the source of David's rest from his opponents, the fundamental rest spoken of in Deuteronomy, Fokkelman suggests.[17] The king's approach to his prophet—Nathan looming suddenly in the way of prophets—is a comment rather than a question and surely not a consultation. It is, rather, the naming of a situation that we come to understand that David considers unsuitable. The prophet issues a blank check, not negotiable for long and not repeated by the prophet in our hearing.

16. A useful, general and wider-ranging study of these materials can be found in Mark K. George, "Fluid Stability in Second Samuel," *CBQ* 64 (2002): 17–36; 19–24 explore some of the "fluid language" of the unit, the wordplay and ambiguity. Detailed rhetorical work is also available in Lyle Eslinger, *House of God or House for David: The Rhetoric of 2 Samuel 7* (Sheffield: JSOT Press, 1996).

17. Fokkelman, *Throne and City*, 209, cites Deut. 12:9–10. Fokkelman makes many wonderful observations about this chapter on his 207–68, relating it with other pertinent issues.

The rest of this unit is God's speech, provided to Nathan for delivery to David, with the narrative choice being for us to hear it as God's directions rather than Nathan's delivery, though the address blurs, a slippage common in prophetic speech. God's assessment is wholly at odds with what David has evaluated, indicating that not at any time before had a house seemed to God preferable to a tent, stability to transience and flexibility. Not once has God complained about the tent or hinted to any of David's predecessors that a stable house would be preferable, never a reproach about the lack (vv. 6–7). That point is preceded by the question that God will invert as the piece develops (v. 5): *you*, build for *me*, a house for my dwelling? Not in my mind, God seems to say, before picking up on it shortly.

God's next words review David's own journeys: called from the pasture following the sheep to be prince of God's people, always accompanied by God, who has cut off all David's enemies before him. And, continues God, "'I will make for you a great name, like the name of the great ones of the earth'" (v. 9), appointing a place for the people and plant them there, safe from disturbance, rest as not experience from before the time of the judges. The stress is on the common journeying of deity, people and prince, and the corresponding rest to be experienced by prince and people at the behest of the deity. The rest, the secure place that obviates the journeys, will be a gift more than an achievement, certainly not forced by the wresting of a house untimely.

YHWH returns to the theme of who builds what for whom: "'Moreover the LORD declares to you that the LORD will make you a house'" (v. 11). So the time for a house is here and now, but David and Nathan have misunderstood the agency or roles, and that error God corrects: God's vision, God's project, God's agency, not David's. God specifies the nature of the house and of the building:

> "When your days are fulfilled and you lie down with your fathers, I will raise up your offspring after you, who shall come forth from your body, and I will establish his kingdom. He shall build a house for my name, and I will establish the throne of his kingdom for ever. I will be his father, and he shall be my son. When he commits iniquity, I will chasten him with the rod of men, with the stripes of the sons of men; but I will not take my steadfast love from him, as I took it from Saul, whom I put away from before you. And your house and your kingdom shall be made sure for ever before me; your throne shall be established for ever." (vv. 12–16)

So not built by David, not built in his lifetime, not a temple; rather a kingdom, an ongoing relationship, lasting onward in time.

This substantial correction indicates a massive misconstrual of God on the part of king and prophet. Related to David's determination to move the Ark, a plan also redesigned by the deity, the king has made a similar error about divine presence again, thinking God's Ark had a need David was the one to fulfill. This is an important moment for the king, with one—perhaps two—resembling it just having occurred and another like it lying ahead. Though David is about to respond well, something lacks, since his recent experience with the Ark has not carried over to this moment, nor will this moment carry much farther.

Back to one of the most extraordinary things we have heard before moving ahead: Who are the great ones of the earth, and how is it that God tells David he will enable him to enter their company? David is made this promise in the midst of a rebuke, a promise extended to him and words concerning his progeny. It is, in fact, the severest correction we have seen so far, and not the last. David is shown to be seeing poorly, responding inappropriately, anticipating little of who God is, perhaps distracted by all he himself seems to have achieved and not hearing the narrator's assessment to readers that all David has achieved is God's gift. The source of all the agency he seems to have misconstrued: who is serving whom, who is guiding purposes, who will build for whom. It is a prominent human miscalculation.[18] Hearts: How David's is like YHWH's is a theme picked up here from 1 Samuel 13. David has been told that he has replicated Israel's wilderness journey and arrived at rest, thanks to God. The narrator, silent for all this time, reports that Nathan delivered these words to David, but not in our hearing (7:17).

k David's Response: 7:18–25:

David's immediate response seems just right. Taking his place where God's presence is most tangible, presumably before the Ark that lives within a tent in the city of David, David responds to what he has heard, turning over the mystery of who he is to have been chosen a recipient of all he has just been promised would be done for him (vv. 18–21). "'Who am I, O Lord GOD, and what is my house, that thou hast brought me thus far? . . . And what more can David say to thee? For thou knowest thy servant, O Lord GOD! Because of thy promise, and according to thy own heart, thou hast wrought all this greatness, to make thy servant know it.'" His prayer stresses his smallness and lack of knowledge, compared with God's greatness and all God has, unaccountably, showed him. In reviewing with God all that God just has reminded him, David indicates that, for the moment, he grasps the incomparability of God and the smallness of himself, David indicates that, for the moment he sees his place.

He moves on to praise God, God's people, God's reputation, God's deeds, begging God to carry out what has just been promised, unsuspected and undeserved though David owns it to be (vv. 22–25). He circles back to praise God's name and repute, to single out for praise that God has told David the plan for his own household and heirs, claiming that only in the shadow of such revelation can he pray that God will accomplish it. David concludes asking God for everlasting blessings on David's house, such as God has sketched it for him. God makes no response, nor does the narrator comment—response is withheld. Difficult days lie ahead, as we know, for David's family and to decide the matter of who will

---

18. The ascription of the title servant to David, along with its being given to Abraham and Moses, underlines this link: the servant—even the best of them—knows little of what the master is about. In absence of that awareness, the temptation is to bully ahead instead of staying small.

be the next to sit on David's throne and, indeed, to build the place for the Ark to rest—until it vanishes forever.

1 David's Additional Achievements: 8:1–18:

This final unit, summarizing the positive and God-guided accomplishments before they cease shortly, is full of details about David's leadership, all approved by the narrator. He defeats (more) Philistines, Moabites, people of Zobah, Syrians, collecting booty and allies, spoils, and achieving repute. God is with David, the source of his success, the narrator opines: "And the LORD gave victory to David wherever he went. So David reigned over all Israel; and David administered justice and equity to all his people" (vv. 14–15). The last three verses offer notes of what we can call administration, telling us what we may already know but need to hold in mind: Joab named as head of the fighting men, Jehoshaphat as recorder, Zadok and Abiathar as priests, Seraiah as secretary, Benaiah as a commander over the foreign troops; and David's sons as priests.

3 Plotting and Narration: David's Later Deeds (21–24)

If these materials were included within the set 2 Sam. 2–8, we might not think them much out of place. Fokkelman, integrating these six pieces—two poems, two lists, two episodes arranged in a rough chiasm—stresses that they are achronic, and they resist our temporal ordering of them.[19] As indicated in the earlier part of this study of a long narrative, it seems important to ask whether we are to understand them as occurring before or after the events involving David's children. But since they seem not to reference those events, I will take them as unrelated causally and hence preliminary to the events of 2 Sam. 9–20, calling attention again to the uncertainty of edges and structure. Alter's comment that the materials are "manifestly written by different writers in styles that exhibit differences from that of the main narrative, and also certain differences in ideological assumptions" suggests he is content to let them rise from the middle of David's career.[20] To theorize more conclusively about their placement lies beyond the scope of this work.

a Bloodguilt Managed: 21:1–14:

The first of them relates back to the general topic of past deeds of Saul, whose impact continues to be experienced, consequences of his life choices still felt, as

---

19. Fokkelman, *Throne and City*, 362–63, also notes that they ready us to meet the David of 2 Sam. 9–20: "We meet David at his peak. He himself speaks in poetry, with a conscience as yet inviolate, in contact with God, as a hero who gets his strength from God" (363).

20. Alter, *David Story*, 329.

we saw in chs. 2–4 and 6. Here a three-year famine prompts David to ask God for the cause and to learn that Saul had wrongly put Gibeonites to death, violating the oath extracted by them previously. Though this does not refer to a Saul narrative we know of (rather to events known from Joshua 9), it enters our narrative now, managed by God, David, and others. That we do not know all we might wish about details is a consequence of now-familiar narrator reticence. We are reminded that serious matters of pollution caused by violation of norms cannot be disregarded as though it had no impact.

When David, informed by God and responsive, consults the surviving Gibeonites as to a resolution of the injustice, they at first evade him but then ask for seven Saulide sons to be given to them to slay, and so David does. There is no hint that this is not appropriate within the norms of this story. Though sparing Jonathan's son, Mephibosheth, from inclusion, David hands over two of Saul's sons by Rizpah and five of Saul's grandsons, borne to Merab.[21] The Gibeonites hang these males, but Rizpah keeps long watch to prevent the corpses from being savaged by animals. The narrative evokes the battle scene of Gilboa, where the bodies of Saul and three of his sons lie unburied for a time before being displayed on Philistine city walls. Perhaps Rizpah does here and now and over these bodies what she could not do then and there, preserving again into the King David's narrative the presence of King Saul.

David, prompted by what he hears of her heroic deed—and perhaps by what he also was not in position to do after the events of Gilboa—gathers the bones of Saul and sons from Jabesh where they had been preserved and reburies them in the ancestral tomb in Benjamin. God, responsive to all these actions, ends the famine. Rizpah's deed of respect, prompted by David's deed of justice, stirred by God's nudging him about the injustice to the Gibeonites, brings a healing to the land, at least within the ethos that the story seems to project. Serious injustice has effects, and once these are recognized, they must be remedied. God is one of the helpers of this sort of justice, making it known when it was not evident by other channels.

b Heroes of Wars with Philistine Giants: 21:15–22:

Though we have already seen in the previous consolidation section, the two narratives of David and Philistines contending—indeed seen the Philistines removed from their land—here feature several more encounters with Philistines, specifically with giants of Gath. In one such encounter, David, fatigued, is nearly killed, but his nephew Abishai intervenes to slay the giant who threatens to kill David. Since his men beg him not to risk his life again, others—including another David nephew—kill other large warriors from Gath, whose names are noted. But as before, David and his men are victorious over the Philistines. Of these episodes

---

21. We register, again, the impact of David and Michal having no child in common, who would be a Saul grandchild. There is textual confusion here, however, and Michal's name is in the Masoretic Text (see Alter, *David Story*, 329).

and companions, we are otherwise ignorant, and the narrated moments are not particularly well developed.

c David's Poem of Praise to God: 22:

This long poem seems distinctive by its genre, except we recall Hannah's hymn in 1 Samuel 2 and David's lament in 2 Samuel 1.[22] We can here do three things: First, "chunk" the structure of the poem; second, note its many links with the longer story we are reading; third, make a few miscellaneous observations prompted by the issue of David's voice speaking here.

The structure: the poem is ascribed in 22:1; in stanza one (vv. 2–4), we hear the speaker in distress, to which the response is a theophany from the heavens (vv. 5–20). The main part of the theophany details the arrival of God (vv. 5–16) and more briefly describes the actual rescue (vv. 17–18). The second section and center of the poem detail how God rewards integrity (vv. 21–31) and the third section describes the triumph of the rescued one as he confronts those who had beset him (vv. 32–46).[23] The coda comprises thanksgiving (vv. 47–51). Granting that the poem seems oddly inserted here (and resembles closely Psalm 18, thus raising various other questions), still we can see that its content overlaps the "narrative facts" of the story we have been reading.[24] In terms of tone, however, the match is not strong, with this poem's outsized imagery resembling the aggression of David in 1 Samuel 25 more than any other unit we have seen.

All of that said, we can also take it as part of the long and diverse narrative about David, as echoing some of the issues we have been tracking and will continue to consider. The genre of psalm of thanksgiving not withstanding, this passage is also an utterance of David, who in distress from opponents, calls on God for vindication and deliverance, and receiving it, claims to use that righteousness to destroy his opponents. As direct discourse, it is largely triumphalistic, perhaps David's most extreme utterance of his own rightness and deservingness of rescue. It is, arguably, the inverse of David's best moments, when less certain, he consults God, or when finding himself in trouble, he accepts critique. God's action is more

22. In tradition, David is "the" psalmist, so again, this is not quite so distinctive and unexpected in a broader context than our present one.

23. Fokkelman, *Throne and City*, 333–55, specifically on 335, orders it by introduction and coda, by three stanzas, three sections and numbers its strophes and counts its words and syllables.

24. Morrison, *2 Samuel*, 287–89, lists these: for example, God chooses David, protects him from opponents, rescues him, and is with him. David trusts God often and is victorious over his foes. Some of the language overlaps closely (perhaps since there are obvious vocabulary choices with the present subject). David verbalizes his thanks and leaves a positive legacy. This is all true at an abstract level and does not take on the topic of where the fit is not so good (e.g., the claim of innocence, which is problematic in the longer story). David J.A. Clines has also worked closely with the two poems: "What Remains of the Hebrew Bible? Its Text and Language in a Postmodern Age," *Studia Theologica* 54 (2011): 76–95.

overt by far than anything else in the whole story. In terms of the sort of agency leading to compassion, there is not much to say here. In a sense, this prayer is problematic.

d Last Words of David: 23:1–7:

These are manifestly *not* the last words of David, since those occur as he manages his heir and legacy. These are more general, perhaps in some way ending or responding to the long poem just recited. They are contextless, wisdom-like, concerned with ruling, stressing fear of God.

e List of Mighty Men: 23:8–39:

Roughly parallel to the deeds of the heroes above (21:15–22), we have here more feats against Philistines, naming men who for the most part we have not known. There is a group of three, another of thirty, and then the narrator sums up that we have heard of thirty-seven heroes. Lists are unstable over time, with adds and drops expected and likely.[25]

f Episode of Guilt and Deliverance: 24:1–25:

A final narrated episode, intriguing and more sophisticated in design than its present fellows, concludes this general unit. Preparatory to examining it under characterization, we can note the role of the narrator and the strings of the plotting.[26]

The narrator provides the framing information (vv. 1, 25): that God is angry about something relating to Israel and nudges David to respond, with the eventual outcome that God breaks off an action already begun as remedy. We see a match for the other narrative of the pair, where the injustice of Saul to Israel's old allies prompts a similar response. The episode also evokes David's first effort to move the Ark and his presumption to build a temple. That we do not know the specific reason for divine outrage, with our only hint being the corresponding passage regarding the Gibeonites, is intriguing but resistant to solution. From God's angle, only partly disclosed to us by a very reticent narrator, the angry reaction of God is all we have. That the passage concludes with God's acceding to David's accepting a limit of some kind. David's response is, again, frustratingly opaque: "So the LORD heeded supplications for the land, and the plague was averted from Israel." Whether God's response is to something we see or do not quite see is the point to explore: who wants what and moves to get it, and how so.

---

25. Fokkelman, *Throne and City*, 299–301. He splits it vv. 8–12, 13–17, 18–22, 24–39.

26. Fokkelman, *Throne and City*, 308–31, provides the basis for many of these insights by his careful work. He psychologizes in a way that I cannot endorse, but his observations about the language are highly useful.

David—not knowing, as we do, that his prompt to count Israel and Judah is itself a response to God's anger over something—gives the order that counting be done. Joab, knowing little as well—though apparently more than David does—intervenes to dissuade his king from the action, but David is not responsive to Joab's intervention. So the census proceeds, named in time and in space (vv. 4–9). The result is brought to the king: 800,000 in Israel, 500,000 in Judah.

Then, and unaccountably, David's heart registers dissent and his lips contrition (v. 10): "But David's heart smote him after he had numbered the people. And David said to the LORD, 'I have sinned greatly in what I have done. But now, O LORD, I pray thee, take away the iniquity of thy servant; for I have done very foolishly.'" Why he so speaks is not clear, despite efforts to name it. Perhaps counting is presumptuous, but the narrative does not really provide such information. David lacks the crucial information that his prompt to count was activated by God's anger—not the reverse. We know but still do not understand the precise dynamics of divine urgency, and all the human not-knowing may be the point.[27] David undertakes a series of actions that in a certain way has little relevance to what God is doing. And yet they are what we have to interpret. God responds to what David has said and done, sending the prophet and seer, Gad, with choices for the contrite king. We learn them along with David (not before [v. 13]): "'Shall three years of famine come to you in your land? Or will you flee three months before your foes while they pursue you? Or shall there be three days' pestilence in your land? Now consider, and decide what answer I shall return to him who sent me.'" The response continues the quasi- or partial responsibility David bears for the counting. That is, though God has prompted the counting for a reason not presented, and though we do not see any but Joab and eventually David himself fault it, the deed takes place. The character God accepts David's sense that the census is wrong and needs requital. Perhaps in the narrative calculus, an act to clear pollution is what is needed, and David is struggling to do what is needed, as he did in ch. 21. Perhaps his heart's feeling and words of sorrow are what counts.

The choice of three lengths of time, three kinds of affliction, diverse participants, and different agents seems well-explored in and outside the text. David, not without expressing struggle, opts for shorter and (implicitly) for divine agency (v. 14): "'I am in great distress; let us fall into the hand of the LORD, for his mercy is great; but let me not fall into the hand of man.'" His preference appears to be for short time length and divine agent. Next, the narrator tells us, it happened. God sends the three days of pestilence, and whether David had anticipated it or not, the pestilence falls on many besides and to some extent instead of himself: seventy thousand of those just counted die, while David survives. Only when the agent of the destruction approaches Jerusalem does God intervene (v. 16): "And when the angel stretched forth his hand toward Jerusalem to destroy it, the LORD repented of the evil, and said to the angel who was working destruction among the people,

---

27. The narrative setup is thus somewhat like the story of Job, where the characters lack key information which we have, though without well understanding its significance. The point may well be that however much we may claim to know, it is not very adequate.

'It is enough; now stay your hand.' And the angel of the LORD was by the threshing floor of Araunah the Jebusite."

After and in addition to God's intervention, David also reacts (v. 17): "Then David spoke to the LORD when he saw the angel who was smiting the people, and said, 'Lo, I have sinned, and I have done wickedly; but these sheep, what have they done? Let thy hand, I pray thee, be against me and against my father's house.'" That is, both deity and king intervene at a certain point in the inflicting of the pestilence, seeing its outcome. Is the three-day period over as well, or does God halt the slaughter early? Is the danger to Jerusalem the main prompt for God, the angel's arrival at the city? These are not matters the narrator makes clear, though the interest of the passage seems spatial rather than temporal. With David still in only partial awareness of these narrative facts and ourselves knowing not a great deal more, we consider the last exchange.

The prophet/seer appears again, presumably sent as before, with new directions (v. 18): "'Go up, rear an altar to the LORD on the threshing floor of Araunah the Jebusite.'" David moves to obey and Araunah to respond to the approach of the king (v. 21): What this character knows is not provided to us, except that he cannot have missed completely the three days of pestilence, even as it is halted just short of his own heritage. Making obeisance to his lord, the Jebusite questions him. "And Araunah said, 'Why has my lord the king come to his servant?' David said, 'To buy the threshing floor of you, in order to build an altar to the LORD, that the plague may be averted from the people.'" Again, we register that David is making causal connections that seem odd to us, with our narrator-provided information. We know that God, who has prompted the whole episode for some presumably necessary reason, has already stopped it. David's intervention comes after God acts, as indeed does the prophet's advice.

The two haggle a bit over conditions of exchange (vv. 22–25):

> Then Araunah said to David, "Let my lord the king take and offer up what seems good to him; here are the oxen for the burnt offering, and the threshing sledges and the yokes of the oxen for the wood. All this, O king, Araunah gives to the king." And Araunah said to the king, "The LORD your God accept you." But the king said to Araunah, "No, but I will buy it of you for a price; I will not offer burnt offerings to the LORD my God which cost me nothing." So David bought the threshing floor and the oxen for fifty shekels of silver. And David built there an altar to the LORD, and offered burnt offerings and peace offerings.

The characters settle that David will pay rather than accept a gift, whether such be relevant or not. As is the case in ch. 21, David's action, worked out by him, may or may not be directly effective. We see it is important to him, whether more broadly necessary or not.

We conclude with the narrator frame: "So the LORD heeded supplications for the land, and the plague was averted from Israel." Again, perhaps a question of reliability: To what is the deity responsive, when, why? But whatever angered the deity seems managed, cleared. We will return to this provocative and enigmatic unit in Chapter 7, realigning it slightly.

This whole set of material has a miscellaneous feel to it, not quite achieving the impression of steady consolidation of the rest of the narrative chs. 2–8 suggests. These events seem midway or later, some plausibly nearer the end of his rule. The quick consideration of them here serves mainly to allow us to consider the ways in which certain of their actants are drawn, and also to review edges, structures, plotting, and narration, preparatory to zooming in shortly with more methodological precision. A summary from which to move is useful: In terms of the design of the implied author, accumulating in many ways across the whole narrative, David's actions show a mix of what God approves and disapproves, leaving us the challenge of discerning the divine heart and its impact on the king's capacities. That God wants David king is clear, but Saul's successor has anything but a free hand. The deity desires and expects to be consulted, as David sometimes does and as Saul so rarely did. Some of God's specific desires remain opaque, at least until they have been transgressed by David's overreacting and excessive agency. The narrator, generally less polished here than elsewhere, shows king and deity collaborating but not always smoothly. God checks David's presumption as needed, and David is suitably responsive, though perhaps not carrying the learning over from moment to moment. To state that point somewhat differently: Insofar as it is not easy for a new king to know what the deity desires, David is shown as acting first and listening to divine response afterwards. In certain cases, his actions are approved, while in other matters—notably cultic—the strength of the rebuke testifies to the seriousness of the lack of alignment between David and YHWH, to David's arrogance in proceeding without consultation.

4 Characterization: Theory

a Scope and Task:

How to manage this most complex of our tools? The process needs to work with the others we are using—not simply be artificially about characterization itself—and also to be in conversation with contemporary theory—both with ancient theory from which much modern theory pushes off and with the nuances of modern theory itself, as informed by the novel. What I offer here also needs to be compatible with this particular project of reading David amid the wide range of other characters. So first we need to talk generally about facets of this characterization challenge, then to open a pathway for proceeding.

Both ancient theory and classic narratives are necessary for the consideration attempted here. Aristotle, never long absent from the theoretical discussion, makes astute observations about what ancient writers did. But various of them did diverse things, and it is not always useful to generalize too globally. "Ancients" includes here the Greeks and Romans, notably eighth–seventh-century Homeric poet(s), and the fifth–fourth-century writers of lives and novels, not omitting the drama of the fifth century, which, though not strictly narrative, does have characters—deep ones. The Hebrew Bible is ancient as well, offering great diversity of narrative style, with the material of 1–2 Samuel being at the most developed end of the spectrum, due both to momentum sustained and subtlety of technique. "Ancient" also includes New Testament texts, notably the Gospels and Acts of the Apostles, whose characters are children of both Hebrew and the Greco-Roman traditions. All of this character/characterization study contributes to our project.[28]

Modern theorists are invaluable, for what they say both about the ancient and modern literature, with contemporary topics often provoking insight indirectly.[29] I do not share skepticism about using modern theory for ancient material, so long as we are careful to avoid gross anachronism. But when modern theorists are accounting for modern literature in particular—notably the novel and also some of the postmodern narrative genres—the theory grows more complicated than is needed for our present narrative.[30] So if ancient theory is not adequate and modern theory can be too arcane and cumbersome, and if my goal (distinct from certain other theorists) is not to set up categories that are generally right or useful broadly but rather particular ones, our theory discussion can be more heuristic. The material under present consideration works, over two biblical books, with the deepest character in the OT and also with many others of near-similar to dissimilar complexity. My hope is to talk about the David material usefully, not to attempt something of broader applicability. So the goal in this chapter is to offer enough theory and some practical tools for talking about minor characters here and clearing the ground for use with major characters is the next two chapters.

28. See Cornelis Bennema, *A Theory of Character in New Testament Narrative* (Minneaplois: Fortress Press, 2014). His ch. 1 surveys the state of the question on characterization rising from ancient biblical and Greco-Roman texts and reviews relevant theory in his ch. 2, laying out the position he plans to take. His object is to call into question certain reigning assumptions and test alternatives, indeed to offer a comprehensive theory for NT characterization (meaning for the Gospels and Acts). Among his most useful general points to push off from (rather than debate here): (1) some HB/OT characters have substantial depth, more so than some Greco-Roman materials; (2) certain of Aristotle's observations do not well correlate with certain HB/OT or NT materials; (3) modern tools and insights are legitimate to use, or cannot be ruled out simply because they are modern; (4) readers inevitably and legitimately infer.

29. For a thorough and accessible review of character and characterization, consult Baruch Hochman, *Character in Literature*; Scholes et al., *The Nature of Narrative*, 160–206; a shorter version, stressing the structuralist contribution, can be accessed in Herman and Vervaeck, *Handbook*.

30. A good example is the whole discussion of focalization, which, though important, threatens like quicksand. For a sample, Manfred Jahn, "Focalization," in *Routledge Encyclopedia*, 173–75. Bennema, *Theory of Character*, 53–56, reminds us that contemporary literary theory has in general moved past drawing primarily on the novel to move to a broader category, narrative, which makes them useful.

b Stipulations and Preliminary Points:

1. Terminology: "Character" refers to what is more authorial, while "characterization" is concerned about how readers construe.[31] As with many other useful distinctions, this one is helpful only to a point, since the two realms are not ultimately separable. Character, then, is the artistic presentation of such actant information, conscious and otherwise, while the characterization challenge faced by every critic is to set it up for discussion comprehensively but as simply as possible. The task of readers is to establish the set of traits composing a character, weigh it as to adequacy in relation to readers' frames of reference, then to engage it, and interpret.[32]

2. Nature: Literary characters are something between simply marks on a page, on the one hand, and people pretty much and unproblematically like us, on the other. To name those extremes is to find ourselves looking between them for nuance, for practical precision. Marks on a page would not account for the tremendous pleasure our human species has clearly gained from reading. Naive realism does not hold up over time, since it is clear that literary characters lack psychology, intentionality, and subjectivity.[33] Literary figures are not, basically, "like" us, though they often seem so—are meant to—and offer us plenty of space for projecting our own consciousness.[34] Baruch Hochman efficiently calls them "substantial hypothetical beings."[35] Even characters who once existed actually or historically are fictive when they appear in narrative.[36] A similar instance is the deity, who exists but is a character when met in literature. "Fictive" implies not false but made. That modern study of the Hebrew Bible has been massively obsessed over the historicity issues is highly limiting and seeps into much commentary, surprisingly. There is

31. Keen, *Narrative Form,* 64.

32. Phelan, *Reading,* 8–12, says that characters are meeting places of certain predications, traits collaborating to suggests persons; readers will decide what they will privilege. This explanation helps us see why one era can find a character believable while another does not. There are external worlds from which traits spring besides the primary literary ones used here, for example, the sociological and psychological.

33. Robyn Warhol, "Character," in Herman et al., eds., *Narrative Theory,* 119.

34. Keen, *Narrative Form,* 57–58, discusses this feature of reading, as does Hochman, *Character in Literature,* 7–9. This may be the place to note that our first reading of a text is different from all subsequent ones, which, in the case of ancient classics, may be many rereadings. We can change our minds about characters, but that is not the same as learning about them for the first time.

35. Hochman, *Character in Literature,* 26.

36. Though I have found much of his work very helpful, I disagree with Bennema in this matter, as he makes a case for the non-fictionality of God and Jesus (*Theory of Character,* 63–72). I wonder if, due to the particular nature of literature that is also accorded the status of Scripture, particularly when it involves Jesus, there is an instinctive avoidance of words related to fiction, lest serious misunderstanding creep in.

a key place for suitable historical and sociological data, but it does not trump the fictive nature of characterization.[37]

3. Reader role: Though literary characters are not like us in one sense, they are recognizable by us, reading, and that link provides our access to interpreting them. They have human-like qualities: physical, mental, and social. Readers make inferences about characters, inevitably, legitimately, as responsibly as possible, naming our assumptions and tools as well as bringing to bear all the relevant information we can manage. One of our ways of reading characters is by joining their discrete moments, ordering them in one way or another, which we need to name if we can.[38] This we do, notably when we are provided with information indirectly and must pose questions or make assumptions in order to proceed.[39] Dorrit Cohn reflects perceptively "that narrative fiction is the only literary genre, as well as the only kind of narrative, in which the unspoken thoughts, feelings, perceptions of a person other that the speaker can be portrayed."[40]

4. Categories for characters/characterization: There seem to be as many ways to name the coordinates of characters as there are theorists. If the question is approached in terms of what there is for us to notice, we can factor character elements to include physical features, cultural traits, relationships, modes of speech, habits, and so forth.[41] Or we can try to systematize at a slightly more abstract level, as Phelan and Rabinowitz do: mimetic facets, synthetic ones, thematic ones, understood (I think) as follows: Mimetic features concern characters as possible people living in a narrative world arguably like our own; thematic features have to do with issues that are cultural, ideological, philosophical, or ethical and are faced by characters; synthetic material draws attention to the more artificial constructs, lining up with our aesthetic judgments. The issue is how these factors collaborate in a particular work of fiction.[42]

Drawing again on the distinction between author and reader, we can both distinguish and overlap character and characterization. This set of data comprises what sorts of questions we, reading, want to probe. Bennema offers three spectra

37. Keen, *Narrative Form*, 56, discussing inappropriate historicism, says that a paradigmatic inappropriate question in English literature is to ask how many children Lady Macbeth had. Biblical commentators often betray this slip when they talk about what likely happened, when the better question is what is being presented for our consideration.

38. One of the limitations of even best of the charts or grids available is that the best readings come from correlating the information, not simply from studying the individual categories, however complete they may be in their way.

39. Abbott, *Cambridge Introduction*, 133.

40. Cohn, *Transparent Minds*, 7.

41. See Keen, *Narrative Form*, 60–64, for an elaboration derived from Seymour Chatman, one of the most influential of modern character-theorists. Subcategories can be constructed, of course.

42. "Introduction," in Herman et al., eds., *Narrative Theory*, 7, and later in their piece in the same volume, "Character," 111–13.

for these features: degree of complexity (ranging from one or few traits to more); development (capacity to change not at all, a little or more); penetration (the degree to which their inner life is available: less to more),[43] while Keen offers the abstractions of descriptive, illustrative, and demonstrative information.[44] Hochman has eight categories, each with an end point named.[45]

5. *Story and discourse:* I continue to find this distinction—like character and characterization—useful, not least so that we do not inappropriately overlap the two. At the level of *story*, that world in which characters exist, act, and have knowledge, we may usefully think of them as woven zones, sets of traits that vary in consistency: tighter at the center and looser at the edges. These character zones are fluid and mobile, seem to be aware, to desire, feel, speak, act, and engage others. When we are looking at them in the story (making story rather than discourse prominent), we can factor them and follow them as they move through the story. As noted when we worked with character plotting, to name what seems to drive characters to their specific plans is a useful way to manage this facet. It remains fruitful to recall that they do not know all that we know and that they may be hinted to know what is withheld from us.[46]

At the level of *discourse*, our concern is the manner in which we, reading, are provided whatever information we are offered, especially as complexity emerges, thickens. We will, as before, work with the following aspects: The narrator, in our case existing outside the story rather than within it, is crucially important. Not a character, the narrator provides verbal information to us.[47] The narrator can be queried in terms of *what* he provides for us (not for the characters) and *how* it is done. The "what" includes things like external information, inner perceptions, words, actions, and hints from the contexts or setting. We can examine several mini-spectra on any occasion when the narrator is active, though trends will emerge, as we have already seen when talking about the narrator role apart from his characters-contribution: Is the narrator more complete or less so? Is he even-handed with characters or prone to partiality (more about some, less about others)? Is the narrator more explicitly omniscient or less so? Is he generally reliable? Is there occasionally some signal that the narrator clashes with some other source of information? Does he tell or show the information, directly or more indirectly—or in between, as is true of all these choices? These factors will shift constantly and must be pressed in each individual moment of interpretation, if they are to be

---

43. Bennema, *Theory of Character*, 73–82.

44. Keen, *Narrative Form*, 60–64.

45. Hochman, *Character in Literature*, developed in his ch. 4.

46. Walsh, in *Old Testament Narrative*, 23–27, observes that we tend to accept characters in the story, suspend our incredulity; but we remain on the watch for ways in which characters violate our expectations.

47. Verbal or "underlinable" information distinguishes the narrator from the implied author, who is responsible for more than the narrator's parts of disclosed information, though theoretically for it as well.

used with precision.[48] Within discourse, characters are sometimes and somewhat analogous to the extradiegetic narrator, providing narrated information, serving as narrators themselves—intradiegetic ones. So in terms of information, in addition to absorbing what we are offered by the narrator, we may scrutinize and organize what we are told by characters and how it is provided. A character may provide information about self or others and be noted or given to do it along similar lines as we have just seen: more complete or less so; more evenly with characters or prone to partiality (knowing more about some, less about others); the character will be more informed or less so, even wrong on occasion; the character's view may be generally reliable or in some clear way clashing with some other source of information; the character will tell or show the information, directly or more indirectly—or in between, as is true of all these choices. Again, the point is to ask these questions as we go and not assume consistency and stability, though patterns are likely. With all these matters, it is to be assumed that readers, though perhaps agreeing on much, will ourselves receive information variously, and for reasons we may benefit by examining.[49] To be utterly complete is neither possible nor necessary.

6. *Focalization:* The fraught and confusing topic of focalization provides us with a way to recognize and manage the relation between what is shown (the range of "whats") and the angle from which they are disclosed. It is in this relation that gaps open.[50] The concept of focalization is a contribution of narratology, that is, the theory developed and articulated by structuralist literary critics (twentieth century) and refined thereafter, once some of that modernist superstructure crashed of its own complexity and blindness, leaving some great remains for reshaping to further use.[51] As the word suggests, the issue has to do with seeing, but in fact, as refined, it has to do with the registering of impressions from all the senses, not simply sight (though sight is the most obvious and prominent). Focalization concerns how impressions are managed from various viewpoints or angles. In shorthand, it is about who sees and who says and how such perceptions, reported, blend as readers interpret.

48. Keen is useful here, *Narrative Form*, 38–44, as is Herman and Vervaeck, *Handbook*, 67–69; see also Cohn, whose whole part I of *Transparent Minds* is on third-person narrative presentation of characters.

49. It is my long experience in teaching the David material that some students come early to dislike or resent, surely to mistrust him. Though a valuable clue, such readers remind us that to simply fall back on judgments that David "is" manipulative, dishonest, and abusive is not adequately critical. The reading angle needs explication.

50. All recent theorists talk about this phenomenon, sometimes using a different terminology: For example, Herman and Vervaeck, *Handbook*, 70–71; Keen, *Narrative Form*, ch. 4, notes 56–57.

51. Genette provides the classic overview in *Narrative Discourse* and *Narrative Discourse Revisited*. Refinements can be tracked in Bal, *Narratology*, Rimmon-Kennan, *Narrative Fiction: Contemporary Perspective* (London: Methuen, 1983).

Focalization has become an arcane topic, and my aim here is to present it simply enough to be useful. Let me start with an example: A visitor from the academic dean's office comes to a class session I am teaching, and as I make introductions, I say to her, "They [nodding toward the students seated around me] really love my syllabus supplements," smiling contentedly and proudly as I make that claim. The visitor, hearing me, also looks around while the sentence is moving from my lips to the ears of all present, my face and expression also available to all eyes present (except my own, of course—unless I were being filmed, in which case I could watch later). What she sees as I speak: About half the students nod their heads in agreement; some few sit stolid, apparently not reacting or with no reaction visible; a few roll their eyes, shake their heads minutely; one shoots a hand into the air; one burps. Multiple angles of reception to read.

Focalization comprises the offering and the receiving and appraising of all those reactions and the angles made by their engagement: the relation between what I (as a sort of narrator) say and what the visitor (as reader/interpreter) registers from the others (quasi-characters) who hear me.[52] So we have three sets of participants: myself, the visitor-witness, the students as participants with me but not quite the same as me. How will the visitor-witness note and gather the information from her two general sets of participants? In some cases there appears to be little slippage between what I say and how some students feel, though even this is inferential; apparently I have reported them accurately—though my summarizing their perception is not the same as their articulating it. But in other cases, there is considerable divergence, tangible variously. It is at once apparent, and reinforced by reading theory, that this is an infinitely complicated matter, and my goal here is not to manipulate the concept until it is lost in a tangle— "intractable ambiguity," as one critic says[53]—but to make it useful for the basically and comparatively simple characterization we have in the story we are reading.

The other players can again be distinguished: The real and implied authors are relevant, in that they offer assertions of many kinds for readers to infer, interpret. How the real and the implied authors build the world of David with many and varied substances is difficult to single out since their text is woven of many patterns. One example would be my claim that the implied author is negative to dynastic kingship and that such a view pervades the story without being able to be simply pointed to. Focalization works more practically and directly when we talk about narrator assertions, which (consistently for us) have been verbal, underlinable. So the question is what the narrator says about and through the characters and how it can be spoken of by readers, who should (by the theory) agree on much but not all. That is, when a narrator provides information concerning a character, what is the angle or are the angles from which it is given: Standing where in relation

---

52. My analogy is not quite right, since literary characters (cf. my students) are not aware of what the narrator (myself as teacher) says, though the narrator knows what characters are doing. But the main point emerges well enough, for the comparatively simple sort of focalization relevant in the David narrative, I think.

53. Jahn, "Focalization," 173–77.

to characters and providing what from that point? Analogously, it is also about characters and how they offer their value-laden perceptions and how all these interact, as perceived by the reader.

The word "filter" is sometimes used, as well as the analogy of the camera. Jahn offers the image of a narrator opening windows (both classic and computerly), giving readers space to register events and perceptions through the screens provided. He also uses the word "montaging" to suggest the fluidity and participative nature of the process.[54] Focalizing, impacted as it is with other narrative tools, is crucial and helpful to explore.

c Characterization Spectra

- **Who** provides the information?
  - narrator
  - a character about another
  - a character about self

- **What** information is provided? (note that some things do not slot so neatly)
  - something external and tangible: gender, age, appearance, dress
  - something internal and hidden: feelings
  - an action or event (more change-making): marriage
  - a situation or quality (more stable):
  - a social role of function: name, gender, ethnicity, age . . .
  - speech of some kind

- **How** is it provided by whoever provides it? [focalization discussion here]
  - directly, bluntly, with little room for ambiguity
  - more indirectly, with more ambiguity (that we should be able to name specifically)
  - inferentially, so that it needs piecing together

- **When** is it provided?
  - in what seems normal time
  - earlier than we might expect it
  - later than we might expect it

- **Why** is it provided, or what is arguably its impact?[55]
  - How changeable is a factor: not very............somewhat............crucially..........
  - How often is the matter attested? not very............somewhat............ crucially..........
  - How disputed is a matter? not very............somewhat............crucially..........

---

54. Ibid., 175.
55. These spectra are closer to Hochman's than has been the previous set.

- ○ How important is a matter? not very............somewhat............
  crucially..........
- ○ How complex or tangled is a matter with other data? not very..........
  somewhat..........crucially........
- ○ How much inner access are we provided? not very............somewhat............
  crucially..........
- ○ How artificial or odd is the information provided? not very..........
  somewhat..........crucially........

5 Sampling Minor Characters

Our next project for this chapter is to converge the implications of what has been unearthed from this part of Davidic narrative with the aid of structures, plotting, and narrator role combining now with character theory, sampling and testing with a few minor characters who appear in this set of material. We will investigate in order of ascending complexity. The challenge is both to sharpen the theory and to see the characters and the characterization process well, all while addressing the matter of David's heart.

a Ahinoam of Jezreel

This character is hardly a trace, yet a brief discussion is fruitful. All the direct information we have is from the narrator, who mentions Ahinoam of Jezreel five times and Ahinoam daughter of Ahimaaz once.[56] Ahinoam of Jezreel is always named in her role as David's wife, linked with Abigail, wife of Nabal of Carmel. She is also named as mother of David's firstborn son, Amnon. So by role, she is wife and mother, potentially queen mother though eventually showing deficit there. She is given no interiority. The only character who provides us anything about her is the distress of David when he learns that his two named wives have been taken from Ziklag with all the other families of his men who had been there while David and his men marched to Aphek (1 Samuel 30:1-6).[57]

Most of what is noteworthy rises from gaps of information—what the narrator does not fully disclose. Is Ahinoam the daughter of Ahimaaz the same as Ahinoam of Jezreel? When and under what circumstances did David's second wife (after Michal) and mother of his firstborn come to marry David, if she did so? That she is referred to by patronym or gentilic rather than by her husband's name would not be surprising, if she began as wife of Saul and ended with David. When does she vanish from the story in which she is hardly more than a name? Is it the case, as some suspect, that David's struggle with Saul involved conflicting loyalties not only

---

56. 1 Sam. 25:43, 27:3, 30:5; 2 Sam 2:2, 3:2. Ahinoam daughter of Ahimaaz, wife of Saul, is named in 1 Sam. 14:50.

57. David's narrated response of distress does not necessarily provide information about his wives themselves, revealing more clearly information about David, deprived.

of Merab, Michal, and Jonathan but also of Ahinoam? If so, why do we not know more, and how do we manage the crumbs we have? If David has the allegiance of Saul's wife as well as, variously, that of his children, what is Ahinoam's role? How is it to be constructed? If such is not the case, does a narrator assume we will not miscue around her? When might we suitably have learned these opaque things, since it seems too late by the time we have her name? Is the substantial negativity associated with Amnon's part of his mother's characterization? Gaps are primarily what construct Ahinoam, and they may rise from simple ignorance on our part as much later readers, or they may be more artistic. There are characters about whom we know less, but not those who are named five or six separate times and who are married to the first king of Israel and Judah.

b Rizpah

Our next character is Rizpah, daughter of Aiah (whoever she may be). Rizpah is a secondary wife of Saul, we learn, and mother of Saul's sons, Armoni and Mephibosheth. There are two brief episodes involving her, both in this role as wife to King Saul and mother to their sons. The narrator provides that brief information (3:7–11; 21:8–11). Two characters act in relation to her: Abner, army commander and assistant of Saul, and Ishbosheth, surviving Saulide son, engage over the allegation that Abner took Rizpah when she was still part of the Saul household. In the second episode she does not speak but acts, protecting the corpses of her and Saul's two sons after David has handed them over to be executed by Gibeonites for some injustice Saul had committed. Each episode can be combed briefly.

We have not heard mention of Rizpah before we hear Ishbosheth and Abner quarrel about her: Ishbosheth says, "'Why have you gone in to my father's concubine?'" (3:7). The narrator does not vouch for the truth of the question/accusation, nor does anyone else. We will examine these competing Saul-men below, but here we have a question riding on an accusation, so two uncertainties, voiced by one man to another, marking Rizpah as property: Did you, why did you? As with David's wives, reaction concerning her does not provide information about her.

Abner's response is equally ambiguous: The narrator first tells us that Abner was very angry at the words, replying,

> "Am I a dog's head of Judah? This day I keep showing loyalty to the house of Saul your father, to his brothers, and to his friends, and have not given you into the hand of David; and yet you charge me today with a fault concerning a woman. God do so to Abner, and more also, if I do not accomplish for David what the LORD has sworn to him, to transfer the kingdom from the house of Saul, and set up the throne of David over Israel and over Judah, from Dan to Beersheba." (vv. 8–10)

Again deferring some of the possibilities until later, we can note the narrator's naming anger (and not some other emotion) and offering not a denial but a counterquestion about status. To be called a dog's head is clearly an insult,[58] and

---

58. For possibilities, see Keith Bodner, "Bakhtin's Pseudo-Objective Motivation and the Demise of Abner," in Bodner, ed., *David Observed*, 48–49 who reviews the "dog's head" possibilities.

Abner imputes such contempt to Ishbosheth (to Rizpah as well), contrasting his own alleged though about-to-be-rescinded loyalty to Saul's household with the behavior of Saul's son. Abner, who boldly and directly withdraws his claimed loyalty, says he will reverse it. The narrator concludes by saying that Abner's response frightens Ishbosheth into silence. So here Rizpah, lacking voice and agency, is the subject or object of a quarrel, whether actual or pretextual, we will consider below. Abner dismisses her status to that of "a woman," which Rizpah is, of course, but also a king's secondary wife and mother of royal sons.

We do not hear of these sons in any of the Saul material but in a later episode opening after his death, where Rizpah's action of respecting the bodies of their sons—performed day and night from barely harvest time until the first rains (late spring until early autumn)—prompts a response from David. The narrator is again our source of this indirect testimony of David to the mother of the dead Saulides: "When David was told what Rizpah the daughter of Aiah, the concubine of Saul, had done," he acts to bury properly the bodies of Saul and others, whose corpses we saw both abused and respected at the end of 1 Samuel 31. Rizpah, verbally silent while acting with persistence and perhaps courage, prompts a good deed from David for Saul, arguably a deed due him. This is more than we have of Ahinoam, but still not a great deal. The gaps emerging differ from those generating Ahinoam, provide firmer status detail and an action to read. Her response to the quarrel between Abner and Ishbosheth and that which involves her will be examined additionally below.

c Ishbosheth

Characterization becomes slightly more complex, though again, the impression may well be that gaps dominate firmer data. The major non-provided information is how a son of Saul survived the battle of Gilboa with no mention of any sort. Always when dealing with "missing information," we have to ask if it was well known by intended readers and hence not needed, or whether uncertainty rises from something more intentionally artistic. I think the Gilboa-survival of the Saul-son who does so poorly starts him under a cloud from which he never emerges. That is a later- and real-reader construction, and other possibilities exist. But I will suggest that as we meet Ishbosheth, he has already failed both to live notably and to die bravely with his father and brothers. So both narrator reticence and timing of the information provided launch my sense of Ishbosheth.[59] And yet, the survival of this Saulide is also an achievement of sorts.

---

59. Another characteral datum is his name: Man of shame, to translate it literally, and whether "boshet" is a euphemism for "baal," the utterance is not good. For more comments on this point, see Bodner, "Crime Scene Investigation: A Text-Critical Mystery and the Strange Death of Ishbosheth," 15–35 in Bodner, ed., *The Artistic Dimension: Literary Explorations of the Hebrew Bible* (London: Bloomsbury T&T Clark, 2013), 19, who says that the narrator's refusal to name Saul's last son directly (calling him Saul's son and by the euphemism, if such his name is) is part of his characterization.

The narrator provides the next piece of information, and in contrast to other information about David: As the men of Judah make David king, Abner, Saul's army commander, brings Ishbosheth to Mahanaim and makes him king over various groups. Ishbosheth is silent, passive, acted upon, giving no assent even from those men indicated. At the age of forty, he has two years to reign, but the narrator reminds us that the Judah-men are actively aligned with David, who has more than seven years attributed to this phase of his rule, more than two stretching ahead. It is not a strong narrative start, nor does it improve as the two royal sides meet, first in some ceremonial and ritual way, where the Israelites stay even with their opponents, and second in subsequent battle, where they lose more men that David's side does (all in 2 Samuel 2).

Intervening for this character is Abner's slaying of Asahel, to be considered below. It is not a helpful move for the Saulide side, prompting Abner in an unexpected way. The next episode involves Saul's army chief and his son exchanging words over Rizpah, with Ishbosheth accusing Abner, who takes offense at both the accusation itself and that it would even be raised if true (3:7–11). Leaving for the moment Abner's possible role, we examine Ishbosheth by listening to his direct discourse: First, though upbraiding Abner, Ishbosheth reinforces his own weakness, since he appears unable to have claimed Rizpah for himself. Second, doing more harm than good, Ishbosheth hands Abner occasion to transfer his loyalty. So, whether the charge is true or false, it weakens Ishbosheth to have accused his right-hand man—though of course if the charge is true, to have kept silence would be a weakness as well. In case we need to be told, the narrator confirms that the responses of Abner frighten Ishbosheth into silence, and he proceeds no farther. Ishbosheth's characterization is thus handled primarily in negative space.

His last bit of detail, provided to him by the narrator (4:1–12), is twofold: First, that Ishbosheth is fearful when he learns of the circumstances of Abner's death (perhaps fearing the progress of Abner's boldly announced transfer of loyalty); second, that he is assassinated in his sleep by two fellow-clansmen who make their way into his house, kill him, behead him, and escape with the head. The gap from Mount Gilboa is freshly activated, as this beheaded son of Saul dies ignominiously, incompetently, as part of events that reverberate as Saul's army chief is handing Saul's kingdom over to David. That is, these two killers (Rechab and Baanah, sons of a certain Rimmon, a Benjaminite and fellow-tribesman of the man they kill) correctly appraise Ishbosheth's life is most valuable to them when taken from him, while incorrectly assuming Ishbosheth murdered can help them as they offer the proof of his death to David. Their calculation is impossible for us to weigh with clear result, though David speaks negatively about the death and kills the assassins. David's words over this dead man's head are not about the man himself but about his manner of dying, may be more about himself than about his rival.

So the narrator, the man himself, and other characters all converge to show that Ishbosheth has little positive filling out his character zone. One way to put that is to ask if there is a single piece of information that can be construed as positive, only to answer in the negative. Ishbosheth has no positive trait, no action that succeeds, no utterance that is effective, no loyal or even competent ally or helper, no surviving kin—except his nephew whose presence is mentioned in 4:4—no feeling attributed to him except fear. Actions are done to him rather than by him, and these all falter short of success. I see no space for ambiguity, no beneficent shadow. When the bones of the slain Saulides are buried in the family tomb, his are not mentioned, his head apparently remaining in Abner's tomb. The larger impact of Ishbosheth's characterization, I suggest, is to add discredit to the house of Saul and by contrast, to promote David's royal claims. And yet, while Ishbosheth (and later Mephibosheth) maintains presence, Saulides have footing.

d Michal

More complex than Ishbosheth though still quantitatively minor in our long story, Michal's presence gives us the opportunity to explore characterization additionally. In the six or seven mentions she has, we can use our spectra more explicitly and comprehensively to see what precisely is on offer, reaching from the small moments of narrative presence to the prominence given to this character to her final scene. There are six (one hinged) distinctive sets of relevant information.

The narrator first provides in a straightforward manner (in 1 Sam. 14:49) that Michal is second daughter of King Saul, indicating or implying briefly her gender, place in the family, status, ethnicity, kin relationships, and so forth. For all the information offered, specificity lacks. The timing of her mention may be a bit odd, with information coming early in Saul's story though in the last episode before his firing.[60] Second, she is spoken about and by category in 17:25 and 27, when Saul's fighters opine that the slayer of Goliath shall (will or ought to) be given the king's daughter. As already noted, that "hearsay" makes complex the betrothal scene negotiated between the Goliath-slayer and the king who failed to kill the Philistine himself.

The third set of information is also provided by the narrator and by story characters, acting as narrators. In each instance, the matter under consideration is also Michal's status as David's wife. In 1 Sam. 18:20–27 she is spoken of, by anonymous persons at court and by her father and by her husband-to-be. In 18:20 that Michal loved David is told to her father, who acts on the basis of what he is told to open negotiations with David. Michal herself has no voice or agency in the communication, and so her focalization angle is minimal. I venture that she does not claim the perception given her, here or elsewhere, and except for the power of this narrated rumor, we might never associate Michal with love for David. Saul and David speak of her (through servants) in terms of her strategic worth and value as they negotiate over David's marriage to her, the process by which she becomes wife

---

60. Often we can see that there is no automatic or natural time to provide background information and there may be no very suitable time. Before we meet David, it is probably good that we know about the family with which he will become so involved. So I will not remark the "when" of this information as odd.

of David as well as daughter of Saul. The negotiation is highly complex, with each utterance ambivalent and ambiguous.[61]

Fourth, we learn, also from the narrator (25:44), that "Saul had given Michal his daughter, David's wife, to Palti the son of Laish, who was of Gallim." Again, her angle is not provided, but she is spoken of as a daughter, as a wife of two (David and Palti), and that the regiver is her father. In 2 Sam. 3:13–15 the marriage brokers are again David and Saul's surrogates: Abner and Ishbosheth. Michal becomes an object in that transaction, with the narrator quickly describing the two moments of the negotiation: her marriage to and her return from Palti to David:

> And [David] said [to Abner], "Good; I will make a covenant with you; but one thing I require of you; that is, you shall not see my face, unless you first bring Michal, Saul's daughter, when you come to see my face." Then David sent messengers to Ishbosheth Saul's son, saying, "Give me my wife Michal, whom I betrothed at the price of a hundred foreskins of the Philistines." And Ishbosheth sent, and took her from her husband Paltiel the son of Laish.

David makes the same demand of both men. We hear that David refers to Michal both as Saul's daughter and as his own wife, though not both relations simultaneously. He also characterizes Michal as a commodity or reward earned for performance of a particular feat. David, approaching each of the two men distinctively, omits other things he might have said of Michal and, indeed, speaks primarily of himself rather than of her. His reasons and plans are not provided. The narrator does not quite coordinate these two facets of the transaction: why ask Abner first and then approach Ishbosheth? But we can see that in no case is Michal herself a subject. We also see that her husband Palti contributes information "around" her, specifically his feelings about what happens: "But her husband went with her, weeping after her all the way to Bahurim. Then Abner said to him, 'Go, return; and he returned.'" Why Palti weeps is not made utterly clear, but it seems safe to infer his sadness at their being parted, so he indicates care for Michal.[62]

The fifth and fuller moment of characterization involves Michal's agency to a greater degree and also her voice. We back up to her marriage to David and its effective dissolution for that scene. In 19:11–17, we hear her speak to her husband of danger David does not seem to have registered. What she offers him is a choice: "Flee tonight or die tomorrow" is concise and urgent, suited to what happens. Michal evinces no feeling of any kind except urgency, though we can add to that concern for one or both of them a broader care about what her father is about to do and its impact. She is also focalized as speaking so as to gain time for her husband and seems unafraid to face her father, once that has to be done. Her language is not

61. See my discussion in *Mighty Fallen*, 301–18 and "Michal Afresh."

62. Tears are hard to read, so though it seems tempting to claim that Palti loves Michal, we must notice that it is not quite said. Palti can be weeping from shame, anger, or any other number of things, the point offered about David's reactions regarding his wives' capture. Narrator reticence reigns.

deferential, in fact, barely polite. Though he is her father, Saul is also a king, and Michal presents herself as daughter, wife, a thwarting if not disloyal subject. Her words to her father—"'He said to me, "Let me go; why should I kill you?"'"—are usually construed as a lie, but that does not seem unequivocally established; we cannot know. Saul makes no rejoinder, leaving her words as dominant. Though we learn later that Michal is given to another man, it is not said to be a punishment of her, more plausibly a situation to benefit her father, the king. We can summarize that Michal provides herself testimony about her qualities, facing danger competently and without hesitation or fear.[63]

We arrive, next, at the sixth, final, and most complex scene, with Michal herself as well as the narrator and another character providing information (2 Sam. 6:16–23). In this scene, she is focalized by the narrator, by David, and by herself as wife/daughter and as a shrewd and independent observer.[64] As David accomplishes a success in bringing the Ark of God into the city of David—preceded by a lethal failure as his first attempt was—all in the city, participating, seem to celebrate while Michal sees and speaks from a different angle. Shown watching from a window a scene where others are participating, her distinctive angle is reinforced. When she speaks, we can reasonably infer that her perception is at odds with the view of others and that it needs to be spoken, though it is not so clear why. The narrator begins by showing us generally what she saw and thought, but then she takes over, speaking her appraisal of it: "As the Ark of the LORD came into the city of David, Michal the daughter of Saul looked out of the window, and saw King David leaping and dancing before the LORD; and she despised him in her heart." The appraisal prompts, though not quite adequately, what we might have otherwise missed, since his words are sarcastic rather than precisely descriptive (v. 20): "'How the king of Israel honored himself today, uncovering himself today before the eyes of his servants' maids, as one of the vulgar fellows shamelessly uncovers himself!'" Distracted as we may be by wondering what the uncovering comprises, we miss the basic literal charge: David has acted for his own glory in bringing the Ark of God into the city of David.

David's response (vv. 20–21) sees and names Michal brutally as a member of a loser-house, not preferred by God while the speaker's own household seems to be thriving. David shows himself as in a powerful position to please others while Michal remains displeased and displeasing. In sum, he focalizes her as a Saul-daughter, not a David-wife, and the narrator agrees, saying that Michal remained childless, implying both divine disfavor and social shame, leaving her able to claim no role in David's kingdom. The narrator weighs in with David's view against hers, though saying something that David cannot have known at the moment. We watch

---

63. By contrast, Jonathan and even David manage Saul very differently from Michal.

64. All of her "markers" are in place: gender, ethnicity, status, experience, and so forth—some sketched within the narrative, others more inferential, whether by readers who know the specifics of her cultural situation or by those who do not. That is, though general readers can have some sense of how "a Michal" might feel, we cannot know precisely what shame and respect markers are operative here.

the various "screens" montaging to appreciate how complex a characterization can emerge in the fifteen or so verses that Michal is given.

To converge the character and characterization facets of this scene underlines Michal's qualitative importance. She is described by the narrator, addressed and spoken of by David, angered at her words, and she speaks for herself. The narrator has presented her once as Saul's daughter and currently and previously as David's wife. That she has been sketched as taken from a man who wept at the key scene of losing her and is reproached by her current lord underlines her status as exchanged among powerful men. As she is shown watching a scene from an angle unshared by others, David included, she addresses him with no sign of fear or desire to please, whatever her slur exactly denotes. That she alone disapproves of his Ark-action prompts us to recall that God did not approve of it earlier and will shortly rebuke David for his next plan to house the Ark. That is, what she says and how she articulates it stands closer to the deity's angle of perception than most have observed. This is her last speech, pronounced at a dramatic moment, with David's reply to her ending her discourse. David appears to know more about royal houses than Michal does, but we, reading, know he does not know as much about his own house as we do. Michal has no sons to lose, while David will lose several and under the most painful circumstances. I hear Michal as consistent in her characterization, since I disqualify the assertion of loving David as her own claim. What they speak of here is crucial to the whole story: God's choice of David over Saul, but David has a lot still to learn, but not today from Michal. We may be more docile.

e Abner

Like Michal, Abner has briefly appeared before we meet him for a final time. Like her, he brings his narrative and focalizing past to the moment we are now considering, interacting with others as well. Abner is listed as Saul's army commander (1 Sam. 14:50) and three times given agency in that role: as David returns to Saul with Goliath's head and Saul asks Abner a question he claims to be unable to answer (17:55–57); when he sits silent with the king at a feast (20:25); when David interacts with Abner and Saul for the last time (26:5–15).[65] In a word, he is shown as Saul's lieutenant, witness to three moments when David bests Saul. In the present set of material, he stands at the crux of two incompatible outcomes: Ishbosheth is to succeed Saul or David is to succeed Saul. With our characterization chart in mind, we look more closely.

As regards source of information (*who* tells), we have narrator's testimony, four sets of characters' information, and data from Abner himself. The narrator provides some general information about Abner, most important, that he is making plans for Saul's surviving son (2:8–9). Other characters construct him, diversely: Ishbosheth (3:7) accuses him of acting dishonorably in regard to Saul's

---

65. How are we to think about Abner escaping death at Gilboa? That gap is part of his characterization, but not easy to interpret.

secondary wife (3:7–8), a charge provoking offending Abner.[66] Joab accuses Abner to David, charging duplicity at 3:24–25: "'What have you [David] done? Behold, Abner came to you; why is it that you have sent him away, so that he is gone? You know that Abner the son of Ner came to deceive you, and to know your going out and your coming in, and to know all that you are doing.'" David, who once accused Abner of inept service to Saul (1 Sam. 26:15–16) eulogizes him at 4:33–34, though ambiguously: "'Should Abner die as a fool dies? Your hands were not bound, your feet were not fettered; as one falls before the wicked you have fallen.'" David's people, as a set, follow the king in his mourning for Abner. In the events after Abner's death, the leaders of Israel credit his plan of allying with David, completing the move. Abner provides information about himself, if indirectly, as he changes sides and when he fails so momentously to suspect Joab. Important to note is the diversity of viewpoint and the degree of certainty with which it is offered and supported variously. Abner is difficult to read.

What we are told is similarly rich and also undecidable: with Saul, with Ishbosheth, caught up contentiously with Asahel and Joab, joining former Saul-men to David, mourned by David when Abner lies dead. We can, I think, get a sense of Abner's status from his position at Saul's court and infer a diminishing status under Ishbosheth, as well as sense both glory and shame attached to going over to David's side, as Abner does. Though exactly what Abner has in mind remains obscure, the transfer of allegiance from the house of Saul to David seems clear. That Abner works for the dispreferred and dwindling house of Saul is part of his characterization, since at no moment is Saul's lineage not bested by David. The circumstances of Abner's killing Asahel are provided, but only to an extent, such that it remains uncertain whether the killing was a war-death or not, an uncertainty that David mentions as late as in his speech to his son, Solomon (1 Kgs. 2:5, 32). Abner is shown by his own speech as unwilling to kill Asahel, and yet he does so. Abner's decision to deliver Saul's people to David is never explicitly approved by any, including the putative beneficiaries. That David accepts what is on offer does not mean Abner's effort to broker is respected. Abner's plans for transferring Israel and Benjamin to David are known but never praised. David's "Good" (3:13) is not so much an expression of approval as it is immediately attached to a condition which Abner must fulfill or show his readiness to accomplish.

The *how* of Abner's characterization is similarly varied. His own speech to Ishbosheth is blunt (3:8–10), but David's speech about him is without clarity (e.g., 3:38): "'Do you not know that a prince and a great man has fallen this day in Israel?'" What David may be supposed to think privately of the man who betrayed

---

66. Bodner, "Demise of Abner," in his *David Observed*, makes other useful comments about Abner's characterization, including that his words to Israel in 3:17–18 are not verified and need not be assumed to be such (51–52), and that Joab's swerving Abner into the city gate and stabbing him in the same spot where Abner had struck Asahel is a sort of justice utterance (56); he also brings to bear several ways to appraise the narrator comment in 3:35–37 (61–62), which various commentators find dubious in diverse systems.

his lord is not disclosed, except that we remark his earlier words to Abner, freshly relevant now (1 Sam. 26:16): "'As the LORD lives, you deserve to die, because you have not kept watch over your lord, the LORD'S anointed.'" The clearest "how" we lack is the certainty about what Abner desires, and whether the death of Asahel can be seen to have forced his hand in ways that were not anticipated or preferred by him. That is, had Abner not killed Joab's brother (David's nephew)—having first tried to avoid it—how might things have proceeded? This is not a matter of "what happened" but of how clearly we are provided information crucial to our understanding of Abner's goals, or are not given it.

The *when* of the Abner characterization may seem normal and natural enough: We meet him when David kills Goliath (17:55) and twice thereafter. We learn of Abner's leadership when his first king is gone and his surviving son, Abner's second lord, is weak. Abner's death sets off the penultimate fall of a Saulide, leaving only Mephibosheth to survive all his people.[67] We may feel his plan of joining Israel to Judah succeeds at 2 Samuel 5, only to fall apart at ch. 20 as Benjaminites will withdraw from David. The most deferred facet of the Abner presence comes when David is still naming him when he addresses Solomon about his duties as king: "'Moreover you know also what Joab the son of Zeruiah did to me, how he dealt with the two commanders of the armies of Israel, Abner the son of Ner, and Amasa the son of Jether, whom he murdered, avenging in time of peace blood which had been shed in war, and putting innocent blood upon the girdle about my loins, and upon the sandals on my feet'" (v. 5), and similar at (v. 32). At the very end of the story this "Abner incident" is still being spoken of, though David seems to have decided Asahel's was a casualty and not a murder.

So a character as minor as Abner provides important gaps for negotiating not only himself but also David. His entanglement with even a few other relatively minor characters provides ambiguity for understanding this character very definitively. To summarize *why* Abner emerges as he does is to suspect it will cause steady trouble between David and Joab.

f Joab

As is the case with all the individuals being lifted out briefly here, Joab's characterization offers us something we cannot well do without, not least as we approach material where he features so prominently in the story of David. So the challenge with Joab, relatively minor in this present set of material but to be gathered from different parts of it, is to see what is on offer that we might otherwise miss if we do not begin our sketch here. I will here simply name ten things about Joab's characterization prompted by our chart but without aiming toward coherence or completeness. The ten insights: First, timing: For being such an important player in 2 Sam. 9–20 and into 1 Kgs. 1–2, Joab appears late on the scene. He is named

---

67. We do find out about Saul grandsons in 2 Samuel 21, and that information seems tardy, irrelevant to the basic storyline we know. They also do not survive. Homologously, the line of lone survivors attaches various Elides to the last Saulide.

in 1 Sam. 26:6 simply to identify his brother who accompanies David to engage Saul. Joab emerges as a character only at the start of 2 Samuel—late, especially given his subsequent prominence in the story ahead. Second and related: Joab is absent from the list of David's mighty men, again except to be referenced to assist identification of three others (2 Sam. 23:18, 24, 37). Alter, reminding us that the names listed do not agree with the total announced, notes that if Joab were included, the numbers would work out.[68] But since that does not happen, the gap is odd. Third is Joab's identification tag: he is consistently called by his mother's name, given a matronym rather than a patronym.[69] We are left with the impression that Zeruiah is familiar to the intended audience, her name dotting the books of Samuel; but of course she is not present except in her sons. Fourth, another relative deficit: The narrator avoids summing up Joab's deeds clearly. By convention, were the narrator to evaluate Joab, the information would be reliable. The episode that most begs for such assistance to our construction is Joab's killing of Abner, an event still rankling as Joab dies ostensibly for that early deed as well as for his last choice. David seems to have come to clarity that the killing was illicit, but the narrator does not venture a clear summary of it. Fifth: David, however, does evaluate Joab's deed in this present set of material, after Joab has confronted the king over the offer of Abner to deliver the remnants of Saul's people with little apparent effect, such that Joab takes the matter into his own hands (2 Sam. 3:27–30):

> And when Abner returned to Hebron, Joab took him aside into the midst of the gate to speak with him privately, and there he smote him in the belly, so that he died, for the blood of Asahel his brother. Afterward, when David heard of it, he said, "I and my kingdom are for ever guiltless before the LORD for the blood of Abner the son of Ner. May it fall upon the head of Joab, and upon all his father's house; and may the house of Joab never be without one who has a discharge, or who is leprous, or who holds a spindle, or who is slain by the sword, or who lacks bread!"

Cursed about as thoroughly as can be imagined, still Joab continues to serve David and in major responsibilities. At 3:39, David exclaims dramatically: "'And I am this day weak, though anointed king; these men the sons of Zeruiah are too hard for me. The LORD requite the evildoer according to his wickedness!'" We lack information as to how custom would guide here, but that David so massively condemns his nephew without removing him from service seems odd. Sixth, Joab's lack of reply to the king's words is mysterious, suggesting what?[70] Enigmatic reticence.

68. Alter, *David Story,* 352.

69. NT scholars suggest that to call Jesus "son of Mary" only calls attention to a problematic paternity. Here it could be argued that the matronym helps make the David link, but it still seems unusual.

70. Keith Bodner, "Crime Scene," 16–17, says, "A brother's death is not so easily forgotten, and certainly not by such a character as Joab."

A seventh point emerges around Joab's plans and plotting: In the material under present discussion, Joab's goal and consequent plan is clear and spoken clearly: to prevent Abner from assisting David. It seems unlikely that Joab would not approve of David adding tribes to his kingdom, so the objection more likely involves Abner's role in David's relationship with Saul's former man. That is, the agency of the transfer affronts Joab rather than the transfer itself. Joab's feelings toward and dealings with Abner are surely the product of Abner's killing Asahel, and so Joab may be characterized as acting recklessly out of conflicted motivation. In the matter of David's children, lying ahead of us, Joab will be more opaque. The central mystery to develop around Joab as he remains central in David's rule is what precisely does he desire and how does he plan for it. Eighth: Does Joab's construction of Abner's killing of Ashael divert the whole "David consolidating" story, such that we can ponder that what the new king might have managed in one way is irretrievably diverted once Abner has alienated Joab by killing his brother? Again, the quest here is not for "happenedness" but for narrative choice points. If, as seems the case, Joab becomes the character most implicated with David in the material ahead, a serious misstep on Joab's part as David is just widening his set of loyal people would remain a sore point between the uncle and nephew remaining in close contact as they do. If Abner had not wanted to kill Asahel, had tried to avoid it but is blamed by Joab for it, that does not help David. Ninth point: Bodner points out that we may infer that Joab's second reason to dispatch Abner would be to protect his own position in view of Abner's fresh advantage with David.[71] Finally, tenth, in the episode of the counting of David's people (2 Samuel 24), what are we to make of Joab's direct discourse to David, courteous beyond anything offered elsewhere (v. 3): "But Joab said to the king, 'May the LORD your God add to the people a hundred times as many as they are, while the eyes of my lord the king still see it; but why does my lord the king delight in this thing?'" Is this a sincere intervention, Joab trying to prevent David from a foolish action, as it turns out to be? How does Joab make such an assessment, and why is this the only moment like it? Alternatively, if David is somehow being prompted by God to clear some pollution that we can barely discern, the Joab's effort to dissuade him is exactly wrong. Both the character and characterization resist clarity while remaining crucial to navigate.

g YHWH

The deity is a character in biblical narrative with a presence generated by many of the same factors as attend the humans, granting a few differences. That I am a committed believer in God is not at odds with this assertion about characterization; that I hold Scripture as revealed and inspired does not change or conflict with my mode of discerning character traits. Representation into language of real beings—God, Jesus, Abraham Lincoln, Sonia Sotomayor—does not, cannot, and need

---

71. Bodner, "Crime Scene," 17.

not correspond precisely with their selves.[72] Language—verbal, iconic, artistic, photographic—can offer powerful access to existents, but it does not comprise them. Some representations of the deity in the Bible may seem more adequate or apt, and are more appealing to us than others. But to classify those traits globally is a difficult call over centuries and millennia. We know there are differences in portraiture: the deity of the so-called Yahwist is not quite the same as that of the Priestly writer, as the Jesus of Luke's Gospel is not the same as that of John's text. Within the 150 psalms, the construction of God varies massively.

The question here is the presentation of YHWH as a minor character in the story we are reading, moving as it does in the long narrative under consideration here. A few things can be stipulated generally, not because they are obvious or clear but, because though there is no space to detail them, they cannot be left with assumptions unnamed. God (as I will call this character) is not a human being like virtually all the other characters and is not tangible in the same way, either in the story or as spoken about. God does, on occasion, speak with prophets (Samuel, Nathan, Gad), and those encounters seem distinctive, not available in the same way to others. Prophets have unique and mysterious access to God, though they may also misunderstand the deity. Priests, especially with the use of the ephod, can learn what God thinks or they may say that they are not getting information they expect (Saul's priest in 14:35–36, cf. the priest Abiathar in 1 Sam. 23 and 30). Characters can claim communication with God, as David does and Saul conspicuously does not, but they may be mistaken or lying, and so each case needs assessing.

God as a character in this narrative has some generally consistent views and preferences, which again, by shorthand, we can say, conform more closely to a Deuteronomic view than to a Priestly one. The character God seems generally tolerant of the social praxis of the Iron Age east Mediterranean culture: the economy functions as it does here without divine critique; some men are more powerful than others, with concomitant obligations to be patrons for others; the patriarchal household seems accepted, with its sexual ethics; certain religious obligations are normative and others proscribed; foreigners are not treated the same as God's people. Most of that ideology is in place for most of the story's duration, or it is at least not fundamentally questioned or disputed. Becoming a bit more specific about our story before looking simply at one chapter: God, though not pleased about the idea of monarchy when it is presented by Samuel agrees to it, is portrayed as working with it, though that effort does not last past the sixth century. God, having once chosen Saul, fires him (though allowing him to remain ostensibly in place) and chooses David, whom he assists on numerous occasions. There is serious divine pushback at least—but not much more than—three times: once in 2 Samuel 6, again in ch. 7, and also ahead in 12. There are other moments of intervention as well, both positive (2 Samuel 23) and negative (2 Sam. 24:1). Even when God does not "weigh in," aside from general assumptions, we cannot

72. For a very different presentation of these matters, see Bennema, *Theory*, 63–72.

construe approval but must concede toleration.[73] Again, as with every other literary character, we can only proceed with what we are provided by the authoring hands.

With all that stipulated, we can take 2 Samuel 7 as a specific excellent instance of divine characterization. The topic of a house/temple emerges new here, but we have had some experience of God with the ephod and the Ark, and we know generally that God has a sensitivity about the land of promise, the heritage land given to God's particular people. Part of the general characterization of the deity feeding in here is that God, spatially distinctive, we might say, somehow shares identity with the Ark, a relationality demonstrated by Elides who severely offended it, as well as by Philistines and even by certain Israelites (all on view in 1 Sam. 1–7). One way to consider that claim would be to suggest that the Ark is a quasi-character. Another is to suggest that part of God's character zone includes some tangible space and is spatially reactive, for good and for bad, when the space is respected and when it is not. David has just (6:1–23) had two Ark engagements (one negative, one neutral) where he experiences this divine reactivity and now has another moment to meet this aspect of God's character.

The narrator, quite distinctively here, only provides information twice (except for tags). In 7:1–2 the narrator gets the episode started, as follows: "Now when the king dwelt in his house, and the LORD had given him rest from all his enemies round about, the king said to Nathan the prophet . . ." At 7:17–18 the narrator provides, "In accordance with all these words, and in accordance with all this vision, Nathan spoke to David. Then King David went in and sat before the LORD, and said . . ." The rest of the characterization is ceded to characters to manage directly in their discourse.

David and Nathan briefly exchange information about God, that God wants or needs a house, but both are incorrect in what they say, marking a limit to what each knows about himself and the other—and about God of whom they so confidently opine. God speaks about self and implicitly about prophet and king, making clear that they have limits on what they know, surely on this "house" topic. What God discloses is information about peripeteity and stability, about a temple and alternatives, about timing, about houses and who builds them, how enduring they are, and so forth. The content is not my main concern here but the characterization of the deity. God's language is highly self-disclosive, as clear as it gets, really.[74] As indicated, God's literary presence is not quite human but human-like, suitably called quasi-anthropomorphic. Though utilizing wordplay on concepts of "build" and "house" and by the repositioning of deictic words,

73. That is, I think we can assume that God remains opposed to idolatry, whether it is explicit or not. I do not assume God approves everything David does but does not engage actively absent some explicit indication of it. We might make a case for God's disapproval of Saul's slaughter of all the priests of Nob, or of David's killing of whole groups while sheltering with Philistines, but direct evidence is scant. What God can be claimed to think of the Ark's coming to Jerusalem shows complexity: not pleased at first, at least tolerant eventually.

74. For an excellent article naming some of these same points, see Kenneth M. Craig, Jr., "The Characterization of God in 2 Samuel 7:1–17," *Semeia* 63 (1993), 159–76.

there is little ambiguity surrounding who is the builder and what sort of house. A house for God—a temple—is not David's to build, nor is the time now. God offers that being templeless has not so far been a problem, and for king and prophet to assume so is incorrect. God quotes what he has never said to stress what he is saying now: No temple. The house God is building for David quite surpasses what the character David can be supposed to know, extending into David's future, as he is made like one of the great ones of earth, and his progeny's and people's future, as God's royal project with David's heirs is spoken of (vv. 10–16).[75] The timing of the information is not particularly odd. God speaks up when David initiates a plan and Nathan agrees. Looked at slightly differently, God might have been a bit more explicit when David was arranging for the Ark, since it seems clear that he misreads it once, if not twice in ch. 6 and then again in 7, as he imagines it needing a house to dwell in and himself able to do such a thing. As often noted (starting from Gen. 2–3 and onward), the deity's clearest speech sometimes comes just after an unfortunate or regrettable human act. The reason for God's speech seems also obvious at the surface: David is not the temple-builder, but with reasons for that ranging from common tradition and opening up in many other directions (e.g., why David did not do so) as well, also not relevant here, or at least not made explicit.

The second characterization scale we are using registers with less ambiguity than usual as well. How changeable is this data? Not at all. How often is it attested? Once will suffice. How disputed is it? Not at all. When David learns of God's words, he goes to sit near where God is (at the Ark, most likely), and speaks, but not to contest. How complex and tangled is the discourse? Again, at this point, not tangled except with the Ark, as suggested. How much inner access to this character? A great deal. How artificial is the information offered? I think, over "Bible-time," we think of God's temple as "there," forgetting that it has a fairly brief existence, or two runs, we might say (first temple, second temple; one by Solomon, one by the returning exiles, counting Herod's efforts as a remodel). The temple seems almost provisional, optional, surely not essential.

The rest of the material in the chapter is David's characterization of the God whose word he has just joltingly learned, and it is language of acceptance and praise, gratitude and humility. David learns, relearns (as he will need to do again) that God is the primary agent in this matter, the "decider," and that David's role is to heed. He expresses a willingness for those roles here. From Nathan we do not hear. That the deity is so unequivocal here, and so unusually clear, instructs us, again, that like David and Nathan, we may be more wrong than we suppose. That, though rarely on occasion God intervenes strongly helps us mind the ongoing characterization of David. Here at the moment of a great success, when David has been given by God rest from all his enemies roundabout, he makes a second serious miscue. Shortly, he will make another, with similar intervention and relevance to the dynasty and kingdom.

75. Later readers can have questions about the "everlasting" claims offered about the house, but those do not really affect the clarity of what God says to David here.

6 *Implications and Transition*

How do these two extended sets of material and particularly the contribution of the minor characterizations contribute to our investigation of David's capacity for compassion? We can first summarize more globally and then more closely. As the absence of Saul advances David's rule, the gain is clear: God approves David's going to Hebron, surely supports David's claims against the rule of Saulide survivors, assists David to accumulate a house of sons (and at least one daughter) and to vanquish enemies on his southwest and eastern flanks (2:1, 5:19–25, 8:14). The ancient city, Jerusalem, is taken and inhabited by the king, without divine rebuke.

But if we see that David gains his kingdom with God's support, it also comes at the price of death, paid many times over by those with whom the king interacts. The mother of David's firstborn is the elusive Ahinoam, whose name activates questions of her relation to Saul and hints of her relationship with her troubled son, Amnon—two shadows in David's life. Rizpah, similarly, is marked by courage that David had neglected to develop until she showed the way (2 Sam. 21:1–10). Death among David's close allies assumes prominence: Asahel dies, as do unnamed combatants of both the Ishbosheth and David groups (2:2, 15–16, 30–31). While in the midst of abetting the transfer of Saul's people to David, Abner dies, as does Ishbosheth, followed by his two assassins (chs. 2–4). Joab emerges to compromise David's achievement by killing a man who should have been safe while dealing with the king, and he retains his own position if under severe curse. David appears less than careful about the house of Saul and its survivors.

Defenders of ancient Jerusalem die (ch. 5), along with at least one man when David initiates transfer of God's Ark into David's city (6:7). Among the several victories David imposes on his enemies in Moab, Zobah, Syria, Hamath, Edom, Ammon, and Amalek are those against Arameans of Damascus, a bitter root ready to produce more trouble as we move on (8:1–14). More Philistines die (21:12–22). Mighty men gain their status in warfare (ch. 23), and David's people suffer from his counting them and then from the punishment he chose (ch. 24). He reclaims his first wife, Michal, who seems unwilling and remains barren (3:13–16; 6:16–23). Having taken Jerusalem, David wrests the Ark from its resting place to house it in his city. Michal, among all the witnesses of the Ark's celebratory arrival at Jerusalem, names the triumph as David's covering himself with glory rather than the act he claims it to be. Granting that being king is not the same as aspiring to become king, I suggest a foundation of carelessness and contempt for other actants shaping these early days of rule.

If we can see that God generally assists David in various ways, we can also see places where divine taciturnity or permissiveness gives way to opposition, when David's arrogations become excessive. Advised to dwell at Hebron, David takes Jerusalem for his home (2:1–2; 5:6–10). Anticipating the bringing of the Ark of God to the city of David, the king acquiesces briefly to divine resistance to such handling of the Ark (6:10). Conceding the Ark a brief sojourn at the home of a man of Gath, David proceeds with what he had planned when circumstances seemed more propitious. He breaks off his effort to build a temple (7:18–29) when corrected clearly by God. And he acts more carefully when he owns fault over the counting of his people (24:10–17). David's willingness to delay his moving the Ark, to accept censure from God over the temple-building plans, and over the results of the three-day plague stand forth provocatively. Prone to overreach, David shows himself willing to give way, back down, admit his own wrongdoing, and implore God for mercy. It is not so small a character trait in so mighty and apparently successful a man. If David's efforts and those of the authors' of his tale have focused here over the front part of the tapestry, smooth and clear as David attains such power so quickly, the knotted and raveled back asks for our attention as well: How will David manage when larger disasters than he has already met overtake him, when his failures come more manifestly from his own excesses than has been the case so far? As we turn to the events involving David's family and continue our work with characterization, we will explore that matter.

Chapter 6

FRUITS OF ARROGANCE: DAVID'S POOREST CHOICES (2 SAM. 9–14)

CONVERGING FIVE TOOLS

1 Transition

Thus far in our consideration of David, we have traced his story from the beginning of monarchy and of Saul's rule, moving through God's choice of David to succeed Saul after the first king's firing from kingship for certain grievous choices. We followed David into Saul's household and accompanied him as he fled it. Entering the wider wilderness region south of Benjamin and especially west into the land of the Philistines, we witnessed David evade Saul's designs on him, with no small or infrequent help from God. Though in a politically disadvantageous situation— allied with a group responsible for the defeat and death of King Saul—David was exonerated from culpability, if not quite from all suspicion. But with the death of Saul and the failure of the lone survivor-son, Ishbosheth, to succeed his father, David comes, by degrees, to be king of Judah and Israel. Moving from Keilah to Hebron and finally to Jerusalem, he achieves a house: a city bearing his name, a palace built by Hiram of Tyre, a dynasty promised by God, a family of sons and daughters. With eventual divine tolerance, David brings the Ark of God to Jerusalem though is stopped from building a house for it. And clearly with God's help, David is shown successful against his enemies, notably Philistines, and he is given rest.

In terms of the thesis of this book—that David grows in a capacity for compassion—we are still in uneven ascent, about to arrive at a crest and a collapse. The shepherd-boy David spoke easily of God's help in his struggles against threats to his flock, and we saw him move with similar sureness into a place of power and intrigue. Shown successful in the eyes of many in the royal household, David aroused the hostility of King Saul himself. Pursued, David managed restraint. Though we also saw and heard him tempted to retaliate—even symbolically rehearsing it—he resisted what he might have been in position to do.

David's agency continues uneven, erratic: Manifesting a certain passivity as those around him act on his behalf, occasionally he proceeds with initiative and decisiveness. Once David emerges from king-to-be to king-in-fact, his struggles with power grow. David's own men are not so malleable as once they seemed, with his nephews most conspicuously resisting his desires. As David moved to consolidate his position, his nephew Asahel, Saul's son Ishbosheth, and the Saulide leader Abner died, and David's claims of innocence were not convincing to all. His wars took a mortal toll, as did his effort to move God's Ark into the city of David. Clearly fundamentally approved and favored by the deity, David was rebuked indirectly at his first attempt to bring the Ark into his city, overtly at the end of his second and successful try, then subsequently stopped from building it a permanent house. The oddly placed episode of the king, the deity, and the threshing floor— eventual site of the temple—offered another occasion to see David out of step with God's desires. David acceded to divine critique, but a pattern is emerging, notably in matters cultic. For rather than consult before acting, David acts and draws back when thwarted. That God is with David is manifest, but whether David is with God, willingly and even docilely moving in concert, is less clear. The former careening from passivity to activity is now a toggling between effective leadership and its thwarting by the intemperate actions of himself and others. Arrogance is likely too strong a word here, but that attitude and practice will emerge from the royal heedlessness coming to attend David.

So far as our tools are concerned, we have five in current use: First, the rich ambiguity and ultimate undecidability of the edges of our story—where it starts and where it finishes, freshly relevant as we manage the narrative of the temple site. Second, and closely related, is the question of the best way to discern the basic structure of the material we are working with from a variety of ways in which it can be seen. Third is the major factor of plot and plotting: how the story is taking authorial shape and how the plans of characters are proceeding and how they are not. A fourth tool is our exploiting the narrator and his choices for providing us information and especially withholding it. Finally, we have considered the palette of characterization devices available, seen how much information can be disclosed in a few words as well as how uncertain a major character can remain despite verbiage. In the present chapter, we will put all these tools to additional use, managing edges and structure first and then watching the narrative of "poorest choices" unfold in terms of plotting, narrator choices, and characterization.

The point to establish now is the fit of David's poorest choices in view of what we have already seen of him. This stretch of narrative, where David makes a number of decisions with disastrous and irremediable effect, needs to be correlated with we have seen before as well as to depart from it. Though this portion of the story is filled with wonderful characters—Mephibosheth and Ziba, Bathsheba and Uriah, Nathan and YHWH, Amnon and Tamar, Absalom and Joab, the Tekoan woman— our focus will remain on David, both in terms of what he plans and how he emerges as a character. Within all the rich detail provided, there is still vast room for readers to differ about interpretations, and I hope this can happen as readers read. My aim is to sketch how the cultic actions David managed peremptorily— though breaking off and even repenting when challenged—continue to suggest an attitude of contempt hosting other actions as well, these now directed at human beings with whom David shared close relationship.

2 Edges and Structure

a Edges

The uncertainty attending the beginning and ending of the David story continues here. Specifically, we can wonder why Saul's grandson, Mephibosheth, emerges and to such little purpose—though we will not be able to evaluate adequately until he disappears in the story portion after this one. We may also query why his first mention occurs so soon: at 2 Sam. 4:4, in the midst of the failure of Ishbosheth to get a grip on his father's throne. As the two assassins creep toward the erstwhile Saulide king's home, we are given basic information about the young man, Mephibosheth: Jonathan's son, crippled as a result of falling while in flight from the events taking place on Gilboa. The single verse seems intrusive in its context of the stalking of Ishbosheth—except, of course, that featured is the resilience of Saul's house. But the Mephibosheth strand, trailing in explicitly from 2 Samuel 4 and persisting until ch. 18, remains anomalous. Another rough edge related to Mephibosheth includes the question of David's sons, a topic also persisting at least from 1 Samuel 18, to persevere past the death of David.[1] Insofar as a basic topic of this David narrative is about dynastic kingship, persistence of his sons seems relevant, sensible.

b Structure

So far as structure is concerned, this present narrative is the simplest set of material we have seen so far. I accept Fokkelman's basic choice to see each chapter as a unit, with particulars noted in his usual precise and fine-grained way.[2] The structure, then, provides a progression from the arrival of Saul's grandson to David's court to the quickly shifting question of David's relations with Hanun, son of old King Nahash of Ammon. The matter of David's unnamed son by Bathsheba seeds the tragedy of Amnon, David's firstborn son and his half-sister, Tamar and the fratricide by their brother, Absalom. Finally come complexities of heir apparent Absalom's return to David's court. The structure, generally or specifically provided, is unusually coherent.

3 Plotting, Narration, Characterization

What remains is to converge these three tools as skillfully as possible in the six scenes of material and then to draw conclusions, before moving on to the next set of related events flowing directly from these present ones. As already noted,

---

1. The thread of David's sons is present every time he either has sons or fails to have them, for example, with Michal, starting from 1 Samuel 18 and tracking into 2 Samuel 6.
2. Fokkelman, *King David*, 23–162. He makes two acts (chs. 9–12 and 13–14), but the units themselves comprise the discrete chs. 9, 10, 11, 12, 13, and 14.

the main focus will remain on David, who is tangled variously with his literary collaborators as well. To be accounted for are David's disastrous choices: why they are shown to have gone so wrong, whether any good emerges. A reprise of the three main and overlapping tools to be used here precedes considering the chapters.

a Plot and Plotting:

We remain managed to no small extent by the implied author of this sprawling narrative and by narrator choices. In character terms, David's plans are primary, interlinked as they are with those of Joab and Absalom in ways not fully apparent to readers or explicitly to the characters themselves. We have actants that are virtually and primarily choiceless, acted upon by others: Bathsheba, Tamar. Between are personages large and small, all contributing to narrative texture.

b Narrator and Narrating:

Crucial here is the basic narrator choice: to provide information himself or to delegate to characters the opportunity to speak their words. In these chapters so crucial to the transformation of David for woe and weal, narrator reticence is the most noteworthy feature. Time after time, vital conclusive information lacks. We need to wonder why, since in this part of the story it is not so likely that the "missing" information would be commonly known and thus not need elaboration. In several instances, character motivation remains shadowed.

c Characters and Characterization:

There are many to watch and weigh, and though our concern will remain with David, they all contribute. Our set of ways in which information is given will allow us nuance and insight. The key David question, I suggest, is the nature of his isolated impulses to disregard and override shading into arrogance and of his responses to the various outcomes of those heedless moments, where he seems to stall and freeze in a way not seen before. What, then, is the shape of David's transformation, and how do we know?

4 David's Poorest Choices

a David's Search for and Invitation to Mephibosheth: 9:1–13

The most obvious feature of the narrative about Mephibosheth is its intermittent distribution from at least 4:4 through 21:7. Mephibosheth's name or equivalent is like a vivid thread, surfacing at intervals in a busy tapestry. Hence my choice is to take that feature as seriously as the content is provided. The Mephibosheth thread arguably emerges at 1 Sam. 20:8–17, 27, 42, where David promises loyalty to Jonathan and his heirs (they pledge mutual loyalty to the other's kin). Mephibosheth will cease mention after 2 Sam. 21:3, when he survives other Saulides. The implied author and narrator, I suggest, challenge us to decide whether David abides by his own commitment—or asks us to assess at what narrative junctures David succeeds or fails to keep faith with his oaths to Jonathan, both how and why.

With the distinctive persistence of the Mephibosheth reference noted as a narrator choice, and with the suggestion that Mephibosheth's narrative presence is a marker for the house of Saul and a gauge for David's commitment to Jonathan's line, we can turn to what is on offer in ch. 9. David's direct discourse opens (9:1), as he inquires, "'Is there still any one left of the house of Saul, that I may show him kindness for Jonathan's sake?'" Since we have already been informed that there is a survivor, we know more than David does and can examine the query rather than being distracted by the answer. That is, David needs information—asks his question twice—while we are appraising a bit differently. Is David quite late to be asking about a son of Jonathan, in narrative terms if not by chronology? With his own house established by a number of measures, only now does David ask about this Jonathan-branch of Saul's house. Narrator timing seems strategic here: David has delayed, even neglected his word to Jonathan. And yet we see that an act of graciousness (Hebrew *ḥesed* [hereafter *hesed*]), even if owed because promised, is on offer.

Before looking at the direct discourse of the characters themselves, we can name a few more narrator choices. As often pointed out, Mephibosheth is referenced as a son or grandson (as a Jonathan- or Saul-descendant). He has been characterized earlier as fallen and consequently lame, a feature repeated summarily in 9:13. Whether the physical trait disqualifies him from some key royal access is debated, but as the detail develops, his impairment surely prevents his being a strong agent.[3] It makes him dependent in a way not boding well for any royal ambitions that might cluster around him. His physical trait of falling is replicated in his self-presentation to David, narrated twice, where he makes obeisance (vv. 6, 8), awkward and excessive though it seem if we envision it. Mephibosheth is also described by the narrator as father to a son, Mica (v. 12). But this reminder that the house of Saul survives into the fourth generation itself shorts out. Mica comes to nothing, narratively speaking. We might find the detail useless, except that we are told it. Although there remains a Saul scion, his existence is moot. Saul's house will not survive Mica, at least in this telling of it.

How do other characters speak of Mephibosheth? What information do they offer, distinct from what the narrator has provided? David's words have, I think, suggested that Mephibosheth is relatively unimportant to him—has been so far and will continue to be so, the royal deeds narrated here notwithstanding. David's initial inquiry for Jonathan's son suggests that David wants to meet his God-witnessed obligation promised to Joanthan's house. David's next words construct Mephibosheth as beneficiary of David's words: "'Do not fear; for I will show you

---

3. The association between Mephibosheth's lameness and the threefold reference to such a handicap in 2 Sam. 5:6–9) is explored by Shmuel Vargon, "The Blind and the Lame," *VT* 46.4 (1996), 498–514.

kindness (again, *hesed*) for the sake of your father Jonathan, and I will restore to you all the land of Saul your father; and you shall eat at my table always'" (v. 7). So David explains what he is about to do and then enacts two instances of it: royal lands restored for the young man's use and a place at the royal table.

Before continuing with David's characterization of Mephibosheth, we consider Saul's servant Ziba, who is brought to speak to the king. After identifying himself, he provides information about the Jonathan-son David seeks: that he lives, that he is crippled, where he dwells. Whether Ziba is short on formal respect for the king is difficult to assess with so brief a scene,[4] but scholars note that the servant presents little of the deference and vulnerability of Mephibosheth, speaking up directly, not prostrating himself, in the know, given charge, said to be the father of many servants and sons (contrastively with the one who has one of each). It is to Ziba that David addresses the words of restoration of the Saul property, to Ziba the charge that he and his household farm the property for Saul's grandson (vv. 9–10). David specifies to the servant that though Mephibosheth will eat at the king's table, his own lands will produce as well. Ziba is thus shown responsible and competent in a way Mephibosheth does not quite achieve. The exchange also positions us for what lies ahead in ch. 16. But for the moment, we see the narrator, David, and Ziba himself all testifying to Ziba's position as well as to Mephibosheth's.

As we focus again on how David and Mephibosheth each construct self and other, we can catch a few more details of interest: Mephibosheth makes no move until the king does, and then speaks and acts subserviently. That David bids him to fear not may be simply a verbal convention, but in this story of the non-survival of Saul's line, I think we are entitled to hear it as more than that. The scene is spare, developing only later, but for this Saulide to be singled out cannot be assumed to be good news.[5] Mephibosheth will survive David's attention to him, but barely, we may think (2 Sam. 21:3 comes to mind). The awkward obeisance may be a plea for mercy as well as or rather than a sign of respect or gratitude, his gestures vivid but inarticulate self-presentations of Jonathan's son to David. Mephibosheth's verbal response is to self-deprecate, using an epithet that we know has been in David's own mouth (v. 8): "'What is your servant, that you should look upon a dead dog such as I?'"[6] Two things here: First, to answer a generous offer with a somewhat self-effacing question comprises neither outright refusal nor acceptance. David has shown himself adept at such ambiguous discourse during the negotiations between himself and Saul for Michal (1 Samuel 18) and perhaps with Jonathan

---

4. Fokkelman makes the case for Ziba's disrespect, *King David*, 29.

5. Polzin develops this point, *David and the Deuteronomist*, 94, building on the possibility that David's lack of knowledge about Jonathan's son is a breach of his oath. A NT reader might think of Matthew's King Herod inquiring about the whereabouts of a royal child (Matt. 2:7–8)—the interest not inevitably benign.

6. Jeremy Schipper, "'Why Do You Still Speak of Your Affairs?' Polyphony in Mephibosheth's Exchange with David in 2 Samuel," *VT* 54.3 (2004): 347–49; Morrison, *2 Samuel*, 125 talks about the expression in its putative ancient setting and points out that the language would have been more offensive to original hearers than it may be in modern ears.

as well (20). When David used the dead dog epithet to Saul, Saul was moved to momentary forbearance, if not generosity in his dealing with David. Here, the question is not answered, but the Saulide property is reiterated—and to Ziba, who has a role in the gift: royal lands made to produce, a place at David's table. The second of these promises is repeated (v. 11), with a narrated rider: "Mephibosheth ate at David's table, like one of the king's sons," ominous though that descriptor may strike us in this particular narrative where many such sons fare so poorly. The beneficiary himself makes no reply, though Ziba does so in general terms. Silence on Mephibosheth's part begs construal, but as the thread continues to present itself, we can see that Jonathan's son has accepted the king's grant, though it will be contested in material ahead. Here, all seems well.

With the narrator choices indicated and the characters' presentation of selves and others provided, we can think about plot. The narrator's placement of the several son-of-Jonathan references makes it difficult, in the end, to argue that David has done well by the words he once swore to Jonathan. Though the implied authorial effort, in my view, is to show highly problematic the matter of royal dynasty—with a contribution made by these threading direct and several more covert allusions to Jonathan's son—still, David fails, in the main, to secure the safety of Mephibosheth.[7] What David the character can be shown to want here remains uncertain. He surely brings Jonathan's son under his observation and plausibly his generosity, but that gesture will eventually prove ineffective, whether the intent is truly to shown a kindness that had been vowed or also to supervise. And whether Ziba, ahead, will speak truth or lie (16:3), the damage is done when the servant quotes his current master, truthfully or mendaciously. David plots poorly here, or carelessly and improvidently—arrogantly—announcing rather than consulting. The action that might have bespoken compassion and protection as once promised and perhaps intended seems flawed, both here and as Mephibosheth will become caught in the snares of David's son. Mephibosheth, in relation with David, becomes another failed Saulide.

b David's Dealings with Ammon: 10:1–19 and 12:26–31

Though we are accustomed to thinking of ch. 11 as its own crucial scene and will indeed treat it carefully, I am in strong agreement with those who see the Ammonite war of chs. 10–12 as the crucial background and necessary context for events happening while it extends through ch. 12. So first here, we will talk about the whole fresh episode of David with the Ammonites, specifically comprising ch. 10 and ch. 12:26–31. Previously as we came to the end of events of David's consolidating his realm, he was given rest from his neighboring enemies. Indeed, this episode rises from an ally, not an enemy. David's dealings with Ammonites

---

7. Various commentators remark and some explore resonance between Mephibosheth and Jehoiachin in 2 Kings 25. See Jeremy Schipper, "'Significant Resonances' with Mephibosheth in 2 Kgs. 25:27–30: A Response to Donald F. Murray," *JBL* 124.3 (2005): 521–29, a relevant topic though outside my present scope.

are loosely connected with what preceded, as tends to be typical of many of the episodes narrated about David, with connections to be inferred.[8]

The narrator provides David's own interpretation of the opening of matter, a shadow or double of the unit we have just considered (vv. 1–2): "After this the king of the Ammonites died, and Hanun his son reigned in his stead. And David said, 'I will deal loyally with Hanun the son of Nahash, as his father dealt loyally with me.'"[9] Again, David is offering a gracious act (*hesed*), part of a network assumed between or among allies. But when David sends his servants to console the new king concerning his father, his clear choice and effort to fulfill obligations of loyalty with kindness are met with overt hostility, if not misinterpretation (v. 3): "But the princes of the Ammonites said to Hanun their lord, 'Do you think, because David has sent comforters to you, that he is honoring your father? Has not David sent his servants to you to search the city, and to spy it out, and to overthrow it?'" Next follows an insult to David's emissaries that reaches his ears. His men he treats with consideration—compassion—sparing their shame while preparing to march against his new opponents.

David goes largely unblamed for these actions, as commentators tend to take his discourse as sincere and true and the Ammonites' reactions as foolish and excessive. In the general honor and shame culture assumed to shape these matters, for a king to overlook such an affront would be unthinkable, and it is not disregarded here.[10] The Ammonites, seeing what has been unleashed (whoever may be at fault) and assessing David's hostile reaction to them, gather ultimately four sets of allies: two groups of Syrians[11] and men of Maacah and of Tob. First Joab and Abishai and then David himself are effective in breaking apart the coalition between Ammonites and allies, adding some of those groups to David's royal territory, reducing the Ammonites to self-reliance and siege in their city, Rabbah.[12]

---

8. Just as the events of 2 Sam. 21–24 are somewhat vaguely linked to other parts of the narrative, so are various scenes narrated elsewhere in the long narrative. Polzin, *David and the Deuteronomist*, 106–07, says that ch. 8 is a summary of David's whole reign, not a chronological contribution to the story that is gathering here. Fokkelman, *King David*, 42, reminds us that an imprecise connection marks the start of a new episode.

9. Nahash was an opponent of Saul in 1 Samuel 11, hence at least logically an ally of David's. The biblical story of Ammon and Israel is, of course, more complex and may be sampled in Genesis 19, Deut. 2–3, Judg. 10–12, all of which maintain the point that there is some sort of quasi-kin relationship between them.

10. Philip F. Esler, "David, Bathsheba, and the Ammonite War (2 Sam. 10–12)," in his *Sex, Wives, and Warriors: Reading Old Testament Narrative with Its Ancient Audience* (Cambridge, UK: James Clarke & Co., 2011), 303–21 helps us understand some of these issues contextually, notably the point that (part of) the relationship between David and YHWH is a patron/client one.

11. There is reference to David's defeat of these Syrian groups in 8:3. Morrison, *2 Samuel*, 126, points out that God was with David then, and so plausibly this is an approved alliance.

12. This outcome is detailed in ch. 10, where the encounter seems to break off until the turn of the year, to be concluded at the end of ch. 12. For closer work on the tactics, consult Fokkelman, *King David*, 41–50 and 64–66.

After a number of other events occur, to be examined shortly, Joab returns to the matter at hand at 12:27–28, capturing the city and demanding that David come finish the formalities: "'I have fought against Rabbah; moreover, I have taken the city of waters. Now, then, gather the rest of the people together, and encamp against the city, and take it; lest I take the city, and it be called by my name.'" Joab, who has had a major David-linked adventure between his initial defeat of the Ammonite coalition and this final scene, orders the king in no courteous language. David, wordless, obeys his nephew and subordinate: Gathering people to Rabbah, David takes the city, replaces its king wearing a heavy golden crown with himself, and despoils the city, enslaving Ammonites there and elsewhere before returning to Jerusalem.

Noteworthy here is primarily the relationship between David and Joab. I want to review what we have seen of it to date and then talk about the ending of the war before going back to what happens between Joab and David earlier in this same war, but also involving Uriah and hence the whole foundational episode of David and Bathsheba. As already observed, though named as David's nephew, Joab does not function as a character in 1 Samuel. The episodes in 2 Samuel featuring him have so far revolved basically around David and his dealing with Abner, who seems to have held with Saul and Ishbosheth the position that Joab comes to have with David: chief military assistant (so in 8:16, Joab is named in charge of David's army). Most relevant is that Joab is Abner's opponent while David's and Ishbosheth's men fight each other (2:13–17); when Abner kills Joab's brother Asahel—however that deed is to be understood—Joab and Abner exchange accusations over it (2:26–27): "Then Abner called to Joab, 'Shall the sword devour for ever? Do you not know that the end will be bitter? How long will it be before you bid your people turn from the pursuit of their brethren?' And Joab said, 'As God lives, if you had not spoken, surely the men would have given up the pursuit of their brethren in the morning.'" Since pursuit is the context for Asahel's death at Abner's hand, I take that as a charge against Abner by Joab. Joab breaks off from his own pursuit of Abner, having taken more lives than he lost, and returns to Hebron.

Abner's turning from Ishbosheth to David seems to proceed without reference to Joab, being negotiation between David and Abner rather than a military event. Though Abner was portrayed as open about his plans, Joab was shown surprised to arrive at David's house to learn that Abner has been there, displeased to learn how far negotiations between Abner and David had progressed (3:22–25):

Just then the servants of David arrived with Joab from a raid, bringing much spoil with them. But Abner was not with David at Hebron, for he had sent him away, and he had gone in peace. When Joab and all the army that was with him came, it was told Joab, "Abner the son of Ner came to the king, and he has let him go, and he has gone in peace." Then Joab went to the king and said, "What have you done? Behold, Abner came to you; why is it that you have sent him away, so that he is gone? You know that Abner the son of Ner came to deceive you, and to know your going out and your coming in, and to know all that you are doing."

We can note the discrepancy in aims between the two men: Abner to deliver Israel to David, Joab to stop some aspect of it. We see the gap in knowledge between David and Joab: David apparently coming close to completing with Abner what Abner had proposed, Joab seeming to learn of it for the first time when it is well-advanced. Joab reproached the king disrespectfully, with none of the verbal padding that often attends speech to a king, particularly if one is disagreeing or criticizing. David, contrastively, made no response. Indeed, Joab has told David that he is being played for a fool, deceived by a man he thinks is helping him. We, reading, are not in a position to judge that matter, except we have heard what Abner has said boldly about his plans, set up as plausible by the narrator. How David is drawn to think and feel, we cannot say in detail—beyond what he says of it after Abner is killed.

Joab's next move was bolder still, as he acts on his own (3:26–27):

> When Joab came out from David's presence, he sent messengers after Abner, and they brought him back from the cistern of Sirah; but David did not know about it. And when Abner returned to Hebron, Joab took him aside into the midst of the gate to speak with him privately, and there he smote him in the belly, so that he died, for the blood of Asahel his brother.

To kill Abner while he was negotiating with David, to kill him unauthorized, to do it with some subterfuge seems a triple-boldness on Joab's part.[13]

The outcome of this braided deed prompted, finally, speech from David (3:28–29), who asseverated his own innocence and denounced Joab soundly for what he has done, cursing his house. The narrator intruded to justify Joab (3:28): "So Joab and Abishai his brother slew Abner, because he had killed their brother Asahel in the battle at Gibeon." The narrator seems to remind us, if not David, that the slaying of a brother is not a deed to disregard—sounding a theme to be developed extensively. David's conspicuous and not necessarily insincere mourning for Abner has also drawn attention to the rift between David and Joab (3:31–35), gathering the people toward his own view rather than to side with Joab. Again, the narrator guided our reading (vv. 36–37): "And all the people took notice of it, and it pleased them; as everything that the king did pleased all the people. So all the people and all Israel understood that day that it had not been the king's will to slay Abner the son of Ner." But that having been said, we hear from David again (vv. 38–39): "And the king said to his servants, 'Do you not know that a prince and a great man has fallen this day in Israel? And I am this day weak, though anointed king; these men the sons of Zeruiah are too hard for me. The LORD requite the evildoer according to his wickedness!'"

---

13. Bodner has pointed out that Joab's "swerving" Abner into the city gate, traditional site for the administration of justice, stabbing him in the same anatomical place where Abner killed Asahel, suggests that Joab sees his deed as a justice-deed that he performs when David does not do it: "Demise of Abner," 38–76 (56) in his *David Observed*.

So with that material reviewed: As we approach the detail of Joab's role with David in chs. 11–12, first here his role in managing the ultimate defeat of the Ammonites, we begin from a place of contestation, narratively speaking, and wonder whether Joab has David's interests at heart. With that uncertainty in mind, we can examine the conclusion of the Ammonite campaign, prior to looking at its famous middle. By way of anticipation here, we can stipulate that Joab has been involved in the protracted Ammonite struggle from the first engagement (10:7–14), influential in the victory of David's men that split their Aramean allies from the Ammonites, allowing David's men to battle with groups individually rather than as cooperation. At the end of the whole episode (12:26–31) Joab brings the siege of Rabbah close to a victory, then sends to David: "'*I have fought* against Rabbah; moreover, *I have taken* the city of waters. Now, then, [*you*] gather the rest of the people together, and encamp against the city, and take it; *lest I take* the city, and it be called by *my name*.'" My added emphasis highlights the potential competition between the two, rather than an alliance. "My David," hearing the challenge, completes the conquest and sets the heavy golden Ammonite crown on his own head, despoils the city and enslaves its people and their people before returning to Jerusalem.

The point I want to suggest, prior to amplifying it, is the skirmishing between Joab and David, with David clearly the uncle and king and Joab the deputy and nephew, but with Joab shown to give orders and David to obey. I want to construct strife between Joab and David, rather than cooperation and show how it works consistently in the material we have. David and Joab are shown seriously at odds, and David's actions here, peremptory and unconsulted if perhaps well-meant, sow discord. Additionally, we have a second deed of mercy offered by David that turns, in time, into a reprisal or contempt.

c *David, Bathsheba, Uriah, and Joab: 11*

The challenge here is to note carefully the manner of visible plotting, the role of the narrator, and the specifics of the characterization. Since the scene is so central,[14] we will move through it in order, managing what comes with the appropriate tools.[15]

The narrator opens by referring to what has just occurred: The alliance of those assisting King Hanun of Ammon having been broken, Hanun stands alone now to face the troops of the king he has insulted. Joab, recently victorious, is sent to manage while David remains in Jerusalem (v. 1).[16] The next few verses (vv. 2–5)

---

14. Alter, *David Story*, 249, calls it a "crucially pivotal episode . . . orchestrated with a richness that scarcely has an equal in ancient narrative."

15. Morrison, *2 Samuel*, 134–49, sorts it into eleven scenes, for which he provides structures.

16. Many think the narrator is rebuking David, while I do not. I find the matter unable to be decided with certainty and not particularly important. Remaining home when battle recommences is not the key deed. What is needed is two narrative scenes at a distance from each other, and those our narrator has provided.

are provided by the narrator with extreme reticence: strong verbs but no other detail. David, rising from sleep to walk on the roof of his house, sees a beautiful woman bathing.[17] Inquiring of her identity, he learns it, sends messengers for her, she comes, he lies with her. That David has been told that she is the wife of one of his fighters and possibly kin to a royal adviser is crucial, intensifying his arrogance in disregarding these ties.[18] That Bathsheba goes to the king when summoned leaves her complicity uncertain, again, without clear resolution possible. *We* know what David has in mind, but she as a character has not seen him see her. To be summoned to the king's presence does not imply that she knows he wants to lie with her. But he does want to and does so, with the verb suggesting that she is an object rather than a partner. She has no agency beyond accompanying the messenger, though nor does she display the verbal resistance we will hear shortly from Tamar (13:12–13). The narrator's comment of v. 4b is difficult to construe as well. It may be an analeptic comment, to explain the nature of the bathing David observed, or a description of Bathsheba's ablutions after sleeping with the king.[19] Bathsheba's first and only time to speak is her informing the king that she has conceived, words delivered in her voice but with virtually no detail. This verbal reticence prompts us to contemplate imaginatively all that remains unsaid. The first point to stress, then, is the lack of verbal drama on the part of all involved, implied author, narrator, and characters. Given the import of the event, we can imagine alternatives to this presentation.

Next we have David's first plan—adopted hastily since one of the most obvious characteristics of the king's taking the wife of one of his soldiers is that it happens unexpectedly. David has acted hastily, though not without one precaution: learning the identity of the woman he has seen and is summoning. But now David plans what next to do, compounding the act begun in an instant. David's character emerges well-exposed here, if more uncertain in the first few verses. David requests, of Joab, that Uriah be sent from the siege of Ammon back to

---

17. A useful study of the scene's ambiguity is offered by Sara M. Koenig, *Isn't This Bathsheba? A Study in Characterization* (Eugene, OR: Pickwick Publishers, 2011). See also J. Cheryl Exum, "Bathsheba Plotted, Shot, and Painted," *Semeia* 74 (1996), 47–73. Exum sees fault almost inevitably projected onto Bathsheba by readers and viewers of art, who tend to find her guilty of tempting viewers because (at least) one of them sins after what he has seen. This is a reading issue: When we see David in this story falling into heinous sin, are we forced to complicity because of what we are presented? I think there is more choice, less inevitability, than Exum proposes, a point offered without my disputing many of the points Exum makes about men and women, art and literature, and life.

18. Uriah is referenced in 2 Sam. 23:39 as one of David's mighty men, a status he must have already gained prior to this, his last days to live. Bathsheba is also identified as the granddaughter of Ahithophel, another of David's enumerated heroes (2 Sam. 23:34).

19. Again, I think this remains undecidable. We moderns, with our precise knowledge of begetting and conception, can take it for a proof that the child conceived is David's, and the rest of this story seems to assume that. Morrison, *2 Samuel*, 140–41, is one who says we cannot know what the narrator's assumptions are in the matter.

Jerusalem (v. 6): "'Send me Uriah the Hittite.'" There is now one more person involved than previously, Joab whom we have been discussing. The narrator summarizes David's inquiries as to the well-being of the commander, the fighters, and the war, with no answer being provided for any. The effect, I think, is to imply that the questions are perfunctory—even specious—and to highlight what the king is about to put at risk: commander, men, war.

Uriah's taciturnity here continues his characterization, sketched more with deeds than speech. David urges Uriah to sleep at home with his wife, a gift of some kind accompanying him (v. 8). But Uriah, leaving the king's presence, does not enter his house (v. 9). When this slight resistance to orders is reported to David, he questions Uriah about it, suggesting concern, whatever its root might be. Uriah's only words are these (v. 11): "'The ark and Israel and Judah dwell in booths; and my lord Joab and the servants of my lord are camping in the open field; shall I then go to my house, to eat and to drink, and to lie with my wife? As you live, and as your soul lives, I will not do this thing.'" We hear Uriah provide a response to both—all—the questions David has asked: How the welfare of the commander, the men, the war—and Uriah adds the state of the Ark as well, with which David was earlier so concerned: All are deployed at the siege. Uriah professes solidarity with those agents, even when he is in Jerusalem, sleeping on duty at headquarters, as it were. We may hear contrast with the king—remembering that we know more than Uriah does about how David has been sleeping. We may hear reproach and critique, even a certain righteousness on Uriah's part, but I do not consider any of that nuance inevitable. Uriah says, basically, that he is on war duty and chooses to do it in a particular, prescribed, way, declining a royal suggestion to the contrary.

An intriguing and well-discussed feature of this narrative is what Uriah can be said to know.[20] The implied artistry of the narrative leaves the matter open. We have heard enough to imagine easily that anonymous others have witnessed events in the palace and shared them. So information may be available for Uriah. On the other hand, the narrator omits any suggestion or even hint that Uriah knows what has happened concerning the king and Uriah's wife. The point, as before, is how we read each possibility. If Uriah is ignorant, do we think him naive, insensitive, harsh, foolish? Or is his loyalty and focus such that he has only the common good in mind? If Uriah is informed, do we think him wooden, manipulative, uncaring, dumb? Or is he slyly provoking the king? And how do we construe David interacting here with Uriah, supposing what? How does "our David" hear Uriah's explanation of how he sees his responsibilities? What do we assume David assumes about Uriah's knowledge?

In any case, David, focused, desperate, or simply out of ideas, intensifies his effort to get Uriah to bed with Bathsheba, perhaps "uncorking" a royal gift in abundance and in advance of sending it so that Uriah will forget his responsibilities and motivation (vv. 12–13). But the narrator reports no change in Uriah's behavior. However we see Uriah's plan in terms of David and Bathsheba, he is consistent that righteous conduct of the war is his primary concern.

20. For a classic study of this matter, see Sternberg, *Poetics*, ch. 6.

So David must move to a second plan, from securing putative fatherhood of Bathsheba's child to achieving her widowhood. Far advanced, now, from an unplanned glance from his roof, David sets up the subversion of the Ammonite war to achieve his purpose, which to restate it, is to cover over his having taken Uriah's wife and begotten a child consequently. It is a grave offense against the woman, a crime of multiple and dire offense against Uriah, involving others who will die when he does, causing or occasioning the child's losing its life. My point is not to fulminate but to underline that for depth, this is fresh moral territory for David. Unlike those who see it as a first major flaw, I see it as distinctive but not singular. It is a disregard that surpasses anything we have seen of David with Saul or with Achish. It seems more heinous than his slaying of groups of people when sheltering with the Philistines. It diverges from while resembling his actions of appropriating the Ark and undertaking temple construction, unbidden.

David once again implicates Joab, and on this part of the transaction we must keep a steady eye. David directs Joab, in some sort of a missive carried by the victim himself (v. 15): "'Set Uriah in the forefront of the hardest fighting, and then draw back from him, that he may be struck down, and die.'" David is well-exposed to Joab here, the words making clear that the primary object is the death of one man, at whatever other "collateral" cost. David has placed crucial information in Joab's hand, which I think we may appreciate signals determination and desperation, since David is typically far more strategic and surely more reserved. This is a really shocking direction, in a number of ways. The narrator takes over the report (vv. 16–17): "And as Joab was besieging the city, he assigned Uriah to the place where he knew there were valiant men. And the men of the city came out and fought with Joab; and some of the servants of David among the people fell. Uriah the Hittite was slain also." The objective is gained, with related harm not avoided. Ours is to think about why and with what effect.[21]

As Joab prepares the news for David, we may hear again a response to David's earlier query to Uriah about the state of Joab, men, and war (vv. 18–24). Joab tells his messenger what to say and how to respond to what Joab anticipates will be David's reply: "Then Joab sent and told David all the news about the fighting; and he instructed the messenger, 'When you have finished telling all the news about the fighting to the king, then, if the king's anger rises, and if he says to you, "Why did you go so near the city to fight? Did you not know that they would shoot from the wall?"'" That is, Joab anticipates that David, hearing the news of the deaths, will fault the conduct of military leaders for making so basic and obvious an error. Joab, in my characterization of him, anticipates how David's anger or at least

---

21. Bodner speculates on Joab here, suggesting him as a reader-response critic, cueing skillfully and attentively to David's moves but with some creativity. In "Joab and the Risks of Reader-Response Criticism," in *David Observed*, 98–111, Bodner makes explicit what we can know Joab did and did not know and offers his sense of how Joab will have consequently construed his own options, modifying to make less extreme the result of the death of some. Bodner like myself recognizes that Joab's dealings with David must be seen in terms of what has preceded since he became an active player after the death of Saul.

indignation will rise, splashing on those in charge.[22] Joab anticipates David citing the episode from what we know as Judges 11, where a king did not foresee similar danger as he might have done (v. 21). But, adds Joab, when the king questions the judgment of the tactics, say, "'Your servant Uriah the Hittite is dead also.'" Joab assesses correctly that such a report will silence the king, redirect his animus. The narrator begins at the report scene, where the messenger is shown to summarize up to the key point (vv. 22–24):

> So the messenger went, and came and told David all that Joab had sent him to tell. The messenger said to David, "The men gained an advantage over us, and came out against us in the field; but we drove them back to the entrance of the gate. Then the archers shot at your servants from the wall; some of the king's servants are dead; and your servant Uriah the Hittite is dead also."

The messenger, I think, is characterized as intent on getting the news out but indicating no sense of the precise timing Joab has exposed for our ears. How the fighting went, how some can understandably have approached the city wall to drive back an attack, and the name of one among others who died. Joab has read David skillfully, better than the messenger does, his slight miscue demonstrating his lack of strategy while highlighting Joab's skill and David's manipulability. For David's response is (v. 25): "'Thus shall you say to Joab, "Do not let this matter trouble you, for the sword devours now one and now another; strengthen your attack upon the city, and overthrow it." And encourage him.'" By first anticipating and then suppressing the indignation Joab had set David up to express, intensified by his callous disregard for the well-being of those in Ammon, we see David display contempt. It seems a brutal response, a naive one, and a foolish one.

The narrator, almost finished with this portion of David's complex planning, reports three more things for our consideration (vv. 26–27): "When the wife of Uriah heard that Uriah her husband was dead, she made lamentation for her husband. And when the mourning was over, David sent and brought her to his house, and she became his wife, and bore him a son. But the thing that David had done displeased the LORD." We are unable to penetrate Bathsheba's mourning for her husband—as both Bathsheba and Uriah are identified—shortly before Bathsheba becomes David's wife and the mother of a living son—events also reported without her focalization. Most important and most famously, the deity is displeased at "the thing" that David had done. The narrator ends as enigmatically as he began, providing us with sparse if crucial information. Bathsheba's descriptors trace her journey relative to other characters but little else. Of David, we have no response past the callous and false words we just heard addressed to Joab through the messenger. These words about the devouring sword will come back to address David additionally. This may be the moment to speculate about why the taking

---

22. Here we may do well to rethink or re-weight the narrative comment in 11:1: When David even hypothetically reproves from afar those in charge of the siege, it may be that he ought have been there himself.

and impregnating of Bathsheba is such a crisis, evoking such an extreme reaction from the king. We, reading, are so accustomed to the impact of this event on David's reign that we might forget that for the king to have taken another woman, even one married to a colleague, would be wrong and shameful—but worth such an extreme solution, I am not so sure. To anticipate a point, the arrogance of the whole action may be the problem, not simply the adultery. God is permissive with David, but every so often—three times already and just ahead—God draws the line firmly. We can rethink this matter when we hear the voice in Nathan's parable communication: More women, others' wives? Not a problem!

Before proceeding, I want to underline my sense of David's gross misjudging of Joab here, his apparent *naïveté* or desperation in handing Joab—putting in writing, we might say—such a revealing and incriminating command. It is difficult to think how the instructions can be construed except as a command to eliminate Uriah. How David entrusts this task to a man as little compliant as Joab seems to me to underline David's desperation. What David has done in this scene repeats, intensifies, his actions with Mephibosheth and Hanun: pronounced, carried out, but with little awareness of consequences, which then are poorly managed.

d David Confronted: 12

As we begin, we might catch up with our character planning, focusing again and for the moment on that most challenging character of all, YHWH. As indicated previously, I think the deity in narrative is constructed like other characters, though with different reference: As a king is not the same as a commoner, a deity not the same as a human. But in terms of norms of narrativity, the process is basically the same. The deity participates intermittently in this narrative but implicitly and by convention is not to be understood as absent or uninvolved even when not acting tangibly and directly. The deity stands in place of a complex set of norms for the story—for all the biblical narratives—and somewhat distinctively in each set. It is difficult to be precise about how YHWH is to be understood within a narrative, not least since the material continues normative for religious believers and the understanding of this deity has evolved (and continues to do) over more than twenty-five hundred years.[23] This particular aspect of the story—how David relates with God—is of particular interest and offers intriguing challenges for readers who consider themselves as attempting the same thing.

As suggested when God appeared as a minor character in the material considered previous to this present set, the deity is shown consistently in favor of

---

23. A brief, profound, and widely ranging article by Karel van der Toorn, "Speaking of Gods, Dimensions of the Divine in the Ancient Near East," in Marjo C.A. Korpel and Lester L. Grabbe, eds., *Open-mindedness in the Bible and Beyond: A Volume of Studies in Honour of Bob Becking* (London: Bloomsbury T&T Clark, 2015), 273–85 surveys the general character of the species "deity" to review the general character of the concept. The most useful insight (279) is his way of situating what are now literary deities in relation to human qualities: superior, certainly, not totally "other" than humans, "perfected humans."

David's kingship, assisting that process in multiple ways. When David consults, God responds, though sometimes—but not always—when David acts on his own, the deity intervenes. Generally tolerant and even permissive of much that may seem dubious, God has stopped David from his first effort to transfer the Ark to Jerusalem and from building a temple. The first of those actions was resumed with apparent success, though a character pronounced that the event portrayed primarily the king's self-glorification. On the matter of the temple-building, God will not change the divine mind, and on the present matter, the deity will also stand firm.

God has used prophets prominently in the story under consideration here, beginning with the pre-born Samuel and culminating with him post-death. Though not all agree, in the main I think Samuel presented YHWH's views generally well enough, and that he was often not heeded exposes an inherent flaw in the deity-prophet system, where God's desires are made known through the words of a fallible human. Even when the prophet presents speech as words of God, couches them in formal prophetic language, accompanies them with signs, there is still no reliable way to compel attention, respect, obedience. A prophet may have misunderstood, been misled; and a prophet can be marginalized and dismissed (arrested, killed) by those who do not want his words heard or heeded.

Nathan may seem to have done better than Samuel did, but David is perhaps more malleable than was Saul. Actually we have heard from Nathan only once before, when he approved a general plan David put to him or endorsed a comment David made. As prophetic pronouncements go, its expression is far from classic and was, in any case, firmly contested by the deity who corrected it in direct words spoken to David (2 Samuel 7). In a sense, Nathan's appearance in ch. 12 is his first prophetic occasion. The narrator, having told us that YHWH is displeased by David's deed, now shows us the texture of that displeasure. Nathan is sent by God, and contrary to other similar occasions, we are not privy to the instruction phase of the prophetic process and thus do not know what Nathan will say until he speaks.[24]

Nathan narrates a story to the king (12:1–4):

"There were two men in a certain city, the one rich and the other poor. The rich man had very many flocks and herds; but the poor man had nothing but one little ewe lamb, which he had bought. And he brought it up, and it grew up with him and with his children; it used to eat of his morsel, and drink from his cup, and lie in his bosom, and it was like a daughter to him. Now there came a traveler to the rich man, and he was unwilling to take one of his own flock or herd to prepare for the wayfarer who had come to him, but he took the poor man's lamb, and prepared it for the man who had come to him."

24. For Bodner, "Nathan: Prophet, Politician, and Playwright," in his *David Observed*, 67–70, whether the initial story is the prophet's or the deity's is an important question for Nathan's characterization, a point I am not able to go with; I do not think we can discriminate the voices in this instance.

The story, as is well known, can be taken—read, heard—in a variety of ways, responsive to a variety of moves.[25] It is commonly observed that since the king is the arbiter of justice and hears cases as part of his role (as we will see also in ch. 14), David construes the prophet's words as a case involving some petitioner for whom Nathan speaks.[26] Another way to put that is to say that David hears a literal deed, brought to him for adjudication—a category and genre mistake, but not unreasonable, in the circumstances. For readers—better informed, less involved, and more familiar with genre than is David—the matter seems obvious, but that may not be the case in a story featuring a king charged with doing justice.

David's reaction to Nathan's small narrative is great anger kindled against the rich man, and he pronounces two outcomes and the rationale for each (vv. 5–6): "'As the LORD lives, the man who has done this deserves to die; and he shall restore the lamb fourfold, because he did this thing, and because he had no pity.'" David's anger at the fictive rich man distracts him, plausibly, and his instinctive feeling for the poor man and for the lamb works in a similar way. Standing outside the narrative, the king seems quick and certain in his sense of what injustice others have done or suffered, and why.

Before listening to Nathan speaking more bluntly and directly for the deity, we can note a few things about this apparently simple narrative. It has four actants, three human (one rich and one poor, two local and one visiting) and a lamb, implicitly of course other humans and herds as well who do not feature specifically. The single lamb is beloved and cared for almost to excess, achieving the status of a member of the poor man's household and providing the only thickness of detail in the brief narrative. The crisis in the story comes when a visitor to the rich man prompts a choice about hospitality: take one of his own animals or the one belonging to another. The rich man's decision is narrated without drama or explanation. If there can be supposed to be more to the story, it is interrupted by the king's outburst.

Nathan's "'you are the man'" changes everything (v. 7). The narrative cannot be a literal case presented for adjudication if "the man" is the addressee. Before the prophet explains how this identification is crucial, we recognize that to be told a narrative ostensibly about others but that actually describes ourselves prompts

---

25. Much of the discussion on the passage begins with the assertion of Uriel Simon, "The Poor Man's Ewe Lamb: An Example of a Juridical Parable," *Bib* 48 (1967): 207–42 that the genre is juridical parable. Whether such a tag can or needs to be named definitively, several useful points emerge from the discussion generated from that piece, notably the extent to which the story details fit well the life-circumstances of the characters, whether the punishments announced by both king and prophet conform to biblical law, whether the point of the genre is to trigger self-judgment. See a good discussion of these points by David Janzen, "The Condemnation of David's 'Taking' in 2 Samuel 12.1–14," *JBL* 131.2 (2012): 209–20.

26. Alter, for example, *David Story*, 257, finds it strange for David to miscue in this way, given the polished literary nature of the "case" presented. Related, likely, is Bodner's wonder that David is slow to see the reference that is plain enough to us ("Nathan," 71).

recognition, however unwelcome, moving us into a genre other than literal. So a story with roles sketched and proffered, some more attractive than others, nonetheless urges an inevitable a moment of recognition. To simplify again, we are now choosing to hear either an allegory, where the details can be pretty closely and clearly matched to participants, or a parable, whose architecture works somewhat differently, though resembling allegory at the surface. Briefly, before listening to Nathan expatiate, we can test each of those genres. If the narrative is an allegory, then the task of the hearers (David and ourselves) is to match the actants and acts of the brief narrative with the longer one we have been reading: A wealthier man with lots of possessions takes from a poorer man the only one of what he had, prompted by some crisis that changes the equilibrium between them. The match is not so difficult to see, though the more precise one seeks to be, the less good the fit is.[27] Though David becomes outraged on the poor man's behalf, the prophet tells him *he*, rather, is the rich man and then rereads the case against him.

If, however, we have a parable, then the challenge is to hear some startling redescription that is compelling, if not welcome. The actant roles may be the pathway, or the contrast between extremes may cue us, or the moment of choice. Identifications may be fluid. Here, the terrain is more uncertain. The resolution of an allegory tends to confirm what is clear; the negotiation with a parable will more likely produce sudden and unexpected, often unwelcome insight before being refused, or accepted. When Nathan tells David he is "the man" in a parable with at least three actants, we still have work to do.[28]

Nathan's next words may help us (vv. 7–9):

> "Thus says the LORD, the God of Israel, 'I anointed you king over Israel, and I delivered you out of the hand of Saul; and I gave you your master's house, and your master's wives into your bosom, and gave you the house of Israel and of Judah; and if this were too little, I would add to you as much more. Why have you despised (*bzh*) the word of the LORD, to do what is evil in his sight? You have smitten Uriah the Hittite with the sword, and have taken his wife to be your wife, and have slain him with the sword of the Ammonites.'"

The prophet's choice of an oracle form indicates that he is reporting God's words, something not so evident in the story preceding the explanation. The speaker, the I-voice, is God, common in prophetic literature. God's main point is that God is the agent (I anointed . . . I delivered . . . I gave . . . I gave . . . I would add more). The implicit accusation is disregard of the giver by the beneficiary, who seems to think he is the agent of his own destiny. Arrogance is more basic than adultery.

27. Janzen, "Condemnation," 209–10.

28. Polzin, *David and the Deuteronomist*, 122, notes that it is not so clear who the rich man is—perhaps the deity, who is featured as taker as the narrative fills fuller in the prophet's speech. A perceptive comment by Jonathan A. Kruschwitz, "2 Samuel 12:1–15: How (Not) to Read a Parable," *RevExp* 109 (2012): 254, that a parable may be a subgenre of the larger category (genre) *mashal*, which is a juxtaposing comparison of some sort.

While we are listening, we may note that the usual prophet-denounced sins are absent: This charge is not about common religious infidelity, so-called idolatry. It is not most basically about abuse of abstract institutional power, nor exclusively about women or war. The deity, speaking through the prophet, mentions while brushing those things aside to get to a deeper point. In fact, God says, if you want more wives of your betters or peers, I would provide them—but ask, do not simply take. And yet, as the deity's words continue, it does concern taking the wife of another man and then killing him—but the point is that David did it himself rather than asking YHWH to provide such prizes for him. God's point is about David's presuming to act on his own, brazenly and grossly. The parable exposes David's culminated arrogance, contempt, and presumption.

We must hear deeper than the specific crimes themselves (the *taking* of another's wife, the deliberate killing of a man) to highlight the basic language used by Nathan, David, and even YHWH to characterize the charge: Nathan at v. 4: the rich man was *unwilling to take* one of his own flock . . . *but he took* the poor man's lamb; David's charge at v. 6: because he *had no pity*; the prophet/deity team (v. 9): Why have you *despised*? . . . (v. 10): you have *despised*; . . . (v. 14): you have *utterly scorned* the LORD.[29] To stop at the specifics disregards this set of charges about David's attitude of basic disrespect for who God is, who God's chosen is. It comes close to the overweening, violent arrogation of certain Greek heroes of their deities, a refusal of proper limits.[30]

The words move from compressed and encapsulated accusation to verdict and consequences, announced here largely as punishment (vv. 10–12):

> "Now therefore the sword shall never depart from your house, because you have despised me, and have taken the wife of Uriah the Hittite to be your wife. Thus says the LORD, 'Behold, I will raise up evil against you out of your own house; and I will take your wives before your eyes, and give them to your neighbor, and he shall lie with your wives in the sight of this sun. For you did it secretly; but I will do this thing before all Israel, and before the sun.'"

God names the sword which will not depart from the house that David heads, evil from within that house itself. What David did to another's wife he will suffer as well, an outrage committed against him by an intimate, and publicly in place of what David attempted to do secretly—now exposed. Most important, God stresses the root sin: contempt.

As God speaks, we hear a match of detail: David took and others will take from him. But God concedes what ended up as David's—another man's wife—does not

29. The two Hebrew words intensify the charge: To scorn (*bzh*) is named twice (12:9, 10) and the verb *n's* is used intensively to suggest callous disregard (v. 14).

30. Esler, "Ammonite War," 316–19, talks in terms of David violating the patron/client relations, which may be part of it. Janzen, "Condemnation," 209–17, points out these basic charges and violations of God's role, without, however, letting them be as primary as I think they are.

begrudge it, would provide more, if asked. So "possessing" is not the issue, most basically. Without eliminating that crime, God reaches deeper: contempt. It is not quite the same as what David assessed above: no pity—but close, with contempt hosting moments of non-pity. This brief prophetic narrative is a parable, its impact rooting in the nature of the offense: David has become contemptuous of God and demonstrated such a demeanor in his arrogations of others' goods, not for the first time but with far more deleterious consequences than before.

David seems to hear and accept the critique (v. 13): "'I have sinned against the LORD.'" We may debate whether I have described the insight aptly, but that David accepts it is clear. If it is his contempt, perhaps spawned from lack of pity or the lack of pity from contempt, we can see how it plays out, continues to pollute. This moment is what the Greeks call *anagnorisis*, the recognition by a protagonist of his wrongdoing and its outcomes. Noteworthy is David's refusal to attempt explanation or exoneration. The recognition is clean, ungrudging, non-alibied, most similar to David's rebuke by God for presuming to build a house for God's Ark.

The prophet, spending no words of approval, moves on to talk additionally about consequences (discarding one of David's sentences—the taker's immediate death—but amplifying the other—fourfold restitution), to specify what has already been said, not to mitigate it but to indicate how it will commence (vv. 13–14): "'The LORD also has put away your sin; you shall not die. Nevertheless, because by this deed you have utterly scorned the LORD, the child that is born to you shall die.'" Nathan also reiterates the root sin: utter contempt. The deity who has been the source of all that David has received now claims involvement in the destruction of some of it. David—and we—allowed no illusion about the nature of the sickness and suffering about to unfold. David makes no further remark here.

The narrator moves us right to the next part of the story, the unfolding of consequences of David's deed, spilling now ever more widely into the lives of those he loves: (v. 17): "Then Nathan went to his house. And the LORD struck the child that Uriah's wife bore to David, and it became sick." David's next actions (vv. 16–23) are narrated for us, with only a bit of direct discourse. The narrator spends no agency on the child, nor in fact on the mother or the prophet. The focus is exclusively on king and deity. The king who is also the father beseeches God for the child, though not in words for us to hear. David's gestures are, we will learn, not the usual or expected ones. David fasts, sleeps on earth, refusing to be moved or to accept food, even when pressed by his people to do so. The attempted intervention by one set of servants and then the direct discourse of a second set help us—generally ignorant of cultural nuance here—grasp what is happening. Since we are not permitted to hear David's words of intercession for the child, we can only read the effect of the actions, tagged as they are as unexpected, startling to those who do understand customs.[31]

---

31. For a useful discussion of the passage, see David Bosworth, "Faith and Resilience: King David's Reaction to the Death of Bathsheba's Firstborn," *CBQ* 73 (2011), 691–707. A central point he offers is that we can understand supplication, fasting, and abstinence from grooming as parts of both supplication and mourning and can see them as expressions

David's words and actions are not able to change the outcome of the words Nathan and God spoke, and on the seventh day, the child dies. The exchange among his servants testifies to their appraisal of matters (v. 18): "And the servants of David feared to tell him that the child was dead; for they said, 'Behold, while the child was yet alive, we spoke to him, and he did not listen to us; how then can we say to him the child is dead? He may do himself some harm.'" We can take them as understanding little of what their master is doing, perceiving the depth of his anguish but not seeing its root dynamics even so clearly as we do, while informing us about what was the cultural norm.

David reads their demeanor and understands what they are unwilling to tell him. "'Is the child dead?' They said, 'He is dead'" (v. 19). Then David reverses his gestures, troubling his servants once again (vv. 20–21):

> Then David arose from the earth, and washed, and anointed himself, and changed his clothes; and he went into the house of the LORD, and worshiped; he then went to his own house; and when he asked, they set food before him, and he ate. Then his servants said to him, "What is this thing that you have done? You fasted and wept for the child while it was alive; but when the child died, you arose and ate food."

In case we missed it, the surprise, even shock, registered by the witnesses of David's gestures suggests not simple intercession but of something more, else: mourning for an already dead one or perhaps deeper penitence. The seven days likely cue us to the latter. "My David" understands that he must "clear" his sin, and that is what he does, not excluding to pray for the child or perhaps on its behalf, over it, not necessarily for its reprieve. We cannot be too certain here, with so much left implicit. That David goes to God's house for prayer is a narrative hint of the mending of that relationship, harmed as it has been through David's contempt and God's harsh words to him. David consoles Bathsheba, and they beget a son, beloved of God, the narrator tells us, named Jedidiah but called Solomon, a reconciling name.

And, finally, as we have already considered, Joab and David bring the Ammonite war to a close. As all agree, the unit—whether 10–12 or 11–12—makes a major shift in the action. We have watched David from 1 Samuel 16 through the end of that book (16 chapters there) and in 2 Samuel 1–10 plus 21–24 before coming to the moments of 11 and 12. It is sometimes suggested that everything bad that happened to David from this point forward was a result of the taking of Bathsheba, but I do not think that is feasible. The more urgent matter is how David was caught so off guard that in an instant he stepped into such a morass. Insofar as deity and prophet have charged David with the condition of scornful arrogance, not a first diagnosis but a metastasis, and David has accepted rebuke, the question is what

of heartfelt feelings and rubrics of ritual, without necessarily being able to parse more precisely. Hence we cannot quite name the exact motivation or objective of David's actions in regard to his son.

path he will now take: he may, as before, fall back into the same condition, or he may change his ways.

e David Easily, Passively Led: 13

Results of David's sin continue to flow, not simply or primarily as punishments administered but as consequences of royal choices, habits, behavior—even conceivably as copied traits. The chapter is well discussed in secondary literature, and we will not repeat all of that work but offer some larger commentary.[32] David, judging the rich man in Nathan's parable, named the sin as sparing his own while taking the goods of another, and as lack or refusal of pity. Nathan, speaking for God, called it despising, and in his own voice named it as utter scorn for God. David, denying none of these charges, begins now to gather the bitter fruits of his behavior. There is a cause-effect dynamic set up, verbally and in deeds, but we will miss the most significant dimension if that is all we are calculating. There are ways in which the numbers balance, so we can see David eventually paying fourfold. But the reality goes beyond such precise equivalence, though including it. The point, I think, is to see that David has, to no small extent, brought significant troubles to his house and realm. He and his people now will struggle to cope, as best as they can, which may not be very well. This episode involving David's firstborn son, Amnon, born to Ahinoam of Jezeel, and David's daughter Tamar, sister of Absalom, is the second of the tragedies among David's children—the unnamed son of Bathsheba being the first.[33]

The episode involves Tamar and Amnon, also Absalom, Jonadab (another nephew of David's), and David. Amnon's rape and rejection of Tamar form the main action, and it is well-commented upon in literature. I want here to focus on David's role in regard to these four characters, consequently shrinking the main action. Once Amnon has disclosed his lovesick condition to his cousin and counselor, Jonadab instructs him and manages the coordinates of the event, whether intending the consequences or not. In this long story, unintended and unforeseen consequences feature prominently, raising the question of what is to be foreseen, by whom, and how it works out, intended or not. Jonadab, anticipating David's coming to see his son who is both feigning and suffering sickness, instructs Amnon how to proceed (13:5): "Jonadab said to him, 'Lie down on your bed, and pretend to be ill; and when your father comes to see you, say to him, "Let my sister Tamar come and give me bread to eat, and prepare the food in my sight, that I may see it, and eat it from her hand."'" Amnon is shown indulged here, by his close

---

32. Remaining classic and insightful in literary terms is Shimon Bar-Efrat's *Narrative Art*, ch. 6, 239–82.

33. When David's sons are listed, it is clear that some of them fall out of the story at once, whether because they have died or because stories do not attend them. Those filial stories featured here are part of the web of consequences attending David the king. The motif of David and Michal's sonlessness may "sound" here as well.

kinsman and by his father—no credit to any.[34] And so it happens (13:7): Amnon, prompted, makes his request and David falls in with the plan: "Then David sent home to Tamar, saying, 'Go to your brother Amnon's house, and prepare food for him.'" Two points here: First, David continues in his roles as judge, hearing and granting this request in contrast with what he will refuse to do at the end of the event; second, as a death-dealing father.[35] The language agreed among the three males about Tamar's going to Amnon's house (vv. 6–7) echoes ominously David's sending Uriah to his house and the lethal consequences ensuing.[36]

We can remark David's culpability here, his so easily acceding to the plan of the shrewd Jonadab and the sick Amnon, whose secrets we have witnessed. David, lacking our perspective, is suggestible and led, not more, to my mind—so far. That David is not very observant is also true, but I think the narrative sets up this crime of brother raping sister as almost unimaginable. David does not see it before it happens—though since we have seen David take Bathsheba, we may be more alert than he is. Tamar, also, seems ignorant of what might happen as she does what her father asks and what her half-brother desires (vv. 8–19). But then, raped, refused her alternatives, repulsed with her remaining life blighted, Tamar leaves Amnon's chamber.

Contrastively, Absalom seems both unsurprised and unsympathetic (v. 20): "And her brother Absalom said to her, 'Has Amnon your brother been with you? Now hold your peace, my sister; he is your brother; do not take this to heart.' So Tamar dwelt, a desolate woman, in her brother Absalom's house." The narrator adds (v. 22): "But Absalom spoke to Amnon neither good nor bad; for Absalom hated Amnon, because he had forced his sister Tamar." That Absalom will eventually respond directly is relevant, but it is also noteworthy that he does not do so here, except to refuse to speak with Amnon and to shelter his sister in his home.

Her father's response: "When King David heard of all these things, he was very angry" (v. 20). But he, also, defers action.[37] The difference between Tamar's two male kin is that Absalom is characterized as planning while David is not so

---

34. Fokkelman, *King David*, 106.

35. Mark Gray, "Amnon: A Chip off the Old Block? Rhetorical Strategy in 2 Samuel 13:7–15: The Rape of Tamar and the Humiliation of the Poor," *JSOT* 77 (1993): 39–54, and Morrison, *2 Samuel*, 175–76.

36. Bar-Efrat, *Biblical Narrative*, 250–52. Johanna Stiebert, *Fathers and Daughters in the Hebrew Bible* (Oxford: Oxford University Press, 2013), 62–63, notes that this negative characterization of David is oblique and proceeds by contrast and with inference and with interpreters continuing to reference Nathan's parable.

37. Again, useful comment at a slightly wider level. Stiebert, *Fathers and Daughters*, 63, reminds us that we are not told, specifically, at what and why David is angry. William H. Propp, "Kinship in 2 Samuel 13," *CBQ* 55 (1993): 39–47, taking the opposite tack from most who comment, reviews the tangle of things that pertain now in David's family and kingdom—rape, illicit sexual behavior between and among family members, incest, improper dismissal of a raped woman, offenses against the male responsible for the unmarried Tamar—and suggests that it is not so clear what David might have done. We are

described. Amnon's further deeds are not provided, leaving the impression that he escapes temporarily, except for the lack of status that Tamar warned him would characterize him (v. 13): a wanton fool in Israel. The narrator does not provide such detail within the story, though readers may internalize it as an assessment of the character Amnon. To add complexity, we can recall that the offense committed by Amnon and Jonadab, abetted by David, includes social as well as personal consequences and that it also engages the competition of David's sons to succeed him.[38] Alice Keefe makes the case for the rape narrative here, as elsewhere, being a metonymy or synecdoche for the larger violence on the loose in the land: "The violated body of a woman functions as a metonym for the social body as it is disrupted in war." She says:

> The effect of the narration is to draw one into this tragedy of Tamar's life, so that it becomes not merely a narrative fact, a device of plot, but an experience of a woman's pain shared intimately with the reader. This intimacy occurs in a narrative context of violence within a family, including not only incestuous rape, but fratricide and a son's war against his father. There is perhaps no more serious breach in the order of human relationships than violence within a family. And because the *nebalah* [foolishly shameful outrage] takes place in the context of the royal family, and the father under assault by his son is also the king, the welfare of the entire nation is inextricably bound up in the drama.[39]

Absalom's plan unfolds over long story time but short discourse time. The narrator provides it (vv. 23–27):

> After two full years Absalom had sheepshearers at Baalhazor, which is near Ephraim, and Absalom invited all the king's sons. And Absalom came to the king, and said, "Behold, your servant has sheepshearers; pray let the king and his servants go with your servant." But the king said to Absalom, "No, my son, let us not all go, lest we be burdensome to you." He pressed him, but he would not go but gave him his blessing. Then Absalom said, "If not, pray let my brother Amnon go with us." And the king said to him, "Why should he go with you?" But Absalom pressed him until he let Amnon and all the king's sons go with him.

back to inexorable conflicts and clashing responsibilities and may feel some sympathy for David's choices.

38. The anthropological and sociological facets are brought out by Victor H. Matthews and Don C. Benjamin, "Amnon and Tamar: A Matter of Honor (2 Samuel 12:1–38)," in Gordon D. Young et al., eds., *Crossing Boundaries and Linking Horizons: Studies in Honor of Michael C. Astour on His 80th Birthday* (Bethesda, MD: CDL Press, 1997), 345–55; they highlight ways in which David is both dishonored by the rape and himself guilty of failing to live up to his own responsibilities of protecting his heritage. They also detail the case for David's sons struggling to succeed him.

39. Alice A. Keefe, "Rapes of Women/Wars of Men," *Semeia* 61 (1993): 79–97 (92).

As before, we see David set up by a planner to permit violence, if not to participate directly. David declines his son's invitation to be present, offering the claim of being burdensome. David, asked by Absalom to permit Amnon to attend, first questions but then allows it. If suspicious, he declines to inquire further. For a second time, David's sons make him complicit with their plans of harm. It would have been worse, arguably, had the king been witness to the killing of Amnon by Absalom, but for him to have approved the plan is painful to contemplate.

Absalom's deed takes place (vv. 28–29), and his servants strike Amnon when he is celebrating and likely not alert, if alert he ever is. The rest of the king's sons flee, and word reaches the king's ears before any witness arrives (vv. 30–31): "While they were on the way, tidings came to David, 'Absalom has slain all the king's sons, and not one of them is left.' Then the king arose, and rent his garments, and lay on the earth; and all his servants who were standing by rent their garments." David, thinking he is bereft of all his sons, mourns, informed by one no less suitable than Jonadab that the matter is not quite so dire (vv. 32–33):

> "Let not my lord suppose that they have killed all the young men the king's sons, for Amnon alone is dead, for by the command of Absalom this has been determined from the day he forced his sister Tamar. Now therefore let not my lord the king so take it to heart as to suppose that all the king's sons are dead; for Amnon alone is dead."

How David can be anticipated as receiving such news is difficult to imagine. Not all David's sons, but just his firstborn slain by his brother, who is now fled to kin across the Jordan. How will David *not* take the thing to heart, and why should his nephew offer such a crass consolation? The surviving sons arrive at their father's house, as is announced to him (vv. 36–37): "'Behold, the king's sons have come; as your servant said, so it has come about.' And as soon as he had finished speaking, behold, the king's sons came, and lifted up their voice and wept; and the king also and all his servants wept very bitterly."

We, if not yet David—who makes no verbal reply here—contemplate alternatives to the events of ch. 13. David's refusal to act in any decisive way dominates the narrative of his children, and in fact closes it in a most complex way. The translation says for v. 39: "And the spirit of the king longed to go forth to Absalom; for he was comforted about Amnon, seeing he was dead." It is a most ambiguous and contested verse in a narrative not short on ambiguity. The uncertainties can be somewhat disentangled as follows: Is the king's spirit positively or negatively reaching out to Absalom, exiled? Is David consoled or changed about Amnon, because he is dead? In other words, does David want Absalom back or not, and with what feelings would he be welcome? Three careful readers opine on the matter: Alter says that it is clear that David mourns for Amnon, not Absalom (v. 37), but that his hostility toward Absalom subsides (v. 39).[40] Fokkelman, confident that David does not long for Absalom, provides his definitive translation: "David longed intensely to march

40. Alter, *David Story*, 274.

out against Absalom, for he was grieved about Amnon, that he was dead. Joab, not, the son of Zeruiah, discerned that the king was ill-disposed toward Absalom."[41] Polzin, alternatively, suggests that the ambiguity is purposeful.[42]

Critics can resolve the language in both ways, and yet a clear decision by each "writerly reader" is necessary as background to what unfolds after this. Before moving on that challenge, we can note that once again David defers action, and Absalom remains in exile for five years (in Geshur, more in Jerusalem but not in his father's presence). David seems unable to choose but rather to let whatever is in motion around him control him. The next chapter adds a comment which might clarify but does not, so that, as we move ahead, we have a major uncertainty.

f David Vaguely Irresolute: 14

We enter more deeply now the aftermath of the scene just witnessed, challenged both to examine its detail and to step back to ask broader questions of it, allowing the nested narrative to reposition what we have been given.

The chapter splits into two uneven parts, with an important decision laboriously made, followed by narration of diverse consequences of that choice. The narrator opens this next event as follows (14:1): "Now Joab the son of Zeruiah perceived that the king's heart went out to Absalom." As already suggested, we are not quite certain. Joab perceives how David felt—truly so? Inaccurately so? How *does* David feel toward Absalom? Will Joab, as we know him, proceed with genuine concern for David? For Absalom? For himself? For what reasons, from what motives, with what plans that we can follow? The narrator has not provided language amenable to definitive resolution, and so readers will proceed as they feel prompted. Since I am seeing David presently as passive and caught, and unable and unwilling to move—though he and we will soon, unequivocally, witness his love for his son Absalom—I will stipulate to David as wallowing in conflicted feelings for Absalom and thus immobilized. My Joab, developing from the struggles between Abner and David's men (and continuing in this vein, as we shall see), does not hesitate to manage David for purposes of his own, whatever those may be. So with David uncertain, Joab acts for his own aims to align with David's if possible but not fearing to thwart them if he must.[43]

41. Fokkelman, *King David*, 126–27.

42. Polzin, *David and the Deuteronomist*, 133.

43. Commentators vary widely on these points and argue as they think best. But those who find the text definitive and their own reasoning obvious to those who are reading correctly seem to me to have overreached. For example, Alter, *David Story*, 276–79 seems in little doubt as to who wants what. Polzin, *David and the Deuteronomist*, 139–40, on the other hand, seems more open to the range of possibilities projected from the narrative and this specific text, asking good questions.

Joab, acting indirectly, brings a new character onto the scene. She, in effect, is a rough Nathan-equivalent, a wise woman whose specific challenge is to influence the king toward Joab's desires, whatever it may be, to persuade him across his resistance, whatever it may be.[44] However, to have been sent by YHWH as Nathan was is not the same as being sent by Joab.[45] Granting that Joab has asked her help and instructed her at least minimally, we need not doubt her integrity or skill, though many do. She outdistances Joab soon enough in any case, and shows herself adept at speaking with, persuading the king.[46] The characterization of David continues to show him passive, manipulable, open to suggestion, willing to agree. It is David we will watch primarily, without disregarding the desires of the woman and of Joab, insofar as those are able to be seen. The woman's story is not quite a parable as was Nathan's, but it is close—a fictive narrative, resembling a judicial case such as might be offered for royal adjudication, designed to induce insight and change of heart about an ancillary though vital matter once a first and fictive situation has been engaged. The chapter moves in ten rounds, with eight exchanges between the two main protagonists, framed by words of Joab to the woman and of the king to Joab. David does not reply to this story as he did to Nathan's narrative, royal rage bubbling up almost before the case is finished. Here, he seems perfunctory, pronouncing generally, willing the woman to leave long before she does, and finally coming to an abrupt end as he turns from the woman to Joab. A closer look at this remarkable scene is instructive, if not necessarily clarifying.

First, the directions of Joab to the woman (vv. 1–2): "'Pretend to be a mourner, and put on mourning garments; do not anoint yourself with oil, but behave like a woman who has been mourning many days for the dead; and go to the king, and speak thus to him.'" So Joab put the words in her mouth. Speak which words, we will soon be asking, with David. The woman does not reply but obviously moves to implement what she has been charged to do. The narrator's omission of Joab's direction removes our knowing where his words stop and the woman's begin, and prevents our knowing precisely what each is doing, saying, desiring. It challenges us beyond what would be the case were we to have heard the basic script. There follows the first exchange between the woman and the king (vv. 4–5): "When the woman of Tekoa came to the king, she fell on her face to the ground, and

---

44. Polzin, *David and the Deuteronomist*, 141, also notes that she is a David-double, her situation resembling his.

45. The fullest study of the many places of ambiguity and undecidability in this portion of ch. 14 is taken up in detail by Larry L. Lyke, *King David with the Wise Woman of Tekoa: The Resonance of Tradition in Parabolic Narrative* (Sheffield: JSOT Press, 1997).

46. An alternative to the case for the woman's wisdom and skill is offered by Patricia K. Willey, "The Importunate Woman of Tekoa and How She Got her Way," in Danna Nolan Fewell, ed., *Reading between Texts: Intertextuality and the Hebrew Bible* (Louisville, KY: Westminster John Knox Press, 1992), 115–31. Willey shows the woman an inarticulate blunderer who may, at best, stumble into a good outcome.

did obeisance, and said, 'Help, O king.' And the king said to her, 'What is your trouble?'"

The presentation proper begins as the woman narrates her situation: (vv. 5–8):

> She answered, "Alas, I am a widow; my husband is dead. And your handmaid had two sons, and they quarreled with one another in the field; there was no one to part them, and one struck the other and killed him. And now the whole family has risen against your handmaid, and they say, 'Give up the man who struck his brother, that we may kill him for the life of his brother whom he slew;' and so they would destroy the heir also. Thus they would quench my coal which is left, and leave to my husband neither name nor remnant upon the face of the earth."

The matter seems clear, not so difficult to judge, but the king responds simply, "'Go to your house, and I will give orders concerning you.'" We do not know what the king is thinking, but he seems to feel able to judge, whenever the moment for it will come.

The third exchange between wise woman and depressed king unfolds in vv. 9–10, with the woman noting that any eventual fallout is hers, not the king's. David agrees. The fourth exchange (v. 11), initiated by the woman, coming closer to the heart of the issue, is similar, concerning reprisal: "Then she said, 'Pray let the king invoke the LORD your God, that the avenger of blood slay no more, and my son be not destroyed.' He said, 'As the LORD lives, not one hair of your son shall fall to the ground.'" She has indicated that the avenger of such deaths might move against her son in any case and begs David to pray to God about it (wise advice!). I hear the woman wanting more time while David is again ready to conclude. She next (fifth) grows more laconically direct, as does he (v. 12): "Then the woman said, 'Pray let your handmaid speak a word to my lord the king.' He said, 'Speak.'"

In this sixth exchange of their dialogue, the woman transcends her narrative, and Joab's, I suggest—now if not previously—to raise what is most apt (vv. 13–17):

> And the woman said, "Why then have you planned such a thing against the people of God? For in giving this decision the king convicts himself, inasmuch as the king does not bring his banished one home again. We must all die, we are like water spilt on the ground, which cannot be gathered up again; but God will not take away the life of him who devises means not to keep his banished one an outcast.[47] Now I have come to say this to my lord the king because the people

---

47. Richard G. Smith, *The Fate of Justice and Righteousness during David's Reign: Rereading the Court History according to 2 Samuel 8:51b–20:26* (New York and London: T&T Clark, 2009), 169–70 tells us there are at least eight ways to translate and thus understand the inference the speaker draws from the spilled-water aphorism (itself not unambiguous). Willey likewise, "Woman of Tekoa," 119–21, helps us appreciate the difficulty of translating and understanding this part of the woman's discourse, calling it strange and garbled in both phrasing and intent.

have made me afraid; and your handmaid thought, 'I will speak to the king; it may be that the king will perform the request of his servant. For the king will hear, and deliver his servant from the hand of the man who would destroy me and my son together from the heritage of God.' And your handmaid thought, 'The word of my lord the king will set me at rest'; for my lord the king is like the angel of God to discern good and evil. The LORD your God be with you."

The king's reply shifts ground similarly (v. 18): "Then the king answered the woman, 'Do not hide from me anything I ask you.'"

The woman has, in effect, said to David: You are the man—with the sons. Against the whole people have you offended in refusing to resolve the matter of fratricidal sons by returning yours to us. As you judge my case, you are judging your own. Her metaphor (actually symbol) helps us follow her insight and reasoning as she addresses the king: We mortals are like water, spilled, that cannot be regathered. But early spilling is not inevitable, is not the only alternative. God will not deprive of life (i.e., of an heir) the father who struggles to bring an errant son back into his family—the point David seemed to offer her in vv. 10–11, by promising her and her son protection from kin wanting to solve the fratricide in some other way.[48] Her argument continues: Your verdict for me and my son is also the judgment for you and your son. The woman then reviews and shares her process, how fear drove her to ask from the king a justice she feared she would not otherwise have. She compliments him, arguably not so much to flatter as to explain why she came to him with her case, hoping that royal wisdom and justice would save her last son—but now, she implies, the king's as well. Insofar as angels are messengers of God, then she is saying that David's judgment is God's own choice and is a divine discernment of how to weigh competing claims. She is praising God's justice, which she expects David to affirm and which he has done. The question for David now is why that speech prompts him to ask her permission for what he next says.

The next frame of the conversation proceeds after David has asked to speak frankly (vv. 18–19): "And the woman said, 'Let my lord the king speak.' The king said, 'Is the hand of Joab with you in all this?'" She speaks again, her final time (vv. 19–20):

The woman answered and said, "As surely as you live, my lord the king, one cannot turn to the right hand or to the left from anything that my lord the king has said. It was your servant Joab who bade me; it was he who put all these words

48. Lyke, *Wise Woman*, 142–46 points out that there are viable alternatives in play for David in regard to Absalom: have him executed, leave it uncertain, reprieve him. Propp, "Kinship," 49–52, points out that there is custom or law which pertains, but it may not be so clear as we might suppose or wish. He ultimately things the matter of "brothers" (the woman's two sons, David's eldest two, and Joab's brother Asahel, slain by Abner who is then killed for it) revolve around the issue of whether their blood was shed wrongly or not. Propp decides here that Absalom's killing of Amnon was not legitimate. I think it is not so clear.

in the mouth of your handmaid. In order to change the course of affairs your servant Joab did this. But my lord has wisdom like the wisdom of the angel of God to know all things that are on the earth.'"

This language rather than her previous reply seems excessive to me, crediting the king with either insight or information to have detected his nephew's words beneath hers. She implies Joab as designer of all her words, which seems unlikely at the surface, since she has clearly enough been improvising to at least some extent. But the salient insight is that David grasps as central the role of Joab, opening again for us the question of what his plan can be. The king does not reply again to the woman but addresses Joab (v. 21): "'Behold now, I grant this; go, bring back the young man Absalom.'"

Joab's response to this royal word is the most lavishly appreciative we have seen or will see from him (v. 22): "And Joab fell on his face to the ground, and did obeisance, and blessed the king; and Joab said, 'Today your servant knows that I have found favor in your sight, my lord the king, in that the king has granted the request of his servant.'" Here he and the wise woman do sound as though they are working from the same script—though that is not necessarily so. That Joab wants Absalom back in Jerusalem and that he wants to be recognized as broker of that move now seem clearer, with his specific and basic motive still uncertain. But the aftermath is perhaps unexpected and disappointing, moving us from what the king wants and what Joab wants to consider what Absalom himself wants—relinking us back to the matter of David's desires and the challenges of discerning them, trying one possibility and then another in order to explore what is happening within the portrait we are being offered.

Joab is sent to bring Absalom back from Geshur but not quite home, since he is made to dwell apart from his father (vv. 23–24). No reason is given, though possibilities abound, adding uncertainty to what any of these characters actually specifically desire and can be planning. No character comments, and the narrator does not explain. Rather, we are presented with fresh information about the young man who is now the eldest surviving royal son: his outstanding and perfect physical beauty, affirmed not only by the narrator but by many summarized as speaking of it. His hair is singled out as emblematic of his physical qualities, evidently admired by himself as well as by others.[49] He is also here made the father of three sons and a daughter, suggesting that a line will continue from him.[50] His naming his daughter

---

49. Commentators note that the hair is mentioned here since it will be the immediate cause of Absalom's death, his inability to escape Joab's lethal darts. Fokkelman, *King David*, 197–98 thinks Absalom is characterized as flaunting his beauty.

50. This contradicts what we will be told in 2 Sam. 18:18 that Absalom has no son. Commentators solve this discrepancy in various ways. One suggestion by Randy L. McCracken, "How Many Sons Did Absalom Have? Intentional Ambiguity as Literary Art," *BibSac* 172 (July–September 2015): 286–98, is that the contrast shows the reversal of Absalom's position of power and influence.

Tamar brings forward the memory of the reason for his banishment, his killing his half-brother for raping Absalom's sister.

In this testimony and during the two years it represents, we are offered no perspective from Absalom, told to remain apart from his father (14:23–28). But beginning at v. 29, we are told by the reticent narrator that Absalom has at least twice asked Joab to intervene with the king, to no avail—in fact, Joab does not meet to hear what Absalom would ask. In a most revealing vignette, we hear an increasingly impatient Absalom instruct his servants to fire a field of Joab, contiguous with Absalom's own land. That done, Joab does approach Absalom, who speaks his request (v. 32): "Absalom answered Joab, 'Behold, I sent word to you, "Come here, that I may send you to the king, to ask, 'Why have I come from Geshur?' It would be better for me to be there still." Now therefore let me go into the presence of the king; and if there is guilt in me, let him kill me.'" Absalom shows himself out of patience, unable to raise a response from Joab except by violence, expressing no gratitude for what has been achieved for him thus far, desirous of at least access to the king (and palace), if not for reconciliation. Joab accedes, again, with his own wishes opaque, the narrator spending a minimum of words on a scene that begs for more (v. 33). Both this long chapter and the preceding one end as father and son meet (v. 33): "Then Joab went to the king, and told him; and he summoned Absalom. So he came to the king, and bowed himself on his face to the ground before the king; and the king kissed Absalom."

Again, lack of precise detail obscures what we would like to understand. Who has gotten what he wanted? But since the quest is not for "what happened" but for how we are offered the rich artistic narrative, we can summarize what we were shown. Joab, with his deepest motives obscure, is shown eager to have David persuaded to return Absalom from Geshur but reticent about managing directly until the king has agreed to the return. Once Absalom is back but not fully restored, Joab seems to have lost interest in Absalom's closer return. Joab is responsive to David, not Absalom. Absalom is easier to read. He wants a full return to the palace, and the narrator scarcely disguises that Absalom envisions more for himself than previously secured. I accept the wise woman as God's proxy as well as Joab's, and take the deity as assisting with the return of Absalom from his flight/exile. The *mashal*, with its language of justice and prayer to avoid reprisal, is a divine prompt. David has, since Nathan's parable, ceased to act unilaterally and decisively—and so here. As in other narratives where his children are involved, David resists decisions and acts with delay and reluctance. His precise motives remain unclear, but the arrogant commandeering is gone. Whether passivity is an improvement remains to be seen, but it marks a decisive change from his former behavior regarding Mephibosheth, Hanun, and Bathsheba.

5 Conclusions and Transition

Focused primarily on David as his long narrative takes firmer shape, observing trends of his plotting and characterization after the deaths of Saul and Ishbosheth bring their people under his authority, we saw him achieve many necessary things and remove certain obstacles to a secure rule, including his clearing of a polluting injustice Saul had left behind (ch. 21), while committing himself an egregious act requiring mitigation as well (24). Chastened variously for his efforts to manage cultic matters, David's initial effort to move the Ark was rebuked. Though a subsequent effort seemed approved, David's wife Michal, appraising from an angle distinct from participants, named it an act of royal self-aggrandizement. David, speaking from closer to the ground, rejected her appraisal, but we, reading, heard it (6). Michal's words seemed to gain credence as David's next worship initiative was even more definitively forestalled by the deity. As we watched David consolidate, the most troubled part of his rule seemed to involve the specifically cultic: the city with its threshing floor, the Ark, a temple. Accepting God's help as well as divine limits eventually if not at first, David seemed poised to rule well.

But as we have in this present chapter followed him into the high summer of his reign, that analysis falls short of adequate. Though we appear to have six fairly coherent scenes, in actuality they resemble more closely a series of flickering scenes, with portions briefly lit before going dark. At first (2 Samuel 9 and 10), David undertook two generous gestures toward allies, and these appeared positive. Royal condescension to Jonathan's son (9) and to Ammonite King Nahash's son (10), presumably well-intentioned but undertaken by David with no consultation or regard for the consequences soon to unfurl, indicate poor seeing, defective judgment, importunate acting. Whatever David's plan and hope, both Mephibosheth (eventually) and Hanun (at once) suffer from these initiatives, as well as clearly enough from their own defects.

The middle pair of scenes, David's glimpsing Uriah's wife, Bathsheba, from the roof of the palace, invites disaster for many: for them, for the men fighting in Ammon, for David's own household, and on his kingdom most serious harm—waves of it, with more ahead (11–12). If David's first impulsive desire might have been understandable, the subsequent choices—beginning from his learning whom he was coveting—move matters into a different realm. The deity, generally tolerant and even permissive with David, draws a firm line again, sending speech to which David attends perceptively, late again though his acknowledgment comes. This time the root of the sin is laid bare for all to examine: not only or so much about objects reached for arrogantly as about the arrogant reaching itself, contemptuous of the good of others and of the deity who has been David's generous benefactor.

Chastised and chastened, we see David fall into passivity and impotence as consequences of his root demeanor invade and destroy people around him. Insofar as he entered an ethical and political thicket with his acts of graciousness, he has become stuck, unable to manage consequences he did not foresee, met by his modes, such as they had grown to be. Almost always opaque and prone to passivity as others act on his behalf, David becomes even more difficult to read, his narrative ambiguity suggesting an ambivalence and irresolution at his depths. Others seek to align him for various purposes of their own. Aimless now himself, David gives way readily in a way that is new. Assisted by a brave Nathan and a wise woman, David nonetheless cannot move much beyond their particular words. We can see the active hand of Joab without quite understanding what he wants from the king, doubt it can be for ultimate good. We watch David's sons, Amnon and Absalom, act to compound the harm their father has done, scrambling for desires of their own, resembling their father in some way while not in others. David seems to have broken the pattern of which he was accused by his advisers—Nathan with his parable, the Tekoan woman with her story—though we have seen him repent before when chastened.

That David sees his ailment now without necessarily yet reaching for the cure, seems to break off his harmful behavior without knowing how to replace it, prompting us to the next part of the story, where harm done continues its effect. The basic issue, gathering, is David's choices regarding his son Absalom. Whether David can move closer to healing and reconciliation remains to be seen. The narrative uncertainty about what David feels in regard to his son reflects well the characteral ambivalence. Absalom's own nature and choices will test David's capacity for compassion in a way not yet explored. That God continues in relation even when David neglects it is promising.

Chapter 7

FRUITS OF SUFFERING: DAVID EXPERIENCES COMPASSION (2 SAM. 15–20)

CONVERGING THREE TOOLS

1 Transition

As we move closer to the end of the narrative, issues seem simpler. The edges of the story are not difficult to see, since the revolt of Absalom flows directly from the material preceding it, and the failure of David to resecure the allegiance of the tribes of Israel results from the collapse of their effort to follow Absalom. The structure is also not particularly complex, with Fokkelman having provided it sensibly as one discrete act, as we will see in the discussion below, moving through the material in six sections.[1]

So our focus will be on particular choices of the narrator, on various plotting strategies, and on insights available through characterization. There is plenty to see. The most urgent topic is David's continuing to manage the learning with which he was presented bluntly by prophet, deity, and wise woman and which he accepted: his pattern of scorning or contemning YHWH and others, his failures of mercy and compassion, his poor choices about taking and sparing. Blunt and accusatory discourse was mingled with gentler though relentless speech of a woman about fratricidal sons, one killing and the other dead. To this language David eventually responded with self-knowledge and with action for *his* surviving son. But if it seemed that contrition and self-implication would heal David's heart, it has not happened, and the present narrative exposes the woods in which David is lost and is floundering. For him to find his way is not easy, particularly as he remains a sitting king as well as a grieving father.

So as we saw in our last chapter, even once David has been presented with his "signature sin" and acknowledged it, consequences of that pattern appear in the king's own family. He must gather fruits of his own actions against deity, kin, and compatriots in brutal act of his son Amnon with his daughter, Tamar, in

---

1. Fokkelman has treated the Mephibosheth materials as a separate set (*King David*, 23–40), but we include them in their narrative order. In addition to his outline as presented and adapted slightly for use on the material being studied here, his chiastic structure of chs. 15–20 is useful (*King David*, 339).

enmity between brothers so badly managed in every way, and surely in the king's violations of his military leadership and the close bonds marking that group of men. Resolutions of these cardinal patterns are not readily at hand. David's most characteristic action in regard to all these challenges has been to do little. From his brief mourning and entreaty for his infant son's life—the one mention we have of prayer to God in our last set of material—his inadvertent and unwilling participation in Amnon's rape of Tamar, his fruitless anger at Amnon, his unwillingness and incapacity to manage decisively and appropriately the complex situation of Absalom, David seems frozen. Since the developing issue is Absalom's situation and that of Joab, we can review where we have come as we begin to consider its next phases.

Absalom first appeared, after being listed third among David's sons, in conflict with his brother over their sister. When Amnon schemed to take Tamar and managed to do so, David's impotent anger was contrasted with Absalom's more ambiguous but also more strategic animus. Seeming to speak dismissively to his sister while refusing to engage with his brother at all, Absalom waited two years before consulting their father to secure his consent to if not participation in the celebration planned to host Absalom's killing his brother Amnon. Remaining unclear, ambiguous and implicitly disputed in the narrative was whether the slaying was licit—anticipated in law—or not.[2] This question dominates the story from our hearing of it onward, and the events of our present chapter rise from its impacted state. But whatever the legalities and ethics, Absalom killed and then fled, seeking refuge with maternal kin outside his father's territory and remained there for some time. The narrator showed David uncertain in the matter of Absalom-in-exile. There seem two distinct issues, though of course they are a blend, strands not separable: How does the father feel in regard to his two sons—one of whom killed the other—and what does he want to do about Absalom—with appropriate justice not a clear thing? How shall the king resolve the matter of uncleared blood, if that is what the situation involves? Again, we are back to the issue of how we are to understand the nature of Absalom's killing—which we may fail to do—and to the king and the father's irresolution and inaction, which we must query and interpret.

Joab, who also looms large in the revolt of Absalom, has been shown desirous of bringing Absalom back to Jerusalem, acting to do so by proxy. The wise woman Joab brought from Tekoa presented to the king the situation of fictive sons, one a slayer of the other, asking reprieve for fratricide, not on the basis of innocence but because the killer is all that remains to her. We heard David resolve her case as she seemed to want but then break off from her. Discerning Joab as instigator of the Tekoan woman's suit, David authorized the return of his own fratricidal son to the royal city but refused reconciliation between them. David, again, indecisive and caught between choices—refused both, avoided either. Absalom was shown to read David thus, and to use increasingly aggressive measures to secure access

---

2. The prequel is the slaying of Abner for the death of Asahel, whom he killed in circumstances liminal to warfare.

to his father, to the king. Joab, who had appeared content to gain the presence of Absalom in Jerusalem without pressing for more, was only unwillingly pushed into the intercession that brought Absalom and David together. The climax of those efforts was David's receiving his son (14:33): "Then Joab went to the king, and told him; and he summoned Absalom. So he came to the king, and bowed himself on his face to the ground before the king; and the king kissed Absalom." So, with feelings not exposed and only with considerable nudging did David greet his son. The feelings of these various characters were shared minimally with us, remarkably so for this intense story of powerful situations.

As the curtain rises on the revolt of Absalom, we can anticipate the plans of the implied author to bring David's rule into its most serious disarray while presenting it, assisted by the narrator's pattern of withholding from us much of the emotional color of the events. We continue to follow the tangled strings of character plotting: Absalom's most ambitious desires will be clear, with little suggestion of any regret for his deeds. Joab's role as David's chief assistant and least respectful and malleable ally will develop, though without our fully understanding his motivation. David, avoiding his most egregious sin, will lapse intermittently into the passivity where others act for him, whether at his subtle direction or as he passively accepts it as was the case earlier in his life. The question to be tracked as we interpret his various moves is David's capacity to exhibit compassion: to feel it, to act upon it, grow it. Joab and Absalom will compound their poor choices and various incapacities. The question, as always, is about how David will interact with the pair of them and with God.

2 The Disintegration of David's Kingship

a Absalom Rebels and David Flees 15:1–16:14

1. Preparation and outbreak: 15:1–12 As we begin to watch the plans of these three principals, the narrator makes vivid and unmistakable to any watching what Absalom desires. In the time intervening between his return to Jerusalem and his sounding the trumpet of revolt, Absalom sets himself up as administrator of justice in place of his father (15:2–4):

> And Absalom used to rise early and stand beside the way of the gate; and when any man had a suit to come before the king for judgment, Absalom would call to him, and say, "From what city are you?" And when he said, "Your servant is of such and such a tribe in Israel," Absalom would say to him, "See, your claims are good and right; but there is no man deputed by the king to hear you." Absalom said moreover, "Oh that I were judge in the land! Then every man with a suit or cause might come to me, and I would give him justice."[3]

3. Fokkelman, *King David*, comments that Absalom is characterized by more talking than by listening (169) but has virtually no God-talk (174)—his vow language being

This overt and egregious usurpation is framed by Absalom's getting himself a chariot and runners and by his insinuating himself as intimate of those who approach him, embracing those who would take his hand (vv. 1, 5). The narrator summarizes what we likely concluded and appraises what we might have missed (v. 6): "Thus Absalom did to all of Israel who came to the king for judgment; so Absalom stole the hearts of the men of Israel." We might say that Absalom wants to be *king* but shows little awareness of what it takes to *be* king. That he has had every opportunity to know the texture of what he is craving seems clear, and yet there is no sign of his awareness of his father's kingly struggles. There is no report that David saw or knew his son's behaviors as habitually manifested, though they are not in any way hidden. If we suppose that David does know of Absalom's doings, there is no effort to oppose him.

Absalom's next move, the last words we hear between them, is the son's request of his father that he (Absalom) go to Hebron, his birthplace, to pay a vow he claims to have made in exile. The king readily agrees (vv. 7–9): "'Go in peace.' So he arose, and went to Hebron."[4] Once there—with no vow mentioned—Absalom sends to his allies throughout the kingdom—presumably those he had greeted as they were approaching David for justice but received instead bracing words and a kiss[5] from Absalom—bidding them to rally to him at the sound of the trumpet and the proclamation (v. 10): "'Absalom is king at Hebron!'" In addition to these willing men, Absalom secures the presence of others who do not know about the trumpet or the announcement until they are caught by them (v. 11): "With Absalom went two hundred men from Jerusalem who were invited guests, and they went in their simplicity, and knew nothing."

The next reference is to an individual, Ahithophel, counselor to David, although new to us.[6] Though most commentators take him as included among those rallying to Absalom willingly, I place him with the "innocent" group, after which he is introduced to us (v. 12): "And while Absalom was offering the sacrifices, he sent for Ahithophel the Gilonite, David's counselor, from his city Giloh. And the conspiracy grew strong, and the people with Absalom kept increasing." It seems ambiguous rather than clear that David's counselor joined Absalom's side knowing

---

specious. Virtually every commentator points out that Absalom is more interested in pleasing the petitioners than in judging fairly. To agree that everyone approaching the gates of Jerusalem for justice has a righteous cause is excessive, highlighting the weakness of Absalom as judge. Keith Bodner, *The Revolt of Absalom* (New York: Routledge, 2014), 58, catches the echo between Absalom's interests and Samuel's warnings about kingship's demands in 1 Samuel 8.

4. Bodner, *Absalom*, 60: David is duped again by a son of his.

5. Alter, *David Story*, 284, connects this gesture with that shown by David to his son at the end of Absalom's long absence, calling it a rhyme.

6. An Ahithophel is named as counselor in 2 Sam. 23:34. See Bodner, "Motives for Defection: Ahithophel's Agenda in 2 Samuel 15–17," in his *David Observed*, 124–39 for his sense of David's counselor as acting from motivation of reprisal over his granddaughter. I am not persuaded and read this character quite differently.

what David's son had done. Ahithophel is literally placed by the narrator between those who know the plan and those who are duped.

2. David's flight: 15:13–33 The narrator now informs us (v. 13) how David learns of his son's revolt, the tidings using the very words of the narrator: "And a messenger came to David, saying, 'The hearts of the men of Israel have gone after Absalom.'" David grasps in an instant what he seems not to have noticed for at least four years.[7] Focal for us, now, is the manner of his response to this double treachery of Absalom, his betrayal of father and usurping of king. David's first, clear, and active choice is flight, a resumption of his long dance with King Saul who also pressed David with hostile moves until, finally, David left the palace, assisted by Saul's son and daughter and arguably accompanied by Saul's wife. This choice to evade and be assisted to evade Absalom is decisive though moderate, insofar as it buys time and prevents capture. David's first plan, then, is escape for survival, avoiding both being slain by his son while also preventing his son from slaying him. It is shown basically a good choice, though not completely or uncomplicatedly so. David gives the order himself, and the rationale (vv. 14–15):

> "Arise, and let us flee; or else there will be no escape for us from Absalom; go in haste, lest he overtake us quickly, and bring down evil upon us, and smite the city with the edge of the sword." And the king's servants said to the king, "Behold, your servants are ready to do whatever my lord the king decides."

David seems to assess that the city of David will be safer without his own presence within it. His people, loyal, are shown willing and even eager to obey. The process of his exiting the city he claimed in 2 Samuel 5 is shown in several moments, as will be his journey back.

First, among those who will not accompany him are ten secondary wives, whom he leaves in the city without explanation, except the narrator's vague "to keep the house" (v. 16), maintain David's claim on it.[8] As David stops at the last settled place at the eastern edge of the city, his own mercenary troops march past him, a second scene of flight we are given. Ittai, commander of the troops from Philistine Gath and who has recently come to David's service, is bidden by David to go back and join "the king," that is, Absalom. But the man demurs and corrects, saying (v. 21): "'As the LORD lives, and as my lord the king lives, wherever my lord the king shall be, whether for death or for life, there also will your servant be.'" The contrast with David's son is patent, and David welcomes Ittai to his quasi-procession from

---

7. Fokkelman, *King David*, 176, notes show close Absalom has gotten before David realizes his danger.

8. For some discussion of this detail, consult Andrew E. Hill, "On David's 'Taking' and 'Leaving' Concubines (2 Samuel 5:13; 15:16)," *JBL* 125.1 (2006): 129–39. As we saw with David's decisions for Mephibosheth and Hanun, this choice turns out poorly for all concerned.

the city, those witnessing it weeping as the king and companions cross the wadi Kidron, moving east (vv. 18–23).[9]

Next (third and fourth scenes) choices arise from the meeting between David and his two priests, Abiathar whom we know and Zadok, whom we have only met in lists. This encounter, also handled directly and decisively by the king (vv. 24–29), results in two main strategic decisions: The Ark of God is sent back into the city, as though its formal presence as David's escort is complete and its role, also, is to hold a space for God's presence against Absalom's plans. David had escorted the Ark into the city, and the Ark now accompanies him out, before returning to its place.[10] We can speculate about reasons for this choice, without any of them being clearly correct. The Ark, somewhat recently, had been with the men fighting in Ammon, or so Uriah implied.[11] David now refuses to commandeer it in his struggle against Absalom, though his willingness to leave it in Jerusalem as Absalom will enter that city before pursuing David may seem risky—or perhaps trusting. At the very least, we observe that David seems certain of this move, which is validated as events turn out. We may also think that David recognizes that the Ark is not his, though he does not consult but informs the priest Zadok, who obeys, perhaps signaling his agreement. David indicates verbally that decisions about the Ark and the king are God's (vv. 25–26): "'Carry the Ark of God back into the city. If I find favor in the eyes of the LORD, he will bring me back and let me see both it and his habitation; but if he says, "I have no pleasure in you," behold, here I am, let him do to me what seems good to him.'" Remarkable, encouraging, a change from his earlier attitudes where his arrogance was manifest in his failure to consult.

The other outcome of the encounter between king and priests is the arranging of how the two sons of the priests, Zadok's Ahimaaz and Abiathar's Jonathan, can be positioned as informants about what happens in Jerusalem, able to be dispatched to David from their fathers, who will also remain in Jerusalem (vv. 27–29). Again, David is clear, shrewd, decisive, even while fleeing Jerusalem in deep mourning, perhaps in supplication—though also opaque in terms of plans about his rebel son (v. 30): "But David went up the ascent of the Mount of Olives, weeping as he went, barefoot and with his head covered; and all the people who were with him covered their heads, and they went up, weeping as they went." The narrator chooses this scene as context for David's learning (fifth small scene) that his counselor, Ahithophel, is "with" Absalom (v. 31). Whether the information about Ahithophel's situation is precisely correct or not, David believes it and responds in prayer: "'O LORD, I pray thee, turn the counsel of Ahithophel into

9. David's language focalizing Absalom to Ittai as "the king" is strategically perspectival, inviting Ittai to make his own construction of "the king" explicit.

10. Fokkelman, *King David*, 186, calls this choice "a surprising gesture of renunciation." I am not sure what he is surprised by, but he may also note the change in David's demeanor about the Ark as his object to manage.

11. As suggested earlier, the Ark is a quasi-character representing the deity, having served as witness misuse and abuse by Eli's sons and Philistines (1 Sam. 1–6) and more recently to Joab and David's treachery involving Uriah (2 Samuel 11).

foolishness.'"[12] Whether the counselor has gone willingly or not, the prayer can and will work effectively.

3. *Three more encounters: 15:32–16:13* David continues to act decisively and with apparent shrewdness as, moving east, he encounters three more individuals: Hushai, Ziba, and Shimei. Each offers us a distinct opportunity to assess David.

Hushai (in the long scene's sixth moment) approaches David in mourning demeanor, while David considers how he might assist the thwarting of Absalom's project. David hands him options and words (vv. 33–34): "'If you go on with me, you will be a burden to me. But if you return to the city, and say to Absalom, "I will be your servant, O king; as I have been your father's servant in time past, so now I will be your servant," then you will defeat for me the counsel of Ahithophel.'" Hushai will also be positioned to coordinate the knowledge and plans of the priests and their sons, serving as double agents. Thus will Hushai assist in two ways, and thus does David initiate action to further his own prayer about the advice Ahithophel might tender to his new king.[13]

David next (seventh) meets Ziba, who appears bringing animals laden with food for the fugitives (16:1–4). After learning the intent of the gift, David's words are about Jonathan's son: "'And where is your master's son?' Ziba said to the king, 'Behold, he remains in Jerusalem; for he said, "Today the house of Israel will give me back the kingdom of my father."' Then the king said to Ziba, 'Behold, all that belonged to Mephibosheth is now yours.'" Ziba's final words are a plea to find favor with his lord, the king. Several points: The offerings, presumably, are goods belonging to Mephibosheth rather than to Ziba himself, though Ziba presents them and speaks against his master, vitiating the gift. The king's inquiry addresses Ziba in reference to his service to Saul (or perhaps Jonathan), also implicitly undermining Mephibosheth, who is always characterized as a subaltern. Ziba's allegations about Mephibosheth make a certain amount of sense in the story of the revolt of Israelites—if there is a time to grab Saul's power back, this may be it—but ring hollow, given what we know of Mephibosheth. Though it seems unlikely in the extreme, surely to most commentators, that the throne of Saul would pass to this young man, Ziba asserts that the young Saulide anticipates it, and David seems to accept his word without evidence of questioning it—again under-seeing the man he speaks of helping. A Saul grandson would not be the last to have unrealistic hopes of regaining a former family status or position. David here judges at least

---

12. For a study on the so-called double-causation of Absalom's defeat—human and divine elements collaboration—see Jonathan Grossman, "The Design of the 'Dual Causality' Principle in the Narrative of Absalom's Rebellion," *Bib* 88 (2007): 558–66, and Michael Avioz, "Divine Intervention and Human Error in the Absalom Narrative," *JSOT* 37.3 (2013): 339–47. I do not disagree that such dual artistry is shown here, but these constructions of the literary technique are not sufficiently subtle about the distinction between punishment and consequences.

13. On the basis of his gentilic, Morrison, *2 Samuel*, 214, identifies Hushai as a Benjaminite; if true, he is a Benjaminite loyal to David, cf. Shimei and Sheba (ahead).

hastily, perhaps badly, but surely decisively, as he will do on his return journey. There is no prayer or consultation here.

The eighth and last encounter is different still, as David and his group meet a Benjaminite who most overtly does not wish him well, cursing steadily while pelting the fugitive king with stones (vv. 5–13): "'Begone, begone, you man of blood, you worthless fellow! The LORD has avenged upon you all the blood of the house of Saul, in whose place you have reigned; and the LORD has given the kingdom into the hand of your son Absalom. See, your ruin is on you; for you are a man of blood.'" These are serious as well as dangerous words, with the man claiming that God is behind the coup of Absalom, punishment for David's deeds of usurpation and bloodshed. Shimei is not the last to reason so. David's nephew Abishai, himself no stranger to such theologizing, urges David to deal with Shimei by silencing him violently, but David restrains him, recalling to us the moment where he did so before (24:4):

> But the king said, "What have I to do with you, you sons of Zeruiah? If he is cursing because the LORD has said to him, 'Curse David,' who then shall say, 'Why have you done so?'" And David said to Abishai and to all his servants, "Behold, my own son seeks my life; how much more now may this Benjaminite! Let him alone, and let him curse; for the LORD has bidden him. It may be that the LORD will look upon my affliction, and that the LORD will repay me with good for this cursing of me today."

Contrasted with his dealing with Ziba, David here shows patience and discernment about both Shimei and Abishai, theologizing himself, though with less self-serving certainty. David's words seem to suggest that what God wants can be known later.

As we watch the scenes that comprise David's flight from Jerusalem, we can hear that besides hoping to survive, he also plans the defeat of the rebellion: by his own resourcefulness, by the loyalty of allies, by repeatedly invoking God's help, by trusting in God's assistance. David is shown most skilled at kingship when his leadership is overtly threatened. The strategies involving the Ark and the priests all assume that David desires to succeed in putting down the revolt. But tangible as well is his recognition and claim that the matter lies in the hands of God, whose favor David does not presume on in any entitled sense, tolerating even Shimei until his interpretation will prove false. No word of reprisal is offered by David or by the narrator, and in fact the king rebukes those who raise the possibility. David is preparing and being prepared for what lies just ahead, except in the matter of the fate of his son.

b Absalom and the Two Counselors 16:15–17:23

Though we will consider, briefly, what each of these speakers has in mind, the larger question to follow is what David designs and what God is shown to support, thus to see the two advisers as playing their parts in a larger drama we are watching, implied by authorial artistry and articulated by narrator skill, of which characters may know little. Absalom is in a game far too complex for him and is easily outplayed by his opponents. David reveals no plan for the matter of Absalom, but it seems clear that the deity does not will the survival of this son, an inference based on the eventual outcome of the piece. That Absalom will be shown deeply loved by his paternal opponent adds to the pathos here, but I think the sympathy (mine, at least) runs more to David than to his son.

1. Council of war: 16:15–17:14 In place, then, as the scene opens are two counselors, each, arguably, at cross-purposes: exposed by David's prayer to God and God's implied response. Ahithophel, even if unwilling or unaware when suborned by Absalom, is compromised in the eyes of David, who (with many commentators), believes him guilty of disloyalty. If, alternatively, he is an unwilling ally to Absalom, Ahithophel is drawn fatalistic, seeking not to reverse or even resist his circumstances but doing what he must before he takes his life, knowing or supposing that there will be no forgiveness for these events. I construct him as unwilling to help Absalom, his advice thus aimed to help David, or at least not to harm him—with God abetting this choice. Hushai, on the other hand, is shown bold and skilled, mouthing words of rich ambiguity and clambering to gain a place he might not have expected to secure with the rebel side, given his apparent loyalty to Absalom's father. Thus counterposed, Ahithophel seems fatalistic while Hushai seems opportunistic. Each is helpful, distinctively.

As Absalom and his followers enter the city David has fled, Hushai presents himself, characterized by both narrator and Absalom as David's friend (vv. 16–19):

> And when Hushai the Archite, David's friend, came to Absalom, Hushai said to Absalom, "Long live the king! Long live the king!" And Absalom said to Hushai, "Is this your loyalty to your friend? Why did you not go with your friend?" And Hushai said to Absalom, "No; for whom the LORD and this people and all the men of Israel have chosen, his I will be, and with him I will remain. And again, whom should I serve? Should it not be his son? As I have served your father, so I will serve you."

Absalom responds to Hushai's words bluntly but naively, thinking that the royal blessing just twice pronounced references himself while challenging Hushai for disloyalty, as though he himself were not thereby accused as well. Hushai's response echoes what David has said, though not in Hushai's presence, the narrator thus choosing to affirm the rightness and viability of David's cause.

Ahithophel has a moment of attention from Absalom, is asked and gives advice (vv. 20–21): "Then Absalom said to Ahithophel, 'Give your counsel; what shall we do?' Ahithophel said to Absalom, 'Go in to your father's concubines, whom he has left to keep the house; and all Israel will hear that you have made yourself odious to your father, and the hands of all who are with you will be strengthened.'" What Absalom reveals about himself by his so open-ended question is amenable to construction. That he has few actual plans for the revolt he has long desired becomes clear, though he may also be testing the man he has so misused.

What Ahithophel intends is also uncertain. As virtually all point out, the recommended action of raping David's secondary wives reinforces the blatant determination of son to supplant and dishonor father—though as the story develops, it is not so clear how David would have reacted, had Absalom survived his own folly. Ahithophel may anticipate that only an egregious and public act will keep David resolute about Absalom's danger. But more importantly, the counselor also speaks words that accord with what Nathan has already told David will happen, helping us see the hand of God in the ruin of Absalom. The narrator sums up the result of Ahithophel's advice to the man who may have been happy enough to receive it. That the violation of ten women "rhymes" with the injury done by Amnon to Absalom's sister is not remarked by narrator or character but lies in plain view. The narrator also summarizes his sense of Ahithophel's reputation (v. 23): "Now in those days the counsel which Ahithophel gave was as if one consulted the oracle of God; so was all the counsel of Ahithophel esteemed, both by David and by Absalom." That is, the advice is skilled, with our challenge being to see how so. It may seem odd that we are not privy to any of this tradition, but the point may rather be that Ahithophel and God are to be seen as a team. This first set of counselor advice is thus shown to readers as synchronized with what God is designing for David and Absalom. Both counselors say more than they may know.

The more famous and strategically substantive counsel comes in the next moment, where each adviser offers his view about how Absalom should manage "the David problem," which is to say, to suggest how David can best be killed by his son. Ahithophel's advice, provided unprompted by any, comes right after the narrator's superlative appraisal (17:1–3):

> Moreover Ahithophel said to Absalom, "Let me [I would] choose twelve thousand men, and I will set out and pursue David tonight. I will come upon him while he is weary and discouraged, and throw him into a panic; and all the people who are with him will flee. I will strike down the king only, and I will bring all the people back to you [as a bride comes home to her husband].[14] You seek the life of only one man, and all the people will be at peace."[15]

The speaker personalizes the plans, offering them in a first-person cohortative, as though Ahithophel were saying what he would do, a possible construction of his verb choices.[16] As is well-noted and generally agreed, however, the advice is

14. The words are difficult. Alter, *David Story*, 296–97, prefers to construe the three difficult words, rather than the metaphor, "for it is one man you seek."

15. Fokkelman, *King David*, 214 comments: "no rhetoric, no flattery, not one flourish."

16. I am not convinced by the claim of Bodner, *Absalom*, 79, that Ahithophel is himself presuming to lead the expedition. He is more convincing when he comments in "Motives," 128, that Ahithophel speaks like one accustomed to being obeyed. Those who construe David's former counselor as bent on revenge over the king's treatment of his granddaughter read him differently from me.

sound, practical and efficient: Move now, move with a small contingent, count on fatigue and discouragement—which are not what we have witnessed but might plausibly have thought to see from David—and kill the one man only, with as little other violence as possible, the better for eventual reconciliation with survivors. Ahithophel does not raise the possibility of the failure of this effort, nor is Absalom shown to think of it. And, appropriately, his words please the man to whom they are offered. Insofar as Absalom wishes to be his father's successor, this tactic seems to advance that plan. Again, what else would Ahithophel say, with his bridges burned behind him by the man who now asks his advice, if not also by himself? Ahithophel need not be guilty of disloyalty for the implied author to have God use his good advice contrarily.

But though the newly and self-proclaimed king is pleased as are his "elders," whoever they may be, Absalom invites his newly (self-)selected adviser to speak as well, an unfortunate choice for Absalom, as things turn out. Though we may see David's prayer to God active here, find God's desires working well with David's "'O LORD, I pray thee, turn the counsel of Ahithophel into foolishness'" (15:31)—Absalom makes this decision as well, from whatever impulse (v. 5): "'Call Hushai the Archite also, and let us hear what he has to say.'" Perhaps Absalom is uncertain, perhaps he thinks another plan may be better. He may be seen as enjoying the process of being served by wise men, co-envisioning and rehearsing aloud the moment when he triumphs over his extraordinary father. Readers provide Absalom with various motives. Hushai, shown assisted by God replying to David's prayer, constructs and baits the son as powerful thwarter of a once-powerful father.

Hushai speaks at length, with elaboration, envisioning grandly (vv. 6–13): "'This time the counsel which Ahithophel has given is not good.'" As noted, the opening words credit the former advice and adviser as well as trumping them, at the moment. But then he elaborates:

> "You know that your father and his men are mighty men, and that they are enraged, like a bear robbed of her cubs in the field. Besides, your father is expert in war; he will not spend the night with the people. Behold, even now he has hidden himself in one of the pits, or in some other place. And when some of the people fall at the first attack, whoever hears it will say, 'There has been a slaughter among the people who follow Absalom.' Then even the valiant man, whose heart is like the heart of a lion, will utterly melt with fear; for all Israel knows that your father is a mighty man, and that those who are with him are valiant men."

Hushai underlines the valorous qualities of Absalom's father: his wily skill and strength, motivated by anger rather than by depression to which Ahithophel alludes. Hushai also pictures for the son the likely effect if any casualties among the rebels are reported back, likely playing to the uncertainty of this young man who seems so short on plans of his own. The picture of father and son being offered seems structured to prompt defensive bravado on the son's part.

That sketch continues:

"But my counsel is that all Israel be gathered to you, from Dan to Beersheba, as the sand by the sea for multitude, and that you go to battle in person. So we shall come upon him in some place where he is to be found, and we shall light upon him as the dew falls on the ground; and of him and all the men with him not one will be left. If he withdraws into a city, then all Israel will bring ropes to that city, and we shall drag it into the valley, until not even a pebble is to be found there."

That is: gather many to your side, picture yourself leading vast throngs, finding the fugitive wherever he may foolishly and pointlessly have gone. Whatever it takes will be the resources by which all will assist and witness your capture of your father. This son, greedy for success, is drawn more realistically than is the father, as Absalom seems to like what he hears (v. 14):[17] "And Absalom and all the men of Israel said, 'The counsel of Hushai the Archite is better than the counsel of Ahithophel.' For the LORD had ordained to defeat the good counsel of Ahithophel, so that the LORD might bring evil upon Absalom." Though the narrator offers reliable information, it is not utterly clear why Absalom accepts it, or why his men are eager to agree, or unwilling to disagree. Picking up the narrator's assessment of Ahithophel's repute and echoing Hushai's careful trouncing of it, the revolt group chooses badly.[18] David and God seem to be doing well, working seamlessly as has been his most effective mode in the past.

2. *Escape of David*: *17:15–23* The first outcome of the advice and consent is Hushai's quick dispatch of the result to David's priests, who send their sons to run the news to David, urging him to move on from where he may have stopped. With high drama, we learn that the two sons are spotted and reported to Absalom, who sends pursuers. But thanks to a loyal and resourceful woman, the pair is saved. The scene begs elaboration, but the narrator provides its bones only, stressing the point that David has brave and shrewd agents on his side, from the deity to an unnamed woman who, Rahab-like, saves the two lives, advances their mission. The danger ends as word is brought to David (vv. 21–22):

After they had gone, the men came up out of the well, and went and told King David. They said to David, "Arise, and go quickly over the water; for thus and so has Ahithophel counseled against you." Then David arose, and all the people who were with him, and they crossed the Jordan; by daybreak not one was left who had not crossed the Jordan.

The second coda to the scene is the inevitable outcome for the counselor who has fallen from a privileged place, by whatever steps and whosoever design. Knowing

17. It seems generally conceded that the advice is unrealistic and impractical as well as suited to the ego of the addressee.
18. These counselor speeches have been studied well and extensively by Shimon Bar-Efrat, *Narrative Criticism*, 223–37.

he has lost credibility with all who once accepted his words, perhaps sensing—whether truly or not—that he has no future with a victorious David, Ahithophel takes his own life.[19]

Before looking at the quickly told result of all this detail, we can sum up our characters and their plans once again. We are watching God, David, and Absalom primarily, though not forgetting the two advisers, Joab, and David's various benefactors. To be stressed is how the deity's putative plans are falling into place together with those of the king. David himself has been shown determined first to escape and then to survive, a plan that seems likely, however the details will fall out. As when he was opposed by Saul, David has a lot of assistance, grounded, it seems, by loyalty. More than a match for Absalom, David protects his own kingship and the future of his dynasty, though with a curious lack of details about how Absalom will fare. Absalom's plan, though never stated quite so bluntly as it might have been, is to kill his father. Part of his characterization is his avoidance of ever saying so. Nothing short of the reigning king's death will leave an Absalom kingship secure. Joab's plans are completely unspecified thus far, so we need to reach back to Joab's earlier efforts to get Absalom back to Jerusalem, if not quite into his father's presence. We can only speculate about, absent any information, what Joab can want now: The defeat of Absalom with his (Joab's) assistance? The defeat of David, with some new opportunity for Joab? That we cannot know does not mean we ought not be thinking about it, given what we know is about to happen. The two counselors, each "misplaced" or situated falsely, seem swept into God's plans. Hushai wills it, and "my Ahithophel" simply does not resist Absalom, except perhaps indirectly. And we have seen many people supporting David, with only Shimei and nameless elders on Absalom's side.[20]

c Battle Results: 17:24–19:1

1. Preparations: 17:24–18:18 Finally, we learn as well the last information about David's assistance as he faces Absalom making poor choices: As David and his people reach Mahanaim with Absalom and his supporters in pursuit, crossing as well to the east side of the Jordan, we learn that Absalom has set over his fighters another of his cousins, Amasa, whose skill is far from adequate, here or later when David offers him another chance to lead fighters. David, we are told, is provided for by three foreigners, offering him "beds, basins, and earthen vessels, wheat, barley, meal, parched grain, beans and lentils, honey and curds and sheep and

19. Bodner, "Motivation for Defection," *David Observed*, 138, observes that it is odd that for all the testimony about Ahithophel's skill, we only see this one place where he is ineffective, at least in the eyes and ears of most present (so to speak). Of course, we can appraise that the advice was right even if not heeded by the foolish man to whom it was offered. If we can see that David does not judge wisely of Mephibosheth, the same can be said of his discernment about Ahithophel.

20. If we believe Ziba that Mephibosheth anticipates a restoration, we have to see that he is not really abetting Absalom in any tangible way.

cheese from the herd" (17:28–29), saying, "'The people are hungry and weary and thirsty in the wilderness.'" Of provisions for Absalom's people we hear nothing.

David next musters his men, who are not few, placing them under the commands of Joab, Abishai, and Ittai, announcing his intent to accompany if not lead (18:2–4):

> And the king said to the men, "I myself will also go out with you." But the men said, "You shall not go out. For if we flee, they will not care about us. If half of us die, they will not care about us. But you are worth ten thousand of us; therefore it is better that you send us help from the city." The king said to them, "Whatever seems best to you I will do." So the king stood at the side of the gate,[21] while all the army marched out by hundreds and by thousands.

The scene again testifies to the active participation of David, his planning and commanding, his willingness to engage—and his acquiescence to another point of view. David has never feared or avoided danger, not earlier and not recently, so cowardice is unlikely to be a factor here. My sense is that, besides prompting lavish testimony from his loyal men, narrative design needs David absent from the ultimate engagement of his people with Absalom, both emotionally and so that we can listen to him give orders and subsequently receive news.[22] His orders come next (v. 5): "And the king ordered Joab and Abishai and Ittai, 'Deal gently for my sake with the young man Absalom.' And all the people heard when the king gave orders to all the commanders about Absalom." We can wonder what "gently" implies, what the king has in mind, but we can be sure it is not to be equated with the outcome.[23] If we venture that David anticipates being himself involved in reprisal against his son, his response to the news of Absalom's death shows it unlikely.

2. Outcome: The battle itself, if long anticipated, is over in three verses (vv. 6–8):

> So the army went out into the field against Israel; and the battle was fought in the forest of Ephraim. And the men of Israel were defeated there by the servants of David, and the slaughter there was great on that day, twenty thousand men. The battle spread over the face of all the country; and the forest devoured more people that day than the sword.

No detail is provided, the metaphor of the devouring forest serving in place of factual accounting. For the narrator hurries on to the only scene we need to witness (vv. 9–18): "And Absalom chanced to meet the servants of David. Absalom was riding upon his mule, and the mule went under the thick branches of a great

21. A royal position, as Absalom seemed to see as well, in 15.
22. David's absence from the battle scene here as in ch. 11 is thus artistic rather than moral.
23. Alter, *David Story*, 304, suggests its root (*l't.*) is most likely to mean to cover, protect. It is not utterly clear what David is asking, but generally that he wants care for his son.

oak, and his head caught fast in the oak, and he was left hanging between heaven and earth, while the mule that was under him went on."[24] Again scanty with detail, the narrator has eyes for the one scene only. How Absalom is alone is a provocative detail, riding, perhaps, an animal we heard of in 15:1, trapped soon by the hair we heard about in 14:26. The two details, more suggestive of the man's character than literally useful, mark the destruction of the royal plans Absalom once entertained. The consuming forest takes a final prisoner, though without itself killing him.

That task is left to a human being:

> And a certain man saw it, and told Joab, "Behold, I saw Absalom hanging in an oak." Joab said to the man who told him, "What, you saw him! Why then did you not strike him there to the ground? I would have been glad to give you ten pieces of silver and a girdle." But the man said to Joab, "Even if I felt in my hand the weight of a thousand pieces of silver, I would not put forth my hand against the king's son; for in our hearing the king commanded you and Abishai and Ittai, 'For my sake protect the young man Absalom.' On the other hand, if I had dealt treacherously against his life (and there is nothing hidden from the king[25]), then you yourself would have stood aloof."

The brief scene is as vivid as any we have witnessed. The confusion of battle is implied as reason an anonymous man knows more than Joab does, unless we may suppose that Joab feigns surprise, as though hoping to avoid what he will, in fact, have to do once Absalom's plight has been called to the attention of all.[26] If we knew more strategically what Joab wanted, it would be easier to read the scene. But its main tactical point is clear. Joab wants Absalom dead, and tells the man he would have paid him to do it. The nameless character, speaking very boldly to his superior, disdains reward, deed, and instigator in scathing language. The strength of the reply makes a great contrast between Joab and at least some others, since the one man cannot be imagined as the only one to see Absalom so vulnerable.[27]

Joab's answer is dismissive, even defensive.

> "I will not waste time like this with you." And he took three darts in his hand, and thrust them into the heart of Absalom, while he was still alive in the oak. And ten young men, Joab's armor-bearers, surrounded Absalom and struck him, and killed him. Then Joab blew the trumpet, and the troops came back from pursuing Israel; for Joab restrained them.

24. Deuteronomy 21:22–23 stresses the curse accompanying any who dies in this way.
25. We may find this an odd assertion, but again it testifies to the confidence David's loyal men have in him, thus adding to his characterization.
26. Alter, *David Story*, 306, inclines toward the view that Joab, striking Absalom with sticks (not darts), does not really wish him dead. I find that out of character with Joab, as he will be exposed shortly by his own words to David.
27. Fokkelman, *King David*, 245, remarks the similarity with the role Uriah played earlier in managing the death of Uriah.

Rather than risking futility—or worse—by ordering another to do the deed, Joab himself further disables his cousin, after which a group of ten finishes the killing and they bury the body before the troops disband and make their ways home. This scene seems proleptic and analeptic at the same time: David's son is buried at once, and his words of a former occasion are recalled: "Now Absalom in his lifetime had taken and set up for himself the pillar which is in the King's Valley, for he said, 'I have no son to keep my name in remembrance'; he called the pillar after his own name, and it is called Absalom's monument to this day." We have been told previously (14:27) that Absalom sired three sons, and though we can suppose they have not survived, the broader point seems to be that the house of David will not be built through the Absalom line. The monument he leaves is not the one he provided. It is a brutal and pitiless epitaph for this son of David, though not his last.

3. *Report and Response: 18:19–33* In narrative terms, this scene ranks with 2 Samuel 12 for impact on our understanding of David, our watching him grow in his capacity for compassion, feeling for another as though for himself, at potential cost to himself. The scene is meticulously provided, by the narrator, by various characters, by David. In contrast with the speed and reticence comprising event of Absalom's defeat itself, we are given a slow and detailed view of how this news is to be communicated, with the various angles of focalization contributing to our understanding of David. In contrast with the more routinized if heartfelt concern for his infant son, David's grief for this so-flawed Absalom will be deep, destabilizing for the father. David's earlier ambivalence and inconsistence about Absalom seems transformed, now, into something clear and deep, manifested without confusion. If we cannot detail *how* the change has come about, I think we can witness *that* it has. But now comes the scene where the king learns the full outcome of his plans.

First we have the two actual runners. One of the priest-sons volunteers to take the news back, specifically calling it good news. His youthful and naive enthusiasm first misperceives what David wants to hear—sharpening it for us: "Then said Ahimaaz the son of Zadok, 'Let me run, and carry tidings to the king that the LORD has delivered him from the power of his enemies.' And Joab said to him, 'You are not to carry tidings today; you may carry tidings another day, but today you shall carry no tidings, because the king's son is dead.'" The alternate messenger, a Cushite, remains silent. "Then Joab said to the Cushite, 'Go, tell the king what you have seen.' The Cushite bowed before Joab, and ran." The young priest-son imagines the outcome in one way, while Joab sees it in another—offering us additional insight into his deed, suggesting as well that Joab anticipates David's response to the news. The Cushite provides opportunity for a third angle. We may think Joab does well here to attempt to dissuade Zadok's son from being messenger of this news, and may wonder that Joab does not instruct the Cushite but frees him to say what he saw. When the young Zadok-son begs again that he might run the news, Joab warns him again, but to no avail:

Then Ahimaaz the son of Zadok said again to Joab, "Come what may, let me also run after the Cushite." And Joab said, "Why will you run, my son, seeing that you will have no reward for the tidings?" "Come what may," he said, "I will run." So he said to him, "Run." Then Ahimaaz ran by the way of the plain, and outran the Cushite.

Before the news arrives, we can think about Joab additionally. How can we understand, construct, Joab's behavior here? Is he empathetic, bold, careless, or resigned? His basic opacity makes it impossible to finalize his characterization or plotting, but he exhibits a concern for Ahimaaz that seems not to extend to the Cushite runner, to David, or even to himself. Joab, victorious in the battle to defeat the king's usurper, is evidently so unconflictedly determined on Absalom's death, so unafraid of consequences that he defies the orders of the king and makes no effort to either cover his deed or explain it. As before—and later—Joab seems unconcerned for David's reproach and untroubled by any of the powerful allies David has, for example, Nathan. That Absalom is killed in war is clear enough—even as he, defeated, flees alone, taking us once again back to the killing of Joab's brother Asahel by Abner. David has remained committed to defeating the revolt while simultaneously and only latterly and tangibly showing care for the well-being of his son.

We—knowing the content of the news—have ample opportunity to envision the impact of its delivery. David, not knowing the outcome, has at least two possibilities to explore. The narrator returns us to David where we left him as his men departed for the battle against the rebels (18:24–27). We recall the last words of the king about his son, and we have heard them quoted again even as violated. David, father as well as king, awaits news, as we have seen him do on previous occasions. The narrator begins to build the scene:

> Now David was sitting between the two gates; and the watchman went up to the roof of the gate by the wall, and when he lifted up his eyes and looked, he saw a man running alone. And the watchman called out and told the king. And the king said, "If he is alone, there are tidings in his mouth." And he came apace, and drew near. And the watchman saw another man running; and the watchman called to the gate and said, "See, another man running alone!" The king said, "He also brings tidings." And the watchman said, "I think the running of the foremost is like the running of Ahimaaz the son of Zadok." And the king said, "He is a good man, and comes with good tidings."

The king and father is shown quick, eager to discern good news in the evidence as it comes into view. One messenger, running alone, is plausibly not a whole army routed into disarray but a man with news. As the runner approaches, the watchman from his lookout feels able to offer an identification of the runner as one who had done well so far, the young Zadokite. The king, apparently making that connection, takes hope. There is, contrastively, no speculation on the identity or significance of the second runner, who he is and why he also is approaching.

The Cushite is a mute if poignant reminder to us of what David dreads to learn, looming even as Absalom's father continues to resist the implications of the battle. The gap between what David knows and what the reader knows has never felt so vast.

The narrator lingers, now, on the arrival and the dispensing of information in its parts. "Then Ahimaaz cried out to the king, 'All is well.' And he bowed before the king with his face to the earth, and said, 'Blessed be the LORD your God, who has delivered up the men who raised their hand against my lord the king.'" Ahimaaz, still not understanding what Joab was trying to save him from, delivers news he assumes the king is eager to hear, only to learn in an instant what had evaded him previously: "And the king said, 'Is it well with the young man Absalom?' Ahimaaz answered, 'When Joab sent your servant, I saw a great tumult, but I do not know what it was.' And the king said, 'Turn aside, and stand here.' So he turned aside, and stood still." Perceiving in an instant what the king is most concerned for, the young runner suddenly says he does not know what happened—strange announcement from a messenger. We may think this awkward evasion should be a warning to David, but time for hope grows short.

For the Cushite approaches: "'Good tidings for my lord the king! For the LORD has delivered you this day from the power of *all* who rose up against you'" (emphasis added). That seems clear enough, but David presses: "'Is it well with the young man Absalom?' And the Cushite answered, 'May the enemies of my lord the king, and all who rise up against you for evil, be like that young man.'" There is no mistaking that news, carefully phrased as it is.

David's reaction is, I think, unlike anything we have seen from him thus far, though it resembles other scenes partially, and is composed of responses we have seen before. The narrator tells us (v. 33): "And the king was deeply moved, and went up to the chamber over the gate, and wept; and as he went, he said, 'O my son Absalom, my son, my son Absalom! Would I had died instead of you, O Absalom, my son, my son!'" We witnessed David angered when his family site at Ziklag was raided, we saw him in distress for Jonathan and moved by the death of Saul. We watched him indignant for Abner, and intercede mutely for the infant son who died. We were present for his wordless anger at the rape of Tamar, shock and grief over the killing of Amnon. This sorrow is different. Before saying more about it, a last construction of Absalom.

Absalom, of course, is beyond planning, but we can summarize retrospectively how deluded his long and lavish vision of succeeding to kingship is shown to have been. Advised several times, rarely well, never effectively, he seems easily defeated by his opponent, overmatched in all aspects of his hopes. That he is characterized by the narrator as dying sonless, a failed parricide, deserted by—or deserting— all who had shared his cause, hanging on a tree, is sobering, to say the least. His military debacle, which he survives briefly to know, has to be the opposite of anything he had imagined or desired. Though we remain conscious of the apparent slowness with which David readmitted Absalom into his presence after the killing of Amnon, so long as Absalom lived, reconciliation and even justice have remained available. That David has partially but inadequately anticipated the likelihood of what would befall Absalom in battle is reinforced by his words to the fighters and his barely concealed anxiety as messengers approach with news. That David had not expected the rebel son's death hints that Absalom likely did not expect it either. To call David dilatory about Absalom is justified, but he surely does not want him dead.

d Various Responses: 19:1–26

We learn with Joab: (19:1): "It was told Joab, 'Behold, the king is weeping and mourning for Absalom.'"

1. David's peoples' response: Before offering us Joab's appraisal, the narrator provides additional participant reaction (vv. 2–4): "So the victory that day was turned into mourning for all the people; for the people heard that day, 'The king is grieving for his son.' And the people stole into the city that day as people steal in who are ashamed when they flee in battle." We hear that David's people respond sympathetically to the king, react as though from his perspective, not their own victorious experience. The narrator takes responsibility for characterizing this group, reporting what they do and then offering an analogy for it—returning as if in disgrace rather than as if triumphant. Joab's analogy likens their behavior to fighters shamed as when a longed-for victory is reappraised as a defeat, once the people learn of their king's sorrow.[28] But we are again shown David as his loyal people see him: "The king covered his face, and the king cried with a loud voice, 'O my son Absalom, O Absalom, my son, my son!'" The narrator's showing us this scene before we hear Joab cannot be without impact.

2. Joab's response: Joab's assessment, both coinciding and conflicting with what the narrator has already said, is provided in vv. 5–7, tempting us, perhaps, to accept it:

> "You have today covered with shame the faces of all your servants, who have this day saved your life, and the lives of your sons and your daughters, and the lives of your wives and your concubines, because you love those who hate you and hate those who love you. For you have made it clear today that commanders and servants are nothing to you; for today I perceive that if Absalom were alive and all of us were dead today, then you would be pleased."

As though having heard the narrator's analogy, Joab accuses the king of shaming his loyal people, in fact of treating them like enemies to defeat rather than as allies to bring success.[29] He accuses David of ingratitude toward those who have saved

---

28. Fokkelman, *King David*, 188, perhaps to counter Joab's accusations, reminds us that all the gestures of loyalty transacted between David and his followers constitute *hesed*.

29. This artificial way of suggesting that a character has overheard the narrator calls attention to the artistic overlap among authoring levels. The narrator, to my view, has not quite focalized the people as shamed while using an analogy that suggests it to us. When Joab characterizes the people as shamed by David, we both hear the corroboration and see the difference. Granting that shame is not simply an inner feeling but an ascribed social condition, still, Joab has claimed more than we have quite witnessed.

his life, perhaps of a grosser disrespect. Joab appraises that David treats friends like enemies and foes like allies. There is truth here but distortion as well, and an ominous echo of the battle that resulted in the death of Uriah. Permissive toward those who do not wish him well, whether from strength or weakness, David is not shown to contemn his allies, except perhaps Joab himself, who as we have seen is a dubious partner. David seems utterly overwhelmed by what he learns of his son's death, that news blotting out any consideration of anyone else—not quite the same as what Joab accuses.

There is nothing gentle or empathetic in Joab's words, no sense that the king's dead enemy is a son. Nor does Joab seem to note that the people are not shown outraged as he himself is. Though he speaks for the group of David supporters whom he says—with some narrator cover—the king has shamed and misvalued, it is hard to discern any link with them in his actual words or indignation. Joab's final accusation, that David wishes the result had been the inverse of what it was, belies the whole narrative we have been reading, where David's energies are clearly and consistently bent toward defeating Absalom's revolt. Joab's final exaggerated salvo discredits, to some extent, the substance of his accusation. His description of the situation, though vivid and direct, does not suit well what we have seen of the king before the battle or the father after it. It is tempting to say that Joab is simply wrong in his reproach to the king, and yet, granting how little we may understand honor and shame, there is likely some truth offered. Even if we, reading, may excuse David for placing what we would call a personal grief over a civic need, the result may in fact be loss of social honor for David's allies, even if they, also, do not register it tangibly, as their empathy overrides their own sense of having been let down. In this long section, filled with contrasts, we must find our way with care.

Moving now past assessment to advice, Joab adds: "'Now therefore arise, go out and speak kindly to your servants; for I swear by the LORD, if you do not go, not a man will stay with you this night; and this will be worse for you than all the evil that has come upon you from your youth until now.'" That Joab makes such a statement under oath adds to its weight, though the narrator provides no information to us that would validate it. We may suspect Joab of aiming to distract from information he does not want known, how it came to be that not only is the revolt crushed but that its leader dead, despite orders given about that matter. Though he appears to have made no previous effort to hide his own role in Absalom's death, Joab's present counterattack may have the intent or effect of shutting off discourse about the manner of it. In any case, we do not ever learn with certainty what David knows about those events, since his thoughts are not verbalized.

The king wordlessly obeys his nephew and commander (v. 9): "Then the king arose, and took his seat in the gate. And the people were all told, 'Behold, the king is sitting in the gate'; and all the people came before the king, all wordlessly. Now Israel had fled every man to his own home." David's men greet their king and are received by him. It is a silent and sober conclusion to the scene, difficult to read, given all we do not see or hear.

3. Broader reactions: As the people loyal to David—having demonstrated it by accompanying him from Jerusalem—thus respond to him, the narrator offers us views of two other groups. First, the failed allies of Absalom reflect (vv. 9–10):

> And all the people were at strife throughout all the tribes of Israel, saying, "The king delivered us from the hand of our enemies, and saved us from the hand of the Philistines; and now he has fled out of the land from Absalom. But Absalom, whom we anointed over us, is dead in battle. Now therefore why do you say nothing about bringing the king back?"

We hear their appraisal and discussion among themselves, to the effect that David had done well by them before the Absalom effort, itself now failed. Why not reconnect with the king who had served them well?

David, though still in the field (in story space and time), seems to be thinking along somewhat the same lines (vv. 11–14), addressing another group of his own tribe, perhaps aiming to provide Judah with an advantage over Israel: "And King David sent this message to Zadok and Abiathar the priests, 'Say to the elders of Judah, "Why should you be the last to bring the king back to his house, when the word of all Israel has come to the king? You are my kinsmen, you are my bone and my flesh; why then should you be the last to bring back the king?"'" These elders of Judah, identified neither with Absalom's revolt nor with those who accompanied the king, are tangibly not with David, outside the city. David's next words seem addressed to the allies of Absalom, whom we heard speculating along the same lines: "'Say to Amasa, "Are you not my bone and my flesh? God do so to me, and more also, if you are not commander of my army henceforth in place of Joab."' And he swayed the heart of all the men of Judah as one man; so that they sent word to the king, 'Return, both you and all your servants.'"

While the Israelite tatters of Absalom's group, quarreling among themselves, continue to ponder their options, David orders his two priests to deal with the Judahites who had neither sided with Absalom nor gone with himself, urging that they welcome their king back—suffering no reprisals—before the others can do so. Repeating words we heard earlier (2 Sam. 5:1), he cites close kinship as the basis for his relationship with them, as something the Israelites may never have, whatever they may desire. As incentive, he names Absalom's failed leader Amasa, also kin to him, as leader in place of Joab, for reasons we can provide, recent and longer-running. There is no response indicated, as the Israelites continue to talk among themselves and we watch the people of Judah greet their returning king (vv. 14–15): "And he swayed the heart of all the men of Judah as one man; so that they sent word to the king, 'Return, both you and all your servants.' So the king came back to the Jordan; and Judah came to Gilgal to meet the king and to bring the king over the Jordan."[30] We hear no words of recrimination, none of apology. Is this wise, or perhaps overhasty?

---

30. We may have assumed, due to the terminology consistently used, that two groups split over David and Absalom, Israelites to Absalom and Judahites to David, granting that

e David's Journey Back: 19:17–41[31]

Having just shown us both David's tremendous grief and his practical initiative, each resulting from his victory over the rebellious forces, the question to be explored as the king returns to the city is how he will greet those individuals whom he met when leaving Jerusalem. In other words, is David-reclaiming-his-city different from David-fleeing-it, and are his interlocutors? The journey of the king and his loyal followers back to Jerusalem is about process rather than endpoint. Since it is already beyond doubt that he will regain his city, our vantage point prompts us to study his post-death-of-Absalom responses as he meets some of the same people he encountered when in flight. Who and what sort of human being and king is David? We have three moments to scrutinize.[32]

1. Shimei: 19:17–24 One man encountered as David moved east was Shimei of Benjamin, who cursing and throwing stones, identified David as a man of blood. David rebuked Abishai for a typical Zeruid intemperate impulse to destroy Shimei, suggesting that perhaps the Benjamin's prompts were of God. Here, now, Shimei approaches with a sizable unit of men, including Ziba and his household, all making haste to greet the returning victor and "do his pleasure," as the narrator specifies. Shimei bows before the king, begging forgiveness for the words earlier shouted. His admission of guilt is thorough, even refreshing (vv. 19–20): "'Let not my lord hold me guilty or remember how your servant did wrong on the day my lord the king left Jerusalem; let not the king bear it in mind. For your servant knows that I have sinned; therefore, behold, I have come this day, the first of all the house of Joseph to come down to meet my lord the king.'" Abishai intervenes much as before, though now from a stronger position, urging that Shimei be executed, only to be rebuked again by his uncle, the king (v. 22): "'What have I to do with you, you sons of Zeruiah, that you should this day be as an adversary to me? Shall any one be put to death in Israel this day? For do I not know that I am this day king over Israel?'" David promises Shimei his life. In strength, David acts no differently toward Shimei than in weakness—though this is not the last word about Shimei. If God was, as asked by David earlier, the judge of what lay between these two protagonists— differing over whether David is under divine sanction for bloody deeds—David seems content to leave matters as God has evidently pronounced now. Whether

---

some of Judah went with Absalom, in ignorance or by choice. But it seems clear, now, that some of the people of Judah not actually among those with David must now be brought back—or David brought back to them. Fokkelman, *King David*, 291, appraises that David has just made things worse with this strategy.

31. Fokkelman's divisions here are not the ones I would offer. He has a chiasm, of the whole unit, *King David,* 339. For a brief but useful study of the symmetry between the two parts of David's journey, see David M. Gunn, "From Jerusalem to the Jordan and Back: Symmetry in 2 Samuel 15–20," *VT* 30.1 (1980): 109–13.

32. Fokkelman attempts something similar when he offers integration sections, as here, *King David*, 275–91. He is reading psychology in a way I am not, so that, though interesting, I do not find his observations directly useful.

restraint is the best choice here is not so clear, nor is it easy to decide whether the king's evenhandedness is active or passive. There is no reprisal and no reward.

2. Mephibosheth 19:23–31 Though Ziba is identified among those with Shimei—redirecting our attention to the great difference between the actions of the present pair toward David as he fled his city—here we with David meet Ziba's present master (Jonathan's son), made so conspicuously absent as David fled. David's earlier question about Mephibosheth's whereabouts had been explained by Ziba, truthfully or not, with assertion that Saul's grandson anticipated Absalom's revolt as his opportunity to restore the Saulides. Now, contrastively challenging Ziba's regretful accusation, we are presented with a young man manifesting signs of grief and distress—his feet not dressed, his beard not trimmed, his clothing not washed, from the day the king departed until the day he came back in safety, the narrator describes:

> And when he came from Jerusalem to meet the king, the king said to him, "Why did you not go with me, Mephibosheth?" He answered, "My lord, O king, my servant deceived me; for your servant said to him, 'Saddle an ass for me, that I may ride upon it and go with the king.' For your servant is lame. [Ziba] has slandered your servant to my lord the king. But my lord the king is like the angel of God; do therefore what seems good to you. For all my father's house were but men doomed to death before my lord the king; but you set your servant among those who eat at your table. What further right have I, then, to cry to the king?"

Mephibosheth counters Ziba's words in several ways, claiming that Ziba refused to assist him to accompany the fleeing king when asked, that Ziba slandered him, and that so far as expecting any restoration of Saul's house, owning that their position was tenable only by David's patronage. Scholars discuss the undecidability of these two feuding characters, but I think, rather, the point is David's response.[33] Asked to judge, David fails to do so, not dissimilar to the situation of Shimei. As arbiter of justice, David should want to disentangle this cardinal dispute. But that is not what we have. Rather, David seems to have become tire of Jonathan's son and his need for the protection we heard David promise as early as 1 Samuel 20 and begin to deliver in 2 Samuel 9: "And the king said to him, 'Why speak any more of your affairs? I have decided: you and Ziba shall divide the land.' And Mephibosheth said to the king, 'Oh, let him take it all, since my lord the king has come safely home.'" David refuses careful attention, and Mephibosheth pushes away recompense from the estate David had already given Ziba, as he once bestowed it upon Jonathan's son. Ziba, of course, was just seen by David and ourselves with Shimei, making no overt presentation of himself.[34] We may think of Joab's words to David about

33. A sample of the discussion can be reviewed in Jeremy Schipper, "Still Speak," 344–51. The matter can be assessed using various methods and criteria, and though some views seem stronger to their proponents than do others, the matter remains open.

34. Fokkelman reminds us, *King David*, 303, that the narrator has given Mephibosheth the last word, and a long one at that, tilting the scale toward Mephibosheth by so doing.

confusing friends and enemies, or even of David's to Jonathan, promising fidelity to his house and think that justice has not been served here.

3. Barzillai 19:32–41 We witnessed David encounter this man with a pair of other foreigners, the trio providing food for David and his companions when they met on the east side of the Jordan. He now has come to greet the king and escort him back across the river. The narrator gives Barzillai's age and reminds us what service he had performed for the king, being wealthy as well as an elder.[35] David's words clearly offer reward:

> "Come over with me, and I will provide for you with me in Jerusalem." But Barzillai said to the king, "How many years have I still to live, that I should go up with the king to Jerusalem? I am this day eighty years old; can I discern what is pleasant and what is not? Can your servant taste what he eats or what he drinks? Can I still listen to the voice of singing men and singing women? Why then should your servant be an added burden to my lord the king? Your servant will go a little way over the Jordan with the king. Why should the king recompense me with such a reward? Pray let your servant return, that I may die in my own city, near the grave of my father and my mother."

Barzillai's reply is that of a wise man, knowing that his end is not so far away and that new pleasures are not likely to surpass those he already enjoys. Barzillai seems untempted by either status or greed, is unwilling to burden the king with a new friend in such circumstances or perhaps be burdened by David's problems. His desire is to accompany David across the Jordan, literally and perhaps to celebrate his triumph. This may be the place to note that none of these people speaks to David about his son. Barzillai, perhaps thinking that David feels the need to recompense and honor an obligation, offers a way to do that by proxy: "'But here is your servant Chimham;[36] let him go over with my lord the king; and do for him whatever seems good to you.' And the king answered, 'Chimham shall go over with me, and I will do for him whatever seems good to you; and all that you desire of me I will do for you.'" David heeds Barzillai, both in what he declines and in what he offers. This justice is not so difficult as the previous two cases, and yet we must draw forward from the final words of David to Solomon the king's admission that this kindness was not considered fully repaid by David as he charges Solomon (1 Kgs. 2:7). So again, a refusal or incapacity of David to manage his charge. The passivity that has characterized him before and will shortly reassert itself to great harm is shown to be reestablishing itself. Shimei is left at large, in Ziba's company. Mephibosheth remains under a cloud, his heritage in disarray. Barzillai's kindness is not quite repaid. Most egregious and unremarked is the matter of David and Joab, given

---

35. Mark W. Hamilton, "At Whose Table? Stories of Elites and Social Climbers in 1–2 Samuel," *VT* 59 (2009): 529–32 examines the two episodes involving this character.

36. Alter, *David Story*, 318, infers that Chimham is Barzillai's son. If so, it adds to the old man's characterization that he does not say so, under the circumstances.

both Joab's success as David's commander and his disobedience to David's clear words about his rebel son. For all the apparent interaction, David is shown to have lost heart. The king shows little appetite or skill for ruling the unruly set of tribes he once managed. As before, his crisis disables him.

f Schism between Israel and Judah: 19:41–20:22

As anticipated before David's reverse journey to Jerusalem is begun, the larger question under negotiation is the restoration of David's authority over those who had either rejected it outright or stood aloof as Absalom's revolt took shape. The king has already—narratively in the midst of his grief for his dead son—made an offer to the leaders of Judah, while the narrator has shown us dissension among the tribes of Israel (19:9–10, 11–14). Since this last episode flowing remotely from David's attempted act of *hesed* to his old Ammonite ally (insofar as all the family situations overflow from events of 2 Sam. 10–11) and more directly from Absalom's revolt will conclude his active rule, it is important.[37] David does not manage this crisis well. That the doomed reconciliation surrounds the resumption of David's rule after Absalom's revolt, we can see the implied connection between the king's grief and his incapacity to resume effective rule. Insofar as the root of instability is the perennial incompatibility of the tribes, weak and divisive managing will not likely be successful.

1. Dispute and Secession: 19:41–20:3 The narrator has already provided us with two sets of plans relevant to what happens in this last event of David's active rule: Israelite tribes quarreling as David is inviting, challenging, or shaming the vacillating Judah people to initiate a return, while offering a path to Absalom's former chieftain, Amasa, as well. That pair of conversations is rejoined now, with the Israelites approaching the king to accuse the Judahites of stealing him (vv. 41, 43)—an ominous echo of Absalom's deed that began the revolt—and the Judahites responding, in place of the king, that their kinship with David is suasive (v. 42). They claim not to be asking anything more than their due. The Israelites counter that their superior tribal count (ten tribes) is more relevant than kinship ties, a claim the narrator then quickly settles: "But the words of the men of Judah were fiercer than the words of the men of Israel" (19:43). The king himself is silent, and we, reading, may feel that the issues of the past revolt have not been adequately rehearsed, let alone resolved. The inadequate justice dispensed on David's return to his city foreshadows this last event of his reign. The spurt of shrewd energy we saw characterize David when he learned of the Absalom disloyalty seems ended.

For a match is set to this tinder of tribal squabbling (20:1): "Now there happened to be there a worthless fellow, whose name was Sheba, the son of Bichri, a Benjaminite; and he blew the trumpet, and said, 'We have no portion in David,

---

37. We can perhaps appreciate again the challenge of where to place the episodes of 2 Samuel 21–24, whether they are meant to come chronologically after this particular failure of David's or simply as a collection of miscellaneous units.

and we have no inheritance in the son of Jesse; every man to his tents, O Israel!'" The narrator's rather rare and blunt characterization of this man, different in type than his sketching of Absalom but with clear impact, lets us anticipate that all will not go well. We next learn that all the men of Israel—just recently claiming precedence—now withdraw from David to follow Sheba the son of Bichri, while the men of Judah accompany their king up to Jerusalem. When the king arrives, he completes the first action we saw of him upon his departure (v. 2): "And David came to his house at Jerusalem; and the king took the ten concubines whom he had left to care for the house, and put them in a house under guard, and provided for them, but did not go in to them. So they were shut up until the day of their death, living as if in widowhood." It is a gesture calling for detail that we do not receive but exposes another instance of David's incapacity to act decisively. Like Mephibosheth, the women might have been treated less fairly, but their loyalty does not appear served as well as it might have been.

2. Joab's Role: 20:4–22 The narrator's choice to show David losing his place in the conversation between tribal groups and acting opaquely in regard to the wives that Absalom had raped seems to abet a choice on the part of the implied author to show David losing—perhaps even loosing—control of his rule, slipping from his recent skill and confidence. Though commentators have been eager to name David as otiose for some time,[38] I think we see it here in a fresh way.

David's first overt action in regard to the revolt of the northern tribes under Sheba is to appoint Absalom's former chief Amasa to gather troops and report back in three days, preceded, we may note, by his divisive overture and his omission of managing Joab more effectively after the death of Absalom. As previously announced (19:13), David's plan is to keep Joab from commanding, but that choice is not carried out effectively for any involved. Joab's replacement with "Absalom's Joab" is not a wise move, and when Amasa fails to meet the obligation David imposes on him, David himself says to Joab's brother (v. 6), "'Now Sheba the son of Bichri will do us more harm than Absalom; take your lord's servants and pursue him, lest he get himself fortified cities, and cause us trouble.'" These are David's only words in the scene, seeing what is amiss but not acting effectively to meet it. Notable is David's avoiding to confront Joab directly and his supposing that the delegation to Abishai can go well. David's consistent discourse with or about Abishai has been to decry the violence of the brothers while continuing to rely on them.

If recognizing the need for speed, David fails to anticipate the outcome of his undercutting Amasa by deputing Abishai, who moves after Sheba with the king's loyal and proven mercenaries. The result is Amasa's death and Joab's successful resurgence, accomplished not least by his killing Amasa (vv. 8–12):

When they were at the great stone which is in Gibeon, Amasa came to meet them. Now Joab was wearing a soldier's garment, and over it was a girdle with a sword in its sheath fastened upon his loins, and as he went forward it fell out.

---

38. Fokkelman's assessment of David as a "born quitter" seems too harsh: *King David*, 316.

And Joab said to Amasa, "Is it well with you, my brother?" And Joab took Amasa by the beard with his right hand to kiss him. But Amasa did not observe the sword which was in Joab's hand; so Joab struck him with it in the body, and shed his bowels to the ground, without striking a second blow; and he died. Then Joab and Abishai his brother pursued Sheba the son of Bichri. And one of Joab's men took his stand by Amasa, and said, "Whoever favors Joab, and whoever is for David, let him follow Joab."

Though Joab's action resembles Abner's killing of Asahel and Joab's dispatching of Abner, this time there is no room for the possibility that the death might be licit.[39] Joab kills a commander appointed by his own king, and once again escapes royal reproach. In a pair of gestures, another kiss and another sword thrust, Joab reclaims his position over David's fighting men.

The rallying cry goes up, again not dissimilar from Absalom's, except that Joab links the king's cause with his own rather than either breaking free like Absalom or serving the king's cause. With the slain Amasa dragged to the side and out of view, Joab and Abishai move north. David's response to these events is, again, conspicuously not provided. The narrator leads us to accompany Joab pursuing Sheba, and arriving to besiege the northern city of Abel Beth Maacah, we witness Joab's dealings with another wise woman, tactical, shrewd, decisive.[40] When the siege grows protracted, the woman negotiates with Joab (vv. 18–19): "'They were wont to say in old time, "Let them but ask counsel at Abel"; and so they settled a matter. I am one of those who are peaceable and faithful in Israel; you seek to destroy a city which is a mother in Israel; why will you swallow up the heritage of the LORD?'" Reviewing her town's venerable credentials, she claims to represent the tradition herself and offers Joab an alternative to the destruction of a tribal city, the solution he accepts while denying that he is a destroyer, and she delivers: the head of the rebel Sheba. Once in possession of the head of the leader, Joab withdraws and returns to David.

In place of the expected encounter between uncle and nephew, king and ex- and self-reinstated commander, the narrator provides only lists, including that Joab was or remained over the army, while Benaiah (whom we are about to spend more time with) leads the mercenaries. As before, Abiathar and Zadok are priests (vv. 23–26). It seems an odd ending to this post-revolt episode, settling Sheba but not Joab. Of mourning for Amasa there is none. Of reproach for Joab, none. This last episode in David's active rule has reinforced material we have seen before: the weakness of kingship, the rottenness within David's own house, the outrages perpetrated by an unchecked Joab, the loss of purpose or direction by David himself.

39. Bodner has underlined the similarity of these deaths in *David Observed*, 38–66.

40. For an analysis of the scene, highlighting the skill of the wise woman, consult Marcia L. Geyer, "Stopping the Juggernaut: A Close Reading of 2 Samuel 20:13–22," *Union Seminary Quarterly Review* 41 (1987): 33–42. She is more generous toward David and Joab than I am, while providing some details of the narrative that I have omitted.

3 Conclusions and Transition

In this sustained and literary method-driven inquiry to search for the well-spring and trajectory of David's compassion, we have now examined all but the last of his moves—that one set when he is old. The quest for constructing and naming David's capacity for compassion—not simply in technical terms as an act of graciousness offered to another and negotiable in a social context, though including that aspect—has sketched two poles along which he has moved.

In his earliest days, David was primarily passive, acted upon by others and did little except to accept and respond. Drawn as the recipient of gestures of loyalty and assistance by others, he became in time the granter of such deeds to others. Young David was characterized as close to God, speaking readily of and to God, responsive to God's direction, serene in that relationship. This first pole of compliant cooperation and reciprocity was stretched primarily by David's reactions to Saul, as he moved gradually to engage his lord more directly, finally to the point of tracking him and breaking off their relationship when David seemed in danger of harming Saul and thus himself as well.

A second pole, developing after David became king in fact as well as by anointment, has been named here in terms of recourse to arrogance and contempt, grasping what arguably lay outside of his competence and right—distinct from engaging, consulting, asking. These matters included David's choices to act as he pleased in cultic matters: seizing and renaming the city Jerusalem, commandeering the Ark from its assigned place, endangering the temple site, arrogating to himself the construction of a temple. Countered and finally stopped by the deity, David acquiesced readily on these occasions, though with little apparent transfer of experience from one situation to the next. More recently, while extending an act of political compassion to an old ally and being rebuffed for it, David retaliated brutally, an event which hosted a still more egregious affront against two human beings directly and toward many others less directly. Consequent upon his military reprisals against the Ammonites and his set of violations of relationship with Uriah and Bathsheba came the cascading disorder in his own family. Faced with such violence, David lapsed again into passivity and isolation, the situation now more harmful than was his earlier tendency to allow events to pile around him.

This present chapter has allowed us to track consequences of this latter passivity and unresponsiveness to what we can call his royal and family obligations, specifically with his oldest children, leading to and culminating in a long and uncertain disaffection between himself and his oldest surviving son, thence to the revolt of Absalom coveting David's kingship for his own. Slow and inconsistent in his handling the effects of the split with Absalom, even when they were clear to characters and readers, David roused himself only when revolt had broken out, acting finally with clear initiative, even with brilliance to reverse the usurpation attempt. In scene after scene, David acted with clear collaboration, drawing to himself a number of loyal supporters willing to risk all to stand with him. David's words included consultation of and prayer to God, as well as with his social allies.

There was no doubt that David wished Absalom's rebellion to be crushed and acted to achieve that goal.

But how he envisioned the aftermath was not made clear at the outset nor even really after the revolt was ended, except that Absalom be spared—for some purpose and plan not articulated. The royal father's directions about the handling of the rebellious son were both clear and opaque: David asked that his followers deal gently with Absalom, implying a choice in the matter, a deferring for later managing of it. The narrator took care that all heard what the king directed, repeated it. But any specific plan for Absalom and especially any glimpse into the source of what emerged as deep feeling of father for son are difficult to tract if unmistakable in their effect. That is, how David's love for this fratricidal and usurping son grew and how David planned to manage Absalom's deeds have neither clear root nor fruit in the narrative, and yet the compassion seems powerful. The killing of Absalom— the direct contravening of the king's order—was shown with conspicuous contrast between Joab and every other character. Absalom himself fled the battle, as it was lost by his allies. Those in a position to kill him refused to do it, represented by one whom Joab reproached but who spoke back with no fear or equivocation. Joab himself, if wishing to avoid the deed, finally moved decisively against Absalom in full view of others watching, making no effort to cover his deed or design the report to the king. Indeed, Joab boldly reproached David for his grief at the death of his rebellious son. If we, reading, were surprised at the king's intensely emotional reaction to the death of Absalom, reviewing the indecision and unevenness with which the father had treated his son, still the grief was impossible to overlook.

But once the upstart son was dead and his plan aborted, David lapsed into his pattern of passivity and irresolution, mishandling the immediate post-revolt situations. He most obviously failed to manage Joab, who blatantly and with no effort at concealment had disobeyed David's order concerning the treatment of Absalom. It might be argued that the rebel died in the battle he initiated, but that Joab expressly disobeyed the king's clear and stressed order is not so easily overlooked. David did overlook it, except to attempt to replace Joab as commander—an initiative Joab refused and David could not or did not enforce. There was no reprisal. Less important, perhaps, but telling, was David's failure to appeal successfully to the former Saul tribes and his apparent incapacity to deal with those he met as he returned, technically victorious, to Jerusalem. David deferred the matter of Shimei's cursing him. He seems, in retrospect, to have neglected his obligation to Barzillai, and it is difficult to see how justice has been done in the matter of Ziba and Mephibosheth. That David will urge his succeeding son to manage two of these and leave the third to fester signals David's lapse from compassion that he manifested all too rarely.

If, or insofar as the clearest moment for us to understand David's capacity for compassion and his depths of love for another who did not wish him well remains his love for the rebellious Absalom, his care that his son not be harmed in the final battle of the revolt, notably his reaction when he learned the news of Absalom's death, these moments remain underexposed by the narrator or the main character himself. That the father's reaction to his son's death is so powerfully drawn, is sketched from several angles, testifies to its importance. We saw David grieve for Jonathan, dead. We witnessed deep care for the young unnamed son of David and Bathsheba before he died. But the grief for the flawed Absalom, following as it does on such poor managing of him, is distinctive, its nurturing hidden from us. That David loved his son is clear, and yet he showed it poorly before Absalom's death. Though David shows a unique vulnerability here, addressing his dead son with the desire that he would have died in his stead, the compassion remains a powerful feeling rather than a practical deed, or a pattern of behavior.

But David has one more crucial action to perform, and to that we shall now turn.

Chapter 8

DAVID GOES THE WAY OF ALL THE EARTH (1 KGS. 1–2)

THE SIXTH TOOL: NARRATIVE ANALOGY

1 Transition

In this final chapter of literary narrative analysis, there are two things to accomplish. First, we need to finish the narrative of David's kingship, tracking it slightly past the death of the hero, as we began our effort a bit before meeting David—taking advantage of the fuzzy edges of the story. How does this David narrative end, how [does it] seed is next portion? Second, we will gather and reposition the insight into David's character we have been exploring, his capacity for conversion to compassion and his lapse from it, naming and using a sixth tool to demonstrate the insight.

As our last chapter ended, David, having thwarted the coup of his eldest surviving son, Absalom, was at once beset by a revolt led by a man of Benjamin, joined by others. Though David managed to keep his kingdom in hand by the end of that episode, he was shown passive and weak, vulnerable to an extent not previously seen. Arguably, the king's separate appeals—first to the people of Judah who had neither resisted Absalom nor assisted David and then to the rebellious tribes to rejoin their relationship with him after Absalom's defeat—were poorly managed, with the result that the ever-fragile tribal coalition fell apart again, as indeed it will do shortly after the death of Solomon: monarchy unstable. The efforts of Sheba, successor to Absalom as opponent to David's rule over YHWH's people, characterized even more dismissively than were those of Absalom, came to nothing quickly. Yet it was not David's skill that thwarted Sheba's revolt—quite the contrary: David mismanaged the episode and his kingdom was salvaged largely by the efforts of his nephews, Joab and Abishai—dubious as such assistance may seem.

To review quickly: After David's words impeded the healing of the breach opened by Absalom, David appointed Amasa in place of Joab, ordering him to gather men to fight. Amasa, not successful under Absalom, managed no better under David, failing to appear with troops at the designated time. By offering no explanation for this failing, the narrator left us to infer Amasa's incompetence and David's as well for a poor choice—by several criteria, perhaps. The lack of skill of Amasa opened a path for the sons of Zeruiah to reclaim their leadership, running right over their uncle to do so, with Joab stabbing Amasa and leaving him mortally injured before finally dragging the body to the side of the road, lest it slow down those hurrying with Joab in pursuit of Sheba. David was shown powerless and wordless during these events, save a single assessment at the start of the revolt, his appraisal that Sheba was likely to do more harm than had Absalom.

Sheba's revolt was settled by Joab, who tracked the rebel to a northern town and laid siege. An unnamed woman negotiated with him to settle for the head of the single leader rather than assault a town needlessly. David had no role to play in these discussions, and the narrative ended without him. The four chapters following, serving as coda to the linked events of chs. 9–20, are, as has been suggested, a nonchronological set of two narratives, two poems, two lists. The plan of the implied author seems to have fizzled David's rule out rather oddly. The leadership we witnessed while reading 2 Sam. 15–19 is thus the last we see of David as king, save for his meager and deficient role in Sheba's revolt. The death of Absalom seems to have marked a turning point in David's life as king, such that we never see from him again the active, skilled, decisive leadership we observed from him previously, characterizing most of his life.

2 David Gives the Throne to Solomon

So it is not a great surprise when we meet David, old and enfeebled, with basically one deed remaining to accomplish in "this exceptionally long story":[1] to set the son of his choosing—and presumably of God's—on the throne to rule in his place, thus accomplishing the building of his house, such as it will be. The design of the implied author, the narrator, and a set of characters (deity, king, prophet, wife, queen mother) culminates, though not without opposition of another royal son and his not inconsequential allies (Joab, Abiathar).[2] The basic structure provided by Fokkelman suggests we see the material as an act in itself (1Kgs. 1–2), with two main scenes (David Decides about Succession: 1 Kings 1; and David's Last Wishes: 1 Kings 2). The last wishes split into four moments: 2:1–12 David Instructs Solomon; 2:13–25 Adonijah's End; 2:28–35 Joab's End; 2:36–46 Shimei's End. Though Fokkelman will nuance this schema, the main divisions remain those.[3] We will track the narrative, then, in that basic order. The point to examine is David's brief but timely recovery from passivity, his spurt of energy for decision making,

---

1. Fokkelman, *King David*, 345.

2. There is no Saulide opponent here, simply opponents from within the David line, though we will revisit the fate of a Benjaminite before the story concludes. We may note a rough similarity with the Book of Judges, where at the outset of the period described, the opponents are external but by the end the struggles arise from within.

3. This structure is printed by Fokkelman succinctly in *King David*, 415. Jerome Walsh, *1 Kings*, 3, offers a slightly different one.

and his capacity to deepen his turn toward God and away from arrogance and contempt—or not.

a David Decides the Succession: 1 Kings 1

King David's enfeeblement is sketched in several vivid ways.[4] The narrator says bluntly that the king is old and advanced in years, unable to stay warm even beneath covers, needing to borrow body heat from another, specifically from a beautiful young woman who lies in his bed, in his arms (1:1–4). David does not know her sexually, nor does he know that his son Adonijah has named himself king, has gathered certain accoutrements of kingship, has secured allies and supporters from among David's household (vv. 5–7). All that the old king does not know about this son culminates at a sacrifice of celebration at En Rogel, near Jerusalem.[5] The narrator adds two specifications: that David had not in the past thwarted any wish of the handsome Adonijah (v. 6), and that Adonijah's supporters include some of David's people (i.e., Joab, Abiathar) and not others (Zadok, Nathan, Benaiah, Solomon).[6] David's not knowing, then, is his basic characterization as the last act of his narrative life begins. Not a wholly new situation for him, it is now terminal, or almost so.

A plan and action for a designated successor, urgently needed, must rise from another quarter. Nathan the prophet is shown conferring with Bathsheba, mother of Solomon, informing her of Adonijah's proclamation of his kingship and prompting her that David has previously spoken of their son Solomon as his choice for king (vv. 11–14). Nathan proposes a plan by which the two of them will present David with news of Adonijah's untimely deed. Commentators split on the plans and characterization of Nathan and Bathsheba here, debating whether or not we are to credit such a royal promise, speculating that this scene is nothing but a palace coup by two people hoping to save their lives when the old king is not there to protect them. Such a construction is possible but not necessarily warranted within the long story of David.[7] That we have to consider at least two possibilities and cannot definitively rule either out is skilled storytelling prompting

---

4. Alter, *David Story*, 363, reminds us that as Saul's household acted to make provision for him in his need, so now David's must do for him. Fokkelman, *King David*, 346, characterizes him as an object demanding care. Walsh, *1 Kings*, 5, points out that David is the subject of no verbs. All of this situation unfolds loosely from 2 Samuel 20.

5. Walsh, *1 Kings*, 6–9 (repeated on 37) argues that Adonijah's deed is more an announcement about his future than a coup, a point I find difficult to accept—and is in any case a distinction that seems irrelevant given the narrative unfolding.

6. Adonijah is characterized in several senses as an Absalom look-alike, says Alter, *David Story*, 369, and Fokkelman, *King David*, 347–51.

7. Though I have high regard for Walsh's capacity to read narrative, his choice here to see Nathan as engineering a "sordid palace intrigue" (*1 Kings*, 10) does not convince me. That Nathan is not named here as prophet as he was before does not necessarily imply that he is not to be seen as acting as a prophet.

intentional reading, allowing this topic of succession to David's throne to continue under discussion. Nathan has been wrong as well as right, but he is a prophet, David's prophet, eventually responsive to God on both the occasions where he has appeared in the narrative. Bathsheba, likewise, has not been characterized as opposing David in any way heretofore. So I will accept the narrator's presentation at face value, take their actions as coinciding with the implied authorship of the book, construe Nathan as speaking for God, David complying as well with what God wishes. Part of David's complex not knowing has been his pattern of deferring action until it is almost but not quite too late—or more precisely, too late for some things but not quite all. Part of God's characterization has been to tolerate David's delay and his arrogance for a long time but not indefinitely.

Bathsheba plays her role skillfully, speaking deferentially and carefully to her royal husband and the father of their child about past words and present realities (vv. 15–20). How she presents Nathan's words, repositioning them slightly and appropriately, is again, well-remarked by scholars.[8] David receives her, bids her speak, listens to her. While that scene is unfolding, Nathan arrives, as rehearsed, and pushes the matter a little farther ahead (vv. 24–27):

> And Nathan said, "My lord the king, have you said, 'Adonijah shall reign after me, and he shall sit upon my throne?' For he has gone down this day, and has sacrificed oxen, fatlings, and sheep in abundance, and has invited all the king's sons, Joab the commander of the army, and Abiathar the priest; and behold, they are eating and drinking before him, and saying, 'Long live King Adonijah!' But me, your servant, and Zadok the priest, and Benaiah the son of Jehoiada, and your servant Solomon, he has not invited. Has this thing been brought about by my lord the king and you have not told your servants who should sit on the throne of my lord the king after him?"

That the plan is rehearsed need not imply it insincere, with the deference offered to the old king enhanced here by the long relationship among these four characters, culminating, now, in a moment of crisis when the king seems least able to manage it. As Craig observes, the whole point of the narrative exercise—that of characters, narrator, and implied author—is to generate adequate response from David.[9]

But David does manage, and for the last time we see him take charge of events.[10] He summons Solomon's mother back to his presence (she leaves as Nathan arrived—the "swinging door" biblical narrative tends to prefer to avoid confusion), addressing her (vv. 29–30): "'As the LORD lives, who has redeemed my soul out of every adversity, as I swore to you by the LORD, the God of Israel, saying, "Solomon

8. Consult Fokkelman, *King David*, 351.

9. Craig, *Asking for Rhetoric*, 171.

10. Alter, *David Story*, 368, thinks David's royal power exceeds his physical presence. That is likely so—that a king's power exceeds his individual self—but David's own characteral capacity exceeds what it seems as he lies chilled even with blankets and a human companion. David's pattern is to rally when he seems least likely to do so.

your son shall reign after me, and he shall sit upon my throne in my stead"; even so will I do this day."'" Bathsheba's response is to bless the king with long life, even as the topic of discussion is precisely his departure from mortal existence. David's next words concern his three loyal men (vv. 32–37):

> "Call to me Zadok the priest, Nathan the prophet, and Benaiah the son of Jehoiada." So they came before the king. And the king said to them, "Take with you the servants of your lord, and cause Solomon my son to ride on my own mule, and bring him down to Gihon; and let Zadok the priest and Nathan the prophet there anoint him king over Israel; then blow the trumpet, and say, 'Long live King Solomon!' You shall then come up after him, and he shall come and sit upon my throne; for he shall be king in my stead; and I have appointed him to be ruler over Israel and over Judah." And Benaiah the son of Jehoiada answered the king, "Amen! May the LORD, the God of my lord the king, say so. As the LORD has been with my lord the king, even so may he be with Solomon, and make his throne greater than the throne of my lord King David."

Walsh notes carefully that there are eight moments in this choice of David to have Solomon acclaimed king.[11]

David's plan is immediate, clear, specific: Delegated to priest, prophet, and mercenary captain, it specifies that Solomon is to be given the king's own mule, taken to Gihon, and, in the presence of others, anointed by prophet and priest and acclaimed by all. David, echoing Bathsheba, pronounces words of acclamation for his son: "Long live King Solomon!" Then led back to the city, Solomon is to be seated on David's throne. Though sometimes characterized as hasty and secret, it is, in fact, quite deliberate and less secret by far than was David's own anointing. It is difficult to suppose that David is not choosing Solomon over Adonijah, or to see it as the act of a befuddled man, *pace* Walsh, who sees it as "a fabrication intended to dupe a dotard king."[12] If never opposing Adonijah before, David thwarts him now.

And so it happens, the narrator recounts (vv. 38–40):

> So Zadok the priest, Nathan the prophet, and Benaiah the son of Jehoiada, and the Cherethites and the Pelethites, went down and caused Solomon to ride on King David's mule, and brought him to Gihon. There Zadok the priest took the horn of oil from the tent, and anointed Solomon. Then they blew the trumpet; and all the people said, "Long live King Solomon!" And all the people went up after him, playing on pipes, and rejoicing with great joy, so that the earth was split by their noise.

The Gihon revelry is heard at nearby En Rogel, with specific details run to that celebrating group as well. Adonijah speaks up to speculate about the source of the

---

11. *1 Kings*, 21–22.
12. Ibid., 25. Craig, *Asking for Rhetoric*, 176–78, lines up the possibilities concisely.

noise, and he is not long left in doubt, taking a last brief hope in good news at the sight of Abiathar's son Jonathan approaching as messenger (vv. 43–48):[13] But:

> Jonathan answered Adonijah, "No, for our lord King David has made Solomon king; and the king has sent with him Zadok the priest, Nathan the prophet, and Benaiah the son of Jehoiada, and the Cherethites and the Pelethites; and they have caused him to ride on the king's mule; and Zadok the priest and Nathan the prophet have anointed him king at Gihon; and they have gone up from there rejoicing, so that the city is in an uproar. This is the noise that you have heard. Solomon sits upon the royal throne. Moreover the king's servants came to congratulate our lord King David, saying, 'Your God make the name of Solomon more famous than yours, and make his throne greater than your throne.' And the king bowed himself upon the bed. And the king also said, 'Blessed be the LORD, the God of Israel, who has granted one of my offspring to sit on my throne this day, my own eyes seeing it.'"

Though news to Adonijah, it is our third recital of the information about Solomon's succession, advancing as well our awareness that David has received and acknowledged congratulations over the event, has blessed it verbally.

There is little hope for Adonijah except to decamp from his coronation site, and so he does, with his guests. He takes refuge at the horns of the altar,[14] where he is reprieved by his brother (vv. 51–53):

> And it was told Solomon, "Behold, Adonijah fears King Solomon; for, lo, he has laid hold of the horns of the altar, saying, Let King Solomon swear to me first that he will not slay his servant with the sword." And Solomon said, "If he prove to be a worthy man, not one of his hairs shall fall to the earth; but if wickedness is found in him, he shall die." So King Solomon sent, and they brought him down

13. We have seen such an error before (at 2 Sam. 19:27), the assumption that a good bearer of tidings presages good tidings. It has the sound of a proverb, but it also suggests wishful and naive, even desperate hope.

14. It is a bit uncertain what altar is envisioned here, since there is no temple. But narratively, this scene (and that involving Joab's similar effort, lying just ahead) is clear enough, and the altar inside the tent David erected for the Ark is able to be understood as a place of refuge where an innocent petitioner should be safe. Jonathan Burnside, "Flight of the Fugitive: Rethinking the Relationship between Biblical Law (Exod. 21:12–14) and the Davidic Succession Narrative (1 Kgs. 1–2)," *JBL* 129.3 (2010): 418–32 (418–20), suggests that we not fall into the anachronism of Western categories, trying to decide whether Adonijah and Joab "qualify" for asylum according to biblical law or not. He suggests (following Jared Jackson) that we distinguish between semantic (more literal reasoning) and narrative (more evocative or imagistic associations) understandings and draw on a narrative sense to understand what is being sketched here. That is, the two men may attempt to find refuge whether (we think) they technically deserve it or not. He also notes that these urgent situations provide cases for Solomon to judge, or to resolve.

from the altar. And he came and did obeisance to King Solomon; and Solomon said to him, "Go to your house."

Solomon has said his first words and accomplished his first act as king.

b David's Last Wishes: 1 Kings 2

The David narrative comes to a close with David charging his son, first in general and then with three specifics, about his obligations. These are cast as the last words of a dying man to his son, of king to successor, of David to Solomon. They need scrutiny, since they seem to many nothing but harsh, vindictive, retaliatory.[15] I think there is more to them than that, and less. Walsh's plot schematic makes visual some of the complexities of the chapter while overlooking a great deal of what might be said about who desires what and moves toward it how, and with what particular results.[16]

1. David instructs Solomon: 2:1–12: The old king's first words are sententious and formal—as befits last words (2:1–4):

> "I am about to go the way of all the earth. Be strong, and show yourself a man, and keep the charge of the LORD your God, walking in his ways and keeping his statutes, his commandments, his ordinances, and his testimonies, as it is written in the law of Moses, that you may prosper in all that you do and wherever you turn; that the LORD may establish his word which he spoke concerning me, saying, 'If your sons take heed to their way, to walk before me in faithfulness with all their heart and with all their soul, there shall not fail you a man on the throne of Israel.'"

David names his mortality clearly, using the formula that also marks a peaceful death. He speaks classic Deuteronomic language to his son, such as we have not heard from him typically. He also, however, cites the words of prophet and deity to him when he was stopped from his plan of housing the Ark in a temple and reminded that God is builder, and of a dynasty for David (2 Sam. 7:12–16). Solomon makes no reply, and of course his father is not finished with instructions. Given this prologue to the specifics David will name, my choice is to hear them as falling within what is licit, even perhaps necessary for the furtherance of David's line, to construct David as belatedly attending to things he has left neglected for too long with attendant harm to his royal project rather than simply rehearsing old grievances, personal and petty. David charges Solomon with specifics about three situations.

---

15. Fokkelman, *King David*, 386–87; Leo Perdue, "'Is There Anyone Left of the House of Saul . . . ?' Ambiguity and the Characterization of David in the Succession Narrative," *JSOT* 30 (1984): 67–84 (73–74); Walsh, *1 Kings*, 37–44.
16. Walsh, *Old Testament Narrative*, 17.

First, he speaks of a set of Joab matters (vv. 5–6):

"Moreover you know also what Joab the son of Zeruiah did to me, how he dealt with the two commanders of the armies of Israel, Abner the son of Ner, and Amasa the son of Jether, whom he murdered, avenging in time of peace blood which had been shed in war, and putting innocent blood upon the girdle about my loins, and upon the sandals on my feet. Act therefore according to your wisdom, but do not let his gray head go down to Sheol in peace."

Moderns are accustomed, now, to the importance of clearing up toxic dumps of long-standing pollution, of resolving political or emotional snarls that have crippled human relations and harmed well-being. That the ancients assumed that the blood shed wrongly had ongoing deleterious effects unless cleared is analogous, if less familiar now.

The relationship between David and Joab has threaded the entire book of 2 Samuel. Indeed, implicitly, the sons of Zeruiah have been with their uncle since he fled Saul's court in 1 Samuel 19. Though some commentators see Joab as loyal and supportive and hence not deserving the words said of him here, I am not among them.[17] In their view, David's words here are undeserved by and punitive toward Joab, simple retaliation on the part of the king who is uncle. My sense of the relationship, rather, is that from arriving on the scene specifically as David's actual kingship begins, Joab has exposed "the David project" to deceit, violence, and bloodshed beyond or outside what can be considered acceptable. Wars there have been, but killings that fall outside of war are not the same as deaths occurring in battle. Joab's first appearance was as commander of the struggle between David as Judean leader and Ishbosheth as surviving son of Saul. When Joab and his brothers pursued Ishbosheth's kin and assistant, Abner, after an encounter of some sort between the two royal factions, and also when Abner slew Asahel who was pressing too close, it became an uncertain situation at least for readers (2 Sam. 2:12–32). Abner was running alone after the battle, with the three brothers in pursuit. Abner, later reproaching Joab after the death of Asahel, says (vv. 26–27): "'Shall the sword devour for ever? Do *you* not know that the end will be bitter? How long will it be before *you* bid *your* people turn from the pursuit of their brethren?' And Joab said, 'As God lives, if *you* had not spoken, surely the men would have given up the pursuit of their brethren in the morning.'"[18] But fighting continues, with David's side slaying more than do Ishbosheth's men. It seems that Abner's killing of Asahel falls within an ongoing war but not in an actual battle—but in any case, a borderline and hence disputable situation. Some characters—Abner—will

17. Fokkelman, *King David*, 386–87, thinks the issue is about revenge. See also Filip Čapek, "David's Ambiguous Testament in 1 Kgs. 2:1–12 and the Role of Joab in the Succession Narrative," *Communio Viatorum* 52 (2010): 4–26 (17), who reminds us how good Joab has been to David.

18. I take this as a dispute about whose fault is the ongoing crisis with attendant deaths; my italicizing the pronouns and adjectives makes this slightly clearer.

plausibly think that the slaying was in battle, while others—Joab—think that it is not. Long-standing events where the status of a deed is disputed will be the more intense than those that seem clear. Our role is not to resolve but to feel the tension rising from a difficult case.

The second and related event is Joab's killing of Abner while he, though formerly closely allied with Saul and Ishbosheth, is negotiating with and hence under the protection of David. That Joab is ignorant of Abner's fresh resolve and does not care about David's honor as host is clear when, after reproaching David for not perceiving Abner's motives, Joab kills Abner. David, who the narrator tells us is not aware of Joab's plan, bitterly reproaches his nephew for the deed (3:28–29):

> Afterward, when David heard of it, he said, "I and my kingdom are for ever guiltless before the LORD for the blood of Abner the son of Ner. May it fall upon the head of Joab, and upon all his father's house; and may the house of Joab never be without one who has a discharge, or who is leprous, or who holds a spindle, or who is slain by the sword, or who lacks bread!"

That Joab construes the situation one way and David another is the stuff of which chronic disputes are made. So the case of Joab's killing Abner is a "perennial undecidable," festering divisively for as long as it is not settled. David is characterized as deferring to resolve matters.

A third Joab-episode concerns Amasa, appointed by David to replace Joab after the ending to Absalom's revolt, but failing to do his job competently (2 Sam. 19:13; 20:4). As the post-Absalom revolt gains momentum, Joab simply eliminates Amasa by approaching him as though a friend, gaining the physical position to stab him as Abner had stabbed Asahel and Joab Abner. Thus the narrator links the three deaths.[19] Of Absalom, there is no mention, since his death was more unambiguously a killing in war.[20] That David never mentions knowing what we know about the circumstances of Absalom's death is a great puzzle. But it is not so startling as we recall how frequently in his time of ruling David defers, avoids.

The point at issue is whether these three illicit killings, which is how David appraises and classifies them, have brought harm on David's rule and by extension on his house and people. Bloodshed of innocent people (at least innocent of what they are killed for) that is not cleared pollutes. David's words to his son suggest that though he himself has not exacted what he ought have done from Joab, Solomon must do it. David is not so much guilty of vengeance and petty reprisal as of moral procrastination, allowing something serious to go unmanaged for too long, with the result that it falls to his son to take care of it. David's personal feelings over what we witnessed Joab doing to Absalom despite what David had ordered is not

---

19. This relationship is demonstrated by Bodner, "Demise of Abner," in Bodner, ed., *David Observed*, 38–66.

20. Readers, surely commentators, often feel that David is remiss to omit this Joab-deed, but since it is a wartime slaying, it seems legitimate. Whether, analogously, it resembles the pursuit of Abner by the three Zeruiah brothers is another matter.

in this same category. David is acknowledging that the illicit Joab killings need to be cleared and it is too late for him to do it, but his heir must see to it, for the well-being of the realm. Why David delayed is not so clear—though a case can be contemplated that Joab is David's most formidable opponent throughout—but that he delays is, I think, evident and characteristic. This is clearly David's last opportunity to shoulder these neglected actions involving Joab, and so he does.

Having finished with Joab, David's second concern names Barzillai of Gilead (v. 7): "'But deal loyally with the sons of Barzillai the Gileadite, and let them be among those who eat at your table; for with such loyalty they met me when I fled from Absalom your brother.'" This situation David had attempted to redress, the recompensing of Barzillai who provided for David's companions when they fled Jerusalem hastily to avoid being killed by Absalom. When the king's people were vulnerable and fleeing adversity, Barzillai provided. When they were returning and David offered his benefactor a position at the king's table, Barzillai declined, though provided David the opportunity to recompense a man named by him (2 Sam. 17:7–29; 19:31–40). If Joab's unjust deeds have been allowed to fester, here a good deed seems to have remained inadequately compensated as well, and David tells his son to see to it. If it may do less harm to neglect good deeds than to neglect to manage blood that is wrongly shed, nonetheless, David seems to be advising Solomon to recompense *hesed* as well as bloodshed. David, determined to return to the city that Absalom no longer threatens, may have too readily moved on past Barzillai with his son or servant Chimham as proxy, perhaps mistaking a bargaining or self-deprecating moment for a final position.[21] Now, he knows more must be done.

Finally, David speaks of Shimei (vv. 8–9):

"And there is also with you Shimei the son of Gera, the Benjaminite from Bahurim, who cursed me with a grievous curse on the day when I went to Mahanaim; but when he came down to meet me at the Jordan, I swore to him by the LORD, saying, 'I will not put you to death with the sword.' Now therefore hold him not guiltless, for you are a wise man; you will know what you ought to do to him, and you shall bring his gray head down with blood to Sheol."

The case of Shimei arises from a similar moment as that of Barzillai: A double-meeting between king and another during the Absalom revolt. David forbids his nephews to harm Shimei cursing David, saying that perhaps God had prompted it (16:5–13), and the king upbraids his nephews similarly when they meet a groveling Shimei on their return to the city, (19:22): "But David said . . . 'Shall any one be put to death in Israel this day? For do I not know that I am this day king over Israel?'" David now seems to think that those words were too permissive and that his son

---

21. The sort of haste and indifference characterizing David's dealings with Mephibosheth is a similar sort of case, but David does not revisit that decision, as seems characteristic of his dealings with Jonathan's son.

needs to find a way to settle that matter.[22] Insofar as our narrative reflects not simply ancient and foundational events but also refracts a situation current at the time of production, this is a triumph of Judah over Benjamin, as has been much of the house of Saul-house of David story under consideration.

The three situations involving Joab, Barzillai, and Shimei are each distinct, likely offered as representative: A bloodshed festering uncleared, a good deed not sufficiently acknowledged, a curse inappropriately tolerated—perhaps as it gave David occasion once again to rebuke Joab and his brother. We, reading, can readily find other things we might wish David to speak of at this last occasion, but these three are representative. As is typical of the characterization emerging in this study of David, his deferral of responsibility is managed by him late, though perhaps not too late. The occasion is also typical: Pushed too far—shadowing God's propensity with David—David finally takes charge. So we have heard the king's last words, which I suggest are more about the discharging of justice than about personal retaliation. David, having said what he presumably needed to say, what the implied author and narrator design, withdraws from the narrative efficiently and with dignity: "Then David slept with his fathers, and was buried in the city of David. And the time that David reigned over Israel was forty years; he reigned seven years in Hebron, and thirty-three years in Jerusalem" (vv. 10–11).

2. Adonijah's end and Abiathar's deaths: 2:13–27: We watch Solomon first manage situations about which he has been given no instructions. Perhaps the issue is whether he can act better than has his father in a situation presented to him. Unlike his father, Solomon seems to deal expeditiously, even mercilessly with his brother as soon as given the occasion, or such is the narrator's arrangement. Reprieved at first by Solomon for his attempt to take David's throne under conditions not very specific, Adonijah's requesting Abishag is clearly construed by Solomon as another move against royal power, and Adonijah dies for it. If David might likely have delayed, Solomon does not. Adonijah is slain at once. A similar situation occurs with Abiathar, David's priest, who has appeared to serve long and loyally until he joins Adonijah's coronation process. As soon as the priest violates the conditions laid down for his amnesty, he, also, is killed. Solomon is showing himself less dilatory than his father, perhaps less tolerant.

---

22. For another discussion on various situations David should be referencing (or that the readers of the narrative might fruitfully bring to mind) as the king instructs his son, consult George G. Nichol, "The Death of Joab and the Accession of Solomon: Some Observations on the Narrative of 1 Kings 1–2," *SJOT* 7.1 (1993): 134–51; J. W. Wesselius, "Joab's Death and the Central Theme of the Succession Narrative (2 Samuel 11–1 Kings 2)," *VT* 40.3 (1990): 336–51 (338–43) also finds problematic that David benefited from some dubious actions, for example, of Joab. But I think the point is not simply all the dead bodies or all the situations where David derived benefit from a dubious action of himself or another but those situations that are technically in need of justice.

3. Joab's end: 2:28–35: The fate of Joab immediately after the choice of Solomon seems uncertain as first presented. But the killing of Abiathar provides the narrative context for Joab's last move:

> When the news came to Joab—for Joab had supported Adonijah although he had not supported Absalom—Joab fled to the tent of the LORD and caught hold of the horns of the altar. And when it was told King Solomon, "Joab has fled to the tent of the LORD, and behold, he is beside the altar," Solomon sent Benaiah the son of Jehoiada, saying, "Go, strike him down."

The narrator positions Joab's end after he and we have had the opportunity to see Solomon quick and decisive over two of his father's opponents, each latterly opposing himself. For King Solomon to send the chief of the mercenaries into the place of sanctuary is a bold move, arguably an unsuitable one. Whatever the case there, and whether Joab is a legitimate candidate for sanctuary or not—the very point the narrative does not quite resolve to our satisfaction—Solomon is not in doubt, does not delay, but explains his move clearly:[23]

> So Benaiah came to the tent of the LORD, and said to him, "The king commands, 'Come forth.'" But he said, "No, I will die here." Then Benaiah brought the king word again, saying, "Thus said Joab, and thus he answered me." The king replied to him, "Do as he has said, strike him down and bury him; and thus take away from me and from my father's house the guilt for the blood which Joab shed without cause. The LORD will bring back his bloody deeds upon his own head, because, without the knowledge of my father David, he attacked and slew with the sword two men more righteous and better than himself, Abner the son of Ner, commander of the army of Israel, and Amasa the son of Jether, commander of the army of Judah. So shall their blood come back upon the head of Joab and upon the head of his descendants for ever; but to David, and to his descendants, and to his house, and to his throne, there shall be peace from the LORD for evermore." Then Benaiah the son of Jehoiada went up, and struck him down and killed him; and he was buried in his own house in the wilderness.

Solomon explains, as we heard David do, that Joab's death is the appropriate outcome of his killing two men illegitimately, his confounding wartime blood with peacetime blood. Joab seems to understand what is imminent, but he does not argue that it is not lawful. Solomon next replaces Joab with Benaiah, sets Zadok in Abiathar's place. Of Barzillai, there is no mention, an omission difficult to construe with confidence. We may note that while Solomon's deeds we witnessed called for negative reprisal, what David nudged for Barzillai was something benign.

23. Burnside, "Flight of Fugitives," 430, suggests that Joab may be shown to flee boldly to the horns of the altar, whether he deserves such sanctuary or not. His characterization is not inconsistent with such a view. On the other hand, Walsh, *1 Kings*, 5–7, suggests that Joab is shamed by needing such a refuge.

4. Shimei's end: 2:36–46: David's third instruction to Solomon concludes our text. Solomon has so far acted on his own twice, and has obeyed one royal paternal command and disregarded (as portrayed for us) another. What, now, with the last man? We hear the new king advise his father's old foe:

> Then the king sent and summoned Shimei, and said to him, "Build yourself a house in Jerusalem, and dwell there, and do not go forth from there to any place whatever. For on the day you go forth, and cross the brook Kidron, know for certain that you shall die; your blood shall be upon your own head." And Shimei said to the king, "What you say is good; as my lord the king has said, so will your servant do." So Shimei dwelt in Jerusalem many days.

Scholars split over whether there are two facets to the directive: Go nowhere, including not across the Kidron; or go nowhere, specifically not across the Kidron.[24] However the man himself can be assumed to hear it, we learn what he does:

> But it happened at the end of three years that two of Shimei's slaves ran away to Achish, son of Maacah, king of Gath. And when it was told Shimei, "Behold, your slaves are in Gath," Shimei arose and saddled an ass, and went to Gath to Achish, to seek his slaves; Shimei went and brought his slaves from Gath.

The narrator presents it as a reasonable thing, pursuit of escaped property, a journey effectively accomplished. But Solomon reads it differently:

> And when Solomon was told that Shimei had gone from Jerusalem to Gath and returned, the king sent and summoned Shimei, and said to him, "Did I not make you swear by the LORD, and solemnly admonish you, saying, 'Know for certain that on the day you go forth and go to any place whatever, you shall die'? And you said to me, 'What you say is good; I obey.' Why then have you not kept your oath to the LORD and the commandment with which I charged you?" The king also said to Shimei, "You know in your own heart all the evil that you did to David my father; so the LORD will bring back your evil upon your own head. But King Solomon shall be blessed, and the throne of David shall be established before the LORD for ever." Then the king commanded Benaiah the son of Jehoiada; and he went out and struck him down, and he died. So the kingdom was established in the hand of Solomon.[25]

Solomon is no David, and his quick justice refracts his father's more dilatory pattern. Solomon's conspicuous lack of any tendency toward compassion redirects back to consider David's capacity once more.

24. For that case, consult Walsh, *1 Kings*, 60–64.

25. Bodner's suggestion, *David Observed*, 175, that Solomon is resourceful as his father was what strikes me as partly true: Solomon is resourceful and determined in a way we sometimes but not always saw of David.

3 Constructing a Common Pattern

a A Sixth Tool: Narrative Analogy

Having worked our way through the long narrative with five comparatively simplex modern literary tools, we can now gather from repeating patterns a sixth, more complex one. This is a subjective choice, with other insights emerging for other readers.[26] David's transformation toward compassion, such as it is, comprises a lifelong pattern of conversion, shown over the space of David's narrative life. Hebrew can supply us with a word, a persistent turning (*šwb*) toward the purposes of God, such as those can be established or their inverses suggested. David's path is not consistent but shows prominent flaws and serious slips, with his turning from compassion as well as toward it. But even lapses woven in to the next turn, so that the overall trajectory is toward deeper and closer relatedness with God across the span of the telling. David is a literary figure, and so we are not talking about his psychology or even "his" spirituality. Rather, I, reading, am intuiting, recognizing, and performing a verbal pattern to establish the figure, David and offer it to others. A great storyteller-artist team—comprising implied author, narrator, and characters—has offered us scenes to view, and these are approached through the language and appropriated, interpreted by readers who want to engage the material existentially and deeply. The question I am tracking is this: Over his lifetime—extending from 1 Samuel 16 through 1 Kings 2—can we discern a *pattern* of David's turning toward an ever-deeper graciousness that is Godlike? How is it shown, and what does it offer? We have already noted two oscillating poles—passivity to initiative, arrogant contempt to collaboration—but is there more?

The discernment and description of—engagement with—the flow of such crucial moments make our sixth literary tool. I will call it *narrative analogy* and claim for it the features of two parents: the type-scene and the *mise-en-abŷme*.[27] The type-scene is a loosely constelling set of conventional motifs, each unexceptional on its own, but able to be recognized and utilized when certain factors tend to associate repeatedly. Though recognizable, they are neither inevitable nor formally exact, having the capacity to draw attention to themselves and offer readers a thickened moment, kin to others sharing resemblance. Related more closely to scene than to character or plot, nonetheless they do have participating characters and short plots. They are characterized by formulaic language, rising at least partially from the customization of common elements expressed with standard

26. Fokkelman offers his own synthesis in *King David*, 411–30 (a new chart on 415). While appreciating it, his is not my way of proceeding.

27. A type-scene, as recognized by Robert Alter, is discussed and exemplified by him in his *Art of Biblical Narrative*, 49–53. The *mise-en-abŷme* is usefully discussed and explored by David A. Bosworth in *Story within a Story*, 1–36. A more elaborated description can be found in Hugh S. Pyper, *David as Reader: 2 Samuel 12:1–15 and the Poetics of Fatherhood* (Leiden: E.J. Brill, 1996), ch. 2.

vocabulary. The clearest example is the betrothal at the well, where a hero meets a marriageable woman and accomplishes a set of deeds marking him as worthy, while she also responds in some ways as to signal a corresponding suitability. Likely related to oral composition and performance and present in Homer as well as in the Bible, these type-scenes both give storyteller and audience a brief respite and allow audiences time to make associations they might not otherwise consider, to recognize patterns below the surface.

The *mise-en-abŷme* is a more complex literary device, often characterized as the repositioning a facet or detail of a larger work somewhere else within that work (at the edge or "abyss," as it were), serving to repeat or refract the original element in a different but recognizable way. In a sense, this feature is a story within a story, though it will often be more fragmentary than "story" implies. The repositioning prompts from a character or reader some insight that might otherwise be missed, made possible as the angle is changed even slightly. The notion of a mirror can be a helpful analogy, as to catch sight of something in a mirror will inevitably involve a change of perspective, often a resizing, fresh seeing. There are a number of ways in which ancient and modern literature make use of the *mise-en-abŷme* and various criteria relevant, but the device is distinguished from some of its possible look-alikes, such as summary, allegory, or vague similarity. Though the device needs to be authorially defensible—point-out-able with some clear set of traces—it is also the product of constructive reading and interpretation. The best analogy for this device may be the murder mystery, where vast piles of evidential data must be usefully sorted and constantly re-combed with an eye to significant but subtle patterning, such that what is repeated is both difficult to discern and clear enough once it has been pointed out.

b Hearts Aligned

My starting point is a pair of texts: 1 Sam. 13:14 and 16:7, where, famously, God seems to wash the divine hands of the Saul-as-king project and resolve to choose afresh, this time a man after God's own heart, the prophet Samuel informs Saul: "'But now your kingdom shall not continue; the LORD has sought out a man after his own heart; and the LORD has appointed him to be prince over his people. . . .'"[28] As God directs Samuel to implement the plan, directing the prophet's choice from the more likely sons of Jesse, God reminds him: "Do not look on [Eliab's] appearance or on the height of his stature . . . for the LORD sees not as man sees; man looks on the outward appearance, but the LORD looks on the heart.'" The question to track, now, is about how and to what effect these hearts of YHWH and David are aligned or not? The thesis I wish to demonstrate is that God's heart toward David is vastly generous, even permissive. God bestows gifts on David, lavishly, almost without restraint—nearly too much, we may think. David accepts and makes good use of these gifts, though on several occasions oversteps and acts

---

28. In 1 Sam. 9:10 the narrator informs us that God gave Saul a new heart, but that is not the same claim as is operative in the David material.

unilaterally, with contempt and arrogance. YHWH pushes back in some tangible way, and David readily gives ground, showing us his capacity for conversion, perhaps compassion. David, for his part, is also generous and beneficent to many, arguably nearly to a fault, aligned with his divine benefactor. But when David is or feels ill-served by those close to him, he is not so adept in checking their excess. David's benefactees seem often to refuse gratitude and graciousness, and David then retracts or reverses his gift. His ambivalence and incapacity to check effectively the excess of those around him contribute to the cause of suffering to many, himself included. David shows us many moments of struggling with this heart murmur, and there is plenty for us to learn.

The Hebrew word suggesting the relationships under scrutiny here is *hesed*, not easily reducible to an English word. Though I speak compassion, what is offered and accepted is actions of love, loyalty, reciprocity—arguably compassion—in response to need. *Hesed* is both divine and human, given for a variety of reasons and on diverse occasions, encompassing what we split as personal and sociopolitical, as feeling and deed, reserved to kin or others. Though basically gratuitous—not tightly owed or forced—*hesed* invites from and engenders in the benefactee an appropriate response of gratitude and respect, a loyalty reciprocating what is offered by the benefactor, who acts from a similar set of relational motivations.[29] Though we may want to separate David's official kingly actions from those affecting his family, such a line cannot really be usefully drawn. The deeds we are about to examine, both God's and David's, are embedded within situations where deity or king acts, in David's integral life as he (narratively) lives it. Though the relevant personal relationships are challenging to navigate, the political aspects are even more dangerous, with the crucial matrix for David's life being his royal and patriarchal household, the monarchy, specifically dynastic kingship, a hazardous and unhealthy neighborhood in which to live. It is my contention that the Deuteronomic viewpoint hosting our story suggests most of the kings do not survive it very well, nor does the kingdom of Israel and Judah. David is the most successful, and his record is none too good. If there is an inherited curse/ problematic social situation with which the hero must contend, it is dynastic kingship. The capacity to extend *hesed* well, to give and receive compassion, is not about arrival but process, and over his narrative life David shows himself open to change of heart called conversion, and draws more deeply from the facets of compassion. His most powerful helpers are the priestly consultation process with the ephod, the communications from God and prophet, and the words of several wise people who speak to the king. David also invokes God in prayer. David's best moments are when he can be influenced by these helpers, but his best moments

29. Katharine Doob Sakenfeld, "Khesed," 495–96; "Love in the OT [{Hebrew letters אהב} {transliterated *ahab*} and [Hebrew letters חסד} *ḥesed*]," in Katharine Doob Sakenfeld, ed., *The New Interpreter's Dictionary of the Bible I–Ma*, vol 3 (Nashville: Abingdon Press, 2008), 713–18. These two articles reference several passages in the material under consideration in this book as well as others.

are attended by many relapses. Though the pattern is toward conversion, insight, compassion, progress is not steady but "strugglous."

So now, we examine certain moments to see consistent constellating motifs that invite us to read this long narrative cumulatively as well as sequentially. We will also note some unexpected repositioning, exposing relationships we might otherwise overlook or undersee. Our project is to work out the correlation or analogy between these two great hearts, each, arguably, offered to us as flawed, for our reflection and insight. God has more success with David than David has with his others, but the point for David and his readers is not to crave perfection but to grow compassion. Such is the track we will follow. Since we have already discussed all this material as length, the review, now, is to expose this longitudinal pattern, prompting us to fresh recognition and insight. Because this is a story, we will go in story order, moving from narrative site to site where these moments of narrative analogy cluster and how they build. We are looking for both recognizable type-scenes and the fresh perspective offered by the *mise-en-abŷme*.

c David's Early Years: Mutual Graciousness

The case for God's lavish generosity to David is easy to make, as we look at seven scenes where David interacts with the household of Saul. Foreseen, anointed, David at once is given God's spirit and becomes armor-bearer and musician to Saul (16:21), achieving success in Saul's household under God's spirit's patronage as well as the king's. David seems equally generous, as the gifted can find easy to be. Scrutinizing the shepherd boy's tactful generosity to Saul, faced with Goliath, we hear him name the problem as an affront to God (17:26), take on the king's job, accept briefly and then refuse the king's armor. "'I cannot go with these; for I am not used to them'" (17:39). The boy fells the giant with his own simpler weapons but reaches for the giant's sword for the beheading (17:51). David accepts, passively and wordlessly, the gift of royal clothing from Saul's son (18:4), and the two of them eventually exchange promises of *hesed*, mutual fidelity to each other's kin (20:12–17 is the most developed passage). David shows constraint while living in the household of Saul, avoiding the king's spear when it comes toward him, serving as military leader (18:11–12; 19:10). Intimate of Jonathan, David becomes the husband of Michal, until he flees for his life, accepting Michal's gift of clothing (19:12–13) and her courageous interposition with an angry Saul (19:14–17).[30] God's protection seems to surround David, who prospers even while threatened by Saul and while assisted by those of the royal household, even to their own cost in Saul's eyes.

Once David has fled Saul's household, he reaches for the weapon of another, reclaiming Goliath's sword (21:8–9). Mindful of God's spirit with David, we may see him protected and graced specifically in proportion to what Saul has lost, attended as Saul is by an evil spirit from God. The flight-from-Saul/pursuit-of-

---

30. Modern films of the scene make it clear that if David is to be lowered from a window, clothing is the obvious tool to be presumed, not sturdy rope from the hardware store.

Saul phase can be seen as marked by a certain restraint and proffering of safety on the part of both players. Though Saul seems intent on pursuit, when he has encounters with David, Saul fails to press as he threatened. We watch David grasp but abandon the king's property twice more: He takes a piece of royal robe without the wearer's knowing it (24:4–11). His showing the snipped fragment to King Saul is at once conciliatory and minatory: That worse might have been suffered does not quite disguise the pressing of advantage. In a similar scene, we observe David remove from the king his royal gear (spear and water-jug), again to return it later (26:12–22). The clothing gift that David ultimately accepts is the priestly ephod, brought to his service by the lone Elide to survive Saul's service (23:6).[31]

We catch the repeated and refracted element in scenes where David is offered the clothing or gear of another: bearing the king's armor, wearing it briefly, accepting Jonathan's royal clothing, using and (proleptically) stashing the giant's sword, assisted by Michal's garments, tearing a scrap from a vulnerable man, taking the royal spear from the man who used to throw it at David—and then returning it—finally becoming reliant upon consulting through the priestly ephod. Ultimately, it is not Saul's or Goliath's armor that David inherits, neither is Michal's nor Jonathan's clothing. If it features David serving Saul's interests while managing to further his own, and shows him being offered gifts and him receiving them lightly, the *mise-en-abyme* alerts us to watch the appropriation of such gifts against the good of those giving them. David's claiming of goods is repositioned, as receiving gives way to taking and returning, finally to actions more disadvantageously for the giver.

In this set of material where everyone but Saul seems eager to assist David and he to receive from them, we can note an increasing complexity in David's relationship with God. As a shepherd boy, he can speak truthfully and confidently if naively of taking on Saul's nemesis as he would a lion or a bear. Hostility from Saul proves a more troublesome thing, and we hear David in the last scene of this set struggle with the possibility that God is behind Saul's enmity to David.[32] David's raising this question, if to dismiss or underexploit it, marks a not-inappropriate change from his youthful sense of God as reliable helper. David's ultimately stepping across the border into Philistia to serve Achish of Gath is marked by a prominent non-killing of Saul but also now by decisive flight from all Saul's house might offer him. God's *hesed* to David, assisted by that of key others, is marked by a certain if diminishing generosity and restraint with Saul but also by brutal raids and total slaughter of other groups.[33]

---

31. Even the Elide service of Abiathar's ephod is ultimately dispensed with.

32. This passage, 26:17–25, get less helpful comment than it needs. Even an astute interpreter like Craig, *Asking for Rhetoric*, 100–05, makes relatively little sense of it. Craig does opine that David does not, ultimately, take seriously the possibility that the problems between himself and Saul are of God.

33. The pivot between David's two modes of managing *hesed* may be his brutal slaughter of whole groups of people, whether for some reason we are not told or for no reason. The narrator provides the information with little or no explanation. That Amalekites seek

d King David Acts with Proprietorial Arrogance but Accepts Rebuke

Reviewing the process by which David enters a kingship that is both given and claimed, we see him settle first with his own Judah tribe and then with more difficulty and controversy be joined by Saul's former adherents. Repeating scenes show David's generally successful efforts at consolidation of his position, but now at some cost to others. There is considerable ambiguity attending David's role in the deeds of his various opponents and helpers, justification for scrutinizing his verbal expressions of regret and even outrage at deaths that ultimately benefit him: Saul's and Jonathan's (both in 2 Samuel 1), Asahel's (ch. 2), Abner's (3), Ishbosheth's, and those of his assassins (4). These scenes, sequentially and provocatively presented, are in my view undecidable in terms of David's complicity in the deaths that so assist his kingship. The accumulating moments are studded as well with notices of God's lavish, unstinted favor to David, some provided by the narrator and others by David himself: He is urged to settle in Hebron (2 Sam. 2:1–20); he becomes the husband and father of many (3:1–5; 5:12–18). David is massively successful against Philistines (5:19–25; 8:1) and conquers others as well (8:2–6, 14). The chapter concluding David's early rulership narrates multiple instances of God's granting David victories over others on his borders: "And the LORD gave victory to David wherever he went," the narrator summarizes (8:14). Craig asserts that it is the very generosity of the deity that makes possible the success of the monarch.[34]

Moving past the question of David's complicity in key deaths that assist him, we turn to four moments of David's taking which occasion rebuke from God. If in David's early years his reaching for what was on offer was tempered, and if even in his various moves of consolidation meretricious behavior remains open to question, in these scenes such restraint lacks. We see David's violations of the *hesed* he has been shown by his divine patron, involving sacral objects and sites, occurring in 2 Samuel 5, 6, 7, and 24, already considered above. We catch the repositioning of the reach of the king as he takes and, as eventually he lets loose what he has grabbed. First, David approaches the ancient city held by Jebusites, seizing it brutally from its defenders, to name it for himself (5:6–11). Leaving without consultation the city, Hebron, to which God had directed him after he departed Ziklag, David makes Jerusalem the site for his own house.

His second arrogant initiative, also not preceded by inquiry of God, is to bring the Ark of God to the city of David. At the surface, this seems a deed of respect for the sacred object already subject to considerable abuse in the story leading to kings. But such a narrative is not quite what we have (6:1–23). The Ark, reactive to abuse previously in the transition time between judges and kings, now occasions the death of one who touches it injudiciously during the transfer and dies of his gesture. David, we learn, is angry "because the LORD had broken forth upon

---

reprisal is also told without the narrator establishing a tight link between David's killing and the raid his people suffered (27:9–11; 30:1–26).

34. Craig, *Asking for Rhetoric*, 153.

Uzzah . . . and was afraid of the LORD that day; and he said, 'How can the ark of the LORD come to me?' So David was not willing to take the ark of the LORD into the city of David; but David took it aside to the house of Obededom the Gittite" (6:8–10). Appraising the king's question, we may think he has misperceived the issue, and we ask for him: Why did God break forth against an Ark-handler, Ark-protector? Shall the Ark of God come to the city of David or not? What shall David do if not bring the Ark to Jerusalem? But when the Ark seems to recover its equanimity and bless its erstwhile host, David recommences his effort to rehouse it in his city. The Ark itself, elaborately accompanied by liturgy, arrives passively and harmlessly to be feted in the city of David. It is David's wife Michal who offers him and us the insight needed. Viewing from above and as nonparticipant outsider as she surely is in David's household, she remarks on David's covering himself with glory, however else he may have been uncovered: "'How the king of Israel honored *himself* today . . .'" (6:20, emphasis added). Refusing her assessment, David cites God's generosity toward him, pointing out all that had been lost by the house of Saul and given to David.

Having refused the insight of Michal's distinctive viewpoint, her pointing out from where she is watching and interpreting how the Ark liturgy serves the king's glory, David moves to his third contemptuous taking: the constructing of a house for the Ark and implicitly for its deity.[35] This scene, perhaps among the most famous in the long narrative of the king, represents as well YHWH's clearest rebuke of David to date. As though concluding that his protégé is resistant to subtle restraint administered through others, the deity sends the prophet to tell the king plainly that he has overstepped, that this time it will not be tolerated. To David, Nathan—instructed—clarifies that the house-builder is the deity and not the king; the house is, for the moment, dynastic and not material; the timing remains with God, not with David, and though the moment is not now, the house-commitment between YHWH and David will be long lasting. David has seriously overstepped in a variety of aspects, and God blocks him clearly, stressing pronouns and adjectives carefully we may hear (7:7–16):

> "In all places where I have moved with all the people of Israel, did I speak a word with any of the judges of Israel, whom I commanded to shepherd my people Israel, saying, 'Why have you not built me a house of cedar?' Now therefore thus you shall say to my servant David, 'Thus says the LORD of hosts, I took you from the pasture, from following the sheep, that you should be prince over my people Israel; and I have been with you wherever you went, and have cut off all your enemies from before you; and I will make for you a great name, like the name of the great ones of the earth. And I will appoint a place for my people Israel, and will plant them, that they may dwell in their own place, and be disturbed no more; and violent men shall afflict them no more, as formerly, from the time that I appointed judges over my people Israel; and I will give you rest from all your enemies. Moreover the LORD declares to you that the LORD will make

35. Ibid., 149–67, makes numerous excellent observations about this section of narrative.

you a house. When your days are fulfilled and you lie down with your fathers, I will raise up your offspring after you, who shall come forth from your body, and I will establish his kingdom. He shall build a house for my name, and I will establish the throne of his kingdom for ever. I will be his father, and he shall be my son. When he commits iniquity, I will chasten him with the rod of men, with the stripes of the sons of men; but I will not take my steadfast love from him, as I took it from Saul, whom I put away from before you. And your house and your kingdom shall be made sure for ever before me; your throne shall be established for ever."

In addition to points already made clear by the divine speaker, we learn two more important things: First, God will not renege on David as here the deity acknowledges doing with Saul. Part of God's graciousness to David is long-range consistency. Here, the permissive deity corrects and chastises, clarifies and constrains, but all without any removal of favor or even threat of it. And second David, we see, accepts what he has been told without demur or cavil, in fact with an extraordinary prayer of acknowledgment and gratitude toward his divine benefactor. This, we may see, is David at his finest turn toward God. Neither the shepherd boy, confident of help defending his sheep from lions and bears, nor the troubled and tempted tracker of Saul, wondering who has incited his rival against him—David here knows great success and power. David has received immeasurable favor from God, but can accept his limit as well.

Related to this "sacral object-set" of scenes comprising David's reaching for city, Ark, and temple, we can also place their reversing episodes, marking David's capacity for conversion. First is David's purchase of the threshing floor of Araunah, done to ensure the city's safety from deity-administered and king-selecting plague (2 Samuel 24). Since we are looking for a freshly represented familiar motif, the king's hand releasing what it has grabbed—each a variant as well as a repeat—we can see this "appendix" episode as a healing of David's arrogation of city, Ark, and house-building project, demonstrating what David has learned about the sacred. Seizing Jerusalem, appropriating the Ark, presuming to build a temple, God's chosen king is now led by a most indirect and confusing-to-us (if not to him) process to the site of the temple Solomon will be given to build. The character God, abetted by implied author and narrator, having managed a complex scenario of David's incitement, blame, contrition, punishment, and compunction, maneuvers the king to cry out on behalf of those who have already suffered from what the king takes as his offense (24:16–17):

And when the angel stretched forth his hand toward Jerusalem to destroy it, the LORD repented of the evil, and said to the angel who was working destruction among the people, "It is enough; now stay your hand." And the angel of the LORD was by the threshing floor of Araunah the Jebusite. Then David spoke to the LORD when he saw the angel who was smiting the people, and said, "Lo, I have sinned, and I have done wickedly; but these sheep, what have they done? Let thy hand, I pray thee, be against me and against my father's house."

That is, though we have been apprised that the impetus for this whole episode is God's unexplained anger at Israelites and a consequent divine inciting of David to take a census, the episode punishing him for it is made up of story events, known to the players. We have witnessed God's, offering the king three modes of punishment and then actually calling a halt before David's outcry, so that the scene of relevance is David's arrival at the threshing floor where he is told by YHWH's prophet to erect an altar.

Though David is king and presumably the lord of his city, he approaches the foreign owner of the site with reverence and respect, negotiating with the owner for access. While Araunah speaks most generously to the king, David refuses the Jebusite's generosity:

> "No, but I will buy it of you for a price; I will not offer burnt offerings to the LORD my God which cost me nothing." So David bought the threshing floor and the oxen for fifty shekels of silver. And David built there an altar to the LORD, and offered burnt offerings and peace offerings. So the LORD heeded supplications for the land, and the plague was averted from Israel (24:24–25).

As the inverse of his seizing the city and insulting its guardians, of bringing the Ark despite rebuke, and of presuming to build additionally, David here acts with graciousness, doing more than is required, since we know that God has already drawn back from reprisal.[36]

e David's Mature Reign: Serious Arrogance and Divine Response

Thus far, a generous deity has given David success at virtually every turn, or so it seems. Even David's three (or four) named overreaches have been rebuked and seem repented of, indeed healed, as David turns toward God. Struggle and suffering have not lacked in these instances of narrative analogy, but they have not prevailed. David seems at the crest of his power, with much accomplished since he was first anointed, then eventually crowned by both Judah and Israel's tribes. Potential opponents have been settled, and David's own household seems to be flourishing. The king's acceding with reverence and gratitude to God's words has been salutary for him, for many.

But as we move to the next phase of David's life, we have the blossoming of two distinct though related narrative patterns, related to the other longitudinal characterization patterns operative. The first involves several scenes where David initiates *hesed* but then retracts it and fails to follow through, to the detriment of all. The second is the compounding outcome of David's sin against Bathsheba, Uriah, and YHWH, its outflow into the entire household and kingdom of

---

36. An incident related to this set will appear in the next portion of the story, where the king, fleeing the city he had taken, returns to it God's Ark (15:23–26), also once (or twice) contemptuously arrogated, saying that the resolution of the matter of Jerusalem's status as the city of David or of Absalom will be settled by God.

David, culminating in his incapacity to manage Absalom in matters familial and wider. Since we have already read this material in story order, here we will look achronically at David's inconsistent *hesed* before turning to the more egregious sin that dominates chs. 9–20. As noted above, we are seeing a recurring type-scene and also glimpsing a repositioning of it, startling us into fresh insight.

1. David's abortive gestures of hesed: David's initiatives of *hesed* in this set of material are several: He, perhaps belatedly, searches for survivors of Jonathan's line as he had sworn to do, finds Mephibosheth and Mica and brings them to his table, returning to Jonathan's son the goods of the house of Saul (2 Samuel 9). The king initiates an act of *hesed* for an old ally, Ammon, sending consolers to its new king, Hanun, on the death of his father (ch. 10). This action reverses at once, thrown back rudely as into David's face. At once David engages Ammon and its allies in war. As suggested above, David need not be faulted for his withdrawing of *hesed* from Hanun, though his doing so was nonetheless a fateful move.

Moving past the other events set within the Ammonite war, we can scrutinize the same basic retractive pattern in actions David performs while leaving and then reentering Jerusalem. David's reversal of loyalty to Mephibosheth is clear in 16:4 and 19:29, where he twice refuses to adjudicate responsibly between contenders, first accepting Ziba's accusation of Mephibosheth and then refusing to judge between the two at all. The gesture of consolation to the Ammonite ally ends in the defeat and subjugation of that people to David (12:29–31). If David intended good to his secondary wives by leaving them in Jerusalem, their actual situation and need are poorly assessed, resulting in harm to them that is not in any evident way redressed (15:16; 16:20–22; 20:3). As suggested above, the willing complicity of David's counselor, Ahithophel, in Absalom's revolt is not presented clearly by the narrator and surely not carefully discerned by the king. If continuing loyal, Ahithophel is badly let down by the king, with his suicide ending the matter decisively (15:11–12; 17:23). Shimei, encountering David twice, is twice reprieved (16:5–13; 19:18–23). But that Shimei's fate is given to Solomon to finish off punitively seems badly managed (1 Kgs. 2:8–9). David's *hesed* to Barzillai, engaged first as the king flees the city and then again as he returns, is also left to Solomon, leaving us to infer that David had not adequately recompensed his benefactor (17:27–28; 19:31–40; 1 Kgs. 2:7). Though we cannot quite see what David did not finish, that he speaks of it at the end of his life suggests it has remained inadequately compensated.

Other people of David, loyal to him as his son gathers his own allies to do harm, accompany David as he leaves the city—Ittai, Hushai, Abiathar, and Zadok and their various helpers, unnamed mercenary soldiers and others assisting (variously within 2 Sam. 15–18)—and are spoken for by Joab after the revolt ends and the king is in a position to reclaim his power. Though we may be disinclined to take Joab's words as truthful, yet still his rebuke of David is apt. Disregarding, for the moment, the circumstances of Joab's words, let us hear them again (19:5–6):

> "Then Joab came into the house to the king, and said, 'You have today covered with shame the faces of all your servants, who have this day saved your life, and the lives of your sons and your daughters, and the lives of your wives and your

concubines, because you love those who hate you and hate those who love you. For you have made it clear today that commanders and servants are nothing to you; for today I perceive that if Absalom were alive and all of us were dead today, then you would be pleased.'"

The narrator agrees with this character that David's loyal people feel keenly the sorrow of the king without quite endorsing the specific harshness of Joab's assessment that they are on the verge of rebellion. But that David acts inconsistently, even perversely, toward those who are faithful to him, demonstrating more overt regard for the single disloyal man than for the many loyal people, seems clear enough. David himself, not commenting on what Joab has charged, accedes to it as he greets his people wordlessly. Their response is not provided, since the story veers off to follow those who resist reincorporation into David's kingdom. Even if Joab's charge is excessive, he has prompted us to consider something we may have missed without him. This turning back of *hesed* already extended is thus sustained over a series of episodes.

2. David with Bathsheba and Uriah and with Absalom: Splitting, for the most part, these extensions and reversals of *hesed* on David's part and distributed among them comes the most notorious action of David's narrative life. In the midst of the Ammonite war, David sees a woman bathing, seeks and learns of her identity as the wife of one of his fighting men, sends for her, sleeps with her, impregnates her, summons her husband, Uriah, back from the war, tries to entice him to violate normative practice by sleeping with his wife, makes him drunk, and sends him back to the siege of Ammonite Rabbah bearing the instructions for his own death—those orders risking the war effort itself (ch. 11). Perhaps our familiarity with this cascade of betrayals distracts us from noting how out of character they are in certain aspects for David, typically and consistently careful, strategic, and self-contained. Knowing as we do what David did, we may no longer be so startled and offended at his actions as is justified.

Casting about for narrative justification of such shocking betrayals, asking how these actions suit the character we know, I see two roots: First, large servings of success and power such as have been given to David tend to corrupt their receivers.[37] That David has multiple women with not a sign of disapproval registered by any voice in the text—God's included—logically opens the way for him to take another as he so desires, this time (if not before) the wife of another. Second and related, that God is characteristically permissive with David, opposing only rarely though effectively at the moment, contributes as well to the portrait as we have it. Points to ponder include both the generosity of the heart of David's benefactor who gives so lavishly, and also the king's persistent tendency toward arrogance and contempt that has come to override David's other demeanor.[38] David is chastised endlessly

37. Unprovable, this seems one of the Deuteronomic assessments of dynastic monarchy.

38. If Homer were our bard, we would expect a powerful simile here: As a grand edifice, having survived many storms while being devoured from within by a small clutch of worms, can in a moment disintegrate unexpectedly in a late spring rainstorm, so David . . .

in scholarship for this deed, and though I do not plan to do that, I do want to underline its egregious nature and its substantially uncharacteristic behavior for David, before considering its effects. Again, at a wider and more general level, we are noting typical patterns and then the anomalous repositioning of them. Though penitent—sincerely so, I maintain—David is not able to recover from this heinous action set, and suffering spreads from it, bringing considerable harm to many. Again, this briefer discussion of material already presented offers the challenge of seeing a motif, re-angled while being several times re-presented: God's indulgence of David—often fruitful and positively contagious in the king's life—this time replicating harmfully in David's incapacities to manage Absalom suitably, wisely, well.[39]

David's most unexpected breach loyal relationships receives his most stinging divine rebuke. Nor is there expressed any awareness of wrong or regret for it by David until he is strongly reproached. In fact, he is shown first smug about his achievement (11:25) and then unresponsive to analogy when offered it (12:5–6). But as before, typically for David and for the deity who interposes so occasionally to stop this protégé from his worst excesses, David readily owns his sin when shown it (12:13): "David said to Nathan, 'I have sinned against the LORD.' And Nathan said to David, 'The LORD also has put away your sin; you shall not die.'" But David, though surviving, does not recover from this taproot flaw. And though the deity does not revoke what has been given to David, the death of this first son begins a pattern lasting until the end of the story. Indulgence leading to arrogance—or arrogance to indulgence—is not easily healed, at least in its effects. If some find that the father of this infant recovers too readily from the child's death, to read on is to see more deeply into what now characterizes this human with the heart like God's. If David learns compassion, its likeliest source is his suffering with his children, his experiencing them recapitulating his own arrogant behaviors. Presenting the outflow of this root arrogance of David's as debilitating to himself and contagious to others, I suggest that the subsequent narrative of the king's life is not a series of retributions, since God does not directly punish David. But David does not recover from his weakness and inflicts it on his household, as tends to happen with human weaknesses. This time the pattern works itself out much more harmfully, as we are shown David's arrogant contempt behavior metastasizing in his children.

We look again at David and Absalom, with Absalom representing as well the elder Amnon and the younger Adonijah (2 Samuel 13 and 1 Kings 1 respectively). David is father to those sons, each in turn to be imagined as succeeding him on the throne. If the narrative representation of David's sin against Bathsheba and Uriah is his worst deed, hosting and seeding this series of flaws or lacks, crimes and sins, the king's incapacity to manage Absalom is the most intense harvest. Though we have looked at it previously, the point here is to show its placement in the repeating patterns of the narrative. A third son named to David, Absalom

---

39. There is a more bitter incapacity of David to check Joab, but I will leave it lying fallow for the present.

becomes heir apparent after his killing Amnon and the narrative disappearance of Chileab (3:3). But as we learn from the wise woman, the fact of the fratricide is a complicating factor, perhaps an unsolvable one—surely in our narrative.[40] The point I wish to offer here is that, while not excusing Absalom for his deeds against his father and king, the father-king's refusal to allow the adjudication of Absalom's situation, his inconsistency in reconciling with Absalom, or submitting him to justice reduces options that might otherwise have been possible to consider. As before, the presentation of David's poor managing Absalom becomes more deadly over time.

After the rape of his sister by their brother, Absalom waits two years before killing the rapist (13:20–37). Speaking minimizingly to Tamar and to Amnon not at all—Absalom's ability to guess the problem at once hinting that he may have seen what was happening—Tamar's brother, failing to get their father's involvement, kills his brother and flees the immediate reach of his father-the-king's justice. The narrator's failure to name clearly what David wants in regard to his fratricidal son may exactly suggest David's state: ambivalence, conflict about how he feels about his sons Amnon and Absalom and what he wants for the survivor (13:37–39): "And the spirit of the king longed to go forth to Absalom; for he was comforted about Amnon, seeing he was dead." How David feels toward his son remains pervasively unclear.

To help us, if not the character, grasp the problem, we have the refraction of the wise woman of Tekoa, offering all of us ever more closely the situation needing resolution, representing it fictively much as Nathan did in his parable. Recalling the king's quick outrage at "the man" in Nathan's story as presented for decision, David engages the analogy of the Tekoan woman with less intensity and personal response than before. Immobilized, David can neither punish nor forgive, remand nor reprieve. The king makes manifest in several rounds his willingness to manage the petitioner's problem but not his own. When finally he cannot avoid recognizing her strategy, he distracts us by naming Joab as perpetrator of the small plotted scene—true enough, but not the main issue for David's resolution. When Absalom is brought back to Judah (14:23–33), we see visually several more rounds of David's deferring to do one thing or another. Even when Absalom is admitted to the presence of David and is kissed by him, we are excluded from much that we would like to see—or what we see is David inconsistent, indecisive. Again, without condoning it, we watch Absalom reach out for what he wants in the clearest way he can manage, with no help from David. That the narrator stresses the young man's narcissism may distract us from the starker reality that Absalom's situation needs resolving. He finally does it himself when, after several years, his father has delayed. That the narrator characterizes Absalom's self-aggrandizement does not quite distract us from the weed David has allowed to flourish—a sprig of bamboo into

---

40. I have thought previously that Absalom wants David complicit in the killing of Amnon, but it is as possible that he wants his father to help resolve the matter, since so long as Amnon lives, Absalom's situation remains uncertain.

a tall, thick hedge. Only when the revolt is imminent does David act—decisively, strongly, drawing people to his side, with what seems a quick success. But the outcome is more rebellion rather than reconciliation. David's actions hinder the serious issues his cardinal choice has precipitated.

Looked at in this way, the details of the revolt and especially of the counselor advice highlight the deeper matter: Insofar as Ahithophel says: act now, while Hushai advises: defer, we see David's situation characterized, revisited. The son may calculate—if wrongly—which plan his father is most likely to anticipate. That the follow through on the advice seems to be that Ahithophel's is followed, but he acts as though it were not, our (characters and readers) hearing the choice may be more important than who actually did what. The narrative goes at once to the words of David (18:5): "'Deal gently for my sake with the young man Absalom.' And all the people heard when the king gave orders to all the commanders about Absalom." The matter is stressed additionally when it is repeated by the nameless who refuses to kill Absalom and is rebuked by Joab (18:12): "'Even if I felt in my hand the weight of a thousand pieces of silver, I would not put forth my hand against the king's son; for in our hearing the king commanded you and Abishai and Ittai, "For my sake protect the young man Absalom.""' David's anxiety over Absalom is also reinforced as we watch him see the approach of runners at the end of the battle (18:24–32).

David's verbal response to the death of his fratricidal, rebellious, thwarted, and unrepentant son is brief but filled with feeling. If so often before we have not been able to know what David is thinking and feeling—nor is he either shown able to know—there is no doubt here. David is devastated at the death of this son and begs to be dead in place of Absalom. He does not say why but simply that, and several times (18:33): "And the king was deeply moved, and went up to the chamber over the gate, and wept; and as he went, he said, 'O my son Absalom, my son, my son Absalom! Would I had died instead of you, O Absalom, my son, my son!'" And at 19:4: "The king covered his face, and the king cried with a loud voice, 'O my son Absalom, O Absalom, my son, my son!'" We may suppose many things: grief, regret, guilt, compassion, despair, but to refuse to acknowledge the depth of feeling here is impossible. David may wish for a different outcome and for different moves that might have occasioned it. What we can see, perhaps with the character, is the vast set of factors leading to the result that must now be faced. David does not articulate these things, with his only other comment being in an entirely different register: at 20:6, he says that the next rebel may do more harm than has Absalom. A capacity for conversion persists, if less resolute than we may prefer. A capacity for compassion, surely so, if late in coming. David's dealings with Absalom, bitter fruit of his injustices in the Ammonite war, both replay and reposition his radical incapacity for managing Absalom wisely. Though eventually shown as deeply compassionate for his son, dead, David has not been able to love him well while Absalom lived. In a sense, David's capacity for compassion, both strengthened and undermined by indecision, shows the king resembling his divine benefactor as drawn in this narrative: matching hearts.

f David's Final Instincts and Actions

What can we say of David's heart, after the death of Absalom, with so little material
left to mine? As already noted, David manages the revolt of Sheba badly, not least
for his incapacity to order Amasa, Joab, and Abishai decisively and effectively. If
permissive is the word, or forbearing, David is not cured of those qualities.[41] We
learn that he has indulged his son, Adonijah, no less than he did Amnon and
Abaslom: The narrator summarizes rather than showing us (1 Kgs.1:6): "His father
had never at any time displeased him by asking, 'Why have you done thus and
so?' He was also a very handsome man; and he was born next after Absalom." The
result is similar, as Adonijah makes a move analogous to Absalom's, taking the
throne prematurely and without sanction. Again, since this material has already
been reviewed, my points to suggest are two: That David's heart remains inclined
toward generosity, even though he might have been cured of it. And second, that
when the deity pushes back, now gently through the prophet and another wise
woman, David is again responsive, doing what is needed, not always so easy for
those in power as they feel its dusk. Old David's heart remains much as we have
seen it: He perseveres in habitual excesses, some negative, some positive—or
rather, an unstable blend. If formerly indulgent toward Adonijah, David must
now retract. As David has previously been responsive to divine guidance, whether
God's spirit or corrective word, here, even old and weak, he is obedient to what his
prophet says. And since he has only to respond and not really orchestrate actions,
he does well. Insofar as David moves to clear some toxic situations polluting his
house, he takes appropriate responsibility rather than leaving all such decisions
to his heir. Solomon, temple-builder, is seated on his father's throne. If we have
longed for decisive action on David's part, we see his son move with more resolve
if not with much suggestion of compassion.

4 Conclusions and Transition

This chapter has sought to do three things. First, we finished a close reading of the
long David narrative, rejoining the king as he stirred from a passivity-become-
incapacity to act appropriately and decisively at his last moment to do so. Moving
in alignment with the implied author's and the narrator's presentation of the deity
and also with the wishes of prophet, wise woman, and loyal people, David secured
the succession to his throne for the son who will build the temple. The choice of
Solomon was made decisively, unambiguously enough that even those who lost
by it did not dispute it. David then, finally, gave his son command to clear the two
most polluting situations of his own long reign: the illicit killing of two men by
Joab, who had confounded war-death with peacetime killing. Insofar as David was

---

41. If the material of 2 Sam. 21–24 were managed here, which I have chosen not to do,
we would be proceeding differently, as David would have more deeds of strength attributed
to him.

responsible for the festering of those deeds, he did well to manage these situations himself rather than leaving them to his heir.

Second, we introduced a new, sixth, tool, a narrative analogy, allowing its more complex structure to help us reread more deeply material already examined. A blend of the type-scene, where repeating elements cluster recognizably, and the *mise-en-abŷme*, where a narrative fragment is freshly repositioned to catch our attention, narrative analogy brought us back over material we had considered earlier in terms of plotting, characterization, and narrator direction. We worked throughout the narrative with the suggestion that David oscillates or toggles along two poles: first, from passivity to a fuller engagement and then to a more serious lapse into passivity; second, from receiving gifts to an arrogant and contemptuous grabbing of them, though also to ready repentance when checked. The type-scene lifted out for examination here featured David's tendency to act graciously toward others but to retract the deed of kindness prematurely so, proffering generosity only to later withhold it. Numerous instances of this patterns were considered. The fresh repositioning of this typical pattern was David's massive inconsistency with his son Absalom and the detailed working out of that matter. If the father/king's trail of failures with his son resembles other scenes where he mismanaged situations of *hesed*, the long-running relationship between David and Absalom produced unexpected and atypical fruits, in both David and in his son. Absalom, unlike most other beneficiaries of David's gifts, retaliates, exposing more deeply for us the harm done by the king.

So the third project attempted in this chapter was the exploration of what, specifically, narrative analogy added to our sense of David's capacity to learn compassion. The study presented here also redirected us to the narrative feature where God claimed that the second choice for king, consequent upon the firing of Saul, would be rooted in a similarity of hearts between deity and king. Though the specific meaning of God's ruminated criterion is impossible to pin down, the general idea is clear enough. Evidently having learned from his dealings with Saul, God's heart toward David was shown lavish and loving, even permissive and indulgent to the point where the king overreached and needed correction, which God administered, if often seemingly too late. David's readiness to turn back to his divine benefactor from steps taken in royal isolation was refreshing, his heart is shown the better for it. Like his own benefactor, David offered deeds of generosity, even if often to draw them back for one reason or another. David was shown as generous and forbearing, more responsive to God and humans than Saul had been before him, indeed, more forbearing with Saul's behaviors than Saul had been with David, whom he was said to love.

But if God can be claimed to proceed in such an uneven and even questionable way, David's pattern, if similar, was more seriously flawed. If David ultimately prospered under such handling while suffering as well—learning from his suffering—the dynamic has not seemed so fruitful when David was characterized as mimicking it. God seemed more adept at turning David toward eventual compassion than David managed with Absalom. If David repented of his cultic overreaching and even of the hydra-headed offense against his loyal people during the Ammonite war, and if God forgave that deed-set, its consequences proliferated, notably for David's children, and no check on those outcomes emerged.

Though we watched David turn back after being rebuked for his arrogance, even though several episodes, David's own struggle with Absalom showed no such fruit in his son. David, then, was shown at extremes with Absalom, at his most permissive and at his most compassionate, strangely replicating the heart of the deity. When Amnon raped Absalom's sister, David, though angry, did nothing. When Absalom exacted his life from Amnon before fleeing out of range, David, though saddened, delayed to act. When prompted by Joab and a wise woman, David allowed Absalom back to Jerusalem but not into his father's presence. When Absalom provocatively refused that situation, David finally received him, kissing him, but evidently doing nothing else to stop Absalom from overt revolt. The king, emerging briefly from his inability to act clearly and decisively, successfully brought the revolt to an end, but with no clear provision for his son except the plea that in the ultimate encounter Absalom be treated gently, for the sake of the father. The result, as we saw, was Joab's scorning this request and seeing Absalom dead and buried. The clearest fruit of David's capacity to learn compassion, brief if intense, was his grief at his son's death, his repeated prayer or desire that he had died in place of his son. If such be David's deepest learning, we were then unaccountably excluded from any more narrative where it might have been explored additionally. David's fresh troubles piled up at once, and then he became, for us, an old man.[42] David's exploration of the fruit of his long life, crowned with his suffering over both Absalom's deficiencies and his own inability to manage those of his son, was not on offer. Insofar as God was still helping David to learn, indeed shaping him into one of the great ones of the earth, as promised (2 Sam. 7:9) it was not simply by being powerful but by learning compassion. But deprived of more in this narrative, we must turn to the psalms to experience it.[43]

Though we have finished our verbal narrative, we will reexamine these matters under current discussion once more as we engage the verbal with a visual work of art.

42. Again we see the importance of the choice around the placement of 2 Sam. 21–24.

43. In the wider biblical tradition, we can engage David as a psalmist to learn about his heart.

Chapter 9

Reception and Construction of David in a Western Painting

Reading Visual Art

1 Transition

The interpretation of the character David to be offered here is achieved with the help of a second compound tool, involving a radical transposition in both temporal/spatial factors and in medium. The *narrative* we have been reading likely emerged into its approximate shape mid-first millennium BCE, while the *painting* we will examine—Giambattista Pittoni's *David Before the Ark of the Covenant*—was painted in mid-second millennium CE—clearly by a much later artist for an audience neither intended nor envisioned by biblical authors. We, presently reading and viewing, were not anticipated by any of the artists involved. Challenges encountered when moving from a verbal to a visual medium are complex, filled with opportunities for insight. While in a sense, this whole book involves transpositions, it has so far remained literary. Though normed by presuppositions and conventions not known explicitly nor systematically to the biblical authors, this present interpretation has risen from principles not alien to those that produced the biblical narrative of David. The fresh question to be explored in this final chapter is how reception and interpretation of a verbal narrative into a painting in post-Renaissance Venice enrich *our* capacity to read both texts. How can we explore David's capacity for compassion more deeply than before as we converge these texts and tools?

To fasten attention on a visual rather than a verbal work—or better, to read a painting while considering the rich story—stimulates interpretation. Catching a glimpse of the figure we have come to know as we find him positioning himself with strong feeling toward God's Ark moves us into a new realm. There is no shortage of art featuring David, and neither this scene nor the artist is the most popular of possibilities for our engagement. I chose the work primarily due to its subject matter, as a fitting way to continue to approach David's capacity for compassion. As we view this work, noting David's focus, unshared by any others visible, we raise new questions, gain fresh insight.[1]

---

1. Every writer feels gratitude for the many collaborators who assist with research, whether they are alive or dead, contribute in one way or another. I am particularly

2 *Methodology: A Seventh Tool: Reading Visual Art*

a *Changing Temporal and Cultural Considerations*

The easier of the challenges from these transpositions is negotiating the difference in era and culture as Pittoni offers us a representation of David. The painting I have chosen to present was produced in the period that art history calls baroque and/ or rococo (so from roughly 1700–1850), the first shading into or overlapping the second.[2] Giovanni Battista (Giambattista) Pittoni's *David before the Ark of the Covenant* is dated *ca.* 1760, oil on canvas, now in Florence's Uffizi Gallery. Pittoni (1687–1767, often called Pittoni the Younger to distinguish him from an uncle) was a Venetian painter associated with the *Accademia di Belle Arti di Venezia*, working during the baroque and rococo periods, producing works from biblical narratives and classic mythology, in roughly equal numbers, historical works as well.

Venice in the period under discussion had enjoyed political and economic status, both now in decline. The location of the city, on modern Italy's northeast shoulder with ready access to the Adriatic Sea, allowed it to meet opportunities and challenges from both west and east. Intervening unsuccessfully in Ottoman Empire politics, visited by devastating plague several times between the fourteenth and seventeenth centuries, and accustomed to relying on water transportation inadequate for emerging world exploration, Venice suffered instability under overlords, being by turns part of Austria, an independent unit, and incorporated into Italy. The city enjoyed prominence and distinction in the arts as well, sponsoring artists like Giorgione, Titian, Tintoretto, Veronese, Canaletto, and Tiepolo, but her greatest glory lay also in the past by Pittoni's time.

As is well known, artists are shaped by their contexts, by particular circumstances major and minor. They set scenes and garb figures in clothing familiar to themselves (rather than recreating historically accurate detail), signifying elements of gender, class, and position, and reflecting tastes and

appreciative of three colleagues who have assisted me greatly with the art in this chapter: Leslie D. Ross, Andrea M. Sheaffer, and Anne Tignanelli.

2. It is commonly observed that the terms "baroque" and "rococo" are not particularly useful (e.g., Fred S. Kleiner, Christin J. Mamiya, Richard G. Tansey, *Helen Gardner's Art through the Ages* (Fort Worth: Harcourt College Publishers, 11th edition, 2001), 719–21. The word "baroque" implies the contorted, irregular, grotesque, arising from the turbulent Reformation times and using light and movement to suggest intensity. The emergent rococo style is softer, lighter, more playful, and more disorderly than Renaissance work, with regional differences being important as well. J. Milam offers:

> Viewers cognizant of narrative techniques established during the Renaissance . . . struggle to derive information from the parts of the [rococo] painting where it is expected to be found—facial expressions are difficult to discern, and the backs of central figures are turned to the beholder. Emotions, therefore, cannot be read. Similarly, gestures lead to areas of the composition, or even outside the frame, where no further information can be derived (*Historical Dictionary of Rococo Art* [Plymouth, UK: Scarecrow Press, 2011], 11).

Figure 9.1 Giovanni Battista (Giambattista) Pittoni, *David before the Ark of the Covenant, ca.* 1760. Oil on canvas. Uffizi Gallery, Florence; Photo Credit: Finsiel/Alinari/Art Resource, NY.

preferences in terms of their own experience. To suggest former or other less well-known cultures, artists added elements that seemed exotic to them. Patrons and artists of the baroque and rococo periods, and presumably viewers as well, still appreciated renditions of great scenes from classical and biblical antiquity, understood them and their referents, and could appreciate ways in which new works both continued a conversation from the past but also rang contemporary changes. Later modernity, for the most part, has not carried forth the past heritage in so enthusiastic and knowledgeable a way.

1. Changing Conventions in Art Ken Vandergriff briefly but helpfully surveys the story of King David in Western literature and art, reminding us how interests and concerns changed over time, from era to era.[3] Early postbiblical interpretation of David tended to consider him and his character traits allegorically, hence showing little interest in drawing out or portraying particularities of his narrative character. Renaissance art featuring David was more eager to portray his physicality, and so scenes beloved of artists show David as a young giant-slayer or as attracted to Bathsheba.[4] Modern studies are less concerned to protect David's biblical status as specially favored, tending to explore his flaws and his complex humanity, notably

---

3. Ken Vandergriff, "Re-Creating David: The David Narratives in Art and Literature," *RevExp* 99 (Spring, 2002), 193–205. Another commentator on this matter is David L. Petersen, "Portraits of David: Canonical and Otherwise," *Interpretation* 40 (1986): 130–42.

4. For a study of this David, see the work of Andrea Sheaffer, "Judith Versus Goliath? Visualizing David as Archetype," *Arts* 25.3 (2014): 5–14.

his tangled relationships with Saul and with Jonathan. Multiple challenges of interpretation present themselves, opportunities for receivers to interact responsibly with what they are seeing, to name and explain as best as they—we—can do. Martin O'Kane offers another summary and characterization of art featuring David, choosing to focus on artists' favorite moments to depict him.[5] Selecting moments of David as *puer* (youth) and as *senex* (wise elder), O'Kane comments helpfully on numerous works of visual art and how they manage their interpretive task.

2. Conventions of Venetian Baroque and Rococo Art A quick consideration of other images of David contemporary with the one to be studied here will be useful. The hero tends to be featured as the youthful giant-slayer,[6] or the harpist, pictured at various ages.[7] Baroque artists favored dramatic color, including use of dark and light; strong perspective effects; figures moving upwards; broken and agitated draperies; loose brushstrokes; heavy *impasto* providing texture; dense and detailed and emotion-provoking compositions. Popular moments to feature included visions, ecstasies, conversions, and martyrdom and death, all offering intense psychological states to render.[8]

Rococo art, by contrast, is more delicate, cursive, more prone to use lighter color and swelling and undulating surfaces, grouped subjects, elegantly attired, engaged in decorously amorous play. Rococo derives its name from the French word, "*rocaille*," referring to rock-work—referring to a style of decoration that swirls with arranged curves and scrolls—a decorative response to the baroque realism. Rococo depictions of David, contemporary with Pittoni, include as well the young giant-killer.[9]

b Changing Media

1. Our previous tools reutilized The challenges of moving from a verbal to a nonverbal medium are even more provocative than those involved when we engage the biblical material in eras different from its inception and from our own time as well, promising more productive insight. As the present study has worked

5. Martin O'Kane, "The Biblical King David and his Artistic and Literary Afterlives," *BI* 6.3–4 (1998): 325–34.

6. For example, Caravaggio (1571–1610) has six studies of *David Victorious over Goliath*, ca. 1600.

7. Examples include Peter Paul Rubens (1577–1640) *King David Playing the Harp*, ca, 1627; Andrea Celesti's (1637–1712) *King David Playing the Zither* (second half of the seventeenth century); Rembrandt Harmensz van Rijn's (1606–69) various studies of David as harpist, for example, *David Playing the Harp before Saul* (1655–60).

8. Tignanelli, private communication.

9. Domenico Corvi (1721–1803), *David et Goliath*; Gaspare Diziani (1689–1767), *David with the Head of Goliath before Saul*; Antonio Balestra (1666–1740), *David and Goliath*; Pittoni's student, Anton Kern (1710–47), has an *Aaron, High Priest of the Israelites* that shares features with the priestly figure in Pittoni's work under consideration here.

with narrative literary tools—determining the edges of the work, inquiring about structure, considering plotting dynamics, narrator role, characterization techniques, and finally narrative analogy—some of those features can be seen to have counterparts in visual representation so that we can consider some of those same matters visually.[10] We can note the basic edges or limits of the painting: the size of the space filled, how is the work both constricted and freed by those, as it were. We will ask where the work begins and ends, in itself and in relation to other things that are to be understood when viewing the work as well as when composing it. The topic of edges is intricately related to the shape or structure given to and taken by the material within its space. We will take note of placement of the scene, relative importance accorded to visuals, relationships among them, and so forth. Flowing from that consideration comes the plot of the work, such as can be discerned. What can we say about the plan of the actual artist, such as it can be recovered, discerned? What can we construe about the artist (actual or implied) of the particular work we will be examining, and what is to be said about outcomes the figures in the work are working to accomplish, or have accomplished? Finally, we will look at the figures involved, analogous to our work on characterization, to see how they are represented, and with what effect. As is true of the narrative we are reading, the visual representation is artificial, or fictive. With the presentation of pigment on canvas, the artist suggests and from that medium the viewer construes.[11]

2. Those matters re-angled With those points suggested, we can consider as well ways in which the visual work *differs* from the verbal one, challenging us to work with facets new to us. The most prominent difference to be exploited is the absence of a narrator. In the story we have read, we have been constantly informed by a narrator reliably providing material for us, to us. Though we remain with many choices, the narrator influences our consideration substantially. There is no equivalent in a painting. Absent as well is temporality, or at least temporality as imposed by the narrator of a verbal text. The graphic artist will make spatial choices about the subject matter, but how we will view the material, in what order, is not constrained. We read, to some extent, by establishing temporal order, inserting or imposing some sort of time on what we see:[12] "It is also this propensity to narrativize what we see that allows painters to achieve some of their most amusing and most troubling effects."[13] The artist will suggest the place from where the viewer engages the scene and direct his or her eyes to focalize it. Concomitantly, factors

10. Useful here are suggestions from art historian Leslie D. Ross, who has designed materials for assisting the analysis of works of art by those not trained to do so: "Looking at Art: Suggested Guidelines for Visual Analysis" (unpublished and unpaginated).

11. Dana Arnold, *Art History: A Very Short Introduction*, Very Short Introductions (Oxford: Oxford University Press, 2004), 91–93.

12. Abbott, *Cambridge Introduction*, 6–7.

13. Ibid., 9. He reminds us also (10) that the root of "narrative" includes knowing, telling, absorbing, and expressing knowledge.

that a narrator can leave somewhat abstract and nondetailed will be made tangible and particular in the visual art. If time is a favored implement of the wordsmith, space is a speciality of the worker-in-visuals. These and other differences in media open fresh questions for us to approach as well. What a literary narrative can suggest verbally will be rendered quite differently by a visual artist using color and line. Reading art, viewers are challenged to articulate their responses with the aid of diverse cues. Reading verbal and visual scenes together will enrich our understanding considerably.

3. Plausible referent: The narrative referent for the painting is plausibly and suitably drawn specifically from 2 Sam. 6–7, where after an apparently successful transfer of the Ark from its place at Kiriath-Jearim to Jerusalem, David proposes to Nathan the prophet that he will build a structure for it, a house (temple) for the deity whose Ark is "homeless." First encouraged and then rebuked for this initiative, we learn his response: "Then King David went in and sat before the LORD" conversing in prayer (2 Sam. 7:18). Conflated with these narrated scenes may also be moments before after the death of the infant son of David and Bathsheba where David prays before the deity (2 Sam. 12:16–20). Rather than split those Ark passages apart or choose one and discard the other, I will take them as related and as both implied in the painting, drawing as well on David's relationship with the God whose Ark is made central here.[14] In fact, the presence of the Ark prompts the consideration of its whole "life," accumulating across the biblical corpus. The scene, then, offers access to the question of David's capacity to learn compassion.

c Description of the Painting:

The painting, oil on canvas, measures sixteen by twenty-two inches (without its border). In roughly spatial terms, we can see that the top of the painting is only generally filled in with classic architectural elements, while the bottom is more cluttered with specific items. The left side of the work is filled with figures, while the right side is dominated simply by the Ark. The painting's background hints of a substantial structure, with columns and pillars suggested in the upper left hand portion, showing details of a classic building along the right-hand side of the scene, with several stairs ascending along the bottom of the work. The action thus takes place within a building, though clearly not within a worship site such as would have been typical of the appropriate biblical setting.

   Intercalated among the hard surfaces and firm edges of the building and various objects are the profusion of billowing cloths and of clouds or cultic smoke making its presence felt, serving to obscure the architecture a bit and lighten the darkness of the building's wood. Two large urn-like objects also fill in the background—one

---

14. If the work were not titled, it might be seen as representing King Hezekiah sharing his troubles before the ark, as narrated in Isaiah and 2 Kgs. 19:14–34. O'Kane, "Afterlives," 317–18, reminds us that a visual scene may well include or imply several episodes of a narrative.

on each side of the central space.[15] Along the bottom edge establishing the ascent to the Ark lies a cushion, draped across two steps, and a large harp, seeming to have been placed or dropped. Like the cushion, the instrument sprawls across steps.

On the left side of the painting are several figures. Two male adult figures confer, and a small boy is playing with a dog, though turning away from its face as it noses toward him. The boy seems to be looking at the back of the king. A priest attends, identified by the clothing he wears and the censer and chain he holds. Even though he could seem at home in such a scene, he seems extraneous to the main figure, behind the suppliant and turned to the side, looking at neither David nor the Ark. All seem casual in relation to the main figure, who is utterly intent on something the rest of them are, curiously, excluded from.

On the right side of the work is the Ark of the covenant, a golden chest with two cherubim, wings touching, on its cover as is described in the directions for the construction of worship apparatus (Exodus 25). The Ark rests on a firm and elevated table-like structure, with a white cloth, flowing down from beneath it to cover the base, allowing us to direct our attention to the Ark. A cloud of smoke billows between the Ark and the edge of the painting.

A triangle constructed by the priest, the Ark, and the king draws our focus to David, crowned, central to the painting. He is crouched or kneeling, with his cloak-like garment trailing behind and beneath him, obscuring the actual position of his legs. His arms are outstretched—not raised but extended horizontally, with fingers splayed—toward the Ark, which he faces. Art historian Franca Zava Boccazzi characterizes the space of the canvas as structured by the arms of the king and priest,[16] and I would suggest as well by the wings of the cherubim. She describes carefully the colors of the various garments: The gold-yellow cloak of the central figure flows from his gray and light-blue tunic. The priest wears his blue upper garment over a lilac robe. The conferring adult males are garbed in dark red and pale blue, the boy in blue-green dress. Close consideration of this clothing shows evidence of shades and tones of color subtly at play. The Ark or altar cloth is a white, emerging from colors of brown and ochre suited to its wooden material.[17]

King David's face is angled slightly as though responsive to deep emotion, as he yearns toward or implores the Ark in some way, for some response, his head twisted as he eyes the Ark. We glimpse only part of his face, white beard, and neck. Though the hair of his head is brown, his beard is white. Zava Boccazzi calls his demeanor vigorous and nervous (*robusta, e nervosa*).[18] The Ark is apparently nonresponsive. Art historian Alice Binion offers that Pittoni was more a skilled observer than an artist trained by a master, though he had studied earlier with

15. Though the point of the narrative is that the temple, as described in Exodus, does not yet exist, awaiting construction by David's son Solomon, the artist has made no effort to suggest how a pre-temple structure might have looked by consulting the biblical text. Historical realism is not the point.

16. Franca Zava Boccazzi, *Pittoni* (Venezia: Alfieri, 1979), 129.

17. Zava Boccazzi, *Pittoni*, 129.

18. Ibid.

his uncle. She characterizes his figures as having "dignified poses, grandiose gestures and elegant robes."[19] Others refer to "dignified poses, crisp handling of the drapery; warm transparent flesh painting; and clear, vivacious colour in which yellow plays an important part, ranging from dull yellow ochre to lemon yellow."[20] Before discussing the painting additionally, we need to move back to consider our last tool.

d Contribution of Theorist J. Cheryl Exum:

Exum is a professionally trained, experienced, and skilled biblical scholar who has become astute and fluent in the study of visual art and consequently in the interface of both media.[21] Her project, as she names it in various publications and as collaborators nuance it, is neither simply *art appreciation* nor the *reception* of the biblical text into another medium, useful as those two fields are as part of what pertains. Though the influence of *historical and social factors* is important to investigate—to catch an adequate sense of what a particular artist would plausibly have represented in his or her era[22]—for Exum, the interpreter's interest must include the *autobiographical* as well, exposing interests of all involved. But additionally she is interested to explore comprehensively the *interlocking* retellings and *afterlives* of Bible and art: both how biblical texts have influenced art and how art has influenced ways the Bible is read, whether readers are conscious of the direction of the influence or not.[23]

Her cluster of concerns can be specified and hedged by a set of questions: How does the text influence the art? How does art contribute to readings of the text, as famous and influential visual work likely surpasses textual data in the imaginations of many viewers? How does general cultural memory influence an artist, and how does art influence cultural memory? How might critically informed

---

19. Alice Binion, "Pittoni, Giambattista," in Jane Turner, ed., *The Dictionary of Art* (New York: Macmillan Publishers Limited, 1996, vol. 25, *Pittoni to Raphael*, 1–4): 2.

20. W.G. Constable and C.H.S. John, "The Italian Rococo at Cambridge," *The Burlington Magazine for Connoisseurs* 42.238 (January 1923): 48.

21. J. Cheryl Exum, *BibInt* 6.3 (1998): 259–65. She introduces and presents an edition of *BI* exploring these issues of representation and interpretation across media.

22. Hugh S. Pyper, "Love beyond Limits: The Debatable Body in Depictions of David and Jonathan," in J. Cheryl Exum and Ela Nutu, eds., *Between the Text and the Canvas: The Bible and Art in Dialogue* (Sheffield: Sheffield Phoenix Press, 2007), 39. An article in the same volume (80–94), Sally E. Norris, "The Imaginative Effects of Ezekiel's *Merkevah* Vision: Chagall and Eziekiel in Creative Discourse," demonstrates how much more information is available for interpretation when an artist's work is well known and thoroughly studied, as is the case with Chagall. It is valuable to note what we cannot attempt as well as what we can do.

23. J. Cheryl Exum, "Toward a Genuine Dialogue between the Bible and Art," in Martti Nissinen, ed., *Congress Volume Helsinki 2010*, VT Supp (Leiden, Boston: Brill, 2012), 473–503. This section is from 473–76.

and sophisticated biblical scholarship contribute to art? And how do skilled artists elucidate the interpretation of biblical texts?[24]

As she describes her general method as well as demonstrates it, drawing on various works of narrative and visual representation, Exum seeks a fuller dialogue between text and image, "a dialogue in which the biblical text and biblical art play an equal and critical role in the process of interpreting each other. . . . I want to know what a work of art can teach me about the text."[25] The flow of fresh insight goes both ways: from verbal to visual and from visual to verbal. Exum focuses specifically on how each artist is challenged to "tell the story," or in the case of the visual artist, to show the story. Subsumed are many other choices about what to include or omit from the reading. Exum names some of the differences between the media, indicating how differences will emerge.[26]

She is interested in narratives and paintings, as am I in the work under consideration here,[27] drawing on art historian Paolo Berdini to the effect that the painter reads the text and then translates his or her reading into a problem in representation, to which the artist suggests, depicts, a solution. The challenge is to stage or construct a dialogue between the two media, using the visual art as comment on the verbal as well as the inverse, making visual criticism part of the interpretive process. The interpreter will choose the central question and then bring it to bear on the art-reading-the-text. The astute reader will construct the representation of the problem. Exum says:

> For me, staging a meaningful dialogue between the text and the canvas is often a matter of identifying an interpretive crux—a conundrum, gap, ambiguity or difficulty in the text, a stumbling block for interpretation or question that crops up repeatedly in artistic representations of it—and following its thread as it knits the text and painting together in complex and often unexpected ways.[28]

24. Andrea M. Sheaffer, *Envisioning the Book of Judith: How Art Illuminates Minor Characters*, The Bible and Art in the Modern World (Sheffield: Sheffield Phoenix Press, 2014), 137, pays particular and sustained attention to ways in which verbal and visual aims intersect. She also calls attention to the intersection of character and plot in both media (7–9); her work with minor characters reminded me to query them in Pittoni's work, granted that we know from the text who is assisting Judith, while it is less clear from the text who might be with David as we view him.

25. Exum and Nutu, "Introduction," *Text and Canvas*, 1.

26. The point, she clarifies ("Beyond Horizon," 262), is not to blame the visual artist for not being a biblical expert, nor presumably not to expect the biblical scholar to become utterly proficient in another medium, but to see how collaboration can be fruitful.

27. Exum tends to explore multiple representations of a text in order to discern the consistent problems addressed. Here, for reasons practical as well as more general, I am simply discussing one text. On the other hand, the extensive study of the text presented here allows for a richness not always possible when the text is shorter or the investigation of its language briefer.

28. Exum, "Toward a Genuine Dialogue," 475.

She amplifies that the problem may be inherited from the text and identified by the artist, or it may be that visualization challenges identify a textual problem that both artists and the reader will work with. The issue is not whether the artist got the matter right or wrong. Exum lists an extremely useful set of questions that might be posed, from which I will select the best for me: Where and how is our attention drawn? What is ignored? Is there a gap in the text to which the artist responds? Does the art magnify a minor issue in the text? Point of view? Is the viewer included in the painting? How so? How are our assumptions challenged?[29] The issues raised by Exum and her work in this emerging field are closely aligned with the general hermeneutics on which this present project relies (though possibly not with the issues of spirituality that explicitly drive my interpretation), though she is, in her work, deeply concerned with making explicit and evaluating critically the ethics of a work, as constructed and as viewed.

O'Kane, approaching a bit differently, also adds to our agenda, reviewing briefly ways in which verbal and visual narratives collaborate, and suggesting that biblical narratives offer four particularly rich moments for depiction of words: pace, intersection worlds of the human and divine, the cyclic or comprehensive material on offer, and the old age, and even last moments of a dying person can be featured.[30] Slightly at an angle to Exum's more abstract points, he reminds us how much there is to observe and query as we read and view.

My choice of Pittoni's particular work as the single image for this study is responsive primarily to the content rather than to other considerations. There is a great deal of visual representation of David, and many of the works are presumably of finer quality or more interesting to view as intense relational dynamics catch the viewer's imagination. But since this study seeks specifically to construct the growth of David's compassion from his tendency to act arrogantly, and since the scenes involving the Ark are central to that matter, this work of Pittoni's serves as entry to the point I am developing.

3 Pittoni's David and 1–2 Samuel's David

a Reprise of David's Capacities

With our seventh tool now in hand, we can approach both the text under long consideration in this book and the single painting by Pittoni. The interpretation emerging from the study of the text has posed the question of David's capacity for compassion, claiming that amid the many positive qualities he clearly demonstrates and despite the many gifts and favors he has received from God—or

---

29. "Introduction," in Exum and Nutu, eds., *Between the Text and the Canvas*, 1–2. Exum's own contribution to the volume, "Shared Glory: Solomon de Bray's *Jael, Deborah and Barak*," specifies these questions on pp. 11–37 (11), which helps demonstrate the value of questions for helping us all see what can be probed.

30. O'Kane, "Afterlives," 313–24.

possibly resulting from such lavish attention from the deity—he falls into a pattern of arrogance and contempt, demonstrated by three main cultic occasions and possibly a fourth: When David claimed Jerusalem as his city rather than Hebron where he—inquiring—had been instructed to live; when he wrested the Ark of God from its place and installed it in the city of David; when he presumed to undertake the construction of a house for the Ark, a temple for the deity; less clearly when his census endangered the site of the future temple.[31] On each occasion, David initiates a cultic action, either without consultation or with inadequate inquiry, disregarding alternatives to his plans until he could no longer do so, given divine resistance to his plans. God is shown as permissive toward the chosen king in many ways, initially trying to dissuade him from these moves by gesture and eventually by direct verbal reproof. The more famous instance of David's contemptuous arrogation, his multiple violations of the persons and positions of Bathsheba and Uriah, costing eventually Uriah's life as well as that of the child so unlawfully conceived, was more an ethical and social matter rather than a distinctively cultic one, though not lacking ritual prescription. The complex set of offenses embedded in the Ammonite war demonstrated even more clearly the flaw in David under consideration here, showing us as well the refusal of YHWH to tolerate David's action. Its consequent outflow among David's children presents their father with further opportunities for response.

As discussed above, divine displeasure at David for his taking Jerusalem and removing the Ark from its place is not agreed to by all interpreters, since David's connection with Jerusalem—so entrenched in biblical materials—becomes difficult to question. The transfer of the Ark is similar, except that there is clear divine displeasure when a man dies during the first effort to move it, slowing but not deterring David. His second attempt seems to go more successfully, with only Michal to object to it—and her perspective on the matter is pretty thoroughly discredited by commentators, which again offers interpreters a point of disagreement.

If the David-as-contemptuously-arrogant image, consistently though not exclusively about cultic matters, can be plausibly suggested and developed, what about the character's capacity for compassion? When David was finally rebuked directly by prophetic word (rather than more implicitly and indirectly by gesture), he acceded at once. Both when God through Nathan unequivocally forbade him to build the house for the Ark and the deity and when the words of the same prophet rebuked him for his injustices against Bathsheba and Uriah, he accepted the charge without alibi, denial, or delay. So if shown to offend, he is also ready to repent, to turn to God even though his narrative disappointment has to be great.

The textual presentation shows him contrite, deeply so. But again as already suggested, David's willingness to own up to his fault does not help rectify it at all

---

31. Three of these passages cluster in 2 Sam. 5–7; the other narrative of David's over-reach with cultic overflow, as examined above, comes in the so-called appendix material, where he ends up negotiating with a Jebusite for the future site of the temple, which his son will erect.

or at once, nor does it remove the consequences of his actions. If his arrogance is checked, as seems to be the case, both the episodes involving worship sites and the long string of tragic events with his own children show him as suffering the results of his arrogance, as indeed they do as well, providing him space for compassion, if he has the capacity. Suffering can be, though need not be, a seedbed for growth in compassion, and David's struggle and eventual fruit can be seen in his refusal to make clear decisions and then at his grief at Absalom's death, the father's expressed willingness to die in place of his son. This is not easy or cheap compassion but the slow and uneven growth in love of others and the willingness to spend oneself, which characterize this profound change of heart. Only indirectly and subtly does the David storyteller expose the fundamentals of the process by which compassion and love may replace arrogance and contempt. The outcome is clearer than the process, and David's achieving compassion occurs late and remains narratively undeveloped.

b Mutual Interrogation: Narrative and Painting

With that fresh summary of work previously demonstrated at greater length, we turn to my specific construction of the visual presentation of David with the Ark of God. If text and canvas are to be brought into communication, what are the most appropriate questions to raise? If Exum's suggestions are to be fruitful, with what representation problem is Pittoni plausibly grappling? What crucial gaps do both visual and verbal media offer the viewer for negotiation, and specifically, what do they offer to this particular interpreter of a David shown struggling to grow away from arrogance and toward compassion? Some questions are offered here, related to and flowing from each other, in order to move in on the central visual challenge: First, how can we explore the encounter between the human David and the divine character YHWH, beyond the participation of the prophet Nathan? Nathan has been messenger between God and David in the verbal narrative but is absent visually. Even in the biblical narrative, the real issue of communication and contention is always between king and deity, even if their interaction is mediated. A major existential issue as well in verbal and visual art is the apt and accurate demonstration and discerning of God's desires.

Second, how can David's engagement with the Ark possibly be convincingly shown as intense, since the Ark, being visually, not verbally, responsive as a character, is offered as a stationary box? Why and how will we be drawn to read a fraught David engaging an inanimate structure? Third, how is the reader/viewer drawn into this encounter, not least since no other character seems engaged in it? The biblical narrative has presented the encounters as rare but clear enough, with God's words evoking narrated and discoursed repentance from David, though wordless at the illness and death of his and Bathsheba's child. A reader can overhear David and YHWH. But visually, with four other humans in the scene and none attentive to David and his evident concerns, how does a viewer connect? Is the lack of engagement of any other with David a specific prompt to consider his engagement with God, represented by the Ark? Fourth, who are the other human figures implied in the scene? Verbally, we can construe characters' identities and desires with at least partial clarity. But visually, this problem of identities and roles of other figures prompts us to query the biblical narrative for others who are conspicuously not involved in what is intense for David. Fifth, how will we read, draw out, and name the emotion or situation of David, engaging the deity through the Ark? If the press of Ark misadventures makes it a particular focus, what is David best (or well) understood to be asking or saying? And how do we infer the Ark's (and hence the deity's) responsiveness—easier in the narrative than in the visual? All these questions actually factor the dissonant aspects shared by the figure of the king and the Ark and between the other figures and King David, potentially thwarting to the reader/viewer. As we read these texts, verbal and visual, can we gain insight into David's capacity for compassion?

c Interpretation Claims

The characters shown on what is the viewer's left of Pittoni's work are incongruous, conspicuously so. To have a child and a dog present where the Ark of God dwells is startling, at least in biblical terms, as is the presence of two men talking evidently about something other than what concerns the king. So what shall we make of these other figures? They are all behind the king, not engaging him or the Ark, none even seeming concerned about what we see happening as king and Ark commune. The crowned figure with the censer is implied as priestly by his blue garment and by the incense he stands ready to offer, though he is doing nothing that contributes to the action of the king and the Ark, nor do they seem to require any priestly intervention. His censer does not emit smoke. The priest thus seems excluded from the scene, except he is there: tall, well-dressed, with arms that also catch the motion of the king's supplication and the cherubim-crowned Ark's rejoinder, such as it may be. The priests prominent in the verbal narrative are Elide scion Abiathar, who ultimately deserts David for Adonijah, and Zadok who remains loyal to David's side. Though in earlier days David was reliant upon the priest and an ephod (not a thurible) for communication with God, that is no longer the case, certainly not here. So this priestly figure is obsolete, otiose, to what David wants and needs, a possibility we can bring to the narrative.

The two men to the priest's right, at the left edge of the painting, are even less engaged with David than is the priest. The visual artist likely had little interest in these specific identities, since conventions of the period prompt the inclusion of such figures for artistic reasons. So the question is not about authorial intent but about readerly inference rising from the consideration of both verbal and visual texts. In the narratives that I am suggesting we see here, the likely referents for these two character are Joab and Abishai, David's nephews, the pair most consistently present in his life and adventures. It is possible to leave them unnamed, but since they are so conspicuously useless to the communication uniting king and Ark, they must be serving some purpose, even if a negative one. If they are suitably seen—by me, not intended by Pittoni—as Joab and Abishai, then they, also, are excluded from whatever is so engaging David, perhaps even planning something contrary to what their uncle has in mind and heart. The child with the dog invites an identity as well, and my best suggestion is that we see it as the young royal Absalom, also unconnected from David's prayer and petition here. David is thus isolated in this work, except as related with the Ark of God, whose response is difficult to read. The visual representation of David, isolated among peers, enriches consideration of the narrative where he seems to have withdrawn from or been abandoned by most human helpers as he struggles in God's presence with the results of his harmful actions.

Finally, and centrally, what is being offered and asked here, between these two main figures: king and Ark? What is offered to us, viewing and interpreting this primary engagement, specifically in view of the fact that none pictured in the scene seems attentive to it? If the priest is redundant, "Joab and Abishai" are communicating with each other, the dog is trying to engage "Absalom," who cannot see what his father is doing, we are driven to look at the Ark and the king.

There seems little doubt that the focus in the painting is on David's engagement with the Ark of God—these disparate figures catching our attention by dominating the space in the center of the canvas. Each is garbed in white and gold, one color cascading from the other, each inversely. David's outstretched arms and the wings of the *cherubim* atop the Ark match each other, though we know that David does not always extend his arms in prayer, while the Ark's angels always take that pose, matching the king's prayer, if involuntarily, though the gestures match David's. But the Ark is God's Ark, so "involuntary" is not quite the right adjective. Though David has his gaze fixed on the Ark, shown by the angle of his head and the eye we can see, the faces of the *cherubim* face each other. Though David's specific posture is not easy to see, due to the drapery of his garments, we can observe that he is not kneeling on the cushion that lies across the stairs, though he may have been doing so. Nor is he at present playing his harp, which seems cast down rather than placed more habitually, carefully. If David's cushion and harp can under different circumstances suggest ease or complacence, even opulence, their present abject position suggests the opposite.[32] So he can be seen as having broken off two more normal modes of communion with God to implore the Ark of God, arms spread, fingers intense, head bent, and body angled perhaps from a position on one knee on a stair.

Is David regretting his plans for the Ark, its being brought by him into a city he seized from the blind and the lame? Is he repenting his disregard for human life, lost when the Ark was taken from where it had been resting after a multitude of indignities? Can we construe the king as facing the arrogance of his own temple-building plans, announced to and approved by his prophet, until they are countered explicitly and at length by God? Is he, perhaps, recalling the devastation wrought and the danger threatening the future temple site, a consequence of his numbering Israel and Judah? Is David shocked and grieved at how seriously he

---

32. The lament of David for Saul and Jonathan offers a similar "visual" detail in naming the shield of Saul lying begrimed and desolate on the mount where the king lies dead (2 Sam. 1:21) David's harp, abandoned, suggests that he needs more than his harp can access.

had misconstrued God's plans about the city and Ark and temple?[33] Do we see David at prayer for the life of the child he has been told will die? Is David thus experiencing contrition, compunction, a firm desire to respond more graciously to what God might be wishing, to turn toward it?

David's feeling is intense, but how to name it? I resist Zava Boccazzi's "*robusta, e nervosa*," vigorous and nervous, at least the "nervous." The king's intensity is at odds with that of every other figure, drawing attention to it. He seems to be imploring, possibly explaining, presenting a desire for something. His feeling is clearly not joy or contentment, nor notably contrition. David seems to me to express something while asking something else, his arms extended both to lack and receive something. His white beard signifies that he has reached a certain age or experience, though he is still vital. His crown and clothing suggest his rank, but his posture marks him as an almost desperate suppliant. He is suitably attended, for a powerful man, but he is oblivious of all others, fixed on the Ark and its referent. It goes almost without saying that the deity is not imaged in the biblical narrative, with an intermediary of some sort making tangible the wishes of God. David, then, is deeply engaged, verbally and visually, seeking God's mercy and perhaps healing from his excesses. To specify precisely the textual referent of the scene is less important than seeing it as part of David's habitual response when he can see he has overreached. As David turns toward God, it is surely in the expectation that God's graciousness has already anticipated his move.

Does the Ark offer a response, and how so? To have the Ark visualized as an interlocutor is not so obvious, except in that it is—has been from 1 Samuel—a virtual character representing or reacting for the deity. So in the present construction of the narrative, if David's arrogance has been directed specifically at the Ark and it has suffered from his contempt and disregard for its persona, the Ark is not only a plausible focus for David but also the most suitable communication partner. Though in the verbal narratives implied in the painting, the Ark along with the deity enthroned there clearly has no formal housing since its loss from Shiloh, its catastrophe-laden travels in Philistia, its uncongenial return to Israel, and subsequent mistreatment and recuperation at Kiriath-Jearim, it has no permanent home in the city of David, where it is temporarily ensconced. It is shown here almost informally, with an imposing building suggested behind it but with a contrasting informality of space.

So is David's prayer answered—responded to by God—or not? How might a response be signified? Sheaffer provides crucial insight here, by calling attention to the cloud of smoke billowing forth from the Ark, toward the right of the scene as viewed. Its most obvious literary referent is the testimony about Moses and his intense participation with the deity, the narrator describing how, when Moses entered the tent where he conversed with God, the space filled with smoke, and all

---

33. I have more trouble thinking of it as David in prayer after the string of actions unleashed following his taking of Bathsheba, since that recourse of prayer seems more peaceful and reconciled than this painting suggests.

those observing understood that Moses and God were in intimate communion.[34] The implication, then, my inference activated, is that in this painting God is shown responsive to David's prayer, and he is mercifully responsive to the suppliant in the presence of the Ark, toward which he has, arguably, on more than one occasion acted arrogantly. David can thus be read as expressing regret for his arrogance, pleading for mercy, hoping for compassion to be both received and engendered in him. The biblical narratives assure us that David's contemptuous actions, when finally checked by the deity and then readily owned by the king, are forgiven. That David has more poor choices ahead of him does not make such a moment unlikely. To regret an action or a series of them and to be prompted to acknowledge a pervasive pattern do not mean it will not recur. But here, David is shown reassured of God's compassion for him, its reaching out to fill the space where David asks it. The compatibility of hearts, the strange resemblance between YHWH's being and David's self, invites us to see David leaning into the process of learning compassion through experiencing it, learning how to extend it by receiving it. That David's recovery from his excesses is occasional and partial is not a surprise.

Our framing both the narrative and the visual with considerations—edges, shapes, plotting, characterization, analogy—and in particular choosing a problem from representation have helped our reading distinctively. How does a human figure communicate intensively with what seems to be an object? How does a viewer engage such a scene? The narrative readies us for a deeper story than the art can show, but the art can stress a feature that lies obscured in the narrative: David's isolation and eagerness for a merciful response from God and granted it.

4 *Conclusions and Implications*

The wager with which I began my study—that textual David demonstrates a growing capacity for compassion—has proved more difficult to develop than I anticipated. But the challenge has driven me back to draw more deeply on the implications of the hermeneutical theory laid out in the first chapter of this work. Intentional engagement of a profound classic of the religious tradition shared by Christianity and Judaism allows and even prompts readers to explore more profoundly human experience offered in language—both verbal and visual—and to be changed by the experience of so doing. The character, David, has been drawn with significant complexity by an ancient writer of whom and whose historical/social circumstances we know little. It is literary tools used here

---

34. Sheaffer, private communication. The relevant biblical passage is Exod. 33:7–12. That the figure is Moses rather than David and that the Tent of Meeting is not really the ark's space seem to me provocative rather than confusing, an intertextual rhyme, so to speak, unimportant, as the artist is not aiming to be literally precise but suggestive. The smoke, coming from the ark and not from the priest's censer, is God's response to the central figure.

in careful, intentional reading that have brought him to life. Distinctive among other portraits offered, I argue, is my readerly construction of his struggles to live his narrative span, facing issues that are in one way or another familiar to other humans as well.

David, as constructed here, began his narrative life with many gifts and advantages, not least with qualities that drew others' love: good looks, musical skill, leadership qualities, and tact. Knowing that he had been anointed, David perhaps had only to wait for kingship to fall to him, but we watch him increasingly endangered as he bides his time. His patron, Saul, though once loving him, does not wish David well and seeks to thwart him. David is forbearing to a point, and then arguably snagged by the jealousy, taking from Saul's side many of his people. David accumulates war and bloodshed. His early trusting sense of God's care for him shifts, appropriately so, as his life seems to diverge from what he has been promised. But in time, while avoiding the temptation to kill Saul and protected by his consultation of God's desires for him, David succeeds to kingship.

Compassion is not much in evidence as David consolidates his position. Once he is king, the character David seems to abandon consultation, acting more unilaterally and with a certain arrogance and contempt for others' good, his placing his own apparent well-being over that of others being the opposite of compassion. I have suggested that YHWH supports and sustains David even in these moments, not least by setting limits to David's arrogation of cultic items and moments to and for his own purposes. David's heart remains capable of a certain simplicity or direct acknowledgment of his own deficiencies when challenged by God, and this tardy if unstinted admission of his sinfulness helps his process of conversion from contempt and turn toward compassion. But lest it seem easy, even with all the advantages David is shown to enjoy, the taking of another human for his own purposes seeds a vast chain of consequences that sends David into suffering—his own and that of others—caused, again, by his own ruthless selfishness. David's capacity for compassion seems to stall, to freeze, as he wallows in indecisiveness, lets it spread within his kingdom and among his family, notably toward his son Absalom, who replicates much of David's weaknesses without the grace attending his father, even amid all his troubles.

If we might hope that David's capacity to turn toward God who extends compassion to him will help with Absalom, we are disappointed. David's inconsistency with his son, along with his incapacity to ask for help or to respond wholeheartedly when it is offered to him, contributes to Absalom's tragic death and to more disarray in his family and kingdom. The grief and sorrow of the king and father at the death of his son emerge, too briefly, as all we glimpse of what David has learned of compassion through love and suffering—given and received—is reflected in a few heartfelt and heartbroken words. And the story turns from giving us greater exposure to what path the father of Absalom and the leader of Judah and Israel traveled to arrive at the moment where we see him clearly, briefly. That compassion is not easier will surprise few readers. Perhaps David has shown us enough, or it may be that we, reading him, have learned enough of compassion to appreciate the depth of what we can see.

The visual art, engaged with the verbal texts of David's intense communion with God, offers us the possibility that God continues to show love and presence to this fallible human, and if to him, perhaps to us as well. The biblical narrative of David is a profound story of a great human being, seriously flawed and yet also deeply loving. To engage it has been transformative over time for Jews and Christians who seek from it not primarily historical information or facile and stale allegory but deeper insight into the ways of the creator and his creatures.

Bibliography

Abbott, H. Porter. *The Cambridge Introduction to Narrative.* 2nd ed. Cambridge: University Press, 2008.

Adam, Klaus-Peter. "Nocturnal Intrusions and Divine Interventions on Behalf of Judah. David's Wisdom and Saul's Tragedy in 1 Samuel 26." *VT* 59 (2009): 1–33.

Alter, Robert. *The Art of Biblical Narrative.* New York: Basic Books, 1981.

Alter, Robert. *The David Story: A Translation with Commentary of 1 and 2 Samuel.* New York: W.W. Norton & Company, Inc., 1999.

Altes, Liesbeth Korthals. "Ethical Turn." In *The Routledge Encyclopedia of Narrative Theory*, edited by David Herman, Manfred Jahn, and Marie-Lauren Ryan, pp. 142–46. London and New York: Routledge Taylor & Francis Group, 2005.

Amit, Yairah. "'The Glory of Israel Does Not Deceive or Change His Mind': On the Reliability of Narrator and Speakers in Biblical Narrative." *Prooftexts* 12.3 (1992): 201–12.

Amit, Yairah. *Reading Biblical Narratives: Literary Criticism and the Hebrew Bible.* Minneapolis: Fortress Press, 2001.

Andersson, Greger. *Untamable Texts: Literary Studies and Narrative Theory in the Books of Samuel.* London: T. & T. Clark, 2010.

Assis, Elie. "Chiasmus on Biblical Narrative: Rhetoric of Characterization." *Prooftexts* 22 (2002): 273–304.

Arnold, Dana. *Art History: A Very Short Introduction.* Oxford: Very Short Introductions. Oxford University Press, 2004.

Avioz, Michael. "Divine Intervention and Human Error in the Absalom Narrative." *JSOT* 37.3 (2013): 339–47.

Bal, Mieke. *Narratology: Introduction to the Theory of Narrative.* Translated by Christine van Boheemen. Toronto: University of Toronto Press, 1980.

Baldick, Chris. *The Oxford Dictionary of Literary Terms.* 3rd ed. Oxford: Oxford University Press, 2008.

Bar-Efrat, Shimon. *Narrative Art in the Bible.* JSOTSup, 70. Sheffield: Almond Press, 1989.

Barnet, Sylvan. *A Short Guide to Writing about Art.* The Short Guide Series. 10th ed. Upper Saddle River, NJ: Pearson Press, 2011.

Barnhart, Joe E. "Acknowledged Fabrications in 1 and 2 Samuel and 1 Kings 1–2. Clues to the Wider Story's Composition." *SJOT* 20.2 (2006): 231–36.

Barry, Peter. *Beginning Theory: An Introduction to Literary and Cultural Theory.* Manchester: Manchester University Press, 1995.

Bennema, Cornelis. "A Theory of Character in the Fourth Gospel with Reference to Ancient and Modern Literature." *BI* 17 (2009): 375–89.

Bennema, Cornelis. *A Theory of Character in New Testament Narrative.* Minneapolis: Fortress Press, 2014.

Biddle, Mark E. "Ancestral Motifs in 1 Samuel 25: Intertextuality and Characterization." *JBL* 121.4 (2002): 617–38.

Binion, Alice. "Pittoni, Giambattista." In *The Dictionary of Art.*, vol. 25, *Pittoni to Raphael*, edited by Jane Turner, pp. 1–4. New York: Macmillan Publishers Limited 1996.

Birns, Nicholas. *Theory after Theory: An Intellectual History of Literary Theory from 1950 to the Early 21st Century.* Peterborough, Ontario: Broadview Press, 2010.

Bodner, Keith. *David Observed: A King in the Eyes of his Court.* Hebrew Bible Monographs 5. Sheffield: Sheffield Phoenix Press, 2005.

Bodner, Keith. *1 Samuel: A Narrative Commentary.* Hebrew Bible Monographs 19. Sheffield: Sheffield Phoenix Press, 2009.

Bodner, Keith. *The Artistic Dimension: Literary Explorations of the Hebrew Bible.* London: Bloomsbury T&T Clark, 2013.

Bodner, Keith. *The Rebellion of Absalom.* New York and London: Routledge, 2014.

Bodner, Keith and Ellen White. "Some Advantages of Recycling: The Jacob Cycle in a Later Environment," *BibInt* 22 (2014): 20–33.

Bosworth, David A. *The Story within a Story in Biblical Hebrew Narrative.* Catholic Biblical Quarterly Monograph Series 45. Washington, DC: Catholic Biblical Association of America, 2008.

Bosworth, David A. "Faith and Resilience: King David's Reaction to the Death of Bathsheba's Firstborn." *CBQ* 73 (2011): 691–707.

Boyle, Marjorie O'Rourke. "The Law of the Heart: The Death of a Fool (1 Samuel 25)," *JBL* 120.3 (2001): 401–27.

Brenner, Athalya, ed. *Samuel and Kings: A Feminist Companion.* The Feminist Companion to the Bible, Second Series 7. Sheffield: Sheffield Academic Press, 2000.

Bright, John. *A History of Israel.* 3rd ed. Philadelphia: Westminster, 1972.

Brooks, Peter. *Reading for the Plot: Design and Intention in Narrative.* Cambridge, MA: Harvard University Press, 1984.

Brooks, Peter. "Narrative Desire." In *Narrative Dynamics: Essays on Time, Plot, Closure, and Frames*, edited by Brian Richardson, pp. 130–37. Columbus: Ohio State University Press, 2002.

Brueggemann, Walter. "Narrative Intentionality in 1 Samuel 29." *JSOT* 43 (1989): 21–35.

Bruner, Jerome. *Actual Minds, Possible Worlds.* Cambridge, MA and London: Harvard University Press, 1986.

Bullough, Geoffrey, ed. *Narrative and Dramatic Sources of Shakespeare*, 8 vols. London: Routledge & Kegan Paul, 1957–75.

Burns, Ken. *The Civil War.* Aired September 23–27, 1990. Florentine Films, WETA TV. DVD.

Burnside, Jonathan. "Flight of the Fugitive: Rethinking the Relationship between Biblical Law (Exodus 21:12–14) and the Davidic Succession Narrative (1 Kings 1–2)." *JBL* 129.3 (2010): 418–31.

Campbell, Antony F., S.J. "The Reported Story: Midway between Oral Performance and Literary Art." *Semeia* 46 (1989): 77–85.

Campbell, Antony F., S.J. "Structure Analysis and the Art of Exegesis (1 Samuel 16.14–18.30)." In *Problems in Biblical Theology: Essays in Honor of Rolf Knierim*, edited by Henry T.C. Sun and Rolf Knierim, pp. 76–103. Grand Rapids, MI and Cambridge, UK: William B. Eerdmans Publishing Co., 1997.

Čapek, Filip. "David's Ambiguous Testament in 1 Kings 2:1–12 and the Role of Joab in the Succession Narrative." *Communio Viatorum* 52 (2010): 4–26.

Carrard, Philippe. "September 1939: Beginnings, Historical Narrative, and the Outbreak of World War II." In *Narrative Beginnings: Theories and Practices*, edited by Brian Richardson, pp. 63–78. Lincoln and London: University of Nebraska Press, 2008.

Chatman, Seymour. *Story and Discourse: Narrative Structure in Fiction and Film*. Ithaca: Cornell University Press, 1978.

Chisholm, Robert B., Jr. "Cracks in the Foundation: Ominous Signs in the David Narrative." *BSac* 172 (April–June 2015): 154–76.

Clay, Diskin. "Plato's First Words." In *Beginnings in Classical Literature*, edited by Francis Dunn and Thomas Cole, pp. 113–30. Cambridge: Cambridge University Press, 1992.

Clines, David J. A. "What Remains of the Hebrew Bible? Its Text and Language in a Postmodern Age." *ST* 54 (2011): 76–95.

Craig, Kenneth M., Jr. "The Characterization of God in 2 Samuel 7:1–17." *Semeia* 63 (1993): 159–76.

Craig, Kenneth M., Jr. "Rhetorical Aspects of Questions Answered with Silence in 1 Samuel 14:37–28:6." *CBQ* 5 (1994): 221–39.

Craig, Kenneth M., Jr. *Asking for Rhetoric: The Hebrew Bible's Protean Interrogative*. Biblical Interpretation Series 73. Boston, Leiden: Brill Academic Publishers, Inc., 2005.

Cohn, Dorrit. *Transparent Minds: Narrative Modes for Presenting Consciousness in Fiction*. Princeton: Princeton University Press, 1978.

Constable, W. G. and C. H. S. John. "The Italian Rococo at Cambridge." *The Burlington Magazine for Connoisseurs* 42.238 (January 1923): 46–49, 53.

Cuddy-Keane, Melba. "Virginia Woolf and Beginning's Ragged Edge." In *Narrative Beginnings: Theories and Practices*, edited by Brian Richardson, pp. 96–112. Lincoln: University of Nebraska Press, 2008.

Dällenbach, Lucien. *The Mirror in the Text*. Translated by Jeremy Whiteley and Emma Hughes. Cambridge, UK: Polity Press, 1989.

Dannenberg, Hilary P. "'Plot' and 'Plot Types'." In *Routledge Encyclopedia of Narrative Theory*, edited by David Herman, Manfred Jahn, and Marie-Laure Ryan, pp. 435–40. London and New York: Routledge, 2005.

Dannenberg, Hilary P. *Coincidence and Counterfactuality: Plotting Time and Space in Narrative Fiction*. Lincoln: University of Nebraska Press, 2006.

Davies, Philip R. *The Origins of Biblical Israel*. Library of Hebrew Bible, Old Testament Studies 485. London: T&T Clark, 2007.

Davies, Philip R. *Memories of Ancient Israel: An Introduction to Biblical History—Ancient and Modern*. Louisville: Westminster John Knox, 2008.

DeLapp, Nevada Levi. *The Reformed David(s) and the Question of Resistance to Tyranny: Reading the Bible in the 16th and 17th Centuries*. London: Bloomsbury T&T Clark, 2014.

Derouchie, Jason. "The Heart of Yhwh and His Chosen One in 1 Samuel 13:14." *Bulletin for Biblical Research* 24 (2014): 467–89.

Dunn, Francis M. "Introduction: Beginning at Colonus." In *Beginnings in Classical Literature*, edited by Francis Dunn and Thomas Cole, pp. 1–12. Cambridge: Cambridge University Press, 1992.

Edelman, Diana. *King Saul in the Historiography of Judah*. JSOTSup 121.Sheffield: Sheffield Academic Press, 1991.

Edenburg, Cynthia. "How (Not) to Murder a King: Variations on a Theme in 1 Samuel 24; 26." *SJOT* 12. 1 (1998): 64–85.

Esler, Philip F. "David, Bathsheba, and the Ammonite War (2 Samuel 10–12)." In *Sex, Wives, and Warriors: Reading Old Testament Narrative with Its Ancient Audience*, edited by Esler, pp. 303–21. Cambridge, UK: James Clarke & Co., 2011.

Eslinger, Lyle. *House of God or House for David: The Rhetoric of 2 Samuel 7*. JSOTSup 255. Sheffield: JSOT Press, 1996.

Exum, J. Cheryl. "Bathsheba Plotted, Shot, and Painted." *Semeia* 74 (1996): 47–73.

Exum, J. Cheryl. "Beyond the Biblical Horizon: The Bible and the Arts." *BibInt* 6.3 (1998): 259–65.

Exum, J. Cheryl. "Toward a Genuine Dialogue between the Bible and Art." In Congress Volume Helsinki 2010, VT Supp., edited by Martti Nissinen, pp. 473–503. Leiden, Boston: Brill, 2012.

Exum, J. Cheryl. "Shared Glory: Solomon de Bray's *Jael, Deborah and Barak.*" In *Between the Text and the Canvas: The Bible and Art in Dialogue*, edited by J. Cheryl Exum, and Ela Nutu, pp. 11–37. Sheffield: Sheffield Phoenix Press, 2007.

Exum, J. Cheryl, and Ela Nutu, eds. *Between the Text and the Canvas: The Bible and Art in Dialogue*. Sheffield: Sheffield Phoenix Press, 2007.

Exum, J. Cheryl, and Ela Nutu. "Introduction." In *Between the Text and the Canvas: The Bible and Art in Dialogue*, edited by J. Cheryl Exum, and Ela Nutu, pp. 1–2. Sheffield: Sheffield Phoenix Press, 2007.

Finkelstein, Israel, and Neil Asher Silberman. *David and Solomon: In Search of the Bible's Sacred Kings and the Roots of the Western Tradition*. New York: Free Press, 2006.

Firth, David G. "The Accession Narrative (1 Samuel 27–2 Samuel 1)." *Tyndale Bulletin* 58.1 (2007): 61–83.

Forster, E. M. "Story and Plot." In *Narrative Dynamics: Essays on Time, Plot, Closure, and Frames*, edited by Brian Richardson, pp. 71–72. Columbus: Ohio State University Press, 2002.

Fowler, Don. "Second Thoughts on Closure." In *Classical Closure: Reading the End in Greek and Latin Literature*, edited by Deborah H. Roberts, Francis Dunn, and Don Fowler, pp. 3–22. Princeton: Princeton University Press, 1997.

Fusillo, Massimo. "How Novels End: Some Patterns of Closure in Ancient Narrative." In *Classical Closure: Reading the End in Greek and Latin Literature*, edited by Deborah H. Roberts, Francis Dunn, and Don Fowler, pp. 209–27. Princeton: Princeton University Press, 1997.

Fokkelman, J. P. *Narrative Art and Poetry in the Books of Samuel*: I. *King David (2 Sam. 9–20 and 1 Kgs 1–2)*. Assen: Van Gorcum, 1981.

Fokkelman, J. P. *Narrative Art and Poetry in the Books if Samuel*: II. *The Crossing Fates (1 Sam. 13–31 and 2 Sam. 1)*. Assen: Van Gorcum, 1986.

Fokkelman, J. P. *Narrative Art and Poetry in the Books if Samuel*: III. *Throne and City (2 Sam. 2–8 and 21–24)*. Assen: Van Gorcum, 1990.

Fokkelman, J. P. "The Samuel-Composition as a Book of Life and Death." In *For and Against David: Story and History in the Books of Samuel*, edited by A. Graeme Auld, and Erik Eynikel, pp. 15–46. Leuven: Uitgeverij Peeters, 2010.

Ganzevoort, R. Ruard. "Introduction: Religious Stories We Live By." In *Religious Stories We Live By: Narrative Approaches in Theology and Religious Studies*, edited by R. R. Ganzevoort, Maaika de Haardt, and Michael Scherer-Rath, pp. 1–17. Leiden, Boston: E. J. Brill, 2014.

Genette, Gérard. *Narrative Discourse: An Essay in Method*. Translated by Jane E. Lewin. Ithaca: Cornell University Press, 1980.

George, Andrew R. *The Epic of Gilgamesh: The Babylonian Epic Poem and Other Texts in Akkadian and Sumerian*. London: Penguin Books, 1999.

George, Mark. "Fluid Stability in Second Samuel." *CBQ* 64 (2002): 17–36.

George, Mark. "Yhwh's Own Heart." *CBQ* 64 (2002): 442–59.

Geyer, Marcia L. "Stopping the Juggernaut: A Close Reading of 2 Samuel 20.13–22". *USQR* 41 (1987): 33–42.

Grabbe, Lester L. "Reflections on the Discussion." In *Enquire of the Former Age: Ancient Historiography and Writing the History of Israel*, edited by Lester L. Grabbe, pp. 263–75. London & New York: T&T Clark International, 2012.

Gray, Mark. "Amnon: A Chip off the Old Block? Rhetorical Strategy in 2 Samuel 13.7–15: The Rape of Tamar and the Humiliation of the Poor." *JSOT* 77 (1993): 39–54.

Green, Barbara. *How Are the Mighty Fallen? A Dialogical Study of King Saul in 1 Samuel.* JSOTSup 365. Sheffield: Sheffield Academic Press, 2003.

Green, Barbara. "The Engaging Nuances of Genre: Reading Saul and Michal Afresh." In *Relating to Text: Interdisciplinary and Form-Critical Insights on the Bible*, edited by Timothy J. Sandoval, and Carleen Mandolfo, pp. 141–59. London and New York: T&T Clark International, 2003.

Green, Barbara. "Enacting Imaginatively the Unthinkable: 1 Samuel 25 and the Story of Saul." *BibInt* 11.1 (2003): 1–23.

Green, Barbara. "Experiential Learning: The Construction of Jonathan in the Narrative of Saul and David." In *Bakhtin and Genre Theory in Biblical Studies*, edited by Roland Boer, pp. 43–58. Atlanta, GA: SBL Press, 2007.

Greenstein, Edward L. "The Riddle of Samson." *Prooftexts* 1 (1981): 237–60.

Grossman, Jonathan. "The Design of the 'Dual Causality' Principle in the Narrative of Absalom's Rebellion." *Bib* 88 (2007): 558–66.

Gunn, David M. *The Story of King David: Genre and Interpretation.* JSOTSup 6. Sheffield: JSOT Press, 1978.

Gunn, David M. "From Jerusalem to the Jordan and Back: Symmetry in 2 Samuel 15–20." *VT* 30.1 (1980): 109–13.

Halpern, Baruch. *David's Secret Demons: Messiah, Murderer, Traitor, King.* Grand Rapids, MI: William B. Eerdmans Publishing Co., 2001.

Hamilton, Mark W. "At Whose Table? Stories of Elites and Social Climbers in 1–2 Samuel." *VT* 59 (2009): 513–32.

Henze, Matthias, ed. *A Companion to Biblical Interpretation in Early Judaism.* Grand Rapids, MI: William B. Eerdmans Publishing Co., 2012.

Herman, David, James Phelan, Peter J. Rabinowitz, Brian Richardson, and Robyn Warhol, *Narrative Theory: Core Concepts and Critical Debates.* Columbus: Ohio State University Press, 2012.

Herman, Luc, and Bart Vervaeck. *Handbook of Narrative Analysis.* Frontiers of Narrative Series. Lincoln, NE: University of Nebraska Press, 2001.

Hill, Andrew E. "On David's 'Taking' and 'Leaving' Concubines (2 Samuel 5:13; 15:16)." *JBL* 125.1 (2006): 129–39.

Hochman, Baruch. *Character in Literature.* Ithaca: Cornell University Press, 1985.

Hogan, Patrick Colm. *The Mind and Its Stories.* Cambridge: Cambridge University Press, 2003.

Holub, Robert C. *Reception Theory: A Critical Introduction.* New Accents. New York: Methuen, 1984.

Holub, Robert C. *Crossing Borders: Reception Theory, Poststructuralism, Deconstruction.* Madison: University of Wisconsin Press, 1992.

Jahn, Manfred. "Focalization." In *Routledge Encyclopedia*, edited by David Herman, Manfred Jahn, and Marie-Lauren Ryan, pp. 173–75. London and New York: Routledge Taylor & Francis Group, 2005.

Janzen, David. "The Condemnation of David's 'Taking' in 2 Samuel 12:1–14." *JBL* 131.2 (2012): 209–20.

Jasper, David. *A Short Introduction to Hermeneutics.* Louisville: Westminster John Knox, 2004.

Jobling, David. *1 Samuel*. Berit Olam Studies in Hebrew Narrative and Poetry. Collegeville, MN: Liturgical Press, 1998.

Johnson, Benjamin J. M. "The Heart of YHWH's Chosen One in 1 Samuel." *JBL* 131.3 (2012): 455–66.

Johnston, Gordon H. "The Enigmatic Genre and Structure of the Song of Songs," Part One. *BibSac* 166.662 (April–June 2009): 36–52.

Kafalenos, Emma. "Implied Reader." In *The Routledge Encyclopedia of Narrative Theory*, edited by David Herman, Manfred Jahn, and Marie-Lauren Ryan, pp. 240–41. London and New York: Routledge Taylor & Francis Group, 2005.

Kafalenos, Emma. *Narrative Causalities*. Theory and Interpretation of Narrative. Columbus: Ohio State University Press, 2006.

Keefe, Alice A. "Rapes of Women/Wars of Men." *Semeia* 61 (1993): 79–97.

Keen, Suzanne. *Narrative Form*. Hampshire: Palgrave Macmillan, 2003.

Kim, Uriah. *Identity and Loyalty in the David Story: A Postcolonial Reading*. Sheffield: Sheffield Phoenix Press, 2008.

Kleiner, Fred S., Christin J. Mamiya, and Richard G. Tansey. *Helen Gardner's Art through the Ages*. 11th ed. Fort Worth: Harcourt College Publishers, 2001, 719–21.

Klement, Herbert H. *II Samuel 21–24. Context, Structure and Meaning in the Samuel Conclusion*. Europäische Hochschulschriften, Reihe 23 Theologie, vol. 682. Frankfurt: Peter Lang, 2000.

Koenig, Sara M. *Isn't This Bathsheba? A Study in Chracterization*. Eugene, OR: Pickwick Publishers, 2011.

Kruschwitz, Jonathan A. "2 Samuel 12:1–15: How (Not) to Read a Parable." *RevExp* 109 (2012): 253–59.

Lamarque, Peter. "The Intentional Fallacy." In *Literary Theory and Criticism*, edited by Patricia Waugh, pp. 177–88. An Oxford Guide. Oxford: Oxford University Press, 2006.

Leander, Niels Buch. "To Begin with the Beginning: Nabokov and the Rhetoric of the Preface." In *Narrative Beginnings: Theories and Practices*, edited by Brian Richardson, pp. 15–28. Lincoln: University of Nebraska Press, 2008.

Leitch, Vincent. "Reader-Response Criticism." In *Readers and Reading*, edited by Andrew Bennet, pp. 32–65. Longman Critical Readers. London and New York: Longman, 1995.

Leslie D. Ross, "Looking at Art: Suggested Guidelines for Visual Analysis" (unpublished and unpaginated).

Levenson, Jon D. "1 Samuel 25 as Literature and History." *CBQ* 40 (1978):11–28.

Lundbom, Jack R. *Jeremiah 1–20: A New Translation with Introduction and Commentary*. AB 21A. New York: Doubleday, 1999.

Lundbom, Jack R. *Biblical Rhetoric and Rhetorical Criticism*. Hebrew Bible Monographs 45. Sheffield: Sheffield Phoenix Press, 2013.

Lyke, Larry L. *King David with the Wise Woman of Tekoa: The Resonance of Tradition in Parabolic Narrative*. JSOTSup 255. Sheffield: JSOT Press, 1997.

Matthews, Victor H., and Don C. Benjamin. "Amnon and Tamar: A Matter of Honor (2 Samuel 12:1–38)." In *Crossing Boundaries and Linking Horizons: Studies in Honor of Michael C. Astour on His 80th Birthday,* edited by Gordon D. Young, Mark W. Chavalas, Richard E. Averback with the assistance of Kevin L. Danti, pp. 339–66. Bethesda, MD: CDL Press, 1997.

McCarter, P. Kyle. *1 Samuel: A New Translation with Introduction, Notes, and Commentary,* AB 9. Garden City, NY: Doubleday, 1980.

McCracken, Randy L. "How Many Sons Did Absalom Have? Intentional Ambiguity as Literary Art." *BibSac* 172 (July–September 2015): 286–98.

McKenzie, Steven L. *King David: A Biography*. Oxford: Oxford University Press, 2000.

McKenzie, Steven L. "Elaborated Evidence for the Priority of 1 Samuel 26." *JBL* 129.3 (2010): 437–44.

Morrison, Craig E. *2 Samuel*. Berit Olam: Studies in Hebrew and Narrative Poetry. Collegeville, MN: The Liturgical Press, 2013.

Morson, Gary Saul, and Caryl Emerson. *Mikhail Bakhtin: Creation of a Prosaics*. Stanford: Stanford University Press, 1990.

Murnaghan, Sheila. "Equal Honor and Future Glory: The Plan of Zeus in the *Iliad.* " In *Classical Closure: Reading the End in Greek and Latin Literature*, edited by Deborah H. Roberts, pp. 23–42. Francis Dunn, and Don Fowler. Princeton: Princeton University Press, 1997.

Murray, Donald F. *Divine Prerogative and Royal Pretension: Pragmatics, Poetics and Polemics in a Narrative Sequence about David (2 Samuel 5.17–7.29)*. Sheffield: Sheffield Academic Press, 1998.

Nelles, William. *Frameworks: Narrative Levels and Embedded Narrative*. New York: Peter Lang, 1997.

Nichol, George G. "The Death of Joab and the Accession of Solomon: Some Observations on the Narrative of 1 Kings 1–2." *SJOT* 7.1 (1993): 134–51.

Nightingale, Andrea. "Mimesis: Ancient Greek Literary Theory." In *Literary Theory and Criticism: An Oxford Guide*, edited by Patricia Waugh, pp. 37–47. Oxford: Oxford University Press, 2006.

Norris, Sally E. "The Imaginative Effects of Ezekiel's *Merkevah* Vision: Chagall and Eziekiel in Creative Discourse." In *Between the Text and the Canvas: The Bible and Art in Dialogue*, edited by J. Cheryl Exum, and Ela Nutu, pp. 80–94. Sheffield: Sheffield Phoenix Press, 2007.

Nünning, Ansgar. "Implied Author." In *The Routledge Encyclopedia of Narrative Theory*, edited by David Herman, Manfred Jahn, and Marie-Lauren Ryan, pp. 239–40. London and New York: Routledge Taylor & Francis Group, 2005.

O'Connell, Robert H. *Concentricity and Continuity: The Literary Structure of Isaiah*. JSOTSup 188. Sheffield: Sheffield Academic Press, 1994.

O'Connell, Robert H. *The Rhetoric of the Book of Judges*. VT Supplements 63. Leiden and New York: Brill, 1996.

O'Connor, Michael Patrick. "War and Rebel Chants in the Former Prophets." In *Fortunate the Eyes that See: Essays in Honor of David Noel Freedman in Celebration of His Seventieth Birthday*, edited by Astrid B. Beck, Andrew H. Bartelt, Paul R. Raabe, and Chris A. Franke, pp. 322–37. Grand Rapids: William B. Eerdmans Publishing Co., 1995.

O'Kane, Martin. "The Biblical King David and his Artistic and Literary Afterlives." *BibInt* 6.3–4 (1998): 313–47.

Olson, S. Douglas. *Blood and Iron: Stories and Storytelling in Homer's Odyssey*. New York, Leiden, Koln: E.J. Brill, 1995.

Palmer, Richard E. *Hermeneutics*. Northwestern University Studies in Phenomenology and Existential Philosophy. Evanston, IL: Northwestern University Press, 1969.

Paris, Christopher T. *Narrative Obtrusion in the Hebrew Bible*. Emerging Scholars. Minneapolis, MN: Fortress Press, 2014.

Pedrick, Victoria. "The Muse Corrects: The Opening of the *Odyssey.* " In *Classical Closure: Reading the End in Greek and Latin Literature*, edited by Deborah H. Roberts, Francis Dunn, and Don Fowler, pp. 39–62. Princeton: Princeton University Press, 1997.

Perdue, Leo. "'Is There Anyone Left of the House of Saul...?' Ambiguity and the Characterization of David in the Succession Narrative." *JSOT* 30 (1984): 67–84.

Petersen, David L. "Portraits of David: Canonical and Otherwise." *Interpretation* 40 (1986): 130–42.

Phelan, James. *Reading People, Reading Plots: Character, Progression, and the Interpretation of Narrative.* Chicago: University of Chicago Press, 1989.

Phelan, James. "Narrative Progression." In *Narrative Dynamics: Essays on Time, Plot, Closure, and Frames*, edited by Brian Richardson, pp. 211–16. Theory and Interpretation of Narrative Series. Columbus: Ohio State University Press, 2002.

Phelan, James. "The Beginning of *Beloved*: A Rhetorical Approach." In *Narrative Beginnings: Theories and Practices*, edited by Brian Richardson, pp. 195–212. Lincoln: University of Nebraska Press, 2008.

Phelan, James, and Peter Rabinowitz. "Time, Plot, Progression." In *Narrative Theory: Core Concepts and Critical Debates,* edited by David Herman, James Phelan, Peter J. Rabinowitz, Brian Richardson, and Robyn Warhol, pp. 57–65. Columbus: Ohio State University Press, 2012.

Pleins, David J. "Son-Slayers and Their Sons." *CBQ* 54 (1992): 29–38.

Polzin, Robert M. *Samuel and the Deuteronomist: A Literary Study of the Deuteronomic History.* II. *1 Samuel.* San Francisco: Harper & Row, 1989.

Polzin, Robert M. *David and the Deuteronomist: A Literary Study of the Deuteronomic History.* III. Bloomington: Indiana University Press, 1993.

Porter, Stanley E., and Jason C. Robinson. *Hermeneutics: An Introduction to Interpretive Theory.* Grand Rapids, MI: William B. Eerdmans Publishing Co., 2011.

Propp, William H. "Kinship in 2 Samuel 13." *CBQ* 55 (1993): 39–53.

Pyper, Hugh S. *David as Reader: 2 Samuel 12:1–15 and the Poetics of Fatherhood.* Leiden: E.J. Brill, 1996.

Pyper, Hugh S. "Love beyond Limits: The Debatable Body in Depictions of David and Jonathan." In *Between the Text and the Canvas: The Bible and Art in Dialogue*, edited by J. Cheryl Exum, and Ela Nutu, pp. 38–59. Sheffield: Sheffield Phoenix Press, 2007.

Rabinowitz, Peter. "Reading Beginnings and Endings." In *Narrative Dynamics: Essays on Time, Plot, Closure, and Frames*, edited by Brian Richardson, pp. 300–13. Theory and Interpretation of Narrative Series. Columbus: Ohio State University Press, 2002.

Reis, P. T. "Collusion at Nob: A New Reading of 1 Samuel 21–22." *JSOT* 61 (1994): 59–73.

Reis, P. T. "Killing the Messenger: David's Policy or Politics?" *JSOT* 31.2 (2006): 167–91.

Reventlow, H.G. *History of Biblical Interpretation.* I. *From the Old Testament to Origen.* Translated by Leo G. Perdue. Atlanta: SBL Press, 2009.

Reventlow, H.G. *History of Biblical Interpretation.* II. *From Late Antiquity to the End of the Middle Ages.* Translated by James O. Duke. Atlanta: SBL Press, 2009.

Richardson, B. "General Introduction." In *Narrative Dynamics: Essays on Time, Plot, Closure, and Frames*, edited by Brian Richardson, pp. 1–7. Theory and Interpretation of Narrative Series. Columbus: Ohio State University Press, 2002.

Richardson, B. "Introduction: Openings and Closure." In *Narrative Dynamics: Essays on Time, Plot, Closure, and Frames*, edited by Brian Richardson, pp. 251–55. Theory and Interpretation of Narrative Series. Columbus: Ohio State University Press, 2002.

Richardson, B. "Introduction: Narrative Beginnings." In *Narrative Beginnings: Theories and Practices*, edited by Brian Richardson, pp. 6–10. Lincoln: University of Nebraska Press, 2008.

Richardson, B. "Origins, Paratexts, and Prototypes." In *Narrative Beginnings, Theories and Practices*, edited by Brian Richardson, pp. 11–14. Lincoln: University of Nebraska Press, 2008.

Richardson, B. "A Theory of Narrative Beginnings and the Beginnings of 'The Dead' and *Molloy.*" In *Narrative Beginnings, Theories and Practices*, edited by Brian Richardson, pp. 113–130. Lincoln: University of Nebraska Press, 2008.

Ricoeur, Paul. *Freud and Philosophy: An Essay on Interpretation.* Translated by Denis Savage. New Haven: Yale University Press, 1970.

Ricoeur, Paul. *Time and Narrative.* I. Translated by Kathleen McLaughlin, and David Pellauer. Chicago and London: University of Chicago Press, 1984.

Ricoeur, Paul. "Narrative Time." In *Narrative Dynamics: Essays on Time, Plot, Closure, and Frames*, edited by Brian Richardson, pp. 35–46. Theory and Interpretation of Narrative Series. Columbus: Ohio State University Press, 2002.

Rimmon-Kennan, S. *Narrative Fiction: Contemporary Poetics.* 2nd ed. New York: Methuen, 2002.

Roberts, Deborah H. "Afterword: Ending and Aftermath, Ancient and Modern." In *Classical Closure: Reading the End in Greek and Latin Literature*, edited by Deborah H. Roberts, pp. 251–73. Francis Dunn, and Don Fowler. Princeton: Princeton University Press, 1997.

Römer, Thomas C. *The So-Called Deuteronomistic History: A Sociological, Historical and Literary Introduction.* New York: T&T Clark, 2007.

Ryan, Marie-Laure. "Stacks, Frames, and Boundaries." In *Narrative Dynamics: Essays on Time, Plot, Closure, and Frames*, edited by Brian Richardson, pp. 366–86. Theory and Interpretation of Narrative Series. Columbus: Ohio State University Press, 2002.

Ryan, Marie-Laure. "Cheap Plot Tricks, Plot Holes, and Narrative Design." *Narrative* 17.1 (2009): 56–75.

Sakenfeld, Katharine D., ed. "Khesed." In *The New Interpreter's Dictionary of the Bible*, vol. 3, *I–Ma.*, edited by Katharine D. Sakenfeld, pp. 495–96. Nashville: Abingdon Press, 2008.

Sakenfeld, Katharine D. "Love in the OT." In *The New Interpreter's Dictionary of the Bible*, vol. 3, *I–Ma.*, edited by Katharine D. Sakenfeld, pp. 713–18. Nashville: Abingdon Press, 2008.

Schipper, J. "'Why Do You Still Speak of Your Affairs?' Polyphony in Mephibosheth's Exchange with David in 2 Samuel." *VT* 54.3 (2004): 344–51.

Schipper, J. "'Significant Resonances' with Mephibosheth in 2 Kings 25:27–30: A Response to Donald F. Murray." *JBL* 124.3 (2005): 521–29.

Schneiders, Sandra M. *The Revelatory Text: Interpreting the New Testament as Sacred Scripture.* 2nd ed. Collegeville, MN: Liturgical Press, 1999.

Scholes, R., James Phelan, and Robert Kellogg. *The Nature of Narrative.* 40th anniversary ed. Oxford: Oxford University Press, 2006.

Sellars, Dawn M. "An Obedient Servant? The Reign of King Saul (1 Samuel 13–15) Reassessed." *JSOT* 35.3 (2011): 317–38.

Sheaffer, Andrea M. "Judith Versus Goliath? Visualizing David as Archetype." *Arts* 25.3 (2014): 5–14.

Sheaffer, Andrea M. *Envisioning the Book of Judith: How Art Illuminates Minor Characters.* The Bible and Art in the Modern World. Sheffield: Sheffield Phoenix Press, 2014.

Shemesh, Y. "David in the Service of King Achish of Gath: Renegade to His People or a Fifth Column in the Philistine Army?" *VT* 57 (2007): 73–90.

Shen, D. "Story-Discourse Distinction." In *The Routledge Encyclopedia of Narrative Theory*, edited by David Herman, Manfred Jahn, and Marie-Lauren Ryan, pp. 566–68. London and New York: Routledge Taylor & Francis Group, 2005.

Shereen, Faiza W. "Form, Rhetoric, and Intellectual History." In *Literary Theory and Criticism*, edited by Patricia Waugh, pp. 233–44. An Oxford Guide. Oxford: Oxford University Press, 2006.

Shields, M. "A Feast Fit for a King: Food and Drink in the Abigail Story." In *The Fate of King David: The Past and Present of a Biblical Icon,* edited by Tod Linafelt, Claudia V. Camp and Todd Beal, pp. 38–54. New York and London: T&T Clark, 2010.

Simon, U. "The Poor Man's Ewe Lamb: An Example of a Juridical Parable." *Biblica* 48 (1967): 207–42.

Smith, Mark S. *Poetic Heroes: Literary Commemorations of Warriors and Warrior Culture in the Early Biblical World.* Grand Rapids and Cambridge: William B. Eerdmans Publishing Co., 2014.

Smith, Richard G. *The Fate of Justice and Righteousness during David's Reign: Rereading the Court History according to 2 Samuel 8:51b–20:26.* New York and London: T&T Clark, 2009.

Smith, Wilfred C. *What Is Scripture?: A Comparative Approach.* Minneapolis, MN: Fortress Press, 1993.

Sternberg, M. *The Poetics of Biblical Narrative: Ideological Literature and the Drama of Reading.* Bloomington: Indiana University Press, 1985.

Stiebert, J. *Fathers and Daughters in the Hebrew Bible.* Oxford: Oxford University Press, 2013.

Suleiman, S. R., and I. Crossman. *The Reader in the Text: Essays on Audience Interpretation.* Princeton: Princeton University Press, 1980.

Thiselton, Anthony C. *Hermeneutics: An Introduction.* Grand Rapids: William B. Eerdmans, 2009.

Tomashevsky, B. "Story, Plot, and Motivation." In *Narrative Dynamics: Essays on Time, Plot, Closure, and Frames*, edited by Brian Richardson, pp. 164–78. Theory and Interpretation of Narrative Series. Columbus: Ohio State University Press, 2002.

Toorn, Karel van der. "Speaking of Gods, Dimensions of the Divine in the Ancient Near East." In *Open-mindedness in the Bible and Beyond: A Volume of Studies in Honour of Bob Becking*, edited by Marjo C.A. Korpel, and L. L. Grabbe, pp. 273–85. Library of Hebrew Bible/Old Testament Studies v. 616. London: Bloomsbury T&T Clark: 2015.

Vandergriff, K. "Re-Creating David: The David Narratives in Art and Literature." *RevExp* 99 (Spring 2002): 193–205.

Vandiver, E. *Greek Tragedy.* Chantilly, VA: The Teaching Company, 2000. DVD.

Vanhoozer, Kevin J. *Biblical Narrative in the Philosophy of Paul Ricoeur: A Study in Hermeneutical Theology.* Cambridge: Cambridge University Press, 1990.

Vargon, S. "The Blind and the Lame." *VT* 46.4 (1996): 498–514.

Wesselius, J. W. "Joab's Death and the Central Theme of the Succession Narrative (2 Samuel 11–1 Kings 2)" *VT* 40.3 (1990): 336–51.

Walsh, Jerome T. *1 Kings.* Berit Olam: Studies in Hebrew and Narrative Poetry. Collegeville: The Liturgical Press, 1996.

Walsh, Jerome T. *Style and Structure in Biblical Hebrew Narrative.* Collegeville, MN: The Liturgical Press, 2001.

Walsh, Jerome T. *Old Testament Narrative: A Guide to Interpretation.* Louisville: Westminster John Knox, 2009.

Warhol, R. "Character." In *Narrative Theory: Core Concepts and Critical Debates*, edited by David Herman, James Phelan, Peter J. Rabinowitz, Brian Richardson, and Robyn Warhol, pp. 119–24. Columbus: Ohio State University Press, 2012.

Waugh, P. "Introduction: Criticism, Theory, and Anti-Theory." In *Literary Theory and Criticism*, edited by Patricia Waugh, pp. 1–33. An Oxford Guide. Oxford: Oxford University Press, 2006.

Willey, Patricia K. "The Importunate Woman of Tekoa and How She Got her Way." In *Reading between Texts: Intertextuality and the Hebrew Bible*, edited by Danna Nolan Fewell, pp. 115–31. Louisville, KY: Westminster John Knox Press, 1992.

Wolde, Ellen van. "A Leader Led by a Lady: David and Abigail in 1 Samuel 25." *ZAW* 114 (2002): 355–75.

Wong, G. C. I. "Who Loved Whom? A Note on 1 Samuel 16:21." *VT* 47 (1997): 554–56.

Zava Boccazzi, F. *Pittoni*. Venezia: Alfieri, 1979.

Zimmermann, J. "*Quo Vadis*? Literary Theory beyond Postmodernism." *Christianity and Literature* 53.4 (2004): 495–519.

INDEX

Abbott, H. Porter   17
Abiathar   93, 95, 97, 151, 177, 222, 237,
    243, 249, 250, 257, 289
    see also Jonathan (son of Abiathar)
Abigail   100, 101, 102–5, 109, 121, 129,
    130, 165
Abimelech   39, 40, 41
Abinadab   43, 131
Abishai   106–7, 145, 152, 190, 192, 224,
    230, 231, 238, 242, 243, 247
    visual narrative/representation
        289–90
    see also Joab
Abner   49, 61, 107, 140, 145
    allegiance to David   141–2, 173, 176,
        191–2
    Asahel killed by   141, 173, 174, 176,
        191, 254–5
    characterization of   172–4
    David opposed by   141
    David's mourning for   143, 173, 192
    David's negotiations with, for Michal's
        return   170
    death of   142–4, 174, 175, 176, 180,
        184, 192, 255
    Ishbosheth made king by   140, 168
    and Ishbosheth's quarrel over
        Rizpah   141–2, 144, 166–7, 168,
        172–3
    Joab's charges against   191
    and Saul   172
ab ovo narrative beginnings   35–6
Absalom   50, 51, 205–6, 216, 276
    Ahithophel's counsel to   225–7, 273
    allies of   237, 241
    Amnon killed by   207–8, 218, 271–2
    appearance of/hair of   213, 231
    David's conflicting feelings
        towards   208–9, 218, 271–3, 276
    David's injunction as to   230, 231,
        241, 245

David's mourning for   234–6, 245–6,
    269–70, 273
death of   229–32, 241, 245, 248, 255
death of, reported to David   232–5
flight/exile and return of   208–14,
    218–19, 272–3
Hushai's counsel to   225, 227–8, 229,
    273
Joab's desire for return of   210–13, 214,
    218, 229
and rape of Tamar   206, 218
revolt of   219–24, 244, 269, 273
as usurper   219–20
visual narrative/representation   290
Absalom's monument   232
Achish   88–9, 108, 115, 119–23
    characterization of   121–2, 123
    support to David   125–7
    see also Philistines
Adonijah   42–3, 274
    death of   51, 248, 257
    as usurper   93 n.71, 249, 250, 251–3
adultery
    David and Bathsheba   194–8, 215,
        270–1, 279, 287
    David and Bathsheba, God's rebuke
        of   197, 198, 199–202, 215, 270–1,
        287
affective fallacy   12, 13–14
Ahimaaz   222, 232–4
    see also Zadok
Ahimelech   85–8, 90, 91–4, 112
Ahinoam (daughter of Ahimaaz)   165
Ahinoam of Jezreel   56, 104, 105, 119,
    121, 129, 130, 142, 167, 180, 205
    characterization of   165–6
Ahithophel the Gilonite   220–1
    counsel to Absalom   225–7, 273
    and God   226
    suicide of   228–9, 269
Alter, Robert   151, 175, 208

Amalekites   116, 119, 122
  David's campaign against   129, 130,
    133
  raid of Ziklag   129
Amasa   229, 237, 241, 242
  death of   242–3, 247–8, 255
Ammonites   287
  David's diplomats insulted by
    190, 269
  defeat of   190–1, 193
Amnon   121, 165, 166, 180, 216
  Absalom's plans to revenge
    against   206–8
  death of   207–8, 218, 271–2
  rape of Tamar by   205–7, 218, 276
ancient classics   157–8
  and characterization   158
  endings/conclusions of   37–8
  real authors of   16–17
  see also narrative/narrativity
Aphek   129, 165
Aquinas, Thomas, Saint   23
Araunah the Jebusite   156, 267, 268
Aristotle   5 n.12, 157
  categories of   23
  on literary criticism   4–5
  on narrative endings   36–7
Ark
  brought to Jerusalem by David   146–8,
    149, 180, 265–6
  David and Michal's conflict over   147–8,
    171–2, 215, 266
  and David's flight from Jerusalem   222
  David's temple plans and God's
    opposition   148–50, 178–9, 180–1,
    266–7
  and God   147, 148, 172, 178, 179,
    180–1, 265–6
  visual narrative/representation   283–4,
    290–1
Armoni   166
armor-bearer(s)
  David as, to Saul   58, 59, 132, 136, 263
  and Jonathan's death   40, 90
  and Saul's death   40, 131, 132, 133,
    134, 135–7
Asahel   143, 145
  death of   141, 142, 173, 174, 176, 191,
    254–5

author(s)
  implied author   9, 17–18, 34, 66, 74,
    113, 161 n.47, 163
  real/actual author   16–17, 113, 163
  triad of text, reader and   14–15
authorial intention   114

Baanah   145, 168, 180
Bakhtin, Mikhail   118
baroque   278, 279, 280
  notion of   278 n.2
Barthes, Roland   9
Barzillai   240, 245, 256, 258, 269
Bathsheba
  adultery with David   194–8, 215,
    270–1, 279, 287
  death of first son with David   203–4, 287
  ewe image of   199–202
  Solomon's birth   204
  and Solomon's succession   249–51
beginning (of narratives)   20, 33–6, 184
  ab ovo   35–6
  of Bible   34
  of David narrative   33, 36, 42–4, 52,
    65, 185
Benaiah   151, 243, 249, 250, 258
Benjamin (tribe)   41–2, 90–1, 142, 168
Bennema, Cornelis   160–1
Berdini, Paolo   285
Bible
  beginning and ending of   34
  narrative structure of   47

OLD TESTAMENT

Judges (Judg.)
6–9   40
19–21   41–2

1 Samuel (1 Sam.)   2–3, 17
8–12   48
8–15   52–5
13–16   48
13:14   261–3
16–18   55–65, 66–8
16:7   261–3
17–19   48–9
19–26   69–109
19:1–7   80
19:8–10   80–1

19:11–17	81	15:13–33	221–23
19:18–24	81–2	15:32–16:13	223–4
20–23	49	16:15–17:23	224–9
20:1–42	82–5	16:15–17:14	225–8
21:1–22:23	85–94	17:15–23	228–9
23	94–7	17:24–18:18	229–30
23–26	49	17:24–19:1	229–35
24	98–100	18:19–33	232–5
25	100–6	19:1–26	235–7
26	106–8	19:17–24	238–9
27–29	119–28	19:17–41	238–41
27:1–28:2	119–23	19:23–31	239–40
27–31	49, 115–37	19:32–41	240–1
28:3–25	123–5	19:41–20:3	241–2
29	125–8	19:41–20:22	241–3
30	129–31	20:4–22	242–3
30–31	128–35	21–24	51, 139–40, 151–7,
31	131–32		180–1
		21:1–14	151–2
2 Samuel (2 Sam.)	2–3, 17	21:15–22	152–3
1	49, 115–19, 132–5	22	153–4
2–8	139–51, 180–1	23:1–7	154
2:1–5:5	49–50	23:8–39	154
2:1–11	140–1	24:1–25	154–7
2:12–32	141		
3:1–21	141–2	*1 Kings (1 Kgs.)*	
3:22–39	142–4	1	249–53
4:1–11	144–5	1–2	51, 247–76
5:1–5	145–6	2	253–9
5:6–16	156	2:1–12	253–7
5:6–8:18	50	2:13–27	257
5:17–25	146	2:28–35	258
6:1–22	146–8	2:36–46	259
7:1–17	148–50		
7:18–25	150–1	biblical study	
8:1–18	151	adaptation of literary study to 13	
9–12	50	*see also* Hermeneutics	
9:1–13	186–9	Binion, Alice 283–4	
9–14	183–216	Birns, Nicholas 7	
10:1–19	189–93	Bloom, Harold 9	
11	193–8	Bodner, Keith 85–6, 88, 91, 96, 176	
12	198–205	Booth, Wayne C. 9	
12:26–31	189–93	Bosworth, David A. 100	
13	205–9	Brooks, Peter 76	
13–14	50	Bruner, Jerome 73	
14	209–14	Burke, Kenneth 73	
15–20	50–1, 217–46		
15:1–12	219–21	Cambridge University (UK) 5, 5 n.14, 6–7	
15:1–16:3	219–24	Cassirer, Ernst 24	
		causality of narratives 77–8, 85	

census   155, 176, 180, 268
characters and characterization   157–8, 184
   of Abner   172–4
   of Ahinoam of Jezreel   165–6
   categories of   160–1
   construction of   20
   in *David Before the Ark of the Covenant*   289–90
   in David narrative   186
   and David's capacity for compassion   180–1
   at discourse level   161–2
   focalization   162–4
   of God   176–9
   of Ishbosheth   167–9
   of Joan   174–6
   of Michal   169–72
   narrating characters   17, 64, 66–7, 162
   narrators' attitude to   114, 119, 121
   nature of   159–60
   plotting of   108–9
   reading of   160
   of Rizpah   166–7
   spectra of   164–5
   at story level   161
   terminology   159
chiastic structure   70–1, 72, 146 n.12, 151
Chileab   272
Chimham   240, 256
clothing and goods
   in *David Before the Ark of the Covenant*   283
   offered to David   60–1, 62, 134, 263, 264
   see also ephod
compassion/love, *see hesed*; *hesed* (David's)
context of narratives   77
   see also functional polyvalence
critical literary biblical study   7–8
critical theory   8–9
cultural criticism   9–10

David   41
   "alibi in Being"   118, 119–23, 127–8, 135–7
   anointed as future king   36, 48, 55, 57–8, 69, 83, 105, 109, 140
   arrogance of   4, 94
   in baroque and rococo art   280

boyhood to manhood   60–1, 67
capacity for compassion/goodness, *see hesed*; *hesed* (David's)
concubines of   221, 225–6, 242, 269, *see also* David: wives of
clothing and goods offered to   60–1, 62, 134, 263, 264
death/end of   44, *see also* David, as king: last wishes of
and death of first son with Bathsheba   203–4, 287
dishonesty and duplicity of   127–8, 136
early postbiblical interpretation of   279
first quoted speech of   61
as hero   59–62
and Ishbosheth contrasted   141
leadership challenged   129, 130, 136
madness feigned by   88, 121–2
passivity of   58–60, 67, 244
refuge with Samuel   81–2
in Renaissance art   279–80
and Saul compared   130–1
sons of   141, 146, 172, 208, 209, 244, 271–2, 274, *see also* Absalom; Adonijah; Amnon; Solomon
wives of   141, 146, *see also* Abigail; Ahinoam of Jezreel; Bathsheba; David: concubines of; Michal
see also David Before the Ark of the Covenant; God; Saul
David, as king
and Absalom's allies   237, 241
active/decisive/skilled leadership of   137, 221–4, 230, 241, 243, 248, 250–1, 257, 274
adultery of   194–8, 215, 270–1, 287
aging king   248, 249
anointed as king of Israel   145–6
Araunah's threshing floor bought by   156, 267, 268
Ark brought to Jerusalem by   146–8, 149, 180, 265–6
arrogance of   146–7, 149–50, 157, 180, 184, 186, 189, 194, 198, 201, 202, 203, 204–5, 244, 265–8, 270–1, 275, 286–7
in art   277
capacity for compassion/goodness, *see hesed*; *hesed* (David's)

310 *Index*

census ordered by 155, 176, 180, 268
complicity in key deaths 180, 184, 215, 265
complicity with/indulgence of his sons 205–8, 218, 274, 276
contemptuous of God and others 202–3, 215, 217, 244, 275
court officials of 151, 243
escape across Jordan River 228
famine ended by 151–2
flight from Jerusalem 221–3
Hushai's valorous account of 227
Ishbosheth's assassins condemned by 145, 168
Jerusalem captured by 146, 265
Jerusalem reclaimed by/journey back to 238–41
and killing of Saulide sons 152, 166
last wishes of 248, 253–9
later deeds of 151–7
length of reign 257
plague ended by 155–7
Saul's bones reburied by 152
Shimei's curse against 224, 256–7, 269
sins of 202–3, 215, 217–18
and Tekoa woman 210–13, 215, 218
temple plans of 148–50, 266
weakness/passivity/irresoluteness of 205–14, 215–16, 240, 242, 243, 244–5, 247–8, 274, 275, 276
see also Absalom; God; Joab
David Before the Ark of the Covenant (Pittoni) 277, 286–92
characters and characterization in 289–90
description of 282–4
narrative referent for 282
Pittoni's David 286–8
David narrative
beginning of 33, 36, 42–4, 52, 65, 185
characterization in 186
dating of 277
ending/conclusion of 38, 44–5, 65, 185, 247
interpretations of 1–4
literary structures of 70–2
macrostructure of 47–51
and narrative analogy 275–6
narrator's challenges in 115–16

and narrator's properties 118–19, 186
narrator's reticence in 121, 122, 131 nn.29–30, 152, 154, 167, 170, 170 n.62, 175, 186, 193–4, 232
narrator's skills in 119–21, 125–6
plotting of 185–6
structure of 65–6, 185
and type-scene 275
"who knows what" 75, 90–2, 95–7
see also characters and characterization; *David Before the Ark of the Covenant*
delayed exposition 35–6, 86 n.46, 91, 93 n.72
Derrida, Jacques 8, 9, 29
disjunction 46–7
Doeg the Edomite 86–8, 91, 92, 93, 112

Eli 42–3, 53, 57 n.59, 65, 85, 93, 108
Elkanah 42, 43
ending (of narratives) 33–4, 36–8, 184
of ancient classics 37–8
Aristotle on 36–7
of Bible 34
of David narrative 38, 44–5, 65, 185, 247
see also David, as king: last wishes of
ephod 87, 92, 93, 95, 96, 97, 105, 109, 124, 129, 130, 177, 264, 289
events 15, 75, 79–80
exegesis 22 n.45
extradiegetic narrator 17, 56–7, 64, 66, 114, 118, 162
Exum, J. Cheryl 284–6, 288

fabula vs. sjuzhet 73
famine 151–2
Fish, Stanley 10, 12–13
focalization 162–4
Fokkelman, Jan 47, 59, 70–2, 115, 116, 128, 139, 141, 145, 146, 148, 151, 208–9, 248
Forster, E. M. 73
Foucault, Michel 8–9
Fowler, Don 37
fratricide 207, 212, 217, 218, 272
see also Absalom; Amnon
Freud, Sigmund 8
Frye, Northrop 6

functions
    functional polyvalence   77–8
    ten-function chart   78, 98–100
Fusillo, Massimo   37

Gad   155, 177
Gadamer, Hans Georg   27–9, 31
gaps (narrative)   76–7, 109, 288
Gath   115, 259
    David at   119–23
    giants of, defeated by David   152–3
    see also Goliath
Genette, Gérard   76
Gibeonites   151–2, 166
Gideon   39, 40, 41
Gilboa   129, 131–2, 133, 135, 136–7, 152, 167
Gilgamesh, Epic of   34 n.3, 38 n.24
God   23, 52–3, 105
    and Absalom's return   214
    and Absalom's revolt   222, 224, 228, 229
    and Ark   147, 148, 172, 178, 179, 180–1, 265–6
    characterization of   176–9
    choice of David   55–7, 67–8, 148, 172, 177, 180, 261, 263–4
    choice of Saul   36, 58, 95, 98–9, 107
    communication/consultation with   56–7, 91
    David helped/favoured by   94, 96, 97, 108, 109, 124–5, 180, 244, 261–3, 275–6, 287, 288–9
    David opposed/rebuked by   180–1, 184, 197, 198, 199–202, 215, 265–8, 270–1, 287
    David's accomplishments under the guidance of   151, 152, 198–9
    David's communication/consultation with   95, 96, 98, 140, 157, 177, 188
    David's contempt of   202–3, 215, 217, 244
    and David's flight from Jerusalem   224
    David's obedience to   146, 181, 274, 287–8
    David's praise of   150–4
    David's temple plans for   148, 266
    David's temple plans for, rejected by   149–50, 178–9, 180–1, 266–7

    famine sent by   151–2
    "fictive"   159
    involvement/interference of   112, 177–8
    and kingship   177
    mutual graciousness of David and   263–4
    plague sent by   155–7
    priests' access to   177
    as primary agent   157, 179
    prophets' access to   177
    and Samuel   56–7, 177, 199
    and Saul   54–5, 94, 95, 96, 124–5, 136
    speaks through Nathan   149, 177, 179
    spirit of   57, 58, 82
    unexplained anger of, David's response to   154–5, 267–8
Goliath   60–1, 64, 65, 68, 69, 107, 121, 169, 174, 279
    sword of   61, 87–8, 89, 91, 92, 93, 263
    see also Gath; Philistines

Hannah   43, 108, 153
Hanun   190, 193, 215, 269
Hebrew Bible   46, 158
    historicity issues   159
    see also Bible
Hebrew poetic tradition   5
Hebron   140, 141, 175, 180, 265
    Absalom at   220
    David anointed as King of Israel at   145–6
Heidegger, Martin   27, 28, 30, 31
hermeneutics   21–2
    development of   22–4
    distanciation   31
    surplus of meaning   31
    theoretical background of   26–32
    turn to language   24–6
    and visual art   278–84
    see also Exum, J. Cheryl
hesed
    David as object of   62, 67, 71, 81, 82, 109, 170–1, 263
    narrative analogy   275–6
    notion of   262
hesed (David's)
    and adultery   194, 201, 204–5, 215, 270–1, 287

and Ammonites   190, 215, 241, 269
and Ark   146–7, 149–50, 180, 184,
    265–8
burial of Saul and sons   167
capacity for   59, 180–1, 183–4, 232,
    241, 244–6, 260, 292–4
complicity in key deaths   180, 184,
    215, 265
complicity with/indulgence of his
    sons   205–8, 218, 274, 276
dishonesty towards Achish/
    Philistines   127–8, 136, 137
injunction as to Absalom   230, 231,
    241, 245
lack of   4, 94, 137, 157, 189, 201, 202,
    203, 204–5, 215–16, 244, 265–71,
    275, 286–7
love for Absalom   234–6, 245–6,
    269–70, 273
mutual graciousness of God and
    David   263–4
recompensation of Barzillai   240, 256,
    258, 269
to Saul   140, 167
search for and invitation to
    Mephibosheth   186–9, 215, 269
unfair treatment of concubines   242,
    269
unfair treatment of Mephibosheth
    215, 223, 239, 240, 269
Uriah's betrayal   194–7, 270, 287
in visual medium/representation   277,
    288–92
Hiram   146
historiography   13
Hochman, Baruch   159, 161
Homer   36, 38
Hophni   65, 93
Hushai the Archite   223
    counsel to Absalom   225, 227–8, 229,
    273

Iliad (Homer)   36, 38
implied authors   9, 17–18, 34, 66, 74, 113
    and dynastic kingship   163
    and focalization   163
    vs. narrators   161 n.47
implied readers   17, 19
intended readers   17

intentional fallacy   13–14
Iser, Wolfgang   10–11, 12, 76
Ishbosheth   40, 44, 134
    and Abner's quarrel over Rizpah   141–2,
        144, 166–7, 168, 172–3
    assassination of   144–5, 168, 180
    burial of   169
    characterization of   167–9
    crowned king by Abner   140, 168, 254
    and David contrasted   141
    David's negotiations with, for Michal's
        return   170
    Gilboa survival of   167
    inadequacy of   141–2, 144, 168–9
Israel   174, 237
    David anointed king of   145–6
    schism between Judah and   241–3
    see also Absalom: revolt of; Jerusalem
Ittai   221–2, 230, 231

Jahn, Manfred   164
Jedidiah, *see* Solomon
Jehoiachin   44
Jehoshaphat   151
Jeremiah the Prophet   54
Jeroboam   44
Jerubbaal, *see* Gideon
Jerusalem   155–6, 180, 267, 268
    Ark brought to   146–8, 149, 180,
        265–6
    captured by David   146, 265
    David's flight from   221–3
    reclaimed by David   238–41
Jesse   55, 56, 57, 58, 61, 84, 90, 91
Jesus   176, 177
Joab   51, 141, 151, 174, 247
    and Abner's exchange of
        accusations   191, 254–5
    Abner killed by   142–3, 144, 174, 175,
        176, 192, 255
    Absalom killed by   230–3, 241, 245
    Absalom's burning of fields of   214
    Absalom's reconciliation with David
        sought by   210–13, 214, 216, 218,
        229
    accusations against Abner   173, 191–2
    Amasa killed by   242–3, 247–8, 255
    Amasa replaces   242, 245, 247, 255
    Ammonites defeated by   190–1, 193

and census taking   155, 176
characterization of   174-6
in *David Before the Ark of the
    Covenant*   289-90
David's curse against   143, 180, 192-3,
    255
and David's mourning for
    Absalom   235-6, 245, 269-70
David spares the life of   145
David's warning to Solomon
    about   174, 254-6
death of   258
first appearance of   254
illicit killings of   175, 254-6, 274-5,
    see also Joab: Abner killed by; Joab:
    Amasa killed by
lack of/spared from royal
    reproach   243, 245
and Sheba's revolt   242-3
support for Adonijah   249, 250, 258
and Uriah's death   194-5, 196-7, 198
and wise women   210-13, 215, 218
see also Abishai
Johnson, Samuel   6
Jonadab   208
and rape of Tamar   205-6
Jonathan (son of Abiathar)   42, 222, 252
see also Abiathar
Jonathan (son of Saul)   66-7, 87
"Abigail-the-Jonathan"   102-5, 109
as advocate for David to Saul   48, 70,
    71, 72, 80
Ammonites defeated by   190-1, 193
David as "brother" of   56, 65, 69, 135,
    263
David offered royal equipment
    by   62, 67
David's ascertainment of Saul's aim
    through   82-5
David's lament for   49, 134, 135
and David's last encounter   96-7
David's promise of loyalty to, and his
    heirs   186, 187-9, 239-40, 269
death of   41, 131
and Saul   40, 53, 90, 96
sons of   144, 152, 189, *see also*
    Mephibosheth
Jordan River   228, 240
Josiah   44

Judah   174, 237, 247
    schism between Israel and   241-3
    see also Absalom: revolt of
judges   52, 53, 54
    see also Gideon; Samson; Samuel

Kafalenos, Emma   73, 74, 77-8, 79, 98, 108
Keen, Suzanne   73, 161
Kellogg, Robert   20
kings/kingship   38-9, 65
    choice of David   55-7, 67-8, 172, 177,
        180, 261, 263-4
    choice of Saul   36, 58, 95, 98-9, 107
    emergence of/Pre-David   39-41, 51-5
    and God   177-8
    and implied authors   163
    "mad king" identity   88-9
    motifs of   39-42
    see also Absalom: revolt of; Achish;
        David, as king; Ishbosheth; Saul

Leavis, F. R.   6
literary criticism
    affective fallacy   12, 13-14
    ancient theorists   4-5
    challenges   13-15
    character construction   20
    critical theory   8-9
    cultural criticism   9-10
    "deconstruction"   9
    intentional fallacy   13-14
    modernity   5-8
    New Criticism/Practical Criticism   6-7,
        8, 11
    reader theory   10-13
    repeating, refracting plot elements   20
    "resolved symbolic"   7
    tools   15-20
    see also hermeneutics
literary gaps, *see* gaps (narrative)
literary structures   70-2
    see also narrative structures
loyalty, *see* hesed; hesed (David's)

Malchishua   131
Manoah   43
Marx, Karl   8
meaning   20
    "indeterminacy"   11, 12

surplus of meaning   31
  see also hermeneutics
Mephibosheth   134, 152, 169, 174
  accusations against Ziba   239
  characterization of   187–8
  David's unfair treatment of   215, 223,
    239, 240, 269
  David's search for and invitation
    to   186–9, 269
  obeisance to David   187, 188
  references to   186–7
  see also Jonathan (son of Saul)
Merab   56, 63, 66, 152, 166
  see also Michal
metaphor   30
Mica   187, 269
  see also Jonathan (son of Saul);
    Mephibosheth
Michal   68, 166
  assistance in David's escape from
    Saul   71, 81, 82, 109, 170–1, 263
  betrothal/marriage to David   56, 63–4,
    67, 68, 69, 84, 94, 122, 169–70
  characterization of   169–72
  childlessness of   148, 152 n.21, 171,
    180
  conversation with David   61 n.72
  and David's conflict over Ark   147–8,
    171–2, 215, 266
  David's loss of   104, 105
  given to Palti   170
  love for David   63, 64, 66, 169
  return to David   142, 170, 180
mise-en-abŷme   45, 53, 98, 100, 260, 261,
    264

Nabal   100–5, 144, 165
Nahash   190, 215
narratee   18
narrating characters   17, 64, 66–7, 162
narrative/narrativity   15–20, 160
  ab ovo beginnings   35–6
  ambiguities and gaps   76–7, 109
  beginnings of   20, 33–6
  context of   77
  delayed exposition   86 n.46, 91
  endings of   33–4, 36–8
  functional polyvalence   77–8
  and time   20, 30–1

narrative analogy   260–1, 275
narrative causality   77–8, 85
narrative obtrusion/deferral   96, 97
narrative structures   45–7, 184
  chiastic pattern   70–1, 72
  of David narrative   47–51, 65–6,
    185
  mise-en-abŷme   45, 53, 98, 100
  repetition   46, 61, 79, 108
  of Saul narrative   55–7
  and visual art   281
  see also literary structures; story/
    discourse distinction
narrator(s)   17–18
  absence in visual art   281–2
  adequacy of   114, 118–19
  attitude of   115, 119
  basic tasks of   114
  challenges to, in David narrative
    115–16
  and characters/characterization
    161–2
  extradiegetic narrator   17, 56–7, 64,
    66, 114, 118, 162
  and mode of presentation   115
  overlap/"tile", capacity to   112, 114
  properties of, in David narrative
    118–19
  reliability of   114
  reticence of, in David narrative   121,
    122, 131 nn.29–30, 152, 154, 167,
    170, 170 n.62, 175, 186, 193–4, 232
  role and skill of   112, 113–15
  role and skill of, in David
    narrative   119–21, 125–6
  and space   115, 119
  status and authority of   114
  and time issues   115
  unreliability of   104 n.92, 119
  visibility of   114
  vs. implied author   161 n.47
Nathan   148, 178, 215
  God speaks through   149, 177, 179,
    266, 271, 287
  parable told by   199–202, 272
  and Solomon's succession   249–51,
    252
necromancer
  Saul's consultation with   123–5

New Criticism/Practical Criticism 6–7, 8, 11
Nietzsche, Friedrich 8
Nob, shrine of 85–8, 89, 112

Obededom the Gittite 266
O'Connell, Robert 46
Odyssey (Homer) 36, 38
O'Kane, Martin 280, 286
Oxford University (UK) 5, 5 n.14, 6–7

Palti 170
Paris, Christopher 96, 97
Phelan, James 20, 37, 74, 76, 160
Philistines
    David's defeat of 146, 152–3, 180
    David's raids against 120
    David's refuge with 49, 89, 111, 115, 119–23
    distrust of David 125–7
    giants of 152–3
    list of mighty men who fought 154
    raids against Saul 95, 97
    Saul's battle against, at Gilboa 129, 131–2, 136
    and Saul's death 107, 117–18, 131–2, 136
    Saul's refusal/incapacity to challenge 60
    threat of 53–4, 80–1, 123, 125
    see also Achish; Goliath
Phinheas 65, 93
Pittoni, Giovanni Battista 277, 278
    see also David Before the Ark of the Covenant
plague
    three days of 155–7
Plato 5 n.12, 23, 29
    on literary criticism 4, 5
plot and plotting 72–3, 111–12, 184
    character plotting 108–9
    in David narrative 185–6
    at discourse level 74
    events of 15, 75, 79–80
    notion of 73
    plot design 84
    at story level 73–4
    temporality of 75–6
    and visual art 281

Polzin, Robert M. 209
postmodernism
    and reader's role 74–5
priest(s)
    access to God 177
    in *David Before the Ark of the Covenant* 283, 289
    see also Abiathar; Ahimelech; ephod; Zadok
prophets
    access to God 177
    see also Gad; Jeremiah; Nathan; Samuel
psalm
    of thanksgiving 153

Rabbah 190, 191, 193
Rabinowitz, Peter 74, 76, 160
reader(s)
    and characters/characterization 160
    engagement with text 10–13, 24–5
    and focalization 162–4
    implied reader 17, 19
    intended reader 17
    and plot/plotting 74–5
    real/actual reader 17, 19
    triad of author, text and 14–15
    see also hermeneutics; literary criticism
reader-response criticism 10–13
    "indeterminacy" 11, 12
real/actual authors 16–17, 113
    and focalization 163
real/actual readers 17, 19
Rechab 145, 168, 180
Rehoboam 44
reliable narrators 114
    see also narrator(s); unreliable narrators
repetition (literary device) 46, 61, 79, 108
Ricoeur, Paul 29–31, 76
Rizpah 180
    characterization of 166–7
    as object of quarrel 141–2, 144, 166–7, 168, 172–3
    watch over her son's corpses 152, 166, 167
    see also Ishbosheth
Roberts, Deborah 37
rococo 278, 279, 280
    notion of 278 n.2

Samson   43, 53–4
Samuel   42, 43, 52, 53, 54, 57, 58, 66, 72,
     81–2, 87, 89, 101, 122
   anointment of David by   140
   death of   123
   ghost of, conjured for Saul   124
   and God   56–7, 177, 199, 261
Saul   40, 41, 42, 44, 71
   and Abner   172
   animosity towards David   64–5, 67–8,
     69–70, 79–80
   attempts on David's life   80–94
   bravery of   132
   cloak cut by David   98–9, 264
   David as armor-bearer of   58, 59, 132,
     136, 263
   David as son of   61, 62
   David a threat to   64–5, 67–8, 69–70,
     79–80
   David avoids the spear of   64, 69, 80–1
   and David compared   130–1
   David dressed in battle garb by   60–1
   David pursued by   58–9, 60, 61–2, 66,
     94–5, 120, 121, 263–4
   and David's battle with Goliath   60–1,
     263
   and David's betrothal/marriage to
     Michal   62–4, 67, 68, 69, 84, 94,
     122, 169–70
   David's lament for   134–5
   David's mimicking of, in his
     failures   118, 122, 130
   David spares life of   106–8
   David's rehearsal for killing   110–6
   death of   49, 107, 117, 131–2, 135–6
   death of, David's absence at   117–18,
     128–31, 135–6
   death of, reported to David   132–5
   death of, responsibility for   133–4
   determination to kill David   82–5
   direct confrontation with David
     99–100
   and God   54–5, 94, 95, 96, 124–5, 136
   God's choice of   36, 58, 95, 98–9, 107
   God's choice of David over   55–7,
     67–8, 172, 177, 180, 261, 263–4
   indecision to kill David   98–100
   information/informants for   95–7,
     123–4

   injustice to Gibeonites   151–2, 166
   isolation of   124–5
   kingship of   52–5
   "Nabal-the-Saul"   100–6, 130
   necromancer consulted by   123–5
   Philistines' threat   53–4, 80–1, 123, 125
   reburial of   152
   refusal/incapacity to challenge
     Goliath   60
   sons' death   152, 166
   see also Ahinoam of Jezreel; Ishbosheth;
     Mephibosheth; Merab; Michal;
     Rizpah
Schleiermacher, Friedrich   26–7
Schneiders, Sandra   26, 30
Scholes, Robert   20
Seraiah   151
setting/production distinction   19
Sheba
   revolt of   241–3, 247
Shimei   51, 224, 229, 238–9, 240, 245,
     256–7
   death of   259, 269
Sidney, Philip, Sir   6
Solomon   38, 44, 146, 173, 247
   and Abiathar's death   257
   and Adonijah's death   257
   anointment as king   250–1
   and Ark   148
   birth of   204
   David's instructions to   253–7
   David's warning about Joab to   174,
     254–6
   first act as king   252–3
   and Joab's death   258
   and Shimei's death   259
   succession of   249–53, 274
story/discourse distinction   19, 45, 63, 67
   and characters/characterization   161–2
   and plot/plotting   73–4, 78, 108
   see also narrative structures
structure of narratives, *see* narrative
     structures
symbol   30

Tamar (daughter of Absalom)   213–14
Tamar (daughter of David)   194, 272
   rape of   205–9, 218, 276
   see also Absalom

Tekoa woman   210–13, 215, 218, 272
text(s)
    and image   284–6
    readers' engagement with   10–13, 24–5
    textual dynamics   74
    triad of author, reader and   14–15
    see also hermeneutics; literary criticism
Thiselton, Anthony   22, 28
time/temporality
    delayed exposition   35–6, 86 n.46, 91, 93 n.72
    and narrators   115, 116
    and plots   75–6
    of production   19
    of setting   19, 75 n.22
    and visual art   281–2
type-scene   260–1
    and David narrative   275

unreliable narrator(s)   104 n.92
    and David's narrative   119
    see also narrator(s); reliable narrators
Uriah the Hittite   222, 270, 287
    David's interactions with   194–5
    death of   196–7
    righteous conduct of   195
Uzzah   147

Vandergriff, Ken   279–80
Venice   278, 280

visual art
    changing conventions in   279–80
    and David's capacity for compassion   277
    reading   278–84
visual narrative   280–1
    criticism of   281–2
    and text   284–6

Walsh, Jerome   16, 18 n.39, 46–7, 76, 77
Warren, Robert Penn   7
wise woman/women   243
    Tekoa woman   210–13, 215, 218, 272
Wittgenstein, Ludwig   24

YHWH, *see* God

Zadok   151, 222, 237, 243, 249, 250, 252, 289
    see also Ahimaaz
Zava Boccazzi, Franca   283, 291
Zedekiah   44
Zerubbabel   44
Zeruiah   141, 144, 145, 174, 175, 192, 224, 254
Ziba   188, 189, 223–4, 238, 239, 240, 245, 269
Ziklag   117, 120, 122, 129, 133, 140, 165

Made in United States
North Haven, CT
29 March 2024

50669007R00180